THE GIFT OF THANKS

The Gift of
THANKS

THE ROOTS AND RITUALS
OF GRATITUDE

Margaret Visser

Houghton Mifflin Harcourt
BOSTON · NEW YORK
2009

For Colin—this token.

For information about permission to reproduce selections from this book,
write to Permissions, Houghton Mifflin Harcourt Publishing Company,
215 Park Avenue South, New York, New York 10003.

www.hmhbooks.com

First published in 2008 by HarperCollins Publishers Ltd

Library of Congress Cataloging-in-Publication Data
Visser, Margaret.
The gift of thanks : the roots and rituals of gratitude / Margaret Visser.
p. cm.
Originally published: Toronto : HarperCollins, 2008.
Includes bibliographical references and index.
ISBN 978-0-15-101331-9
1. Gratitude. I. Title.
BJ1533.G8V57 2008
394—dc22   2009014018

Printed in the United States of America

DOC 10 9 8 7 6 5 4 3 2 1

CONTENTS

INTRODUCTION

Nothing orders our lives so smoothly and so subtly as the almost invisible ordinary. The simple habit of saying "thank you," and the notion of gratitude that underlies it, can be a key to understanding many of the basic assumptions, preferences, and needs of Western culture. Yet most people think surprisingly little about gratitude, unless they are in the middle of experiencing it intensely, or until they feel seriously hurt by other people's failure to be grateful when they should be. We often express dismay at an apparent drop in the "standards" of gratitude in society as a whole (people have always tended to complain that gratitude seems to be dying out). But it continues to be a common virtue; otherwise, our society would show far worse signs of disintegration than it does. Ingratitude is excoriated today, as it always has been. And gratitude remains an omnipresent knitter-up of the fabric of modern life. We are rarely grateful enough for it.

My hope in writing *The Gift of Thanks* is to draw attention to the complexities as well as the importance of what happens every time gratitude is felt or its absence deplored. The book takes seriously the plural form of the English word *thanks*. Through the variety of its contents it reflects the multifaceted nature of gratefulness, starting with the simplest and apparently most trivial of its expressions, which is verbal thanking, and ending with gratitude at its highest levels.

A major theme running through the book is freedom. This should be made clear from the start because, as we shall see, the old idea that gifts are freely given and gratitude is a free response has come under attack. True, saying "thank you" still fulfills a requirement of conventional good manners: it is usually in our own self-interest, therefore, to produce signs of gratefulness, whether we are genuinely moved or not, for a favour done or a gift given. And the words "thank you" are so easily said that people who "know the rules" comply with scarcely a thought. Other people—and not only givers—expect them to do so. Requirements, rules of etiquette, and a feeling that we "have to" certainly point to obligation rather than freedom. Yet a cardinal rule of gratitude remains: no matter how desirable it may be, a truly grateful response cannot be exacted. Gratitude must be freely given; otherwise, it might be a polite show, but it is not gratitude.

Trying to define and explain thankfulness has helped me understand my own reactions to many different encounters with other people: of admiration, disappointment, humility, relief, outrage, and amazement. I came to realize that gratitude (or the lack of it) was often involved in such episodes of feeling. Yet the closer I came to grasping what exactly gratitude was, and was not, the more complicated this emotion seemed, and the more implicated with other factors not obviously related. No sooner had I zeroed in on one facet of thankfulness than another appeared. The notion shifted, depending on which side of a transaction (the giver's or the receiver's) was considered, and from what point of view. Was gratefulness a virtue—or simply an emotion, for which one could not be held responsible? Was it an action (repaying a favour)—or a feeling? A spontaneously joyful reaction, a sense of relief—or something one was expected to produce on cue? Could one demand thankfulness from someone else? If so, why were people (myself included) so often and so blithely ungrateful? If not, why was I furious when I wanted gratitude and did not get it? Was it base of me to desire it?

Beginning to read around the subject, I was startled to discover how little had been written specifically addressing it. An enormous amount of modern research had been conducted into gifts, most of it treating giving either as irrational where it was not conventional, or as calculating, even downright hypocritical. We are supposed to be grateful for receiving gifts, yet thankfulness did not seem to be part of the story; gratitude nearly always went unmentioned. Where the subject was raised, it was often with suspicion, and with the presumption that gratitude must be something false, the product merely of social pressure. Perhaps giving thanks seems to such writers to have something archaic about it, the phrase itself bringing to mind religious liturgies or traditional events like Thanksgiving. But there have been exceptions to the unspoken rule, and these, almost as surprisingly, tend to exalt gratitude beyond measure. In the early twentieth century the German sociologist Georg Simmel claimed that gratitude is what in fact holds all of society together. He called it "the moral memory of mankind."

I decided to try to answer questions arising from my own observations, starting with the insistence with which we as parents teach our children to say "thank you," and considering the very different roles "gratitude" can play in cultures other than our own. There has been almost no attempt to bring together a consideration of thanking not only from a modern point of view, but also historically. So this book moves into the pre-literate past to look for signs of gratitude there, and goes on to examine not only modern writings in our own culture, but ancient ones as well: the Bible; the Greek and Roman philosophers, historians, and poets; medieval, Renaissance, and Enlightenment sources; folktales, novels, plays, and films. For giving and gratitude create and sustain memories; they and their opposites are natural drivers of myths and stories. These in their turn help us understand what thankfulness, and unthankfulness, can mean to us in everyday life.

Thanks are given to others, and, properly understood, are themselves a gift. One cannot adequately discuss gift-giving, therefore, and especially giving in return, without taking gratitude into account. The idea that being grateful is a source of pleasure is inscribed in the very etymologies of some of the words signifying gratitude. Does this meaning offer "happiness" as a reward for obeying social hierarchies—or does it point to something pro-foundly true? Under what conditions may gratefulness produce authentic happiness? Certainly gratitude can reach a pinnacle of human virtue, and when it does, its nature and reasons are astonishing, but clear. The lower levels, the ordinary instances of this feeling, on the other hand, are confused and murky, in need of elucidation.

In the end I found myself agreeing with Simmel that gratitude is of ines-timable importance to all of society. I would go further and claim that it also contributes to the spiritual well-being of every person, but especially of those who are thankful—in the true meaning of the word. These days we have a new and particular take on gratitude, and an urgency about rediscovering deep sources for it that is all our own. Our modern society stands in special need of the gift of thanks.

∞

I want to thank everyone who encouraged me to engage in writing this book and helped bring it to fruition. Many pages in it were written with particular friends in mind, remembering discussions with them on the subject of grati-tude, and out of my experience of our relationships. I would like particularly to thank my agents Linda McKnight and Zoë Pagnamenta, my publishers Iris Tupholme of HarperCollins Canada and Rebecca Saletan of Houghton Mifflin Harcourt in New York for their loyalty and support, my copy editor Allyson Latta, and my proofreader Rebecca Vogan. My thanks, too, to the John P. Robarts Research Library at the University of Toronto, for continu-ing to provide research facilities that are not easily matched elsewhere. Finally, I am grateful for the beauty of the countryside where this book was written, and for the presence on the horizon of Mont Saint-Barthélemy which pre-sided over the entire process. *Deo gratias.*

PART I

∞

Saying

I

"What Do You Say?"

People whose native language is English traditionally feel that gratitude is a good thing, that "the least they can do" for people who help them, give them presents, or do them favours is to thank them. To begin with, they usually have the habit of saying "thank you" drummed into them at an early age. And linguistic custom requires them to produce "thank you" and "thanks" not only when they feel gratitude, but also when it is thought they *should* feel grateful even though they do not. Indeed, they often feel obliged to say "thanks" in situations where gratitude is irrelevant.

This constant reiteration of "thank you" seems very odd to foreigners—even to other Europeans. The Spanish become suspicious if, translating English mannerisms directly into Spanish, an Anglo-Saxon keeps saying "thank you" to them: the constant thanker looks, at best, insincere. His interlocutor may suspect that such exaggerated politeness hides ulterior motives, that attempts are being made, for example, to exert pressure or artificially to impress. Constant thanking can actually create distance between a foreigner and a Spaniard. Another idiosyncrasy that is judged strange by non–Anglo-Saxons is the automatic production of "I'm sorry." An Englishman, according to the French, is someone who is jostled and apologizes, who says "I'm sorry" when somebody else steps on his toe.

Polite native speakers of English who commonly mix with others like themselves may say "thank you" a hundred times or more every day. Most of those occasions involve little or no grateful emotion. It is true, of course, that lots of English people fail to say "thank you" when they should; but the convention remains strong. In fact, precisely when people feel, as they increasingly do in our day, that mannerly behaviour in general is on the way out, as they become less and less willing to enact the previously ordained formalities that constitute politeness, the few rules that do remain take on unprecedented force. "Say 'thank you'" is one of these. You ignore this example of "the last few rules that remain" either because you are indifferent to whether you associate with others or not, or because you wish consciously to break with aspects of your own culture. Actual premeditated rudeness, of course, is utterly different: it breaks a rule but depends upon that rule being clear and in force. It is a strategy that relies on total understanding between the two sides, on agreement upon ends and means. "Insolence" is literally "what is unaccustomed" (from Latin *solere,* "be used to"). The unaccustomed is recognizable as such only by those who are well schooled in the widely accepted customary: in what is, and therefore what is not, "done."

Thanking, in English, is like greeting, apologizing, and politely requesting in that it is achieved by means of what linguists call "conversational routines." These include conventional phrases, iron-clad in their invariability, commonly said in a preordained order, and often hard to account for through traditional grammar. "Thank you" means "I—or we—thank you": "thank" is a verb spoken without its subject. The further abbreviation, "Thanks," stands for something like "I offer you my thanks." "No, thanks" is an expression that appears to have arrived during the late-nineteenth century. Mrs. Humphry announces in 1897 that "'No, I thank you,' is a form of words no longer heard in good society, having some time since been replaced by: 'No, thanks.'"[1] The word had become a noun—in the plural.

These words and other routines like them are learned as phrases, or references to phrases, even when the original expressions are unknown to their speakers. As spoken phrases, they often remain unbreakable chunks of words, so much so that they have each become more like one word than a phrase. "How do you do?" seems to be a question, but the speaker really does not require—or even want—an account of how the other is doing. The equally fixed response is to repeat "How do you do?": the two parties have simply and formally assured each other that they belong to the group of those who can be expected to be polite. They are doing what is customary, not "insolent," and correct. Other conventional greeting and parting rituals involve saying "Good morning," "Good evening," "Good night," and "Good-bye," or "Bye-bye," the original and literal meaning of which is "God be with ye." "Please," tied as it is to a request, is less common than "thank you" but may be even more rigorously required. It means "If you please," which sounds archaic nowadays. The whole phrase may therefore, when found, and especially with a strong stress on the first word, be sarcastic: "*If* you please." For "please" we would now say (but we do not), "If it would please you, or at least not inconvenience or trouble you," and the idea includes "It would certainly please *me.*"

The routine phrase "thank you" is far more difficult to account for than "please." Its meaning is so involved and complicated, indeed, that this booklength treatment of the idea will not exhaust its complexity. For example, nobody is supposed to do a kindness or give a present in order to receive thanks. We are very likely to be enraged, however, if thanks are not forthcoming. Gratitude—we feel—ought to be felt and must be expressed. Yet a person owed thanks often feels constrained to protest that the debtor owes nothing. "Not at all," he or she will protest. "It was nothing." What meets the eye, when we talk of thanks, is merely the tip of an iceberg.

The first paradox, however, because it affects us earliest, is the fact that being grateful is apparently not natural at all—yet evolutionary science speaks of gratitude in terms of genetic adaptation. We shall look at the second proposition later. One proof of the first may be found in the real difficulty young children undergo in grasping the concept of gratitude. Parents spend years and years demanding from their offspring the saying of "thank

you." Children who have been brought up to say these words do not manage to produce them spontaneously until sometime between the ages of four
and six. In our culture thanking is believed to be, for most children, the very
last of the basic social graces they acquire. The first unprompted "thank you"
is momentous enough to count as a kind of initiation into a new level of
human consciousness—into distance and therefore perspective, into intentionality, understanding, recognition, deliberate relationship, and memory.
After all, when a creature has a need, it suffers until the need is filled. When
satisfaction arrives, nothing is more natural than pure relief. There is no *need*
to think of anything else, no necessity that one should turn to one's benefactor and display gratitude.

Children have to be "brought up" to say they are grateful. The verb is
passive: they *are brought,* they do not bring themselves. And they move "up,"
to a higher level. The following is a conversation recorded by social scientists
who were observing how parents perform the duty of up-bringing in the
matter of thanking.

FATHER: Whaddya say to Susan? Say "thank you" to Susan.
CHILD: [*mumbles*]
FATHER: Say "thank you" to Susan.
ASSISTANT: That's all right . . .
FATHER: Richard, I want you to say "thank you."
CHILD: No.
FATHER: Richard, that's not nice.[2]

The parents of twenty-two middle-class children, eleven boys and eleven
girls, had agreed to participate with their offspring in a study of "parent–child
interaction." Parents did not realize that the point of the study was in fact
what methods they employed and how hard they tried to teach their children
to say "Hi," "Thanks," and "Good-bye." The "assistant" was in the know about
the real purpose of the investigation. Gratitude is notoriously difficult to pro-

duce under laboratory conditions. This particular experiment was comparatively benign and successful; it did not aim too high. Indeed, it was about the
learning of politeness formulae, and not about actual gratitude at all.

Each family was videotaped for thirty minutes while the parents and
child played together, thinking that this was the point of the exercise. The real
experiment began when the assistant appeared at the end of the session and
gave the child a toy. The assistant spoke from a script. She turned to the child
and said, "Hi, I'm [assistant's name]. Hi, [child's name]." There was a pause to see
how the child responded, and what the parents said if there was no answering
"Hi!" Then the assistant said, "Here's a gift for you for today's visit." [Pause.]
Would the child say "thank you"? Later, there was a "good-bye" and a pause.
The results of the experiment were then tabulated.

These children spontaneously said "hi" 27 percent of the time, "good-
bye" 25 percent of the time, and "thanks" only 7 percent of the time. Parents
prompted 28 percent for "hi," 33 percent for "good-bye," and 51 percent
for "thanks."[3] The experiment went on to analyze the efficacy of fathers as
opposed to mothers in these reminding sessions. Parents not only prompt
their children, but act as models of polite behaviour. During the periods of
play, the conduct of the parents themselves was monitored. Mothers were
much politer than fathers, spontaneously saying "thank you" 50 percent of
the time, while fathers said it only 18 percent of the time. Insistence on *their
children's* polite behaviour was especially important to these parents (knowing as they did that they were being experimented upon for interaction with
their children). That their children should say "thank you" was of particular
concern, partly because the children already said "hi" and "bye-bye" often,
without prompting. The sociologists were of the opinion that since middle-
class parents treat their children "permissively," parents in other social classes
might make even stronger demands for routine politeness.

Children learn "hi" and "bye-bye" much earlier than they learn "thanks."
One reason is that "hi" and "bye-bye" are said in response to other people
producing these words first, whereas "thanks," with no prompt, has to come

out of the child's own head: there is normally no verbal cue for it. The greeting formulae correspond to the physical facts of meeting and parting, with other people joining in. But thanking in no way resembles receiving, so copying cannot produce the correct response. Furthermore, one is expected to say "thank you" even if no gratitude is felt. It is hard to remember to "be nice," to remember when to carry out the routine—and to do it immediately. One might remember when it is too late.

MOTHER: Bye-bye. Thank you, Susan. [*Assistant leaves.*]
CHILD: Thank you for my . . . for my toy. [*To closed door*]
MOTHER: Yes. Thank you for the toy. That was nice of you to thank her. Maybe if you see her again you can tell her in person.[4]

Here, the mother says the words she hopes her child will reproduce on appropriate occasions. The child obediently complies, but says the words too late, and her mother points out the important fact that the whole point of thanking is *the other person*. Now the child will have to remember not only to say "thank you" but to say it later on, to the "assistant," even when the toy is no longer in her arms to remind her of what happened earlier. Learning to say "thank you" is a complex exercise in remembering.

Another reason why "hi" and "bye-bye" are learned long before "thanks" is the custom of making physical gestures to accompany the words, such as hand-waving—so easy for a child to do, so charming, and so exciting for adults to enact, to witness, and to repeat. "Thanks," on the other hand, is usually triggered in childhood not by gestures but by objects—the arrival of things asked for or given. The most useful setting of all for learning "please" and "thank you" is the dinner table, which is a kind of stage for the daily rehearsing of social interaction.[5] Everybody is interested in food. Eating and drinking are done mostly in sharing groups, and this interaction entails asking for things, responding by passing things, and receiving them—with thanks, if the company agrees to insist on the thanking.[6] It quickly becomes obvious that you must say "please" or you probably won't get what you want. And now that you have what you want, either remember the obliging attentions of the dinner companion who gave it to you and thank him, or annoy him by your failure so that he may be harder to persuade another time. At the table, the activities of giving and receiving occur in rapid succession: concrete experience, and repetition both constant and immediate, make for effective learning. Children in our culture learn manners at the dining table, and not manners only. It is believed that falling away from the cultural custom of eating with others at table three times a day can cause backwardness in all of a child's speaking skills.

According to a traditional English custom (one observed in my own British family when I was a child), the business of giving and receiving is provided with its own word, to be said to a child before it can even talk. "Ta," says the adult, giving something to a child or asking for something to be given. "Ta," after "Ma" and "Pa," is among the earliest words learned. It means "we are giving and taking":[7] this is a scenario, a human drama in which both parties are engaged. Later on, the word can be used for either "Please give" or "I have received": one word, but two different actions. The idea of saying a special word when requesting has been introduced. Later on it will be replaced by "please," and at that moment "ta" is understood to mean only the satisfaction of receiving, and the meaning "please" falls away. "Ta" now becomes a simple form of "thank you," to be said before the child can pronounce that difficult series of sounds. Adults prompting for "ta" say the word loudly and clearly, with an intonation requesting repetition of the word, or the action, by the child. A different intonation expresses satisfaction when the word and the action are complete. Adults hold out a hand to proffer an object and also to receive one: the sign supports the production of the word, doubles it, and accompanies it.

Giving and receiving, then, before the child can talk, are a basis of interaction. With "ta" the child begins to give and not only to take. With saying "ta" on taking, an introduction has been made to thanking. This extremely early and intense socializing occurs because of the importance placed in Anglo-Saxon culture upon saying "please" and "thank you." A study in England in 1988 asked parents to draw up a list of what was thought most desirable in children's manners learned at table. "Please" and "thank you" appeared at the top of the list. Farther down came the correct use of tableware; not bringing books and toys to table; refraining from making a noise at table; and asking permission before leaving.[8]

"Say 'thank you'!" parents cry over and over again. "Say" introduces the correct phrase in this and other cases of teaching polite formulae. "Say" is like a flag, introducing the words of the ritual. Children learn what they have to say as though it were a kind of spell, before they know what it means. They come to recognize that this scene is like a previously encountered scene—even though it may involve another place, different gifts, not the same people. And then they must produce the right words. Eventually, when they have matured and been further educated, they will come to be able to feel the emotion that the words express. The words come first, the feelings later.

When parents are aware that "Say 'thank you'!" has been said enough, and their own modelling of the phrase has been witnessed a sufficient number of times, they begin to prompt without supplying the words required: "What do you say?" they typically ask. The time has come, they warn the child. Do you recognize the situation? Do you remember what the script demands? To elicit "please," the question asked is often "What's the magic word?"—that is, the button to press in order to get what is wanted. The final moment—the triumph and the initiation—comes when the child is given something and says "thank you" without being reminded to do so. Parents do well to notice this event, for which they have worked so hard: it marks a whole new stage in a child's development. Later still, the child will recognize that a kindness that does not involve an object given also warrants thanks. Adults may eventually learn that something as apparently "normal" and to be taken for granted as another person's attention to us in times of affliction might be worth more gratitude than almost any present.

Saying "please," "thank you," "hello," "good-bye," and other phrases like them is demanded of us from the beginning, and harped on dozens of times a day, thousands of times a year, at our most impressionable age. Such phrases become so ingrained in us that they last when almost everything else has been forgotten. In states of aphasia, or in people suffering from Alzheimer's disease, these little phrases often survive the shipwreck of all other memories.[9]

2

No Thanks

Given all the work that goes into getting children to say "thank you," it is plain that people brought up in European and North American cultures greatly prize gratitude—and not only gratitude but its prompt and appropriate expression. Children do not thank unless they are taught to do so, however, and must therefore be induced to provide the words expected by adults. But we are also forced to realize that thanking is not "natural" behaviour when we discover that many other societies are found not to practise it.

Taking for granted the desirability of gratitude for civilization in general, explorers, anthropologists, and other European travellers from the sixteenth to the twentieth centuries reported their horror when they came across groups of people, whole societies, who never thanked them. We might feel comfortably tempted, from our post-colonial vantage point, to find an explanation in the fact that the natives had reason to feel resentment rather than gratitude towards their unlooked-for "guests." But then, the natives did not thank each other, either. Many languages have no word for "thanks." And those that have one do not necessarily mean what we mean by it.

"The natives are ungrateful," travellers exclaimed over and over again; they were also selfish, obstinate, and sly (Europeans rarely thought them unintelligent).[1] "The Northern Indians," wrote Samuel Hearne in the 1770s, "seem to be entirely unacquainted even with the name of gratitude."[2] Richard Burton believed that there were no words for gratitude in any of the many "Oriental languages" known to him.[3]

Often the behaviour of the inhabitants seemed absolutely outrageous to Europeans who encountered them. "One of them wanted my waistcoat," wrote an eighteenth-century French visitor to Tasmania, "the bright colours of which had attracted his attention. He had already several times demanded it of me, but I had so positively refused that I did not think he would return to the charge. However, one minute, when I was not paying attention, he seized hold of me by the waistcoat and pointed his spear at me, brandishing it furiously. . . . I had hardly escaped this danger, when I found myself threatened, if not as perilously, at least as disagreeably. One of the large gold earrings which I wore excited the desires of another savage, who, without saying anything, slid behind me, cunningly slipped his finger through the ring, and tugged so hard that he would undoubtedly have torn my ear had not the clasp given way. It must be remembered that we had given them mirrors, knives, coloured glass beads, pearls, handkerchiefs, snuff boxes, etc; that I had stripped myself of nearly all the buttons on my coat, which, being gilt copper, had seemed specially valuable to them on account of their brightness."[4]

The writer saw greed as the cause of this violence. He may well have been right: we cannot think of pre-modern non-Europeans as *ipso facto* innocents. But whatever the morality of the situation in the Tasmanian's mind, it is beyond doubt that this writer experienced a flagrant impropriety, a flouting of his own rules of courtesy; added to which, the man was obviously ungrateful. The Tasmanians, however, were said elsewhere to have been "not ungrateful" when they received medical help, for instance, although it was not explained how this lack of ingratitude was expressed. Another account, of new English arrivals in Tasmania in the nineteenth century, described how they tried to eat toad fish, and the natives, "perceiving its preparation for food, endeavoured to show, by gestures, that it was not to be eaten, and exhibited its effects by the semblance of death."[5] They also saved the lives of Europeans on several recorded occasions from drowning and from fire. Nevertheless, after many breakdowns of communication and violence on both sides, a "war of extermination" eventually wiped out the Tasmanians.

A few observers insisted that the foreign societies they were describing did have words for thanks. "Among some Indian tribes," wrote Washington Matthews in 1899, "it is said there is no word for thanks, but the Navahoes have one, and use it as we would."[6] Medical help was repeatedly reported as having been gratefully received, as when, in North-Western Canada in 1793, a Scottish doctor came across an Indian with a festering hand and a thumb hanging from it by a small strip of flesh. The young man's life was in "a state of hazard," and his wound "in such an offensive state, and emitted such a putrid smell, that it required all the resolution I possessed to examine it. His friends had done every thing in their power to relieve him; but as it consisted only in singing about him, and blowing upon his hand, the wound, as may be well imagined, had got into the deplorable state in which I found it." The doctor, using methods only somewhat more advanced, managed to heal the wound, washing it with the juice of the root of a spruce fir tree, wrapping it in the root's bark ("a very painful dressing"), cleaning it three times a day, and applying to it Canadian balsam, wax, and tallow from a burning candle. The thumb was removed with the aid of vitriol. When he was well enough, the healed Indian joyfully set off on a hunting expedition and brought back with him the tongue of an elk, which he offered to the doctor, and there were, when the doctor finally left, "warmest acknowledgements" from himself and his family.[7]

The Inuit, explorers said, often failed to have "the courtesy" to thank people when gifts were offered them. But these unacknowledged presents were often remembered for long periods of time, in fact, and their givers were astonished when, much later, they were suddenly offered presents in return. A visitor to the Bushmen of southern Africa in 1822–24 admitted that he could not understand their language, but when he gave them food, "their looks" expressed their thanks; the women were more expressive than the men. And he added that he felt ashamed to receive so much gratitude for having done so little.[8]

Many cultural systems, in controlling everyday behaviour among their members, simply do not call for people to say "thank you." Even where thanking formulae exist, they are often kept for purely formal use—for deference before strangers, for instance, who might possibly prove to be unpredictable, dangerous, hostile, or overbearing. In family groups, within the household, or the band, or the tribe, it is often actually rude to thank: people feel the practice to be cold and distant, not the way people close to each other and who understand each other should speak. Members within the family or the extended family or the carefully defined group are obliged to help one another and give to one another whenever there is a need. And the required actions are not expected to result in thanks.

"I have often watched toddlers," wrote Audrey Richards of the Bemba of Zambia, then Northern Rhodesia, in the 1930s, "starting on a slow and arduous progress from hut to hut, wherever they might expect to find dainties and knew they could take them without rebuke. Within this circle of relatives the child early realizes that he is only getting what is his due." And conversely, the child was learning who the people were from whom he could definitely expect to receive. One day Richards asked why a young man who had received a present from his relatives simply took it without saying thank you. She was told, "He doesn't thank because they are his own people. If it had been an outsider, he would have said: 'Thank you, Sir,' because it would have been from pity they gave to him. To one's own people one does not thank, not at all! You say that is good. That is all."[9] Outsiders gave "from pity" because they were themselves moved to give, although they were free not to. Insiders did so because they had to. "That is good" was all one said to one's own: there did exist a necessity of expressing satisfaction at the supplying of one's wants.

People in groups where such obligations exist may complain if they think they have not received enough. Both they and others might discuss the transaction, and criticize any lack of generosity or impropriety in the giving—taking too long to comply with a request, for example. People are allowed to ask, and they expect to get what they asked for. Others outside the transaction have the task of exerting pressure to ensure that duty is done. "Gratitude" within such a system is irrelevant.

Members of small, self-sufficient traditional groups must share what they have to eat. Those who live by hunting depend on the luck of the hunt. Victorious bringers-down of game for meat have from time immemorial carried home their catch, first having eaten the most perishable bits of the animal—the liver and the other innards—immediately after the kill. They then proceed to carve up the animal and give pieces of it to their relatives and the members of their hunting band, each of whom may have a right to a particular piece—a flipper, a foreleg, a rib—whatever the nature of the beast and the pre-established rules of the group. Each of these pieces is then cut up again and given to people dependent upon the receiver.[10] Nobody can be said to be grateful for receiving his or her part. There may be thankfulness, however, for the fact that an animal has been provided to feed them, and when this is the case, a piece of the creature may be offered to the people's divinities, who in this way are given their shares, just as human beings in the group are granted theirs.

The Inuit hunter hauling back a seal he had killed was required to give away all but his own carefully defined portion of the meat. He knew that he had been lucky, and he enjoyed his good fortune and the honour it brought him. He was praised for the skill with which he hurled the harpoon—but not thanked for kindness or generosity in sharing out the meat. He gave almost everything away in the knowledge that somebody else, not he, might be lucky next time. Then it would be his turn to receive—indeed, to expect—gifts in kind from the latest catch. Such behaviour constituted a sort of insurance, a security for everyone. In 1824 William Parry commented that "the regulation does credit to their wisdom, but has nothing to do with their generosity."[11] Ethnographers constantly reiterate that the sharing principle is not dropped when there is little to eat; it is maintained, rather, with more vigilance than ever.[12]

Children are "brought up" in such societies to share, just as our own off-spring are made to say "thank you." Audrey Richards describes how infants were taught in the African society she studied: "An unexpected present or find must be divided with any other babies sitting near. Any European food, such as an orange or a bit of bread, that I might happen to give away was torn into the tiniest fragments, and mothers who are such lax disciplinarians in other respects, speak quite sharply to their children on this one issue. I have seen a woman seize a lump of pumpkin out of a baby's hand and say in most vehement protest: 'You give some to your friend, you child, you! You sit and eat alone! That is bad what you do.'"[13] Eating is not something one should do alone. Food is not merely nourishment, but also an expression, in its sharing, of relationship. The sharing is not a matter of how one feels: it is demanded, and the demand is enforced by parents and later by everybody in the group.

Africans today who travel abroad must take home presents for family and friends left behind. Huge suitcases full of goods are hauled onto airplanes; very little inside may be for the traveller himself. A Congolese man I met was spending two more years in France although he badly wanted to go home: he had not accumulated enough presents yet to return decently to his family and friends. A Solomon Islander, according to an ethnographer writing in the 1880s, would return from working three years on the plantations of Fiji or Queensland, and everything he came home with would be taken, as a matter of course, by others.[14]

People have often created a network of security and excluded violence among themselves by not being possessive about what they owned. They have felt they could ask for, and get, what they wanted. The ethnographers and others who arrived in ships on their shores, and who were shocked at signs of a lack of courtesy, failed to realize that, as outsiders, they simply were not implicated in any of the existing gift-giving and sharing networks. They appeared to the inhabitants bizarre in the extreme, hostile or foolish strangers who could not be imagined fitting in. Not the least odd was their refusal to part with the goods people wanted. They did offer their beads and knives and handkerchiefs, but they inexplicably refused their waistcoats and earrings.

And they came, after all, with so much. William Parry saw that his ships, with their wood and iron—substances as valuable to the Inuit as "hoards of gold and silver" to a European—must have been a temptation, and so he allowed for a certain amount of pilfering: "We must not fail to make due allowance for the degree of temptation to which they were daily exposed, amidst the boundless stores of wealth which our ships appeared to them to furnish." (An earlier traveller, however, the Comte de La Pérouse, despised the Indians of Hudson Bay whom he invited to visit his boat, and who "never disdained to steal a nail or an old pair of trousers" while they were on board.[15]) But Parry admitted disappointment when he found that the high degree of honesty the Inuit showed at first gradually relaxed "as they grew more familiar with us."[16] Apparently, neither Parry nor La Pérouse could see that, to these people, he who has much is expected to give his surplus away; that a stranger is to be treated with respect (that is, distance), but someone known begins to join the group, with its attendant requirement that he should share. If somebody who is "one of us" wants something, the "courteous" thing to do is to give it to him. In the Solomon Islands, they went further. When someone was asked for a thing, he gave it because "by a refusal he will incur the enmity of the person who has made the request."[17]

H.B. Guppy described the "disposition" of the Solomon Islanders in 1887: "Often when during my excursions I have come upon some man who was preparing a meal for himself and his family, I have been surprised at the open-handed way in which he dispensed the food to my party of hungry natives. No gratitude was shown towards the giver, who apparently expected none, and only mildly remonstrated when my men were unusually voracious."[18] Sharing, in other words, went on not only within the (family) group, but also between the group and visiting outsiders—even should strangers arrive unexpectedly. "Open-handedness" of this kind is what we call "hospitality." It is offered by hosts to guests—by those at home, who are expected to give to those who are away from home (and by definition "foreigners" to the hosts), and who *therefore* receive. They receive because they are in need, and also for the same reason that the Inuit seal hunter gave most of his meat away: because one day the host himself might be travelling and need assistance either from this guest or from somebody else who keeps the rules of courtesy. Furthermore, this sudden guest—or even a previously invited one—is, at least relatively speaking, unknown. He is a possible threat, a potential enemy. He is to be placated, therefore, honoured with attentions, and if at all possible given what he wants.

In languages that have developed from Indo-European roots, the words *host* and *guest* come from the same stem, which contains both the *g* of *guest* and the *h* of *host: ghostis.* Hosts and guests play different roles, but they are actors in one "play," a hospitable action. *Ghostis* also provided us with the word *hostile,* so close is the idea of hospitality to the possibility of animus lurking in either host or guest, or both. (A *hostage* is a person forcibly, and therefore discourteously, detained by a group not his own. Originally the word meant a person held as guarantee to a treaty of peace between two previously antagonistic sides.) A guest is an outsider who has been ritually "domesticated," made temporarily part of the host's *domus,* or house. He is given food, offered gestures of affability, and sometimes presented with gifts on his departure—for he must be free to leave. There may be genuine interest in him and delight in his company. But underlying the performance is the formal and primary aim of "disarming" him, of forestalling any likelihood of violence or resentment.[19]

No matter how "ungrateful" the inhabitants seemed to their European visitors, according to early ethnographical reports, they were nearly always credited with generosity when they were allowed the role of hosts: they were at home, giving, while the foreign adventurers accepted the role of guests, away, receiving. For ritually speaking, the host is always the powerful one in relation to the guest. He is on home territory, and the guest is likely to be outnumbered in the encounter. The guest is treated well on that very account, so that the host can show his magnanimity, his self-control, and his authority over the others in his group.

The other side of the same coin that is hospitality is the fear that can accompany the arrival of another, especially of an unknown other, inside one's own house. That person must be turned into a guest, given a guest's role, with the rules attendant upon it: accept your host's attentions, be seen to receive them passively and admiringly, and do not attempt to advise your host, order his family about, or criticize him. Look pleased by his kindness. And finally, show yourself disposed to invite your host back one day: you shall then be the host and he the guest. If there is a place for gratitude, it is here, on the part of the guest. A host, in turn, often feels that guests in his house honour him and give him pleasure by their presence. This too could be construed as something like gratitude. He should certainly show pleasure at their presence, whether he feels it or not.

There is every indication from travellers' tales that they received plenty of hospitality. "Both as to food and accommodation the best they had were always at our service," William Parry wrote; the Inuit showed hospitality and "good breeding." "The kindly offices of drying and mending our clothes, cooking our provision and thawing snow for our drink, were performed by the women with an obliging cheerfulness which we shall not easily forget."[20]

Of the Ila of Zambia, Edwin Smith and Andrew Dale wrote in 1920, "Baila houses are open; a visitor may enter by the open door without speaking or knocking, though it is considered more polite to ask permission to enter." The host then had food prepared especially for the visitor. The neighbouring Barotsi had a duty to give all guests presents of uncooked food to take away with them, but the Ila felt that wives should cook food for guests—it showed less compulsion and less perfunctoriness, especially when the head of the house or one of his wives served the food in person. The host tasted the food first, within sight of his guest, to prove that there had been no tampering or witchcraft: the guest was recognized as possibly being even more nervous than the host. It was rude to make the guest eat alone; one of the villagers had to share his meal. "On receiving food the visitor is not expected to say anything," but when he had finished eating he announced, "I am satisfied. You have given me food. *Nda lumba.*" We are not told the literal meaning in English of this phrase, but it is translated in this text as "I return thanks."

Though he had received hospitality, the guest was permitted to give a present to his host only if the guest was a hunter or a passing trader. Ordinary people, while they were guests, were on no account to give anything in return for hospitality. The host would be offended. He would say, "Do I sell food?" The guest, on the other hand, was supposed to show pleasure, and a desire to come again and visit: "*Ozona ozona!*" he might exclaim: "Tomorrow and tomorrow!" meaning "Give it to me again and again." For, as the Ila say, "The fly that loves you is the one that sits on you": one must visit and so show affection. (Nothing is said of how irritating flies can be.)[21] In hospitality, first one gives, and then, later on, it is the other's turn to do so. A guest must agree to be passive. One should accept, give nothing, and save up all of the obligation one has incurred. One must then pay it back—with interest—on some future occasion.

A web of obligation is created over time. It is a form of security—but it can also cause resentment. One carries around a need to pay somebody else back: where the duty is strongly felt, it can seem like a menace. This metaphor of weight being borne exists in European languages: when we carry out an obligation, we say we "discharge" it, lay it down, and so relieve our aching backs. Peter Freuchen said he was put straight by Sorqaq, an Inuit host, on the matter of thanking: "You must not thank for your meat; it is your right to get parts. In this country, nobody wishes to be dependent on others. Therefore, there is nobody who gives or gets gifts, for thereby you become dependent. With gifts you make slaves just as with whips you make dogs."[22]

This statement questions various European assumptions about "societies of the Gift," as such groups are often called. First, according to this Inuit host, his people see themselves as independent. They are not simple, blind, ant-like components of communal patterns. Second, Sorqaq, at least, refused to call the sharing of meat "gift-giving" because to him gifts meant subordination. They were therefore painful to receive and degrading. He would have much preferred to feel that giving and receiving were obligatory. And so a foreign man had to be advised to refrain from repeating his entirely inappropriate ritual of thanking.

3

It's Only Natural

Cultural patterns can apparently induce gratitude in people, or reduce its likelihood, or make it merely irrelevant. It seems to be the rule, at any rate, that the more obligatory giving is, the less receivers feel grateful. Thankfulness, viewed from the point of view of culture, may seem therefore to be neither necessary nor natural. Gratitude does not "come naturally" to children: they have to be taught to express it first, and later to understand what it means.

Sociobiologists, however, take a totally different view. For them, behaviour patterns are innate and physically determined rather than culturally induced—a matter of nature rather than nurture. Most of the scientists adhering to this discipline, therefore, systematically discount all possibility of giving for any reason other than the giver's own material benefit or self-interest. The notion of free or disinterested giving to people one does not know or whom one dislikes is dismissed as absurd. Apology and pardon also have no motivation other than that of self-interest, and gratitude is nothing more than a reward for benefits received and a hopeful prod for more in the future. Since gratitude is commonly found, it must be useful and therefore inscribed in our genes.

A particularly forceful example of this general stance can be found in Robert L. Trivers, "The Evolution of Reciprocal Altruism."[1] Trivers defines *altruism* as behaviour that benefits another creature not closely related to the giver, while being apparently detrimental to the latter's interests. It is therefore behaviour that needs to be accounted for. The phrase *not closely related* is essential to the definition. One would be altruistic if one leapt, at risk to oneself, into the water to save another person from drowning. But the act might be entirely explicable in terms of self-interest (that is, of natural selection) if the person saved were one's own child: the saviour then "may merely be contributing to the survival of his own genes." Trivers accordingly sets out to show how behaviour that appears to be selfless, even to the point of saving genes that are not one's own, can be explained in terms of the survival of the fittest. The answer, of course, lies in the adverb *apparently* applied to *detrimental*. If behaviour that seems costly can be shown to be in fact advantageous, then selection for it ceases to be surprising.

Trivers takes as an example the conduct of the cleaner wrasse. This fish, the length of a human finger, grazes over the skin of larger fish, eating the parasites that suck their blood and thereby cleaning them. Some of these parasites, which cause acute discomfort to their host fish, are microscopic crustaceans, described by a recent investigator of their habits as "all tiny body armour and biting mouthparts."[2] Their larvae latch onto fish and feed on their blood, and it is these creatures that the wrasse delight in consuming. In so doing they bring comfort to the fish that host the larvae. The big fish, for their part, live on fish the size of these wrasse—but never eat their benefactors.

Wrasse, like other cleaner fish and cleaner shrimp, have evolved distinctive colouring. They attract fish to be cleaned, and make themselves further recognizable as cleaners rather than as fodder by swimming up to their clients and performing a dipping and rising "dance." A fish wishing to be cleaned will approach a cleaner, often swimming to a place where one particular wrasse habitually operates. It slows down and sometimes "flops about awkwardly," showing by these gestures that it has no aggressive intentions. It may even "bow" to the cleaner, with its head down and its tail in the air, "just begging to be cleaned," according to a human observer.[3] Some client fish will change colour for the duration of the cleaning process. Watchers reported seeing a fish, remaining its normal pale colour when it was supposed to become dark bronze first, approach a cleaner that was already busy with one of its fellows. The fish that was being cleaned, and that had turned the correct shade, immediately chased the pale fish away and so presumably saved its useful cleaner from being eaten. The bronze colour clearly signifies, in a potential predator, "No harm intended; I need service."[4]

A cleaner fish sets swiftly about its business, picking off blood-sucking gnathiid (from the Greek for "jaws") isopod larvae, about 1,200 of them per day, servicing about three hundred fish in six hours. The larvae constitute 95 percent of its daily diet: the problems of the big fish clearly benefit the cleaners. The big fish, meanwhile, open up their gill chambers to allow the little fish to go in and out, and spread their fins to let them do their work. They hold their mouths open wide, and the wrasse swim deep inside. When a big fish needs to leave the "service station," it makes a sign, closing and opening its mouth; the cleaner swims out; the fish shakes itself from side to side and then moves off. Even if the human watchers frighten the big fish, it never omits the warning signs.[5] Another big fish arrives at once to take its place.

The surprising part of all this for the scientist is that evolution "ought," in the big fish, to have favoured first letting a cleaner remove the parasites and then taking a further advantage by eating it. After all, there are lots of good wrasse in the sea. After further study, researchers concluded that each particular wrasse is worth more to the host fish alive than dead. The cleaned fish wants to come again to be serviced later. There is evidence that satisfaction with a cleaner prompts a client to return to the provider's proven services and its conveniently known habitat (cleaner shrimp are known to spend weeks and sometimes months within a yard of the same spot). Swimming about looking for a new cleaner can be dangerous, and also a tiresome business when a fish is tormented by gnathiid isopods. Thus there has been strong natural selection to avoid eating one's cleaner. The fish is "grateful" to be relieved of its itching, and "in return" refrains from swallowing the wrasse; the cleaner is "grateful" to be supplied with food, and can be relied on "as a result" to do its best on this and future occasions. Both parties benefit. (No suggestions are advanced as to what the isopods must think or feel.) So nature has given rise to "altruism" and to "gratitude." Of course, as Trivers admits at the beginning of his discussion, "Models that attempt to explain altruistic behavior in terms of natural selection are models designed to take the altruism out of altruism."

Trivers moves next to human beings and their so-called altruism. Human actions, like the actions of the cleaner wrasse, are the result of natural selection. But what about feelings? Trivers writes that human altruism is "regulated" by a psychological system that is itself the result of natural selection. This "system" includes friendship, dislike, "moral aggression," sympathy, trust, aspects of guilt, some forms of dishonesty and hypocrisy—and gratitude. All of these are said to have evolved as underlying emotional dispositions in order to induce us to help one another, so that in this symbiotic process our genes might be preserved.

Reciprocal altruism is to be found in nearly all known human cultures—perhaps in all of those not in terminal decline. People do come to each other's aid in times of danger. They often help the weak—the old, the young, the sick, and wounded; they share food and implements and knowledge. These actions are believed to occur because they meet the essential criterion of natural selection: that of "small cost to the giver and great benefit to the taker."[6] Human beings—like cleaner wrasse—have a sufficiently long lifespan for reciprocity and repeated services to take place before death. It has been highly unusual (at least in traditional societies and until recent times) for people to move away from others in their group and never see them again. They experience a long period of parental care, which provides them with examples of and opportunities for (possibly reciprocal) altruism among close kin.

Human beings know all about dominance, but nevertheless engage in food sharing as a method of survival, for if the weak—especially women and the young—are not fed, the community will die out. They are less devoted

to dominance than are groups of baboons, in which food sharing is not practised and the dominant males normally get all the meat, and more like chim-
panzees, where food is not automatically pre-empted by the most powerful.[7]
Symmetry at some level is required for reciprocity to occur. A difference
through dominance in a human grouping can be reduced in combat: the
many then become necessary to the few. War, according to this reasoning, has
a useful aspect, that of levelling within the group. All of these factors mean
that we live in conditions where reciprocal "altruism" is thought naturally to
arise—is, indeed, selected to do so.

Trivers defines guilt as a kind of debt, incurred by a "cheater," one who
tricks others into giving when they need not, or who fails to reciprocate
"altruism." The others must punish him in order to bring him into line. If a
"cheater" finds all future aid from others cut off, "then the cheater will have
paid dearly for his misdeed. It will be to the cheater's advantage to avoid
this, and, providing that the cheater makes up for his misdeed and does not
cheat in the future, it will be to his partner's benefit to avoid this, since in
cutting off future acts of aid he sacrifices the benefits of future reciprocal
help . . ." Pardon is therefore thought to be a matter of pure self-interest, and
cheaters are "selected" to make a reparative gesture so as to mollify others,
for in this manner the rupture of reciprocal relationships is prevented. The
emotion we call guilt or remorse has arisen to help this to happen, through
natural selection.[8]

Guilt leading to reparations must occur, according to this view, mainly
when everyone knows what the guilty person has done. In 1966 a laboratory experiment produced this conclusion by setting up a piece of expensive
equipment so that it would automatically break when handled by some—
but not all—of the human participants. All of them were then asked if they
would care to volunteer for an experiment that would cause them to experience pain. The ones who had "broken" the expensive machine were more
likely, out of guilt, to sign up than those who had not—but only if they
thought their transgression had been discovered.[9] If people feel remorse for

something nobody knows they have done, they do so entirely because many transgressions performed in private are *likely* to become public knowledge.

People often try, out of "guilt," to repair the harm they have done by helping, "engaging in reparative altruism." But they often help a third person rather than the one they have actually harmed. And sometimes they help the original victim only if they will never see him or her again. An explanation is given for this behaviour. People who have done wrong wish to allay guilt feelings—but would rather not let on that they realize the extent of what they have done. They do not want to "trigger the greater reparation that recognition of the harm might lead to." Or they want to allay their guilt and at the same time appear to be "genuinely" altruistic, because people warm to those they perceive (albeit mistakenly) to be helping without calculating for return favours. The previously guilty therefore offer help—but to a third person, in order to appear to have no ulterior motive.[10] People who prefer others to act without calculating for return favours merely engage in wishful thinking; they keep wanting to believe in a non-existent "altruism."

Unfortunately, it often pays to cheat: subtle cheating itself can be adaptive. If the other person won't find out, or if he will not discontinue altruistic behaviour even if he does find out, or if he is not likely to live long enough to take revenge—in all such cases, the cheater wins. Natural selection responds by evolving in us, first, acute abilities for the detection of cheating, and then the indignation and "moral aggression" that make us do something to stop it. Gratitude is thought to have emerged because people have been selected to be sensitive to "the cost and benefit of an altruistic act, both in deciding whether to perform one and in deciding whether, or how much, to reciprocate." Gratitude involves many more calculations. For example, people have been shown to think they feel more gratitude, the more valuable the altruistic act has been to them and the more the act is judged to have cost the benefactor.[11] One experiment induced more reciprocity entirely because the original act was believed to be "expensive" for the giver: people were more disposed to be grateful for a gift of 80 percent of one dollar than for an offer of 20 percent of four dollars.[12] Cheaters, however, are always ready to take advantage. They are capable of learning to mimic gratitude in order to encourage a giver by making him think he will be reciprocated.[13]

When sympathy motivates altruism, scientists like Trivers have concluded, it is always accompanied by a calculation of the likelihood that it might issue in a future benefit to the recipient: "The greater the potential benefit to the recipient, the greater the sympathy and the more likely the altruistic gesture, even to strange or disliked individuals." The reward is then forthcoming: the recipient feels grateful and may offer a "tribute" of thanks, and even "considerable reciprocity."[14]

In human beings, motive is what normally produces action. Gratitude involves not only deeds, but thoughts and feelings as well. That is one of the reasons for its complexity, a complexity with roots in the phenomena of altruism. And even if we remove moral freedom and any thought of transcendence from consideration—if we attempt to explain human kindness by using "models designed to take the altruism out of altruism"—the intricate labyrinths of human motivation that remain are vast. Trivers himself is constrained to wonder "to what extent the importance of altruism in human evolution set up a selection pressure for psychological and cognitive powers which partly contributed to the large increase in hominid brain size during the Pleistocene."[15]

Such is the picture that, until recently, we received from researchers whose underlying assumptions were that nothing exists but force, necessity, chance, and battles for advantage. It followed, of course, that genuine altruism could not exist. There is nothing, the wisdom went, to suggest that human beings are in any respect superior to animals. We are a living species like any other, in no way better than, and merely different in certain respects from, say, birds or lizards.

However, many scientists seem at last to be awakening from a long, cold dream, a censored consciousness that insisted, among other things, that freedom was a mere hallucination. It is beginning to be acceptable again to notice that a gulf separates human cultures from those of other species, that a richness and even a uniqueness exists that should not be underestimated and remains to be accounted for. Merlin Donald[16] points out how utterly different it is to remember having seen something, as apes do, and actively to seek to retrieve a memory, as human beings do. Even in childhood, human beings go on not only to remember but to reflect on many events and to imagine others. They learn. They rehearse and deliberately refine their skills and responses. And this is to say nothing of speaking, reading, writing, calculating, inventing, theorizing—and rethinking inadequate theories. Human beings may even altruistically "resist evolution," for example by protecting those with disabilities, thus helping them to survive "against nature."

Though it is indisputable that we gradually evolved through chance mutation and natural selection, Donald reminds us that when we began reading and writing a mere five thousand years ago, there can have been no genetic change involved: there simply was not enough time. What had evolved instead—and with astonishing and gathering speed—was culture. Now, the great difference between natural selection and culture is that where genetic variation is random, culture is systematic and shot through with intentionality. A fish that opens its mouth for a cleaner wrasse will do so even if it needs no cleaning. In a laboratory experiment, when a fish raised in a tank was supplied with too many cleaners, it suffered pain from their attentions and tried—in vain—to escape them. The big fish still would never eat them, although it was accustomed to snapping up anything else that was dropped into the tank. For its part, a cleaner wrasse was observed to graze over the big fish even though there were no parasites on it and the cleaner had previously been fed to satiety.[17]

Donald says nothing about morality and carefully disclaims any interest in teleology.[18] He believes that genes provided us with the brain's plasticity, and that culture and incremental knowledge did the rest. This refusal to account for our behaviour entirely in terms of genetic imperatives and evolutionary processes—to see ourselves as "wired" and therefore strangers to freedom—opens up the possibility once again of seeing gratitude as more than mere self-interest, and as a phenomenon that cannot be accounted for entirely in material terms. The question remains, however: why did our brains evolve their enormous size in the first place? "What," after all, as biologist Harry J. Jerison demands, "is so great about being so smart?"[19]

4

"I'm So Sorry"

Reciprocity, which is an important part but still only a part of gratitude, can be found among animals: we have looked at an outstanding
example of interlocking benefits among fish. But this is not exactly what we
mean by reciprocity and gratitude in the human sphere, where memory is
required, together with a sense of justice and a practised desire to appreciate,
keep in mind, and (one day) give back—even where nothing forces us to
do so. Human beings, like other animals, depend upon each other for survival. But the vast variety of the ways in which people live this dependency,
and their freedom to decide what to do and how, amount to a wholly new
order of consciousness, where intentionality directs behaviour. For example,
every human culture invents its own signals and their meanings, and people
then decide when to use these, and when not to, in their dealings with one
another. A group may opt to change the meanings of those signals or invent
new ones. Individuals may manipulate the signals for specific purposes, often
in order to disguise their true feelings and intentions. Saying that "reciprocity evolved" is correct, as far as it goes. But human experience and learning
from experience, human feelings, and what one might still be permitted to
call "free will" remain unaccounted for by any theory that suggests the way
we behave is merely predetermined.

When we turn to scraps of information gleaned from ethnographical reports, such as the ones I presented earlier, we cannot but acknowledge that they too are—of necessity—crude. One of the ironies of modernity is that, just as modern human beings are at last learning to live with, understand, and even sometimes to accept peoples different from themselves, most cultural differences are in fact being wiped out. Variations survive among human cultures, but homogenization, driven by all the usual suspects—technology, transport, communications, mass marketing—is blanketing the earth. Alternative ways of being and behaving are being lost, together with the wisdom and stimulus they could offer all of us, so quickly that we can actually register their disappearance. Hundreds of languages, for example, are dying out as I write—each one of them an immensely rich, intricate, and unique way of apprehending reality.[1]

Of course, we can always turn to the Past to find Otherness. We can read about what travellers saw who discovered societies and peoples that had never come across "us" before, and that lived by rules very different from our own. But the trouble with the Past as Other is that the Past cannot answer back. It may be more rewarding to consider examples of behaviour in modern societies that function differently from ours, where we can ask the people themselves what they think and feel—and let them correct us when we have misunderstood them. We then have a hope of appreciating the choices, complexities, and intentionalities that constitute every human social system. We can, for example, consider the thanking rituals to be found in contemporary Japanese society, and listen to what the Japanese themselves say about these phenomena.

If I were to offer something—a cup of tea, for instance, or some soy sauce—to a Japanese person, he would be likely to say not "thank you," but "I'm so sorry":

A: *Shooyu o totte moraemasen ka.* (Please pass me the soy sauce.)
B: *Hai dozoo.* (Here you go.)
A: *Doomo sumimasen.* (I'm very sorry.)[2]

This response is a comparatively small matter, but (for Anglo-Saxons, and Europeans and Americans generally), a baffling oddity nonetheless. Florian Coulmas raised this point, well known as it was but never so incisively put, in an article on conversational routines published in 1981.[3] A flood of academic treatments—probably hundreds—began to pour out in response to Coulmas's article, in Japanese and other languages. The debate continues today.[4]

Takeo Doi, in *Anatomy of Dependence* (1973), describes how, when he was a new student in the United States, his university supervisor "did me some kindness or other—I have forgotten exactly what, but it was something quite trivial. Either way, feeling the need to say something, I produced not 'thank you,' as one might expect, but 'I'm sorry.' 'What are you sorry for?' he replied promptly, giving me an odd look. I was highly embarrassed. My difficulty in saying 'thank you' arose, I imagine, from a feeling that it implied too great an equality with someone who was in fact my superior. In Japanese, I suppose, I should have said '*doomo arigato gozaimasu*,' or '*doomo sumimasen*,' but, unable to express the same feeling of obligation in English, I had come up with 'I am sorry' as the nearest equivalent."[5]

Doomo sumimasen literally means "Oh, this does not end" or "This goes on and on." (*Sumimasen* is the polite negative of the verb *sumu*, "to be over.") The obligation is the point. "It is hard for me to be placed in this position," exclaims the speaker, "for I am fully aware of my debt to you. I can never repay it." *Doomo*, added for emphasis to *sumimasen*, is like "how" in "How dreadful!" *Doomo* can also be used to express pure deference, and then it is often translated "I have no excuse." The word can be, and often is, used on its own: foreigners commonly (and mistakenly!) think *doomo* means simply "thank you."[6]

An offer of a cup of tea to a Japanese person might also elicit the exclamation "Oh, this poisonous feeling!" (*Kino doku*). First, exclaiming that you feel uncomfortable is said to make the discomfort easier to bear. Second, the recipient of the favour feels ashamed. This is because it is always better to be the first to give, to the point where if I fail to be first, I feel—or at least say I feel—diminished. A much less powerful expression, also used where Westerners might say "thank you," is *arigato*, "Oh, this difficult thing." (The word comes from *ari*, "exist, have" and *gatashi*, "difficult.") This expression was originally a compliment to the giver, an acknowledgement of his or her superiority qua benefactor: it is always hard to admit one's inferiority. The word is now extremely common, its painfulness gone. It is employed, for example, by staff in department stores, who use it to exclaim at "the great and rare benefit the customer is bestowing on the store in buying." The word has become a matter of form. But words like *arigato* or *kino doku* or *sumimasen* have not become conventional utterances by chance. They contain within themselves the history of the culture, and remain pointers to assumptions and thought patterns.

Before we can begin to understand why the Japanese say phrases that may be translated as "I'm terribly sorry," or "This is poison to my soul," or "I feel ashamed," when a member of a Western European or North American culture should say "Thank you," we have first to stand back and look at the construction of Japanese society as a whole. In a famous book that has sometimes, in recent years, been branded "politically incorrect," Ruth Benedict set out after the end of the Second World War to explain the Japanese mind-set to the West.[7] The book is said to be dated because attitudes in Japan as elsewhere are changing fast. Still, some of the principles need to be understood, even today. In the course of the book Benedict lays out major differences between Japanese attitudes and those of Westerners.

Where North Americans, she says, think of themselves as heirs of the past (that is, that the ages culminate in themselves), the Japanese feel they are *debtors* to the ages—to everything that has gone before and especially to their immediate ancestors. They feel—their culture pressures them to feel—equally indebted to everyone in their society today. Righteousness, therefore, is recognition of one's place in "the great network of mutual indebtedness that embraces both one's forebears and one's contemporaries."

One of the Japanese words for obligation is *on,* which Westerners translate variously as meaning loyalty, kindness, and love, as well as obligation. It means all of those and none: *on* is a Japanese word, and no English word or phrase can really capture its significance. *On* is felt as a load, placed on your back by others; one is said to "wear" an *on*. The burden is acceptable if the person who thus encumbers you, your "*on* man," is in a position in society that is superior to your own, for superiors are regarded as being by nature well-wishers towards those inferior to them. If an equal, on the other hand, makes you wear an *on,* he probably makes you uncomfortable, even resentful. The power of *on* overrides all personal preferences; the individual should be ready to sacrifice himself for the group. And an *on* is vast: "One can never return one ten-thousandth of an *on.*" People are naturally unwilling to have *on* imposed on them by just anybody. They therefore try to avoid casual favours, for these might entangle them in *on*. And conversely, it is taking advantage of others to help them or give to them if one has no appropriate authority to do so.[8]

We in the West think of both debt and repayment as external to the essence of ourselves—as two parts, each time they occur, of one specific drama, which ought to come to an end when the curtain comes down. For Japanese, debt underlies everything, and repayment is activity on the surface and in time. Obeying the law, for example, is the repayment of a permanent indebtedness to others and to one's country; one should never stop obeying the law.[9] Westerners think they can "manage their own affairs" without concern for the debts they owe others. This belief, to the Japanese, is the world upside down, the world disconnected, behaviour that is childish, selfish, and confrontational. Another way of putting this is to say that Westerners are content with temporariness in human affairs, whereas Japanese want things if at all possible to be stable, to continue.

We can begin to understand the famous traditional Japanese "confusion" between thanking and apologizing when we realize that, in our own culture, thanking and apologizing do have something in common, and it is nothing other than indebtedness. With thanking, expressing gratitude is not enough.

One should give something back; the intention to return a favour must be present or one's words are merely empty. An apology, similarly, entails a desire to make amends. Both gratitude and apology involve awareness that relationships are at present unbalanced—that something needs to be done to restore an equilibrium that is an aspect of justice. And it is up to the receiver of a gift, or to the apologizing offender, to take the initiative and do something about it.

This is precisely what the word *sumimasen* ("it never ends") accepts and promises. It assures the benefactor that he has given to a thoroughly schooled and polished person, one who understands perfectly that obligation is everlasting. But that is not all. When Japanese scholars set about explaining what happens when somebody says *"sumimasen,"* they lay out a dazzling network of subtleties and intricacies. It is worth considering some of these, so that we may never forget the complexities of human behaviour, even in a domain as conventional and therefore pre-set as that of politeness routines. We might also look back at the facile judgments made by European travellers to foreign worlds about what was going on in the heads of people whose customs and languages they barely understood.

Japanese say that they feel quite different when they are at home from when they are "in public," that is, conversing with strangers or semi-strangers. The outside world of politeness and ritual gestures has its own word, *soto,* while the inside world of casualness and true feelings is known as *uchi.*[10] When in public, one displays one's social self and veils one's private self in discretion. *Sumimasen* is a public word, not taught in the beginning to children, who first master the words *arigato* and the intimate-sphere *gomen,* which are closer, respectively, to thanks and apology than is the ambiguous *sumimasen.* A person who has become adequately educated has learned to build up a public persona and a social "face." He or she is then fit to enter the public realm, the place of *aisatsu,* which is described as something like "decorum" or "greetings and farewells." (Japanese say there is no word in English that can fully express what *aisatsu* signifies.) This is when one starts saying politely apologetic phrases like "I will get in the way"—*ojama shimasu*—on entering a room. And one will begin to use the far-reaching and complex word *sumimasen*. You would never say "*sumimasen*" in private: you would sound full of distance and therefore insincere, superficial, ironic, or sarcastic.[11]

Sumimasen can mean a straight apology, where the speaker really feels he has done something that could offend. There is no thanks in it: *Okurete sumimasen*, "I'm sorry for being late." This is what sociolinguists, in terminology introduced by Erving Goffman,[12] call a "remedial" statement. It mitigates the trampling upon another person's "territory," the set of expectations that he feels, as a person of honour, ought not to be disappointed or "invaded." There is no question that I ought not to have been late; the fault was my own, and I must smooth the possibly ruffled feathers of the person kept waiting. Saying sorry offers a measure of compensation because apologizing is "reducing" one's own honour and thereby increasing the extent of the other person's.

But often *sumimasen* is used to mean both thanks and apologies:

RECEPTIONIST [*who does not have change*]: Do you have sixty yen?
CLIENT: Yes, I think I do. [Starts to count coins]
RECEPTIONIST: I'm very sorry. (*Sumimasen*.)[13]

The receptionist feels embarrassment (mild shame) at not having, when she should have had, change. She is both sorry to have made the client poke about in her purse, and grateful to her for being helpful and for not being annoyed. The receptionist is further grateful because the client has saved the speaker's "face," wrapped up as it is in her efficiency at her job. She needs to express unbounded indebtedness ("it never ends"). (Saying "*sumimasen*" is quite wrong where the speaker feels no particular indebtedness: in such a case, "*arigato*" would be sufficient.) Protesting undying obligation in this example adds "a humble tone," underlining the client's higher status. Of course, this being a routine matter of politeness, there is no necessity for the receptionist to *feel* deeply sorry or profoundly grateful; it is sufficient that she should *say* she does.[14]

Florian Coulmas pointed out—and the Japanese themselves concur—that "the Japanese conception of gifts and favors focusses on the trouble they have caused the benefactor rather than the aspects which are pleasing to the recipient."[15] Here are three examples, where the Japanese apologize and we would say "thank you":

WOMAN: I sent the fax for you yesterday, Mr. B.
MAN: I am very sorry. (*Doomo sumimasen deshita.*)[16]

The man is thinking of the trouble the woman has taken. It is worth pointing out that he is deliberately being "unnatural." He leaps over an intermediate step, the obviousness of which makes it "not worth mentioning": of course he is pleased to receive this service. What could be more natural than to think of himself, what he wanted, and the satisfaction he has been accorded? But Japanese politeness makes him shift his attention away from himself and his own pleasure, and consider the woman who has performed the action.

A: Would you like me to carry your luggage?
B: I am very sorry. (*Sumimasen.*)

"*Sumimasen*" implies that B is accepting the offer. She could also have used the much less ambiguous word "*arigato*"—which could be said even if she refused help. *Arigato* would thank the person for offering aid even if none were needed. However, B could not refuse the offer and use *sumimasen,* because this word must refer to the other person's action; it implies that that person would be carrying the luggage. The receiver of the favour expresses a feeling of regret for trouble caused, because a superior and polite person like her interlocutor could not but show his kindness to her:

[*On the bus, a man to a woman who is getting off*]

A: You forgot your umbrella! Your umbrella!

B: Oh, I'm very sorry. (*Aa, doomo sumimasen.*)

B is sorry she has been the occasion of the man's having to cry out. But also, *sumimasen* thanks people who remind us, advise us, or tell us what we are forgetting to do. It thereby declares that such urgings amount to substantive help, as well as the taking of trouble. People depend upon each other, and Japanese politeness formulae make them express appreciation of this fact.

When, say, a shop assistant acts within his role and performs a routine service, the customer says *arigato*, and as we saw, the assistant similarly thanks the client. But when the assistant does more than his duty, or offers more than was expected, the polite response is *sumimasen*:

[*A customer at a liquor store is buying drinks for a party.*]

CLERK: That'll be (so many) yen. The paper cups are on the house.

CUSTOMER [*handing over the money*]: Ah, I'm sorry. (*Aa, sumimasen.*)

It apparently often happens that when a superior does his duty, he is treated as though he has gone "over the top" and receives polite deference for it: *sumimasen*.[17] A stranger gets similar treatment: if you ask him the time in the street and he gives it, you behave as though what he has done is beyond duty (he might have ignored you and rushed on): *sumimasen*.

When in our culture people apologize in a polite context, it is rude not to accept the apology; there should be at least a pretense of morality. For us, forgiveness is a moral ideal. Japanese *sumimasen* can similarly reveal an underlying morality:

DOCTOR'S RECEPTIONIST: Sorry to have made you wait.

PATIENT: *Sumimasen.*

Here, the patient has to make some reply—that "goes without saying." She chooses *sumimasen* because the receptionist has "lowered" herself by apologizing. The patient remembers her "place"—that she is here to seek help. She therefore murmurs her awareness of the obligation she is under with a ritual acknowledgement of hierarchy, and thankfulness for the benevolence of superiors. Even if one has been kept waiting, one thinks of the kindness and expertise of doctors, not of one's own discomfort or inconvenience.

And finally (in this short and crude discussion of a matter that is far more complex than I have made it sound, and moreover concerns only the word *sumimasen* and none of the other ways of apologizing and expressing the obligation called *giri* in Japanese), conversational rules ordain that if one says both *sumimasen* and *arigato* in one exchange, *sumimasen* shall be said first and *arigato* second:

[*A woman asks a man to take a picture of her.*]
MAN: Sure.
WOMAN: I'm sorry. (*Sumimasen.*)
[*The man takes the picture and returns the camera to the woman.*]
WOMAN: I'm so sorry. (*Doomo sumimasen.*) Thank you very much.
  (*Arigato gozaimashita.*)

This exchange, like thousands of others in Japan, moves in three stages. First, there is an "occurrence of imbalance"—the woman interrupts the man's life and asks him to do her a favour. She "repairs the imbalance" by apologizing in advance, and then again after the man has taken the picture. Finally, the woman says "*arigato,*" a general term covering the entire exchange and marking an end to it. During the double *sumimasen* stage, the woman has denied herself any vulgar expression of her own satisfaction, and focused her attention on the man who has been so kind. He is not a person fulfilling a social role. He did not have to help her. He has done her a favour, she is grateful (that is, emotion has entered into the exchange), and she has done what she can to repay him, by offering him honour. He is honoured because she has "raised" him, treated him as her superior. *Arigato,* once also a word expressing obligation but now far "flatter" than *sumimasen,* brings down the emotional charge of the encounter. Now the two people can properly separate.

It is not sufficient, when we think about human behaviour, even the relatively simple and traditional conventionality that is politeness, to look merely at functioning conversational routines. For human behaviour constantly changes. It can seem almost impossible to keep up with the latest fashionable expressions and the fluctuations in their meanings. Today, we are told, many Japanese have decided to differentiate thanks from apologies in the Western manner. Very up-to-date people with experience of the international scene have brought two new words into their language, *sankyuu* and *soorii.*[18] These are considered to be extremely casual expressions and emotionally cool. Meanwhile *sumimasen,* in all its richness, considerateness, and diversity of application, is said to be gradually dying out.

5

"Thank You Very Much Indeed"

The intricate strategies of *sumimasen,* and the myriad other possibilities offered by politeness formulae in Japanese, are hardly to be looked for in the far more humdrum usages of Anglo-Saxon and other European cultures. But there are two outstanding characteristics of thanking behaviour in English. One is the invariability and simplicity of the words *thank you* and *thanks.* The other is the frequency with which we keep thanking each other, something we tend to do even when speaking in their own languages to foreigners who are unaccustomed to being constantly thanked.

A common problem for people learning foreign languages lies precisely in the control and management of routines such as thanking. Where a person's own language has a totally different phrase ready for when a certain situation arises, or (and even more so) where one is accustomed simply to saying nothing on some occasions, it is difficult for a foreigner to remember to enter into the right routine, to know what—or what not—to say. Yet to get these conventions wrong is to risk appearing "awkward, eccentric, impolite, or ridiculous," in the words of a student of politeness in Arabic.[1]

Arabs offer wishes and blessings when we would say nothing at all. They exclaim "With health!" when somebody has just had a bath, declare "May God forgive you!" when coming upon one who is smoking, or pronounce a desire for "Goodness and peace!" before another speaker may embark on a story or begin to recount a piece of news. A Moroccan waiter is said to have exclaimed "*Bon appétit!*" when he brought the bill after a restaurant meal. But his customer, a sociolinguistics expert, realized that the waiter had artlessly assumed that this French formula resembled *bsshha*, "With health!" which is correctly said after as well as before meals (or baths) in Arabic.[2] "Thank you" in Arabic is often *shukrun*, or *barakallahufik* ("God bless you!"), because people commonly perform thanks by uttering a blessing and calling on God. But different phrases may be used depending on what the gratitude is for, and one of these may not be substituted for another. Examples are "May God strengthen your income!" for money, "May God replace it!" for money or a meal, "May God give you health!" or "Health to your hands!" for manual work such as cooking or repairs, "May God bless you!" for certain kinds of good wishes, and "May God keep you safe!" for others. "Forgive me!" is for the taking of trouble, as when someone has helped a passerby to find his way (and here Arabic is like Japanese in requiring "sorry" for trouble taken, where we would expect "thank you"). Arab women (but not men) presumably make forgiveness sweet when they say, "I cut it from your mouth with honey."[3]

English "thank you" is a bald phrase, quickly uttered. It is also rigidly invariable, apart from the even briefer form, "thanks." It cannot be turned into the passive voice ("you are thanked"), nor can "thank" be replaced with a synonym. All that is allowed is intensification by means of a lengthening ("Thank you very much") or a greater lengthening ("Thank you very much indeed") or by imbedding it in a formal sentence ("I wish to thank you . . ."). We are allowed to add to "thank you" or substitute for it in the form of certain compliments or exclamations of delight ("Thank you! What a marvellous idea!") or both surprise and delight ("Oh wow! *Thank* you!"). Exaggeration also helps express gratitude: "I *love* it!" or "This is a lifesaver!" An English speaker may occasionally say with some solemnity, "I am grateful," to show that strong emotion underlies—or at least hovers around—the words spoken, precisely because he or she has said something other than—and so gone beyond—the ubiquitous because sternly required minimum, "thanks."

"Thank you" can also be said in a sarcastic manner, depending on the context and the intonation. "*Thank* you very much!" said very fast with a strong emphasis on the first word can be a powerfully dismissive expression: "I told them, 'You can count me out, *thank* you very much!'" The second expression shows so much superiority, so much rejection through sarcasm of any idea of gratitude, that the speaker is unlikely actually to have said it to people who invited her, unless she intended to end the relationship there and then. "*Thank* you very much!" often implies, "Don't think you can give me anything, because I don't want it. Don't you realize that I already have what you are attempting to offer?" A routine thanking formula, with this special speed and intonation, both negates its original meaning and implies far more than a plain refusal would have done.

Routines, in any language, have important uses. They reduce the extreme complexity of everyday conversational encounters. (Linguistic scientists assure us that we daily engage in verbal interactions of a complexity they struggle to describe, let alone explain.) Routines give people a chance to think and size one another up while producing, in due form and patterning, words they know by heart, much as a Homeric bard produced sets of hexameters he and his audience knew already, providing a kind of pleasurable mental breathing space until complexity and creativity began again. Routines occur at difficult moments of transition, when people are relieved to know how to react properly: at greetings and farewells (which Florian Coulmas compares with the formalities of opening and terminating moves in chess[4]), apologies, requests, and thanks. Soothing responses are produced and rapport established without speakers' having to become inventive every time such moments occur. (The word *routine* comes from *route:* one knows the way, laid out as it is in advance, as on a map.) The repetition, because of their usefulness, of conversational gambits helps them harden into unchanging agglomerations of words.

The "thank you" formula has become so pre-set and so conventional that it defies grammatical analysis. A whole new linguistic science has been invented, partly in order to explicate simple, routine word sets. It studies such matters as the contexts of words and phrases, to whom and when they may be said, how routines and repetitions are inserted into and help shape conversations, how words and ready-made phrases are adapted to circumstances, recourse to intonation and timing in order to influence meaning—in short, how words are used, as opposed to what traditional grammar analyzes into nouns, verbs, adjectives, prepositions, and adverbs. This new science, called pragmatics, sees *thanks* as neither a noun nor a verb, but a stem, susceptible of expansion, compounding, and ironic subversion. It may also conceal more than it says, as when a woman murmurs "Thank you" (with a rising tone) to a man holding out her coat and means, "I can do the rest of the putting-on by myself, but I do appreciate your polite manners and your kind intentions, and indeed your help with the first and more difficult part of this operation—that of finding the left sleeve while my back was turned towards it."

Pragmatics sometimes calls *thanks* a "behabitive," meaning that it lets others know that the speaker has adopted an attitude. Here, thanking once again resembles apology, and also expressions of sympathy, compliments, applauding, criticism, greeting, wishing, cursing, and challenging.[5] Thanks, like apology, is an "expressive speech act," announcing the speaker's stance regarding either something happening or another person. It is also said to be an "Illocutionary Force Indicating Device" (an IFID), which classifies it as something showing both speaker and addressee to be involved in an illocution (examples of which are warnings, promises, thanksgivings) in a state of affairs that the speaker believes to be a fact. Practitioners of pragmatics are interested in what people's intentions and decisions are, even during the employment of conventional turns of phrase. But pragmaticists are not allowed to let the obvious pass. They explain that one does not thank for something not done by the addressee, or perceived as not having benefited the speaker. Also, the speaker must either be grateful or have decided to behave as though he or she were grateful.[6]

Pragmatics takes from artificial intelligence the concept of "frames" for its stems. Frames are "knowledge representations of communication situations"[7]—in other words, the experience that the speaker has gathered of various social occasions, which leads him or her to choose certain routine phrases and not others. For example, during a restaurant meal one speaks in set phrases that have to be learned in foreign languages: "What are today's specials?" "*Cobrame por favor,*" "*On partage l'addition,*" and either "*Bitte sehr*" or "*Bitte schön*" depending on who is speaking to whom and what is happening at the table. Gratitude frames include the reason for gratitude, the speaker's perception of the size of the favour, the age, sex, and extent of familiarity one has with the interlocutor, all in addition to the specific demands, constraints, and conventions of the situation.

Conversational routines are seen, further, as various sets of "turns" or "moves," a game with amazingly rigid rules. If someone begins such a game and others do not join in, the consequences can be catastrophic. A sociolinguistics professor performed an experiment in his office to prove it. When he arrived for work one day and his secretary said her obligatory "Good morning," he merely looked at her and said nothing in reply. Then he strove to carry on normally after that dreadful breaking of the norm of "turns." The next day he did the same. Tension mounted in the office as the days went by. He received "strange looks" from his colleagues. Eventually his nerve failed him, and he dropped the experiment for fear of an "explosion" if he dared to continue. Greeting behaviour includes a relentless insistence that one "good morning" deserves another: immense hostility can build up if this tiny symbol of benevolence is ignored.[8]

Rigidly required greeting behaviour immediately arouses Darwinian excitement: animals also "greet." Correct "greeting"—a bow from a night heron or a cheep from a turkey chick—can identify the performer as a member of the group, whereas non-performance might mean death to the creature diagnosed as a non-bowing, non-cheeping stranger. (Experimenters proved this by deafening a female turkey, who then murdered her young because she did not hear them cheep. A night heron returning to the nest failed to bow in the required manner, whereupon his own offspring killed him.[9])

Failure to greet, among human beings, normally has strict but less dire consequences, quite apart from the fact that we usually recognize people we know even if they are behaving oddly. We have, it is true, invented precautions, such as the secret password, knowledge of which could save your life among people who have never met you, and the elaborate allowances made for messengers from the enemy, who would probably be killed if they were not official badge-bearing, sign-making messengers. But greeting behaviour, which for human beings includes language as its most significant dimension, makes two demands: first, response to the other person, and second, knowledge of when and how to greet properly (an entirely cultural matter, and in large measure a reassurance for others that one has been taught how to behave). Even the opening greeting "Good morning" is mainly a response, a paying of attention, a mark of respect for the other person's presence. That person is then expected to reply in a similar spirit.

Erving Goffman has reminded us that thanking, like returning greetings, is a matter of balance. Someone makes a request, interrupting the other person's thoughts and actions in doing so, "upsetting the equilibrium" of the relationship by creating, as it were, a gap, a space that needs filling:

A: Would you pass the milk?
B: Here.
A: Thanks.

B has filled the need. A thanks him, not only for the milk but also for returning him to self-sufficiency and restoring the original "balance." A simultaneously brings this exchange to an end by saying "Thanks." Goffman calls the one who asks the "offender." When his request has been granted, the "offender" must thank.[10] We have seen that in Japanese interchanges, often the "offender" must apologize. (And furthermore, it is not "self-sufficiency" a polite Japanese person is seeking, but recognition of human interdependence and obligation.) *Thanks* may be a simple word, but it does not stand alone; it always forms part of an exchange, however trivial and however brief.

The saying of "thanks" is so important in English interchanges that the person who has done a favour often goes on to help the receiver to thank him. "I hope it fits" is a remark that makes it easier for the recipient of a sweater to exclaim, "It fits perfectly! How did you know my size?"—and a whole conversation is launched. "That'll keep you warm" prompts thanks and a further enumeration of the present's advantages. Other cues offered by givers might include, "It should be washable—machine washable." (*Pause.*) Or, after providing hospitality, "It was lovely having you." (*Space for a response.*) Then, "We're going to miss you." (*Now what do you say?*)[11]

The point is that thanking either expresses or provokes interaction. In our culture, thanking and being thanked are essential for expressing both recognition of others—all others, both strangers and intimates—and respect for them. This inclusion of those close to us more than doubles, in English, the number of times that thanking is performed in many other cultures where, as we have seen, one does not thank intimates. Conversely, not thanking at all among intimates whose language is English—where people are on good terms, of course—can express exceptional closeness. It is highly likely that English usage insists on constant thanking in part because of the relative separateness with which people in our culture usually live their lives. This separateness (we also call it "individualism") is something both imposed on us and chosen by us, in the mixture of constraint and choice that constitutes culture. Thanking has an important compensatory role to play, to the point where it becomes an almost compulsory routine. Bilingual Hindi-English speakers in India thank more often in English than they do in Hindi: people who are equally at ease in two languages will allow the language being spoken to dictate customs as well as grammar. In Hindi-English circles, a man will repeatedly say "Thank you, darling" to his wife when using English. But he would not, while using Hindi, say "thank you" to her in the English manner unless he "desires to be sarcastic or is a terrible tease."[12]

A study of compliments in North American English may shed further light on the rigidity and simplicity of English thanking.[13] Compliments are often added to thanks, to expand them and render them more personal. But most of us would be surprised to learn that the outstanding characteristic of compliments in American English is their lack of originality. We think we are being spontaneous and therefore in no way imitative when we offer praise to people, when in fact we unconsciously follow strict and limiting rules.

For example, "nice" and "good" (together with fashionable intensives of these, like "terrific" or "fabulous") are used in nearly half of all compliments: "I love your shoes! They're terrific!" "That chocolate cake was amazing." Other almost inevitable adjectives, all of them quite meaningless except that they demonstrate approbation, are "pretty," "beautiful," "great," "wonderful," "lovely," and "grand." As for verbs, an even narrower compass is preferred. "Like" and "love" occurred in 86 percent of a sample of 686 compliments. And where an even slightly unusual verb or phrase is used, it tends to be intensified by "really": "You've really made a difference to this place." "Just" is similarly added to adjectives if they are less than totally predictable: "Your contribution's been just staggering." Nouns are preceded by the "positive" but almost meaninglessly conventional "quite a" or "some": "That was quite a party." A further characteristic of North American compliments is that they carefully point out what is being praised, and they directly address the person being complimented: "I love your skirt and your blouse."

Researchers found only nine patterns for complimentary sentences. The first three of these make up the majority of them: (1) "——— is/looks (really) ———" ("Your living room looks wonderful"); (2) "I (really) like/love ———" ("I really like those shoes"); (3) "——— is/was (really) ———" ("This was really a great meal"). Less common are (4) "You ——— (really) ———") ("You did a really terrific job"); (5) "You (really) ———" ("You really handled that situation well"); (6) "You have (really) ———" ("You have really beautiful hair"); (7) "What a ————!" ("What a lovely baby you have!"); (8) (adjective plus noun) "———— ————!" ("Nice touch!" "Good shot!"); and (9) "Isn't ———— ————!" ("Isn't it gorgeous!" "Isn't your ring beautiful!")

Compliments are not only relentlessly but also deliberately formulaic. In the flow of conversation, compliments can be dropped in without warning. This unpredictability explains why they have to be so carefully directed to the person and specific about what is found pleasing:

A: Anyway, I've been working pretty hard . . .
B: That's a really nice sweater. It looks great on you.
A: Thanks. I've finished most of the work already.

Compliments can also be used to start a conversation. Anything new that is being worn is good for such a beginning: "That outfit's really nice. Is it new?" And looking thin, being a great sign of acceptability in the culture, is another: "Hey, Joe, you really look good. You've lost weight."

Such compliments are little caresses, signs of affection that need not bear any relation to what else is being said—if anything has yet been said at all. They refer, via kindly observations, to uncommitted, unspecified, but friendly dispositions underlying the words spoken. Compliments of this peculiarly modern kind, like the even more formulaic "thanks," are produced often. They must of necessity be specific, yet chosen from a narrow set of possibilities. Manes and Wolfson, the authors of this report, believe that one reason for these constraints is that "there is little or no similarity of background, and only the most general of cultural values can be assumed to be shared."

The lack of originality in complimenting behaviour is useful in other ways. The word *compliment* is from Latin *complere,* via Spanish *cumplir,* meaning "perform what is due." Now, inventiveness and surprise are rarely "what is due": people sometimes wish to be perceived as peculiar, but not often. And it is essential that the person complimented remain in no doubt that a compliment is what is being proffered, even though there may be nothing to lead up to or prepare for the statement:

A: That's an interesting dress.

B: Gee, is that supposed to be a compliment, John?

A: [*Embarrassed*] Well, sure. I didn't say it was dull, did I?

No offence would have been taken if A had said "great" or "beautiful" instead of departing from the script by producing "interesting."

Three different reactions to a compliment are possible. One may either say "thank you" for it, or one may play it down: deny its truth, protest, or suddenly change the subject of the conversation. The third alternative, outright refusal, is always rude, and usually takes the compliment to have been improper. A Frenchwoman might say in such a circumstance, "*Tes compliments tu peux te les garder*" ("I don't want any compliments from you"—literally "You can keep your compliments"), and even resort to brutal expletives, flinging any semblance of politeness to the winds.[14]

North Americans are famous for saying "thank you" when complimented. Europeans, including the British, traditionally do not thank on these occasions but prefer to play down complimentary remarks. This reaction is changing, as more and more people opt for the modern strategy of the simple, flat, and unmistakably laudatory compliment. There is widespread automatic imitation of American behaviour, but it is also true that the same conditions that first produced the formulaic compliment in America are spreading. As societies adopt egalitarian attitudes, they naturally become unceremonious and blunt of speech. And there is a need for more clarity, less indirectness, and less unspoken subtlety as people increasingly meet others with whom they have little in common and few shared but unspoken assumptions to lean on.

And there is a further reason. As saying "thank you" for it implies, a simple compliment has come to be perceived as a gift. Forcing compliments into token-like regularity of form turns them into symbols of generalized benevolent intent. They are then used simply to show attentiveness, or to lend conscious support to a friendly attitude. These are not trivial matters, even if the compliments themselves are merely formulaic; indeed, we give thanks for the kindly disposition revealed (at least apparently) by compliments. "Thank you" as a response to a compliment leaves little room for expansion, however, unless the admirer is very determined. The compliment having been given, benevolence established, the interlocutors wish to move on. They like feeling they are busy and pragmatic—but still friendly.

To play a compliment down—the alternative and more traditional strategy with compliments in European cultures—is not to refuse it, but to refuse to revel in it publicly:

> INTERVIEWER [*to Brigitte Bardot*]: Your beauty—I mean, it can't always
>   have made life easy. . . .
> BARDOT [*interrupting him*]: Oh, I'm not beautiful. Not really.

Her breaking in to prevent further effusions and her disagreement are typical responses to compliments. Here the compliment is not considered to be a gift, but (merely) an opinion. It might be true or false: either way, there is nothing to be thankful for. Its formulation might be conventional, but there is far less rigour and limitation than in the American examples where the one complimenting is forced to show approbation and approbation only. A person who receives a compliment is not supposed to agree with or endorse the complimentary opinion—as Bardot would have appeared to do if she had replied with "Thank you." There are exceptions to this rule, but they are always at least slightly shocking.

Disagreement, on the other hand, can serve to make one seem more admirable still: one remains cool, unconcerned with one's own merits; one never crows. To protest, however, immediately provides opportunities for further interaction. More might be said in the same vein, or arguments produced to support the original assertion:

A: I love your necklace.
B: Oh no, it's just a piece of old junk. I found it on sale somewhere.

A French speaker in an equivalent exchange is likely to claim madness in the one doing such praising: ("*T'es folle!*" "*Tu rêves!*" "*Tu délires!*") or to behave as if he is joking ("*Sans blague!*" and so forth), in order to turn the compliment aside.[15] Of course, if the necklace really is a piece of old junk and has elicited a compliment, the reason must be that it is one's person that has lent beauty to it. At the very least, to have seen something exceptional in a cheap thing, passed over by others as ordinary, means that its buyer must have outstanding discernment. It is the prowess in the admired person—or the magnificence of the object in her possession—that is assumed to be the subject of the entire gambit, not a vague kindly disposition in the one who offers the compliment. This assumption explains why old-fashioned compliments are commonly "fished" for:

A: I'm afraid the kitchen looks very cluttered—my husband's china
   collection had to go somewhere!
[*B is expected to say something at least as extended and inventive as it is
   admiring.*]

Once again, a small instance from another culture may sharpen our perception of our own attitudes. In Japan, to compliment someone is to engage in not one but several exchanges of praise and ritual denial. Humility in one complimented is essential; even if it is not felt, it must be expressed. And conversely, humility must be ritually rejected, the admirably humble one "raised up" by the one who praises. A Japanese scholar visiting the United States encountered a colleague who commented, politely by American standards, on his new bicycle:

A: What a beautiful bicycle you have.
B: It's nothing; it's the cheapest thing I could find.
A: I like it. Have a nice day.

The Japanese scholar, watching his interlocutor abruptly and cheerfully depart, was left to wonder why she did not like his bicycle (and perhaps also why she was so brutal about it).[16]

Modern North American complimenting behaviour, by contrast, allows those complimented to say "thank you" without a blush:

A: Your eyes are just glorious, you know.
B: Thank you.

Admiration is accepted as freely bestowed readiness to see beauty in others and a sign of fondness in the speaker, rather than a perceptive response to excellence. (The person with glorious eyes might agree that she is peculiarly gifted; her conventional response to having this pointed out, however, veils her self-satisfaction.)

But modern thanking (as opposed to complimenting) behaviour may often lead a benefactor to turn aside his beneficiary's thanks:

A: Thank you so much. You've been so kind.
B: Don't mention it.

English and other European languages have various phrases for turning aside thankfulness: "That's all right," "Not at all," "*De rien,*" "*Pas de quoi,*" "*Keine Ursache,*" "*No faltaba más,*" "*No hay de qué,*" and so forth. All of these expressions can be used as well to deflect an apology. They protest that thanking (or apology) was unnecessary, that there was no need to say anything (although there almost certainly was).

Often languages demand, after "thank you," a response that means "please":

A: *Grazie.*
B: *Prego.*

B's response means, "Please do not thank me. Do not feel you owe me anything." It might further imply, "It is I who say 'please,' and therefore you are not the 'offender'—I am." In Swedish, the response "Please" or "Be so good" seems to give the hearer the option of whether or not to accept the offer made.[17] To the German "*Danke schön*" the response is "*Bitte schön,*" where *schön,* literally "lovely," is an intensifier and therefore optional, and *bitte* is "I beg you" or "please." In Iraqi Arabic, the response to "thank you" is "*mamnoon.*" When I asked an Arab friend the literal meaning of this word, he said, "It means *thank you* twice': thank *you* for giving me the opportunity of doing something for you which has caused me to hear you say 'Thank you.'"

Of course, no one thinks all this when routinely saying "*Prego*" or "*Bitte,*" "*Je vous en prie,*" or "*Mamnoon.*" But the feeling is very strong that something should be said after thanks have been expressed. Such interjections exist to lessen the extent of the imbalance incurred by a kind act. Everybody knows that "thank you" is not enough repayment, that in the future there will probably have to be deeds done in addition to these words said, if gratitude is to be proven. The polite giver therefore seeks to lighten the burden of obligation, at least temporarily, by denying that it exists. Similarly, when someone is given a present, she might exclaim, "You shouldn't have!" meaning that the giver should not feel that there was an obligation to give anything. The gift is entirely the giver's idea; the receiver claims to have expected nothing. Another strategy for the giver is to say that there is nothing to be grateful for because he enjoyed giving ("It's a pleasure" or "My pleasure" or simply "Pleasure") or that giving cost him little.

> A: Thank you! They're so beautiful! I love tomatoes fresh from the garden.
> B: Oh, it's nothing.
> A: Oh, but—you shouldn't have!
> B: No, really, I have plenty.

In a minority of languages—one of them is British English—there is no felt need to say anything after one has been thanked. "Not at all" is possible, and "Oh, that's OK," and other responses that are equally acceptable after an apology. But there is nothing in English like German *bitte* or Italian *prego*. North Americans, however, commonly say "You're welcome" after being thanked (and once again this custom appears to be spreading to British English). It seems possible that foreign immigrants to North America, feeling a dreadful hole in the conversation—nowhere to say "*prego*" or "*bitte*"—every time someone thanked them, supplied the missing response with "You're welcome." (Incidentally, "You're welcome" cannot be used after "Thanks" for a North American compliment. "I love your boots!"—"Thank you!"—"You're welcome!" would either be improper or involve sarcasm. It would make the one praising sound like a cold-blooded sycophant. Compliments are not, then, exactly like gifts.)

North American English also presses thankers to assure their benefactors that reciprocity will occur: "I'll pay you back as soon as I can." "You must come and see us sometime. We'll give you a call." "Next time it's on me." In other cultures it is not always necessary to promise to repay. It might indeed be thought politer not to: people often feel that something so obviously to be expected should not have to be mentioned at all.

The Japanese, ceremonious as they are, often do not say anything in response to thanking. This is because the Japanese thank by using a declaration, expressing their awareness that there exists an obligation to repay. "*Sumimasen*" ("This is not the end") is one example. And such a sentence, as a piece of information, does not call for a response.

In British English as well, "thank you" is often followed by silence. The reason has to do with the special frequency of saying thanks in the language. "Thanks," especially in British English, has many uses that have only a tenuous relationship, or none at all, with gratitude. In modern Anglo-Saxon custom, British as well as North American, thanking is rather like complimenting behaviour in that it is a sign of connectedness in an often disconnected world, a mark of goodwill, a brief gesture of respect. Like the compliments described, it often aims past the actual transaction or the gift or the offer of a gift, to address itself to the person behind it. "Thank you" need not express depth of feeling. It is neither inventive nor creative in its expression, but does demonstrate a minimum of respect. This minimality in itself makes a lapse in this highly mechanical ritual of thanking a serious matter, just as failing to say "Good morning" in response to "Good morning" is a breach that will later need to be repaired if relations are to continue. Often the simpler and the fewer the rules, the more strictly they are kept, and the angrier people become when they are not.

"Thanks," then, is said not only when one accepts an offer but when one refuses it: "No, thanks." At table, the French do not even say "*Non*" but only "*Merci*,"; the thanking for an offer being raised thereby to more importance than the wishes of the person declining. A gesture or a tilt of the head, so slight that it could easily be missed by the unaccustomed, is all that expresses the refusal; acceptance of the offer is expressed by "*S'il vous plaît*" and receiving, followed by another, gestureless "*Merci*." When one refuses something for a good reason, one may explain what that reason is but should still express gratitude: "I'm afraid I work on Wednesday nights. Thanks all the same." Thanks are due for the benevolence expressed by the offer even should it not correspond to what is wanted. And when someone asks about one's welfare, it is rude not to thank him or her for asking:

A: How are you?

B: Fine, thanks.

Other languages commonly make a distinction between forms corresponding to French "*vous*" and "*tu*," the plural form being formal and the singular form intimate. The English language has rejected "thou" and "thee" and kept only "you"—plural and therefore respectful. "Thanks," the informal alternative to "thank you," has appeared because the English language can no longer distinguish between distance and familiarity by using a pronoun other than "you." Calling everybody "you," on the other hand, is an egalitarian move in a culture that nevertheless emphasizes respect.

The Latin word *respicere,* the root of *respect,* means literally "to turn around and look at." Respect involves regard (a word that literally means "a look"), an admiration sufficient to make us stop in our tracks and turn around; it implies a distance between the observer and the one looked at. (In a culture that despises the obediently conventional and even the irreproachable, "respectability" has come to be devalued; "respect," however, has if anything grown in demand.) Respect is most obviously felt for people we consider admirable and therefore above us. Respect for all is, however, one of the ideals of our culture. Constantly saying "thank you" and "thanks" is one expression of that ideal. It has been suggested that every time we say "please" or "thank you," we express respect: "Pass the salt, (*you are worthy of respect*)." "(*You are worthy of respect*), have some more."—"No, (but) (*you are worthy of respect*)."[18]

Thanking is so widely used partly because "thank you" is easy to say and can offend no one. It is useful, therefore, in public notices. When telling people in general, such as clients or passengers, to do something, thanking may be chosen nowadays instead of commanding. It sounds more respectful, the directive less overbearing: "Thank you for not smoking." Apology, on the other hand, is often felt to be a kind of abasement. One can avoid saying sorry for any inconvenience to the public created by work in progress, and at the same time offer a possibly mollifying respect, by displaying a sign saying THANK YOU FOR YOUR COMPREHENSION.

Thanking is also done ironically, sarcastically, or brusquely. It can be a reaction to a compliment that is no compliment, whether it is rudely meant or a joke:

A: This sweater rolls up in the middle.
B: And you don't need that!
A: Thanks.

Gratitude is expressed for a big favour, of course, but also for a little or even a tiny one, such as being handed something. ("Here you are." "Thanks.") It can assure a benefactor of one's future gratitude, or dismiss a person whose services are not needed. Thanks (effusive or mechanical, according to circumstance) are said on receiving offers, arrangements, and suggestions, and on accepting or rejecting them. Sometimes a rejection might offend and therefore needs special work, perhaps with a compliment thrown in:

A: You can have a spoonful of cream with these if you like.
B: I really won't. Thanks awfully. They're terribly good!

In British English, "thank you" can be used simply to end a verbal exchange, which may be why the English traditionally say nothing after "Thank you": the exchange is over and there is nothing further to be said. Telephone conversations—where words are everything because there are no external signs to help in making judgments, and facial expressions cannot be seen—have evolved elaborate rituals for verbally ending an exchange without offence. Cutting the other person off without warning is very rude, and especially to be guarded against because hanging up is so very easy to do. Thanking-as-an-ending is brought into play as a preparation for hanging up, and often offered twice or three times during the ending ritual. Other ending strategies include taking time, making strategic repetitions, and taking turns. There are rules, and we keep them, complex as they are and even though we are in the main unaware that rules exist, let alone that we obey them.

When a telephone conversation is nearly over, the speakers gradually converge upon an ending. This is done by confirmations of what has been agreed, then an agreement to close, then a pre-closing "Thank you" and finally the ritual "Good-bye." (It is possible to end an exchange with a bare "Thank you" but that is very dry and formal, and reserved for people who do not know each other or with whom we are seriously annoyed.) Here is a typical example:

A: Well, as near two-thirty as possible, then.

[*The agreement made previously is recapitulated. This constitutes a suggestion that the conversation might close soon.*]

B: Yes.

A: All right. That's fine. Thank you very much. That'll ensure that we'll get some kind of daylight [*laughs*] even if it's raining—

[*The thanking constitutes a preparation for ending the conversation. There follows a lightening of mood with a little joke, possibly because A has made this potentially offensive move.*]

B: Yes—that'd be good. Yes.

A: Yes. OK, fine.

B: Fine. Excellent.

[*Time is taken to feel satisfaction at the conjuncture achieved; the repetitions are also confirmations. Each waits for the other to make the first definitively closing move.*]

A: Thanks very much.

[*A has done it. The penultimate move is finally taken: they are about to close the conversation.*]

B: Thank you. Look forward to seeing you.

[*B begins the farewell.*]

A: All right. Bye then.

B: Bye-bye.

[*A has completed it, B confirms it. Both have displayed amiability and a good relationship. The curtain comes down when they hang up.*][19]

In this conversation, thanking does retain a hint of gratitude. But it is also "pragmatically" used to move the conversation towards closure. Thanking almost invariably precedes final goodbyes on the telephone. Thanks as an ending occur also in discussions, on radio or television, for example, where a host wants to stop somebody talking and move on to another speaker. This is a transcription from a radio program:

A: We should remember those of our ancestors that we can find out about and take an interest in them because out of them came everything that we are . . .

B: Thank you very much. Let's ask the psychologist . . . [20]

Anglo-Saxons are capable even of making an interaction out of nothing but repeated thankings. In the following exchange a train conductor has taken a passenger's ticket and stamped it. He now hands it back with thanks, perhaps for the passenger's cooperation but perhaps to show he has finished with the ticket. The passenger says "Thank you" on receiving the ticket. The conductor makes an end of the transaction before moving on:[21]

CONDUCTOR: Thank you.

PASSENGER: Thank you.

CONDUCTOR: Thank you.

PART II

Giving, Receiving, Returning

6

Why Give Back?

Before we go deeper into thanking—into what it means, its consequences, and what people feel when they are grateful—it is important to take into account what people say "thank you" for. Gratitude is a response; it invariably comes second. Something has first to be given or done; this action performed or object bestowed inspires people "on the receiving end" to react. The response itself has predictable aspects to it: not only spoken thanks, but usually a deed or a gift given in return. Since ancient times, the very idea of gifts, and the sequence of giving, receiving, and giving back, have been considered extremely important for the functioning of society. But modern speculations and theorizing on the subject have become unusually urgent and conflicted.

A gift is, to modern eyes, an anomaly: an object that should be a commodity but claims to be more. Why—and how—is it not a commodity? After all, in our culture at least, it has been bought, hasn't it? And in exactly what sense can it be said to be "more"? Gifts are commonly thought of as bestowed freely. Now, we can think of lots of things we give because of the conventions of the occasion, because we are under pressure to do so. Where then does freedom come into it? Modernity understands commodities: it is built on money, it admires money made out of things sold, and it regulates buying and selling by means of obligations, written down in advance as contracts. There is nothing free about contracts, and there is apparently nothing mysterious about commodities. They are clear and "above board."

In contrast, "below board," in the dark hold of the ship, as it were, lies the world of gift-giving. This enormous area, essential as it is to all human beings, went largely unmentioned by the secular intelligentsia after the Enlightenment. Nietzsche called gift-giving "the unnameable" from the point of view of the market.[1] It is said that modernity (the most visible and polished part of it, at least—that is, our system of commodities) created itself, quite deliberately, in opposition to this world of the gift,[2] and as an ideology has often had trouble forgiving itself for not having managed totally to demystify and so discredit this "below board" phenomenon. As a matter of fact gift-giving, as anyone who thinks about it may immediately observe, is everywhere in our society. We buy each other so many presents that businesses all over the world would be ruined if we stopped doing so.

And within this endlessly questioned realm of gift-giving, nothing puzzles recent investigators more than the phenomenon of receivers "giving back" something for a favour received. We saw in Part One that when receiving a gift, we normally express gratitude by thanking one another. This habit cuts no ice with social scientists: in the hunt for the secret reasons for our giving in return for receiving, feeling grateful and expressing thanks are scarcely mentioned. We *say* we are thankful, but that simply cannot be the reason why we do favours in return for what we receive from others. It must be something else: we feel inferior for having received and wish to equalize, for example. Or there is "a norm," mysteriously enforced by society, which ordains that everyone who receives shall, willy-nilly, give back. More recently, we have been told that behaviour such as giving, receiving, and giving back must be instigated by our genes.[3] It is my contention that gratitude (once we are clear what it means and how it operates) is essential to any explanation of what happens when we give, receive, and give back.

The puzzlement of social scientists, however, is genuine, and many highly intelligent people have worked hard turning over every stone to find an answer. It is typical of our culture, of course, to set about explaining by focusing on objects and the responses to them rather than on other kinds of favours given: helping other people, for example, or spending time visiting them, or listening to accounts of their problems. Material gifts can be converted into manipulated commodities more easily than can non-material actions. Gifts as objects can be counted, measured, and priced, and so lend themselves easily to scientific investigation. But gifts are also poetic, symbolic, concrete. I myself will often, in this book, let material presents re-present, or be shorthand for, other kinds of favours. We owe it to the suspiciousness and the industry of the social scientists that we have, in the course of the past hundred years or so, learned a considerable amount about what happens when gifts are given. What is certain is that gift-giving behaviour is far from simple, and definitely not to be taken for granted.

It was Marcel Mauss, the nephew of Emile Durkheim (one of the founders of sociology), who was responsible for formulating the question of Giving Back in such a manner that it became for most of the past century a problem for endless academic reflection and discussion. A new relevance has been discovered recently in his book, *Essai sur le don* (1925), retranslated into English as *The Gift* (1992),[4] because Mauss seems to oppose aspects of Social Darwinism. For the notion walks again, "philosophically creaking but technically shining," as Mary Douglas puts it, that "the survival of the fittest" applies to human social life just as it does to the evolution of the species.[5] Douglas feels that Mauss can help us make a counterattack upon the intellectual presuppositions of Social Darwinism.

Marcel Mauss (1872–1950) lived at a moment of imminent change in Western social history, and he did not like what he saw coming. He was an anti-Utilitarian, who especially hated cold-hearted calculation of profit alone, and the privileging of individualism over social interaction. (His name is honoured today by the acronym of a French institute called M.A.U.S.S., Mouvement Anti-Utilitariste dans les Sciences Sociales.) As modern people often do when they want to solve their own social problems, he turned for help to what was known—or thought to be known—about ancient societies and pre-modern societies, expecting them to teach us who we are and what we are capable of becoming. He felt that if only we could forget all our philosophizing and analyzing and categorizing, putting all things "back into the melting pot once more," we might achieve a state of wholeness and be happier for it.

Before Exchange, says Mauss, was the Gift, and not vice versa. This was his first revolutionary proposition, which he derived from the anthropological fieldwork of others. Pre-modern peoples did not live by barter, as had previously been believed, but by gifts and counter-gifts. What in our culture would be commercial exchange was effected by these people through bringing gifts to others, who always gave gifts in return. Gift and Return were not, as we imagine or would wish them to be in our own culture, free and voluntary acts. Three obligations always obtained: Give, Receive, Reciprocate.

For a gift economy human beings later substituted exchange on the basis of contracts, which stipulated in advance what the price of a commodity would be. The invention of the externally valued, impersonal abstraction that is money made such contracts possible. And the contract was underwritten by law: if you did not pay for your commodities, you would be punished by an external agency in accordance with clear, impersonal laws. A gift economy, on the other hand, had no written contracts, no written laws. The gift system existed for a very long time before there was any writing. And it has nothing to do with money: it was flourishing well before money was invented. But always, in these systems, people who had received gifts gave gifts in return. What made them do so, if there were no laws to enforce reciprocity?

Having shown that gift economies preceded contract systems, Mauss went on to universalize the rules he found in these "societies of the Gift." There is, he claims, not only in these societies but also in our own, no such thing as a free gift. There are, rather, three unspoken but mysteriously binding obligations: to give, to receive, and to reciprocate. And the most puzzling of these is the obligation to give back. For his astonishing explanation of the power that invariably underwrites this last obligation, Mauss relied upon a single Maori informant named Tamati Ranapiri, who was asked by the anthropologist Elsdon Best in 1909 to clarify for him the meaning of the Maori term *hau*. "I will speak to you about the *hau*," began Ranapiri, and proceeded to explain that it was "the spirit of the gift." It was that which caused *utu*, or reciprocity. If *utu* did not take place, then serious harm, even death, might come to the refractory person who had received a gift. The spirit of the object itself would take revenge.

People in societies like that of the Maori, said Mauss, did not distinguish, as we do, between givers and gifts. Things given away carried with them something of the self of the giver, and this piece of the giver's self demanded to be returned.[6] Gifts always remained the possession, in some sense, of the giver. More recently, some anthropologists have discovered a clear distinction between "alienable" and "inalienable" property. People in many societies reserve as "inalienable" certain objects they own, while designating others as objects that can be let go for the purposes of exchange (these are "alienable"). We give—but we also keep, and make others aware of what we have not given, but kept.[7] From this point of view the eighteenth-century Tasmanian who tried to grab the Frenchman's waistcoat and earring[8] had failed to understand that the foreigners had brought with them objects designated as gifts (beads, mirrors, handkerchiefs, and the rest), but they did not consider their clothing and earrings "alienable" things, "for giving away."

Best's informant Ranapiri never claimed that the Maori *hau* actually uttered words, but the idea of anxious gifts complaining is found in other anthropological texts adduced by Mauss, where gifts have names, personalities, souls, histories, and desires. Copper objects given away in the American Northwest potlatches were said to "groan" and "grumble," demanding to leave their present owners when they felt it was right to do so. Eventually the gift's warden would relent and send the gift on its way.[9] The ensouled object did not go home directly in the case of the Maori, but was passed to a new temporary possessor first, and only eventually found its way back to its "birthplace." Hunters who had killed birds in the forest gave some of their catch to the priests, who cooked their portion of birds at a sacred fire, ate some of the meat, and returned the rest to nature, a "return gift," to ensure future abundance.[10]

The First Nations of the Pacific coast of North America did the same thing for the salmon, where the fish swim down the rivers to the sea, disappear, and—a yearly miracle—return in the spring. They fight their way upstream, having returned to the very river they had left for the ocean, until they reach their original spawning grounds, lay their eggs, and die. The people gave an elaborate welcome to the first salmon to reappear. Lewis Hyde describes it:[11] "A priest or his assistant would catch the fish, parade it to an altar, and lay it out before the group (its head pointing inland to encourage the rest of the salmon to continue swimming upstream). The first fish was treated as if it were a high-ranking chief making a visit from a neighboring tribe. The priest sprinkled its body with eagle down or red ochre and made a formal speech of welcome, mentioning, as far as politeness permitted, how much the tribe hoped the run would continue and be bountiful. The celebrants then sang the songs that welcome an honored guest. After the ceremony the priest gave everyone present a piece of the fish to eat. Finally—and this is what makes it clearly a gift cycle—the bones of the first salmon were returned to the sea. . . . The skeleton of the first salmon had to be returned to the water intact; later fish could be cut apart, but all their bones were still put back into the water. If they were not, the salmon would be offended and might not return the following year with their gift of winter food." The salmon would remain plentiful, Hyde explains, *because* they were treated as gifts; the Indians had and ritually expressed a gift relationship with nature that acknowledged our participation in, and dependence upon, natural increase. The year was a cycle, and so was gift exchange: give, receive, give back.

The most famous instance of a circular journey of the Gift remains that of the Melanesian *kula,* where precious objects—shell necklaces and arm-

lets, things for adornment but of no practical use, unlike the much low-
lier objects exchanged in the markets—are carried in canoes around the
Trobriand Islands in two circles moving in opposite directions.[12] Armshells
are created by breaking off the top and the narrow end of a big, cone-shaped
shell, and then polishing up and decorating the remaining ring. Necklaces are
made with small flat disks of a red shell strung into long chains. The red shell
necklaces are thought of as male and worn by women; they move clockwise
around the islands. Armlets are female, worn by men, and move counter-
clockwise. During their journeys (it takes between two and ten years for each
of these ornaments to complete its round of the islands), an armlet meets a
necklace; they "cross over," as it were, and then may be exchanged.

When an important man who engaged in *kula* (for the *kula* was an aristocratic activity) received one of these gifts, writes Mauss, he proved his
nobility by showing no interest in it, but rather mistrusted and disclaimed it
(in other words, there was no saying "thank you"), while the bearer of the
gift displayed "an exaggerated modesty" as he carried out his mission. On its
arrival a highly prized shell ornament would be unceremoniously thrown at
the receiver's feet; he responded by taking it up for only a moment. Having
impassively accepted it, and after its bearer had left, he kept the gift for a
good while—the amount of time was his to decide—enjoying its company
and savouring his state of blessedness. He gained "a great deal of renown"
through the object, joining as he did the list of honourable people through
whose hands it had passed. He exhibited it to others, recounted to them its
story and how he obtained it, and derived pleasure from planning to whom
he was going to give it when the time came: "And all this forms one of the
favorite subjects of tribal conversation and gossip." Eventually he would feel
constrained, by something like a *hau,* to pass on the object, and it would set
off again by canoe for another chieftain on another island. The gift must not
be stationary for too long; it must above all move on.

The *kula* continues today. Shirley Campbell (2002) gives an account of
the aesthetics of the practice. One of her photographs[13] shows a man wearing

a gorgeous, high-ranking, long-circulating female armshell named Nanoula. He also wears a spectacular necklace called Kasanai, given to him by its previous owner in hopes of luring Nanoula away from him. Notice that Kasanai is said to have been given *in hopes;* no obligation to give Nanoula in return is mentioned.

Mauss chooses not to ask what people were thinking of when they returned gifts, but prefers to look at the matter from a "pre-analytic" point of view: "What is it *in these things* that caused them to be returned, or passed on?" This question was in one sense prophetic: modern people are more than ever entranced by the "pre-analytic" properties of things, what we call the "image" that objects have it in their power to confer.[14] Karl Marx, too, looked for the secret concealed "in these things": he spoke of modern commodities as fetishes, circulating apparently without external control or purpose, but serving to conceal the truth of the matter, which, he explained, is the workers' poorly remunerated time and effort and their exclusion from the bright world of "autonomous" objects that they have in fact produced.[15]

Writing of our own culture, Mauss points out that unreciprocated gift-objects, whatever they might be, still have a habit of hanging around as standing reproaches, not exactly grumbling perhaps, but nevertheless making us feel uncomfortable until we have given something back to whoever offered them. Status, from a sociological point of view, is an irresistible motive. In our culture the giver is higher than the receiver, and the receiver will recover standing only when she reciprocates: she will therefore obey the imperious rule of return. As we all know, courtesies (such as opening a conversation with "Good morning!" or "Lovely day, isn't it?") demand a response. Invitations should be extended to hosts fairly soon after dinner parties have taken place, and people invited must come unless they offer excellent excuses. Saying "thank you" for an offering of hospitality is not enough: something more tangible must be returned. Mauss concludes that we continue to live, in part, in an economy of the gift. He would have us believe, moreover, that we can recover social health by returning to the joys of obligatory giving, and in particular of public giving to festivals and spending on the arts—to all things that are not merely utilitarian, and which serve to draw us together. We must re-mix our categories, and re-learn what was once an undifferentiated amalgam of the juridical, the economic, the religious, and the aesthetic. After all, human beings only recently became economic animals. In his own way, Mauss is looking back to the days before modernity was founded upon its battle with the world of the gift.

Mauss's analysis, his extrapolations from picturesque foreign or ancient customs and beliefs, and in particular his enthusiasm for the *hau,* have been subjected to much criticism and debate. His little book (only 107 pages in the recent English edition, with 84 pages of footnotes) has become a foundation stone of the social sciences. Its influence has been extraordinary, as much in need of explanation, perhaps, as is the implacable demand of the *hau.* Huge numbers of articles continue to be written mostly as footnotes to Mauss. All books on gifts—the very number of these being a phenomenon in itself— begin with, reconsider, or repeatedly invoke Mauss. Ranapiri, the Maori who spoke to Elsdon Best in 1909, described the *hau* in 207 words (in the English translation, the accuracy of which has itself been questioned[16]). He ended his brief statement with the phrase "*Kaata eenaa*"—"But enough on this subject." He would have been amazed to learn that he could never have said enough. His words did far more than impart interesting information: they initiated, through Mauss, in our own culture (the culture of the anthropologists) an outpouring of insistent self-interrogation. The perennial custom of exchanging gifts suddenly became intriguing again,[17] and enigmatic. The question for social scientists remained: do we have an equivalent of the *hau* that makes us give back? And if not, what is the mechanism at work?

The fascination with Mauss's book (and Ranapiri's words) points to a distinct malaise in modern Western society. Mauss provokes questions we find especially pertinent today: What are things doing to us? Is it things that keep us going as societies? What keeps us—so far—from falling apart? Should we just relax and watch the spectacle provided by the commodification of everything, including our ideas and even ourselves? How and where and why has gift-giving managed to survive in our culture?

Before we try to answer these questions and others like them, we shall first look at one instance of our own behaviour when it comes to gift-giving: wrapping presents up. Why do we take the trouble? The ancient Greeks and Romans took the actions of giving, receiving, and giving back so seriously that they actually personified them; we shall see next that modern reflections on these three serenely Classical figures will raise many more questions than they appear to settle.

7

All Wrapped Up

W hen we present a gift, our culture, despite its preference for low decorum and informality, nevertheless pressures us first to wrap up the object. We are so accustomed to conforming to this rule that we rarely wonder at its meaning or purpose. People in other cultures may feel no need to wrap gifts at all.

The Melanesian *kula* gift, haunted by power and fame, was, as we have seen, flung unwrapped and unadorned at the feet of its new owner. Maori gifts, if not too bulky, were placed at the feet of the one to whom they were offered, with a gruff expression that meant something like "This is for you." Dress cloaks—important gifts—were laid on the ground, outspread like the receiver's shadow, with the collar end farthest from and facing him; weapons as gift offerings were displayed with the haft towards his hand.[1] Care was thus taken in presenting gifts, but wrapping was not part of it. The response from the recipient was often a perfunctory one, the aim being not to show any pleasure, indeed any emotion, at all—which does not mean that there was no real appreciation of the gift. Remaining impassive was etiquette.

For us, on the other hand, a gift ought normally to be wrapped. We call it a "present" because it is presented; but also it *is present* in its wrapping-costume during its time "on stage," during the small drama of gifting. A gift, especially one put to use or on display, goes on to "represent" the giver, reminding the receiver of who gave it. Special objects brought and presented as gifts used to be enclosed in chests, cases, or bags, or sewn into cloth coverings for protection during transport. The word's origin recalls the cloth coverings: *wrap* comes from the Greek for "to sew."[2]

Today, we use paper to cover our gifts, and it is not primarily because they are in need of protection that we wrap them. If we mail a gift, we first carefully wrap it in special "gift" paper—the prettier, the better—and then enclose it, as a safeguard during the journey, in something sturdy and commonplace like brown paper or a plain envelope. Gift wrappings are folded with care. The string that binds a mere parcel becomes, for a gift, a ribbon, often with bows and rosettes added—anything to replace with embellishment the toughness of workaday knots. Extra trouble is taken because of the need to declare that, whatever it is, the thing thus enclosed is not a commodity.

A gift nowadays has almost invariably been bought. As such, it is certainly a commodity, but one that is summoned now to become something else. The wrapping is a sign that the object has changed into a gift. When, on increasingly rare occasions, we give something we ourselves have made—edible gifts mostly, such as jams and chutneys and cakes—we often feel little compulsion to wrap them. We occasionally enfold but fail to hide them, by covering them in something revealing such as cellophane. Not hiding by wrapping means that this present was not bought in a shop. It was made to be given away, not to make money; it does not need, therefore, to be converted into a gift.

We do work at shopping, however, quite apart from having first saved the money to buy gifts. As Christmas draws closer, we spend time fighting our way daily through the shopping crowds, returning from each expedition exhausted, with arms weighed down and aching feet. And we complain. Christmas has gotten out of hand, we say. It has become too commercialized. We are all so greedy, so demanding, and so exigent nowadays. It really is too much. These objections may be true, but our struggles and complaints mean in part that the gifts we have bought have manifestly cost us trouble. We may not actually have made them, but everyone is aware—

our own grumbling making sure it is understood—that work, freely undertaken, went into their acquisition.

If we give a very large present, one too big to wrap up—a car, a piano—we still feel constrained to make a gesture towards wrapping it, or rather designating it as a gift: despite the obvious generosity of the offering, we nevertheless decorate it in some way, write a pretty card and attach it, or—more extravagantly—present it in a particular *mise en scène*. Always, of course, we remove the price from a gift: presents, unlike commodities, are price-less. But we attach cards with names and brief messages that are meant to be carefully read before (though sometimes after) the gift is opened. This practice assures the person that this present was meant for him or her alone, and usually it is important that givers make themselves known: a gift describes a relationship between a giver and a receiver.

The wrapping paper—merely decorative, gratuitous, not at all "useful" except for its meaning—is material proof of the trouble taken. Care for the present within symbolizes the giver's caring about the recipient. The gift inside should itself, if at all possible, prove this caring: in the case of a personal gift (as opposed to objects handed out to clients or to their personnel by a commercial company), it will have been chosen with the specific receiver in mind, taking into account her tastes or needs as they arise from preferences and pursuits, and even demonstrating "insider" knowledge about what she possesses already, what (therefore) she lacks, and even what she would like even if the very nature of the object lies, until now, outside her experience.

Sometimes, however, gift-givers feel constrained to ask people what they would like to receive. People in our society have so much already; often we do not know others well enough to be able to gauge their taste or know what they have not acquired. Whether we are too lazy to find out, or have too little time to discover an object that nobody can reasonably be expected to possess before being given one, or whether we are too anxious to guess and possibly be mistaken, we forgo, by asking what somebody wants, two important elements of modern Western gift-giving: the receiver's surprise, and the giver's own decision-making. But even when the recipient knows what we have bought, we still feel we should wrap it up before presenting it. Two rules of gift-giving having been broken, the wrapping replaces a little of the aura of what should have been a surprise and a declaration of our estimation of the gift's receiver.

The personalizing of gifts is very specific to our culture. In other societies there may be rigid rules about what is to be given. These can depend upon complex questions of rank, on the occasion on which the gift is given, on the cost that is considered appropriate. It may be perfectly mannerly to display the price of a gift on the package.[3] The gifts themselves might be prescribed, as when a Japanese engagement to be married has been settled and presents must be made of tea in a magnificently decorated box, sake, and a sea bream.[4]

In Japan, the wrapping paper for presents given on auspicious occasions is decorated with an emblem called a *noshi,* a hexagonal tube of paper containing a piece of abalone shell, or a printed picture of this ancient symbol of purity. The wrappings for gifts of condolence, on the other hand, should be printed with motifs such as lotus flowers. There are many significant ways of folding the paper, often layer upon layer of it for the addition of refinement. String comes in eight different combinations of colours, and there are various ways of tying it, each with a meaning or a level of formality.

Wrapping in Japan goes much further than merely covering gifts. Often the wrapping—which proclaims what the gift "says"—is more significant than the gift itself. Where the receiver knows what should be inside the parcel, the actual opening—the revelation—is not the point. Westerners who attempt to understand Japanese culture make the mistake of trying to "get through" the wrapping to "the essentials," which to us lie concealed inside. This is cultural bias at work: a hunt for "the hidden truth" is a typically Western obsession, ranging from the Freudian slip to our apparently endless fascination with whodunit novels. This disposition can cause us to miss the point (although we surely admire its beauty) of the Japanese wrapping itself, in which so much structure and meaning reside. One traditional Japanese covering for a gift is a *furoshiki:* a cloth so pretty, and so thoughtfully chosen, that it is itself a gift. The "outside" can be as important as—or even more important than—the "inside."

Indeed, the entire culture of Japan has been analyzed in terms of wrappings. Its system of honorifics in speech has been described as "a kind of armour" for the purposes of protection and distancing; women are wrapped in several layers of gorgeous silk, then tied with an extravagant cummerbund like "human parcels"; houses and gardens are designed with depth and layering in mind. Even sections of time are "wrapped" in elaborate, formal beginnings and endings. Where gifts are not purely formal and prescribed, Japanese wrappings are permitted to conceal surprising contents. The polite behaviour of givers and receivers then provides "wrapping" and cushioning. Wrapping can be thought of as a "cultural template," an organizing principle of the whole of Japanese culture.[5]

But such formal predictability can also be manipulated. The anthropologist Harumi Befu tells us how Japanese wrappings can force other people's behaviour because total reliance upon the mysterious force of reciprocity is taken for granted: a gift demands a return and will not take no for an answer. In Japan, one never opens a present until the donor has left. One must not in the presence of the giver show too much interest even in an unexpected gift. Etiquette demands as well that the giver must always play down his gift. "It's only a small thing," he says, and the receiver, knowing that this protestation is entirely conventional, bows and sets the carefully wrapped gift aside. He can have no idea of its actual value, and propriety forbids him to find out before the giver has departed. If later an inordinately expensive present should emerge from the wrappings, the recipient will know that an equivalent favour must now be forthcoming: the present demands a response. The only question is what exactly is being pressured to happen.[6]

When it is a culturally enforced rule that the donor should leave before a gift is opened, it is clear that witnessing a personal reaction is not the point of the transaction. It might be considered crude to display emotions in public, in which case polite givers withdraw to allow the opening of the present to occur in private.[7] There would, however, be an emotional reaction (carefully dissimulated by the polite) should a gift not be given when it ought to be, or fail to be what obligation requires. An obligation to give, and the rules governing what a gift should be in precisely these circumstances, might be strict enough to preclude entirely both surprise and gratitude.

Gifts can be given on almost any occasion, of course. But many of them, in all cultures, arrive on special days, examples in our own society including birthdays, graduation days, partings, or retirement from a job. Such occasions are initiations, arrivals at definite stages in one's life journey, which others acknowledge and celebrate by giving gifts. Other presents are given and received by all who participate on seasonal, culturally agreed gift-giving days such as Christmas.

Like other gifts, Christmas presents must be wrapped. These paper coverings, easy to cut and fold, are specially manufactured for the season. They may be shiny, in order to reflect the candlelit ambience of a Christmas celebration, and to remind us of glittering snow and ice (even if we live where it never snows or freezes). Or the paper is green, red, or both—the colours of Christmas worn by the tree and Santa Claus.[8] The paper may have small Christmas symbols printed on it, and we might add stickers and other attachments bearing symbols—holly or bells, puddings or carollers, or even small pictures of wrapped presents, which are themselves conventional signs, like the other typical references to "the season."

In North America, mounds of gleaming wrapped gifts are commonly photographed without people present, before the ceremony of opening the presents begins.[9] The amount of them and the beauty of the ensemble represent an achievement of sorts; it expresses both the family's material success and the size of the group of family members and their friends. As the mound is made up of separate presents, so we as a group of individuals constitute the family. The word *individuals* means "not-divided"; individuals are self-sufficient "wholes" that are (therefore) separate, just as each personal, message-bearing gift is separate in its package. When we want to say something is finished and complete, we call it "all wrapped up"; we "wrap up" a meeting, for instance.

All Christmas gifts must be wrapped because, since everyone gives together, no one should know what anybody else is giving. Surprise for us is an important part of the gift-giving effect. But it is also one of the cardinal rules of Western gift-giving that when you give a gift in return, then, as will be explained later, you must give back something different from what you received. This stipulation is easy to observe when presents are one on one: you give; I receive, open, and see what the gift is; and then, when I give back, I can be sure not to give you what you gave me. This knowledge, however, is usually unavailable on occasions when all give together. But since the contents of gift packages, thanks to their wrappings, are unknown to all save their givers, if two people give each other the same thing, it is clear that a mistake has been made; the rule has not been deliberately broken. We can even laugh about it, and note what similar tastes we have and what similar perceptions of each other. For the choice of a gift supplies information about what giver thinks of receiver.

When people open their Christmas presents, they are often individually photographed doing so.[10] Hiding gifts by means of wrapping controls the drama of opening presents, and its timing. Wrapping makes a gift inscrutable before its contents are "dis-covered." The wrapping hides the gift in part to produce surprise—the dramatic moment that cameras are brought out to catch. For in our culture the response of the receiver rewards the giver, to the extent that giving a surprised and delighted response might have to be enacted even if it should not be felt.[11] Genuine surprise is a catalyst of emotion—here normally intended to be pleasure. And gratitude. One of the purposes of gift-wrapping personal presents is to provoke a sentiment of gratitude. When the gift in its wrapping is handed over, the receiver says "Thank you." This gratitude cannot be for the object, since the receiver does not yet know what it is. Thanks is for the giving—for the kindness in itself, apart from the actual thing given. It is for the trouble freely taken, and for the thought, which is what "counts." The wrapping having been torn open and flung aside, there will be a *second* "Thank you," together with exclamations and perhaps compliments of the creative kind, or congratulations to the giver on his or her insight into the receiver's preferences. Wrappings make receivers say "thank you" twice.

Christmas is a festival, and as such it must end. Feasts are by definition not ordinary time. To go on and on feasting would turn a festival into its opposite, which is normality. Great care is accordingly taken not to let this happen, because it would destroy the possibility of holding other feasts, on other occasions. The wrapping on the presents expresses both the "up" time that is festivity, and the closure of the festival, when we clear away the torn coloured paper, now unwanted débris,[12] and get ready to begin living ordinary time again. Another custom at Christmas is decorating the room containing the tree, where presents are given out. A further ritual, corresponding to the wanton destruction and sweeping away of gift wrappings, is taking down the decorations and throwing out the tree. The meaning is the same: Christmas is over. Celebrating it next year depends upon our decisively ending it now.

8

The Three Graces

The ancient Roman Graces were three beautiful, young, naked (or, in ear-lier times, skimpily dressed) virgin goddesses. They were shown dancing with their hands entwined, sometimes in a circle but usually in a row, with two facing forward and the middle one backward. Seneca, writing a massive treatise on gift-giving in the first century AD, mentions the Three Graces irritably and in passing. He had to bring them in, he complains, because all writers invariably discussed what the Graces meant—as if they *meant* anything at all—when they talked of gifts. These people (whose writings have not come down to us) kept asking, says Seneca, why there were three of them. Why were they sisters? Why were their hands interlocked? Why were they happy, youthful, and virginal women? And why did they wear so little clothing?[1]

The Graces, it was generally agreed, represented the social obligations of giving, receiving, and returning gifts and favours. They danced holding hands because a benefit passes from one person to another and eventually returns to the giver. This was so firmly believed that many did not think primarily of the *giving* of the first giver, but habitually jumped a step and called her "the one who earns benefits": she gave, but would eventually get something back.[2] The Graces are girls because both *Gratia* and *Charis* (the Greek for "Grace") are feminine nouns; abstractions are commonly feminine in European languages, and therefore tend to be embodied by women. Their beauty is the elegance of an uninterrupted sequence: they represent gifts circulating without hitch. They are happy because the whole cycle is joyous, virginal because gifts must not be bribes but rather "pure and undefiled and holy in the eyes of all,"[3] and young because the memory of a gift should not "grow old": it must not be forgotten but should provoke a response, and not too late.

The clothing worn by the Graces in earlier times was loose because nothing should restrict the flow of gifts, and transparent because favours when granted "desire to be seen." The Graces later undressed completely; they became proverbial for their nakedness. "*Nudae Gratiae*" was a phrase a Roman would sagely produce in conversation: "Naked are the Graces."[4] It meant that one should be open-hearted and without hidden intentions when giving, receiving, and returning gifts and favours. Erasmus, who comments upon the adage, adds that "some apply the proverb to ungrateful people, because they strip the Graces, as it were, by always accepting kindness in some form and giving nothing in return. It will thus be appropriate for those who are reduced to want by their generosity, because whatever they get they give lavishly to their friends."[5]

The Graces were three, and all alike: Giving was a Charis, Receiving a Charis, and Returning a Charis. But Seneca now brings up an important point: the *first* giver is more honourable, he says, higher and better than the other two; she is "the eldest sister."[6] This idea has inspired—but also haunted—gift-giving, in the West at least, for two thousand years. Locking onto the Obligation to Return (the third Grace), it declares that even when—as he must—a receiver becomes himself a giver by returning a gift, the second giver can never match the virtue of the first.

In this model, to give first is to give without obligation, and therefore to be more virtuous, and also to place oneself in an impregnably powerful position. The receiver repays later on, but always because he or she is obliged, by the mysterious law of reciprocity, to do so; only the first giver gave freely. Subsequent giving can never erase the superiority of the one who gave first, any more than a younger sister can catch up with an older sister's age. In the early twentieth century, Georg Simmel, another of the founders of sociology, expressed the apparently still operative rule as follows: "Once we have received something good from another person, once he has preceded us with his action, we no longer can make up for it completely, no matter how much our own return gift or service may objectively or legally surpass his own. The reason is that his gift, because it was first, has a voluntary character which no return gift can have . . . The first gift is given in full spontaneity; it has a freedom without any duty, even without the duty of gratitude."[7] By "the duty of gratitude" Simmel meant not feeling thankful, but the obligation to "give back."

It follows that giving somebody something or doing something to help another (always because of the iron law of reciprocity) can actually be an aggressive act. We saw an example in the Japanese gift-giver who forced a man to do him a favour by means of his gift.[8] This, in a culture with a powerful preference for modesty of demeanour, is the reason why the irruption of one's gift into another's life demands to be salved by conventional deprecations. The Japanese habitually say, when handing over a gift, that it has little value: *Tsumaranai mono desu ga,* "It's not worth having, but . . ."[9] And offering a tidbit they murmur, "Although this does not taste good, please have it."[10] We ourselves respond to expressions of gratitude from the receiver with "Oh, it's nothing" or "Don't mention it." A donor must always behave as though the receiver is self-evidently worthy of a gift, and therefore has no need to return anything. And etiquette, whether Japanese or Western, demands both modesty and a show of reluctance to create the first link in a chain of obligations to return. An assurance that there are "no strings attached" means that we wish the receiver to feel no obligation to give something back. The metaphor we use is that of being "bound" by obligations. The rule of reciprocity, we should note, is so widely known to be constraining that there is no reason to mention it: in saying "No strings attached!" we offer (adding to our generosity in giving) our polite release from what are understood to be its "ties." The word *obligation* itself derives from Latin *ligare,* "to bind," as in "ligaments."

Is giving-in-the-first-place merely a bid for higher rank? Or does it express a higher rank already held? (It is necessary, after all, to have the means to give.) Granted the higher status of the donor, the receiver can reduce, in giving back, something of his or her subservience. But what if people receive gifts and have little or nothing to give back? Should they not rightfully experience resentment at being forced to accept a lower status, to acknowledge a gap that they cannot close between their social position and that of the benefactor?

Mary Douglas's introduction to the new translation of Mauss, *The Gift,* is called "No Free Gifts." The title is not only a statement of what she believes to be the truth about gift-giving, but also prescriptive, no matter what donors like to think. Douglas says that people who receive charitable donations, including anonymous ones, should not be made to feel that they have received gifts at all. They "do not like the giver," for they have no personal relationship with whoever it is and are allowed to have none. And a receiver, especially one denied a chance to "make up for" the gift by reciprocating, is relegated to a lower status.[11] Ralph Waldo Emerson, in 1844, used similar words, but emphasized not the donor's but the receiver's wish for independence rather than relationship: "We wish to be self-sustained. We do not quite forgive a giver. The hand that feeds us is in some danger of being bitten."[12]

Aristotle, four centuries before Seneca (who does not mention him), conceived the Graces as equals: he sees no "eldest sister" more powerful than the other two. Aristotle thought that the very existence of the State depended on exchange and proportionate reciprocity—good for good and evil for evil—and that the Graces embodied Exchange, the necessary underpinning of society. "This is why," he continues, "we set up in a public place a shrine to the goddesses called *Charitai,* to remind men to return a kindness, that being a special characteristic of *Charis*. It is a duty not only to repay a service done one, but another time to take the initiative in doing a service oneself."[13] In other words, the first Grace was not an expression of power or of a freedom others could not equal, but of duty to the State: the Obligation to Give. The question then arises (for it is not enough for us today to say merely that "it is a duty"): what is it that underwrites such an obligation, there being no law that one must give? And why does anyone give in the first place? The second question might be thought to be as perplexing as "Why give back?"

Plato gives an answer to "Why give back?" in the course of his dramatization of Socrates' decision to die rather than disrupt the functioning of the laws in Athens.[14] Socrates had been tried, then unjustly condemned to death; his judges could not understand the worth of his mission to seek the truth. But he refused to run away and avoid his sentence. He could have done so—he was offered a clear choice—but he decided freely to lay down his life instead. Socrates' reasoning was that it is a citizen's obligation to obey the laws of his city out of gratitude[15] for benefits received from the order provided by law, and from the state generally. Socrates demonstrates, in the course of the *Crito,* that Athens had indeed benefited him, in the past and on the whole, before the moment came when it condemned him to death. He had at any rate chosen to live in Athens, under her laws. Socrates knew that in running away he would not have been true to his own principles, and also that, in the end and when all was understood, his death for his convictions would benefit Athens: his death is therefore a gift. The point is carefully made that Socrates' "gift" to Athens is in fact a response made in freedom, to gifts already given. Gratitude is also shown to be in part a predisposition and a principled desire not to damage the interests of somebody—or some institution—that has benefited us. It was gratitude that motivated Socrates to offer, in the form of a "return" to Athens, the paradoxical gift of his obedience to the sentence of an unjust death—misunderstood as it was, for the time being, by all but a few.

The second Grace—the middle one, with her back to us—is the Obligation to Receive. But why should we feel obliged to accept a gift? It can be imperative, in fact, not to do so. In an American prison in the 1950s, for instance, inmates who wanted to dominate certain others in the jail were observed using all their ingenuity to smuggle cigarettes into the cells of their victims. It went without saying, apparently, that to accept these gifts was to admit dependence upon and subservience to the giver; return favours would be required: "These intended victims, in order to escape the threatened bondage, must find the owner and insist that the gifts be taken back."[16] Similarly, a woman may well feel that in accepting a gift, she is being pressured into offering "favours" in return and is perfectly entitled to turn it down.

Receiving can be dangerous—even, and sometimes especially, should gifts appear to supply one's wants. In accepting gifts we should be selective, even wary. *Nec omnia, nec passim, nec ab omnibus,* the ancient and medieval adage had it: "Not everything, not everywhere, nor from everybody."[17]

Normally, the "obligation" to receive will include expressing thanks and showing consideration for the person giving. Manners decree that a person invited, for example to a meal, must reply as soon as possible, if only to make some mendacious excuse for turning the invitation down. For failing to respond *is itself a response,* and a hostile one. Refusing a gift usually signifies rejecting not merely a thing, but the person offering it. It deliberately breaks off the possibility of a link that the other wishes to forge. To push the gift away is to refuse the relationship, or to destroy it, in some cases definitively. This risks making not a friend, but an enemy. When a couple's engagement breaks down, the woman returns the engagement ring she was given; the action, with great economy, symbolizes the end of the connection.

Manners in all cultures are rules that cause us to pay attention to others and consider their feelings. We saw how the Japanese, who say "I am sorry" instead of "Thank you," are made by means of this convention to realize how their own presence has obliged the giver to give. And we, in giving presents, have to work hard to imagine what it is that the other would like to receive. In return the receiver must appreciate the trouble taken. She is constrained, by good manners, to thank the giver, and if possible to say how much and why she is pleased—even should the gift not be what she wants at all. Above all, the receiver of a gift is not supposed to criticize it. "Never look a gift horse in the mouth," we say, meaning "just take it and be pleased, or pretend to be so, even if it is an old nag." For the gift itself is not the point; the giver is. A Japanese adage goes

As a gift, a wadded garment is
acceptable even in summer.[18]

And it is up to the receiver to make distinctions (and not confusions) among the thing, its giver, and the giver's intention.

Giving a first gift breaks into somebody else's life; it decisively changes a relationship between the two people involved. Claude Lévi-Strauss describes a popular French restaurant where a fellow diner would introduce himself to a neighbour eating at the same table by filling the other's glass with wine, emptying into it his own small bottle. His glass was left empty, and the other had either to respond by filling it with his own wine and so enter into conviviality, or to eat his lunch with a very frosty diner opposite him. The first gift had irrevocably destroyed both anonymity and neutrality. The giving was not requested, yet the giver's glass, should it remain empty, constituted a standing reproach.[19]

Charles Lamb in his *Essays of Elia* complains about the annoyances that unwanted gifts can cause. A gift requires a return, and human beings are always capable of trying to get back a lot after having invested little. Lamb denounces the unfairness of having to receive and then being required to give back. (He gives as an example "a copy of a book which does not sell, sent you by the author" who "expects from you a book of yours which does sell, in return.") He says it is simply stupid having to show appreciation, as we customarily do, by displaying gifts received. "Not an apartment in the fine house of a friend," he writes, "but is stuffed up with some preposterous print or mirror—the worst adapted to his panels that may be—the presents of his friends that know his weakness; while his noble Vandykes are displaced, to make room for a set of daubs."

That we ought to put up with this sort of thing is, he says, a popular fallacy.[20] We might ask ourselves, however, whether we would wish to live in a world in which the "fallacy" no longer holds at all. Just because accepting a gift brings with it almost ineluctably a future relationship with somebody else, receiving can be a generous act. Accepting is agreeing. It can therefore be a form of giving. A friend of ours, a French curé, always displays in the middle of his dining room table a large, gaudy soup tureen, covered in china flowers and pierced with holes so that it can be used only as an ornament. On being asked why he never removes this "tasteless" article from his table, he replied that it was a gift from his cleaning lady. And he added, "She has plenty of taste, even though it might not be the same as ours."

Social scientists have begun to realize only fairly recently that Mauss was wrong to see his model of the Gift as universally followed.[21] A Chinese student of anthropology, first being introduced to the study of Mauss in the 1980s, received with a shock the news of the manifest superiority of the giver and the iron obligation to return—which was felt, he was told, the world over. Yanxiang Yan was twelve years old when, during the Cultural Revolution, his father was accused of being "a class enemy of the people." The family was driven out of Beijing in 1966, and Yan went to live for twelve years in farming villages in northern China. At seventeen Yan was living on his own in the village of Xiajia. When he was eventually able to leave China and began to study anthropology, he remembered what he had seen: he knew that the rules of Mauss did not always apply. He returned to Xiajia to do fieldwork in the 1990s, and this resulted in a book called *The Flow of Gifts* (1996).

Gift exchange, Yan explains, has been central to all of Chinese culture throughout its long history. From time immemorial in the villages he knew, gifts have been obligatory at all ceremonies—at weddings, for example, on birthdays, or at the lunar New Year. Social networking, rather than social institutions, continues to structure Chinese life. Reciprocal gift-giving still plays an important role among circles of people who are more or less equals.

However, in China people of lower status also customarily give to those higher than themselves. These gifts in no way raise the givers' status. On the contrary, they add to the prestige of the recipient, and the more gifts received, the greater the prestige; there are far more donors than receivers. Furthermore, higher-ups need never give anything back. They have to be "kept sweet"—that is, not irritated by failure to receive gifts they consider to be their due. They are very capable of harming a non-giver.

"Face" or honour underwrites the system of gifts flowing in one direction, to the powerful. In former times Chinese tenants would have to give presents to landlords on ceremonial occasions. The landlord would in return throw a banquet for his tenants—which he would not attend because his "face" was "bigger" than theirs. The Communist Revolution replaced landlords with cadres, and the upward flow of gifts continued. Cadres were invited to celebrations and conferred enormous prestige if they came, but they seldom did consent to come, and if they did, they never brought gifts. They themselves, meanwhile, were kept busy collecting the wherewithal to give to people higher than they were in the Communist hierarchy. In addition, the State designated "four bad elements" and placed them beneath everybody's feet. The four were former landlords, rich peasants, counter-revolutionaries, and a vague category known as "rotten elements." Rejection by the State as well as complete social isolation was their terrible lot.

Yan says that the formation of a market economy is changing everything in China. But his account—should what he describes become merely "an ethnographic account of the past," as he says it will—remains an important reminder of what the alternatives are to certain"inexplicable" customs of gift-giving. In China, Yan shows, compulsory gifts to superiors were alienable: there was no "spirit," no *hau* adhering to them. Where such is the case, the mystery Mauss drew attention to falls away. What could be more natural than to take if you can and give nothing back? To be compelled to give to the powerful hoping to placate them? What sociologists call "inalienability" in a gift, or the presence of a *hau* that ensures that reciprocity will follow, belongs to exchanges where people's status is approximately equal. Such equality is not "natural," however: it cannot be achieved without considerable energy and intelligence expended on achieving and then supporting the arrangement.

Until not long ago in Europe, as in China, country tenants had to supply their landlords regularly with gifts of their produce, such as game, poultry, and fruit.[22] A relationship did exist, certainly, and was reinforced through things offered and received. But the idea was also that people lower in status owed respect to their betters, and gratitude if their superiors decided to be benevolent. They had therefore to offer their employers and patrons "gifts" of appreciation. A further tightening of this syndrome is achieved in the situation described by one of the subjects of the oppressive Duke of Savoy: "We are not so much offended with the Duke for what he takes from us, as thankful for what he leaves us."[23]

As social equality spread in Europe, what remained of the custom of gifts automatically passing from people of lower status to those high up gradually died out. It was consciously and specifically abolished in the United States: people can choose which customs to keep and which to discontinue. A Society for the Prevention of Useless Giving was organized in 1912, with the purpose of eliminating presents that department supervisors in retail stores expected to receive from all clerks working under them. People realized that these presents were symbols of the clerks' subordinate position; they were "gifts unsupported by true affection." The society eventually succeeded in its aim, but felt it had to begin by calling gifts to superiors "useless" in order to attract people's attention and secure their support for abolishing the custom. Later on the organization proclaimed that these had not been *gifts* at all, because they were often almost compulsory.[24] A belief in social equality notably coincided with a conviction that gifts must be freely given.

The third Grace was often depicted holding hands with the first Grace, and so making the dance of the *Charites* a round, a circle. This arrangement in itself expresses a major problem with reciprocal and in-group giving: a circle is a closed figure, as indeed is giving and returning from one to another and back again. One has to be a participator in order to benefit from cycles of gift-giving. And human beings—for the usual reasons, of status and class, of racism and sexism and "ageism"—are always capable of excluding others from the "dance," and also of convincing themselves that it is perfectly right and reasonable to do so.

Yet it is possible for the image of the three Graces dancing in a round to mean something very different. When somebody gives *without* expecting reciprocity, the object given is his no longer. It begins a journey where it is passed along from one person to another, provided that each is generous, as the first person was. The gift may be a service or some other sort of kindness. Continual motion is essential to this picture: anyone receiving and then not giving—who refuses or otherwise fails to "pass on" the gift or favour—cuts off the flow of giving. The principle is that a person gives because once given to, and not in order to receive anything back. The dancing circle of the Graces proclaims moreover that when people are relating well with one another, such a giver will one day find herself on the receiving end: perhaps unexpectedly, and often in a surprising manner, the gift will "come back."

But for this to happen, the gift must first have been "lost" to its original owner—given *away,* as we put it in English. There being three Graces, not two, can express the "disappearance" of a gift when it is bestowed on another. The dancing in a ring would signify the gift's return, not through obligatory reciprocation, but as the result of a series of free givings. "It is as if the gift goes around a corner before it comes back," writes Lewis Hyde. "I have to give blindly. And I will feel a sort of blind gratitude as well. The smaller the circle is—and particularly if it involves just two people—the more a man can keep his eye on things and the more likely it is that he will start to think like a salesman. But so long as the gift passes out of sight it cannot be manipulated by one man or one pair of gift partners. When the gift moves in a circle its motion is beyond the control of the personal ego, and so each bearer must be a part of the group and each donation is an act of social faith."[25]

Not "keeping his eye on things," not calculating for a return, both holds each giver in relationship and sets him free.

9

Give It Away

When a gift is an object rather than an action, "mannerly" people usually work hard on granting as little importance as possible to the thing in itself. Take, for example, the way people commonly organize meals together. They try to remember that food should not be the entire reason for the gathering. No one denies the relentless necessity of being fed, but human beings attempt—once they have secured for themselves a regular supply of food—to make mealtimes into something more: occasions for meeting, for talking and sharing, and incidentally for dramatizing their agreements about how people should behave in company, all in the course of considerable enjoyment, to say nothing of relief and gratitude that there is enough to eat. Concrete objects other than food are also essential to our lives and our well-being. But again cultural wisdom often decrees that human attachment to such objects should be played down.

Many societies do this by consciously placing honour above material satisfaction, provided, of course, that material need is sufficiently supplied for a space to be created in which people might work on displaying nobility. We have already seen examples of people being offered gifts they greatly desire—but disdaining to show any emotion whatever.[1] It is considered "low," and certainly unwise, to be thrilled: to grab what is proffered and exult. A noble person's demeanour is unmoved, impassive; his or her sights are on "higher things."

There may also be a determination not to lose one's "cool" simply because it is agreed that tranquillity is effortlessly "high" while excitement, its opposite, is "low." A noble person should be free from greed, magnanimous, and immune from the pressures of base desires. The restraint of the honourable is "refinement," which is artificial and therefore difficult to learn and hard to keep up. It requires turning down immediate satisfactions of a material kind and preferring simplicity, stillness, self-control, dignity, *hauteur*. "The aim . . . is to display generosity, freedom, and autonomous action, as well as greatness," Mauss writes of the Trobriand Islanders' *kula* exchange. He dismisses these aspirations as in fact a subterfuge: "Yet, all in all, it is mechanisms of obligation, and even of obligation through things, that are called into play."[2] It is the external structure and its enforcement that interest the social scientist, rather than the feelings of the participants themselves; Mauss focuses on the obligation rather than on the *kula* chief's desire to rise above his own base impulses.

A noble man accepts subservience to another only in extremity. He is "great," which most obviously means "large"—"larger" than others. The comparative degree is important because it is most easily in comparing that others are able to judge, it being the opinion of others that is the decisive factor where honour is concerned. The greatness of a conqueror needs to be displayed and is commonly dramatized: he will be depicted on a monument (as Great Men were in ancient Egyptian and Assyrian art), posing with his foe, who might be depicted as much smaller than he, crouching at his feet. A man of honour will prefer, of course, that this foe be himself an honourable man, for the greater the fallen enemy, the greater his conqueror. Honour can be "taken from" others; it is added thereby to one's own stock of honour. One would rather "take" a large amount of honour than the little possessed by a puny enemy.

The Three Graces wore little clothing or none, Seneca says, because benefits "desire to be seen": favours given want to be admired by all. People believe that part of "paying back," of showing gratitude, is telling everybody about the benefit one has received, and so enhancing the reputation of the giver.[3] We still say in English that we feel "beholden" to someone who does us a large favour. Most of us today would take this word simply to mean "obliged." In fact, its origin is the same as that of the verb *to behold:* one beholden was "being watched," held under the gaze of others who have firm ideas about how we ought to react. And, where honour reigns, that is enough to create obligation.

When a Trobriand nobleman is the protagonist in the drama of receiving an extremely prestigious ornament, he remains apparently unmoved because to show pleasure and pride would be to "reduce" himself. It would mean that another has the power to grant him what he longs for. (Although honour is no longer the mainspring of action in our own culture today, honour syndromes still make themselves felt from time to time. We might resent saying "thank you" out of an obscure suspicion that to show gratitude is to accept a reduction in status.)

For protagonists in the *kula* exchange, things—even famous shell ornaments—should not have the power to make a great man lower himself by displaying desire or gratitude for them. As for pleasure, it can be expressed later, when the gift bearer has gone. Meanwhile, the bearer flings down the shells and shows "exaggerated modesty": he too is constrained to behave as though the handing over of the treasure were no great matter. Honour is a prickly, sensitive thing, quick to be aroused to anger. A modest demeanour is therefore wise in the gift giver, however important the gift.

In all this Mauss thought the "mechanisms of obligation" most impressive and important. Certainly the man "could not but" accept the gift after its long voyage by canoe, and would one day feel "constrained" to hand it on to someone as highly favoured as himself, just as its previous owner had had to let go of it and send it to him. One could also say that he had an obligation to behave with admirable restraint because such behaviour is what defines a noble man (*noblesse oblige*). But perhaps we should be impressed as well by the will to avoid the natural reaction, which would be simply to seize with exclamations of joy and carry off the longed-for object. Openly to welcome the present at once as an expression of esteem would have been "common sense." To recognize the gift for what it "really" was, namely useless bits of seashell, would have been more commonsensical still. Shame is the opposite of honour, but also honour's prerequisite, the reverse side of the same coin. What honour is *not* is common sense. We express our own commonsensical culture when we insistently ask for what things "actually" are, and what the power play is, or the greed, that many of us feel must invariably be the point of any transaction.

Honour deems that it should not be the thing but the meaning that counts—the meaning that inflates the great man's "size," his honour. And this honour can never be constituted by merely material riches, even though having things might sometimes be a prerequisite for the expression of honour. He who gives with generosity, in such a culture, is magnified in the eyes of watching others, whereas he who receives with a satisfaction too manifest is diminished. In any event, within a group of men "of honour," both the natural and the commonsensical are averted. An honour system avoids forced "giving" to the powerful; it prevents receiving from being more advantageous than donating; and it denies permission to the powerful to return nothing.

An outstanding example of things counting for less than honour is the North American Indian potlatch. Here First Nations chieftains and other nobles struggled to establish and readjust rank among themselves. Many guests—the witnessing crowd that is essential to the recognition of honour—were invited to a dinner and a potlatch ceremony. Should the existing ranking not be a foregone conclusion, a contest would begin, in which one man would destroy a certain amount of his property—say ten blankets—and challenge his rival to respond. As though he had received a gift in seeing his counterpart's blankets burn, the other contender, because of the battle of comparison, had to burn a larger number of his own blankets, say twenty. "The most valuable copper objects are broken and thrown into the water, in order to put down and to 'flatten' one's rival," writes Mauss. "In this way one not only promotes oneself, but also one's family, up the social scale."⁴ The destruction of possessions went on, rising in fury and in amount, until one of the rivals was forced to give in because he had nothing left to break or burn. The winner, in the sight of all, had gained the higher rank.

The potlatch struggle has often fascinated Europeans because there seems to have been nothing in it of "common sense." Large numbers of objects had to be collected before the ritual began, and it was true that given great determination on either side, the chieftain with the greatest resources won. Clearly it was not the accumulation of things that made a man great, but a daring readiness, in the pursuit of honour, to divest himself of every-thing. The Canadian government fought to stop what it saw as an entirely reprehensible, "crazy" waste of goods. But for the First Nations, mere stuff counted for nothing in comparison with honour. The emotions felt while the "big men" fought with property included pride, of course, but also fury. Anger, like pride, is an emotion that inflates one's "size." Rage (which we commonly describe as "towering") typically causes other people to cower, to make themselves "small." Honourable heroes are often transported with fury. ("Rage"—*menin*—is the first word in European literary history. It opens Homer's *Iliad,* an epic whose subject is honour and rage and heroism, and which sings to us of rejection upon rejection of "common sense.")

Another instance of detachment from things is the custom, found in many cultures, that if someone admires one of your possessions, you must imme-diately and without a sign of regret give it to her. The obligation to return might hold for this gift as for any other, and modern Europeans (typically) speculate that the requirement that something else should be given back must soften the fact of having to give something away simply because someone else expressed a liking for it. (Not surprisingly, polite people in these cultures never say they admire other people's possessions. Usually only foreigners are uncouth enough to do so.)⁵ But an important aspect of gift-giving becomes clear here: someone who receives a gift in return for something given has no control over what that return gift will be. To have admired something, say a locket, is to get that locket. But the locket-giver cannot be sure what gift might take its place—unless she is herself rude enough to praise some object she likes among the other's possessions.

Raymond Firth, describing the behaviour "beneath the crust of social decorum" of the New Zealand Maori, says that after a first present had been given, a tacit understanding was created between the two people concerned as to the nature of the return gift, and what its quantity and value should be.[6] Firth believes that this practice of dropping hints as to what return gift would be acceptable, by means of praising things "in a significant manner," gave rise to the custom of giving away something that had been admired. Interestingly, giving away what has been admired always takes place *at once*—the locket is snatched off the neck then and there and handed over—whereas, as we shall see, gift return usually requires time to elapse first.[7] In the case of the admired object, the owner's honour is engaged. There must be no question about a detached attitude to mere personal possessions, and therefore no time is taken—none needed—to consider what the response should be. A Maussian anthropologist would no doubt be convinced that such giving is merely an instance of "the obligation to give." If we were to listen to the person giving away the locket, however, we would hear her say that she gave because she was free from attachment to possessions—and had proved it.

In traditional Maori culture there appears to have been a powerful obligation to give when a hint was made. Firth recounts the story of a man who was "of such greedy disposition that when anyone was passing up or down the valley with fish or other products he always hailed him, saying, 'I am very fond of that food.' This was equivalent to a direct request for it, so of course the food was handed over to him. So tiresome became this practice that at length the people of the district, to end his begging, sent a war party against him and slew him." Firth concludes, "One is almost entitled to conclude from this that in old Maori days true politeness demanded that one should slay a man sooner than hurt his feelings by refusing him a request."[8] What was presumably being safeguarded, however, was the continuance of

the possibility of asking and giving within limits and in an honourable manner, through "hints"—not requests—that left the other free to give. The man,
taking advantage of the honour game, had placed an intolerable burden upon
people's resources: insatiably repeating his trick, he had become a sort of
highwayman and a shameless beggar, with the honour of travellers along the
route as his pressure point.

Two types of beggar exist in Spain, and no doubt elsewhere as well. There
are those who kneel quietly on the pavement with their money-box before
them and a written notice enumerating their misfortunes; and there are those
who run along beside their prey, nudging and cajoling. The first are honourable, the second shameless. The first leave it to passersby to give or refuse; they
rely on people's consciences and try to arouse pity; they "make hints" through
giving information but asking only by making non-aggressive, non-verbal
signs. The second kind are deliberately and physically bothersome. They take
advantage of irritation and even fear, and they ask outright; they have no
honour and "no manners," and run the risk of vociferous or violent refus-
als. There was, if the story of the shameless Maori is to be believed, a greater
taboo in that society against shamelessness than there was against killing.[9]

An honour system is one way of making people play down possessions
and exalt noble behaviour instead. The reward for doing this is not only the
satisfaction that arises from being noble oneself or from witnessing nobility in others, but also the achievement of peace, by means of exchanging
goods while reducing as far as possible a fixation on the things themselves.
In a different kind of society, the group may simply share with one another
everything they own. Egalitarianism will be the hub of this kind of social
system, rather than honour, which is by definition hierarchical. And where
people cannot be said to own any material objects, there is little danger of
their becoming too attached to things.

Lorna Marshall's exemplary study of the Bushmen of Nyae Nyae in
South Africa, published in 1961, shows how methods may be worked out by
small groups of people, who have no avenues of escape from one another, to

cast out violence and maintain goodwill among themselves. The methods involve talking, sharing, and giving. In this society giving is obligatory. Things are "on the move" always, passing through people's hands, but always on their way to somebody else. Violence being the greatest fear, immense efforts are made to lower temperatures and disarm hostilities—wherever possible, in advance. A great deal of learning, understanding, practice—in short, of "up-bringing"—needs to be undergone by everyone to keep things on an even keel. But it is felt to be worthwhile, for this carefulness is believed to be vital to everybody's survival.

To begin with, the Bushmen talked, says Marshall, all the time: they were "the most loquacious people I know." Conversation was "a constant sound like the sound of a brook." The main subject was the availability of food and the giving and receiving of food, and about gift-giving in general, and the persons to whom they had given or proposed to give gifts: "They express satisfaction or dissatisfaction with what they have received. If someone has delayed unexpectedly long in making a return gift the people discuss this." When gift-giving is done incorrectly—not enough, not to the right person, without a proper return—other people talk, and complain, until matters are sorted out. Then they can all "start again in peace."

Speaking could be shouting in alarm, all together, "in extremely loud, excited voices, volcanic eruptions of words" when there was a powerful common emotion such as fear. When all did it at once, there was no dissension. Or it could be an individual's long, murmured repetition in the presence of others, a lament out of a sense of injustice: "In an extreme instance we saw a woman visitor go into a kind of semi-trance and say over and over for perhaps half an hour or so in Toma's presence that he had not given her as much meat as was her due. It was not said like an accusation. It was said as though he were not there. I had the eerie feeling that I was present in someone else's dream." The woman was in no sense arguing; there was no reply from Toma. But she made her feelings known; the controlled performance, insistent but low-key, was a release of tension, "keeping pressures from building up until they burst out in aggressive acts." People were expected to control their tempers and did so to a remarkable degree: "If they become angry, aggrieved, or frustrated, they tend to mope rather than to become aggressive, expressing their feelings in low mutters to their close relatives and friends." Indeed, "any expression of discord ('bad words') makes them uneasy." Marshall reminds us that deadly poisoned arrows, the Bushmen's hunting equipment, were always at hand; tempers could not be allowed to get out of control.

The Bushmen's table manners strike Marshall as extraordinary: nobody revealed eagerness to eat, or took more than a modest share of food. "I found it moving to see so much restraint about taking food among people who are all thin and often hungry, for whom food is a source of constant anxiety," she writes. "We observed no unmannerly behaviour, no cheating and no encroachment about food." Once again we hear about the need to share everything, but food in particular: I have now, but later I might desire your goodwill. "People are sustained by a web of mutual obligation." It would not be possible, in this small and sharp-eyed group, to kill an animal secretly and eat it oneself, because "actions are printed in [the] sands for all to read." There was no fighting about whose poisoned arrow actually killed an animal, because each hunter got a share of the meat anyway: sharing prevented tension. Once everybody had received an obligatory portion of meat, he or she was free to give bits of it away at pleasure. This convention, says Marshall, had "the quality of gift-giving"—but the person who received such a gift was obliged to make a return gift later. The motives for giving were "to measure up to what is expected of them, to make friendly gestures, to win favour, to repay past favours and obligations, and to enmesh others in future obligation." Marshall admitted that she could not know when or if feelings of "genuine generosity and real friendliness" existed, but she is sure that they too would have been expressed by giving.

Gifts circulated constantly among the Bushmen: "Everything a person has may have been given to him and may be passed on to others in time." Artifacts, well made and carefully looked after, "last for generations and move in a slow eddy among the people." Marshall describes how she gave a neck-lace of cowrie shells, unavailable to the Bushmen, to each woman as a fare-well present when she left the band in 1951. In 1952, when she returned, there were no necklaces left, hardly a shell to be found in the band itself; the necklaces had been broken up and every shell given away: "They appeared, not as whole necklaces, but in ones and twos in people's ornaments to the edges of the region."

Every object was known within the group, and also who had given it to whom in the recent past. (Unlike some other peoples, this Bushman group was not given to placing value on antiquity, or to holding the distant past in mind.) They traded, but only with outsiders, never among themselves: trad-ing with each other was considered undignified, too likely to stir up bad feel-ings. The visiting anthropologists did not receive gifts in return for what they offered: "They gave us a few things spontaneously which they thought we would enjoy—python meat, for instance." They were outsiders, and therefore not included in the sharing that drew the group together.

Stealing simply never happened: it was practically impossible in any case because everybody knew each person's footprints, the whereabouts of every object, and who was at present using it. More importantly, one Bushman said, "stealing would cause nothing but trouble. It might cause fighting." Things were for giving, for creating bonds and relationships. Jealousy and envy were strong, but there was always a remedy: if an object should be the cause of dissension, give it away. People who had more than others needed especially to give, to pre-empt jealousy. The two unbreakable rules of gift-giving were these: never refuse a gift, and be certain to give one in return. Refusal to make a return gift made a giver exceedingly angry. Not returning a gift was also noted by other people, and censured in the incessant talk that went on.

It was permissible for a giver to ask for a return gift, and even for some-one to ask for any particular object he or she wanted. One man said that a person could ask for anything. He did, he said: "He goes to a person's fire and sits and asks. (I could imagine him with his black glancing eyes sitting and asking!) He asks usually for only one or two things, but if a person has a lot he may ask for more" and, he said, "to be refused too many times makes a person very angry."

Lorna Marshall says she saw no signs of altruism, kindness, sympathy, genuine generosity, or desire to help the weak in Bushman behaviour. Giving back, however, was obligatory and underwritten by the insistence and the possibility of deep disapproval of others in the group; social obligation precludes gratitude, which is never mentioned in Marshall's report. The "worst thing" was not being ungrateful, but not giving in the first place. Other bad things were not accepting a proffered gift and hanging on to something when somebody else had asked for it. The Bushmen aimed at achieving security, closeness, and peace; and this they did to a large extent through constant, obligatory giving and receiving. "The worst thing is not giving presents," said one of the Bushmen. "If people do not like each other but one gives a gift and the other must accept, this brings a peace between them. We give to one another always. We give what we have. This is the way we live together."

As we have seen, the price of refusing to give something back to a donor often means hostility. Refusing to receive also wounds, while refusing to give in the first place prevents a cycle of exchange from beginning. Human societies *must* engage in exchange (as Aristotle saw).[10] If they do not, they fall apart and collapse into violence. Being fixated on possessions is exceedingly dangerous. The philosopher René Girard shows that people learn to desire objects by watching what other people do and want, and learning from them what it is that is desirable. If they start fighting over who will own the things in question, they soon turn to hating each other so violently that the objects initially coveted almost drop out of view in the heat of a battle to the death.[11] Traditional societies have always set out to discourage a fascination with possessions; ancient experience told them that the consequences of a failure to avert covetous desire were potentially catastrophic.

A peculiarly modern solution to our propensity to what Girard calls "mimetic violence" is to make large numbers of the objects desired. We actually incite people, through advertising, to desire specific objects, to find them "indispensable": we are so sure of ourselves that we feel we can run this risk. (The main method of advertising, of course, is inducement through mimetic desire: showing us other people enjoying the object to be sold to us.) "Demand" having been built up, mass production then steps in to ensure that there are enough identical examples of the commodity to go round—for those, at least, who can pay for them. The solution is brilliant—provided that enough people have enough money to feel they are part of the charmed circle of buyers, and that have-nots can be kept quiet. We are increasingly and painfully aware that we shall reach material limits to "growth" sooner rather than later. Then—or perhaps before that happens—we shall realize that there is no sustainable alternative: we shall have to share what we have, or rather what is left, among all of us. Human beings must either give, or fight.

10

The Give-and-Take of Everyday Life

For historical and practical reasons, and also by choice, modern Western cultures are very different from those "of the Gift." Money, rather than the reciprocal transfer of goods, is the medium of exchange. We insist on contracts drawn up in advance of a transaction: written documents, clear, binding, and above all impersonal. The clarity and transparency of rights seem preferable to the uncertainties of dependency on the goodwill of others. Private property is for us a *sine qua non* for the giving of objects to others: we feel that one cannot give something away unless one possesses it. The societies "of the Gift" are small and close-knit; our own are huge and anonymous. We could not possibly relate closely with more than a tiny percentage of the people we happen to encounter.

We are also a mobile society, to an extent unprecedented in history: we can get away from one other. When social arrangements begin to fall apart, we are often able simply to move away, so that we are not always forced at a personal level to rectify breakdowns and misunderstandings through endless negotiation and peacemaking. To people who are serious about living in close and continuous reciprocal social systems, we can seem lazy and rather primitive in this regard. "Naré enjoyed reminding me in a joking way that whites had an easy time of it," reports an anthropologist studying the people of Mende, Papua New Guinea. "All we had to worry about was feeding and clothing ourselves, and perhaps writing our books, whereas his people had all sorts of hard work. From his point of view, *we* were the ones with the 'subsistence system' [whereas] his society was the one concerned with exchange."[1]

Some have suggested that our social system has suffocated gift-giving by means of an omnipresent commercialism, squeezing it into an exiguous space where it can hardly be expected to flourish. Commercialism is often given as an explanation for our relational superficialities. But one could also argue that the intimate spaces where gift-giving normally takes place have become exceedingly important to us, precisely because of the rampant commodification of our world: personal relationships remain vital for human well-being. And modern people are capable of giving *en masse* to those suffering because of natural or man-made disasters, provided that the media can succeed in horrifying us enough and in assuring us that our gifts will be useful. Many people offer, out of a desire to do so, assistance to the needy. As Claude Lévi-Strauss has complained, we give massively to each other at Christmas: he thinks of Christmas as a huge, competitive, wasteful annual potlatch, almost entirely in the service of commerce.[2] But we give on many other occasions as well. And if we shift our attention from concrete presents to what cannot be bought and sold, then gifts such as friendship, love, helpfulness, or sympathy must play a pivotal role in any schema that could be taken to represent our culture.

In societies "of the Gift," people are regularly obliged to give things away. An Australian Aborigine cuts and shares a kangaroo brought down in the hunt: his relatives know in advance that they will receive specific parts of the animal.[3] A Bushman may ask any one of his fellows for what he wants, and the other must give it, on pain of bitter reproaches should giving fail to occur, and out of fear of sparks that might ignite violence. In such societies sharing is directly and palpably responsible for the survival of everybody in the group. We should notice that it is precisely in societies where giving is compulsory that words for what we mean by "gratitude" seldom occur.

In our own culture, gifting behaviour normally takes place in areas of benevolent social interaction that are not covered by contractual obligations. An act of giving may, of course, be driven by conventions, social pressures, several kinds of motivation, and by the fear of costs in terms of personal relations if the pressures are not obeyed. But there must be a fundamental part of a gift or favour that is not precluded by any of that. The word *benevolent* means "wishing well." That wish can come only from a donor's freedom; the giver must be willing. The same is true of receiving. One does not, for example, have to accept a gift that seems to entail unwanted consequences: if an "entailment" is believed to exist in the mind of the giver, the potential victim may get out of the involvement in advance. A gift starts a relationship, and we feel free to turn down some relationships just as we can choose to initiate others. A receiver may well want to give or do something in return for a gift that pleases. That could be out of love and gratitude, or because she does not want to hurt the giver's feelings by not responding. If she *does* want to hurt him, there are few more wounding weapons than failure to respond.

Giving in modern society is by definition unofficial and non-obligatory—yet, as we shall see, without it social life would quickly become impossible. Giving "must," therefore, no matter what the competition with contracts and commerce, continue to take place. But in the end people are free to "behave"—or not to. This freedom is reflected in the emotion we call "gratitude." A gift that has no motivation behind it other than convention, promotion of status, or force will not elicit gratitude. And gratitude itself cannot be forced from anyone.

Before we turn to the history, springs, and meanings of gratitude, it will be useful to make a brief tour of six aspects of the gift, with emphasis on modern attitudes but including areas in which our behaviour resembles that of all gift-giving. For the sake of brevity we shall stay mostly with concrete presents. They represent many other kinds of benefit, however, throughout.

A. Gift-Giving Is a Ritual

An essential characteristic of a good deal of gift-giving is its ritual dimension. We accompany the gift with quasi-ritual words spoken, gestures and manner, facial expressions. We communicate messages through the medium of gifts, and just as people speaking need not be aware of the grammar they are using, we follow the abstract rules of gift-giving even though we seldom analyze what they are. Language is explanatory as an object given cannot be, but a present remains present as a sentence spoken cannot. Ritual is therefore usually both a thing said and a thing done. The very fact that a gift parcel is an object handled in a special way gives it ritual status: a gift object always stands for far more than itself. Its meanings are there to be "unpacked." But owing in part to its inscrutable status as a thing, a gift can also conceal the truth of the matter—which is mostly to be found in the motives and intentions of its giver.

Formal gift-giving, because it is a ritual, is performed, but also *performs*. If the giving is of a first gift to a person still relatively unknown, the ritual can start a relationship and so influence the future. Most gifts, however, are given to known others: they serve to maintain links already forged, but which would weaken should gift-giving cease. The work of a gift is tracing the link, as a person walking travels along an existing road: the object follows a trajectory that is a "tie" between two people. Or else it is the first attempt at a tie, as a lasso might be thrown across a chasm as the first stage in constructing a bridge.

Giving a gift in return retraces the trajectory already performed. The return is the completion of the ritual. Here is one answer to Mauss's question, "Why give back?" Asking why is like asking why, in an antiphon, one half of a choir responds to the other half: the song is simply incomplete without the response. Seneca likens the giving of gifts to playing handball: if the ball has been thrown to you, then it is your turn.[4] The ball's in your court: throw it back. If a gift does not result in a return, then not only has the giver been rejected, but the receiver's "side of the net" turns out to have been invaded by an unwanted gift. The return is the rest of the ritual, no more and no less; it completes the song or continues the game or finishes the sentence; without it, the meaning of a ritual action is rendered incomplete, and perhaps either incomprehensible or outrageous as well. Resentment—quite possibly on both sides—might be the outcome, and perhaps a complete breakdown of a relationship between two people. For it is people who give and return. The gift is, first, an object, and continues to be one, complete in itself. In addition, it is the ritual symbol of what is meant by giving. We manipulate the gift; it does not make demands on us. But it does bear the memory—in our minds, and not in itself!—of the persons who gave and received it. And so we make a gift objectify preceding social relationships, or represent an attempt to create new ones.

Rituals that "work" often express contradictions. Rituals are especially powerful when the contradiction expressed reaches to the roots of the culture and is capable of calling important aspects of social arrangements into question. For example, gift-giving makes the following claim: "Loss of something (by handing it over to someone else) results in gain. Subtraction eventually adds." This, especially in our commonsensical and quantifying culture, is a saying that is difficult either to understand or to accept. A whole strand of our cultural discourse, indeed, expresses revulsion against the very belief that gift-giving (that is, giving freely) could occur at all. Gifts are judged to be impossible, precisely because they generate more. Givers, therefore, who protest that they want nothing back must be liars: people who give always get something out of it, whether it be a return gift, or somebody else's pleasure in their gift, or even their own self-satisfaction at being so good as to give. And this fact—including knowledge of this fact—is thought to disqualify the gift in advance of its giving.[5] It is typical of successful ritual that it has the capacity to baffle and enrage.

The ritual of gift-giving and gift-returning states other contradictions as well, and overcomes these too by containing the terms of the contradictions in itself. For instance, with us a gift is usually a bought thing; yet it serves a social purpose that has nothing economic about it. People in our culture are free to give or not to give; but at the same time we feel we *must* give, receive, and return. We have worked hard to provide ourselves with autonomy and independence from others; but at the same time we deeply desire connections with other people. Thus gifts are freely given—but seek to create and maintain links and bonds. All these neuralgic points, and others as well, are designated, expressed, and transcended by being included in gift-giving.

B. Gift-Giving Creates Links Between Persons

Through the transfer of things and of favours, back and forth, we enter into relationship with one another. Many a link begins when one person asks another for assistance. A professional British adviser on social behaviour, telling her readership how to make a desirable contact, suggests that a good start would be to ask that person for a favour, and then let him or her play *le beau rôle*:[6] in our culture it is the giver, not the receiver, whose *rôle* is *beau*.

Lending and borrowing can forge links just as giving and receiving can. The advice of Polonius in *Hamlet*, "Neither a borrower nor a lender be," is that of a "foolish prating knave"[7] because to follow it entails cutting oneself off from relationships with others. A person might opt, for example, to own absolutely everything he uses, including buying himself expensive objects he might never need twice. The people who live nearby, meanwhile, are often willing, even eager, to lend him one of these things and so begin to create a neighbourly link with him. But the man insists on buying a huge snow-blower or a professional-quality tile-cutter or a cement mixer, when he could easily have borrowed one. He might be an agreeable fellow otherwise, even one who is willing to help others. But he prefers, Polonius-like, to keep a distance between himself and them. He does this by buying everything he wants, and an important part of what he wants is never needing or being indebted to others. If everyone behaved as he does, there would soon be no sense of community, no real neighbourhood left.[8]

True, as Polonius points out,

> . . . loan oft loseth both itself and friend
> And borrowing dulleth edge of husbandry.[9]

Borrowing entails an obligation to return, since the object handed over (in this it is unlike a gift) still belongs to the lender. The "obligation" has little force, however, apart from the threat of ruining a personal relationship, which is the point of the first part of Polonius's remark. But there is a similarity to giving in lending, in that a decision is freely taken to make a loan in the first place. Lending is "making" or "giving" a loan, while borrowing is "taking" or "receiving" one. Loans are risky: goods can be lost, and people can disappoint.

But never lending is denying oneself many a friend in the first place, and borrowing can in fact be a form of husbandry: everything depends on the borrower's and the lender's attitudes and intentions. In Spanish there is no word for "to borrow"—only *prestar*, "to lend."[10] As we saw earlier, the English terms *host* and *guest* both derive from one Indo-European word, *ghostis*, which reminds us that what we now differentiate as "hosts" and "guests" were once thought of as people involved in one action, namely hospitality, and so they shared one designation. Similarly, the Spanish see borrower and lender as participating in one transaction: a loan being made and received. And again, giver and receiver are end points of one "line," or "link," that is a relationship forged and encouraged by passing objects back and forth.

In modern societies most of the things we possess are bought. For this very reason, gifts must be deliberately provided with their extra significance: as we saw, wrapping them is symbolically adding to them this load of meaning.

We thereby remove such objects from everyday life—our daily struggle in a flood of commodities—and devote them especially to the expression of personal affection and respect. The mobility of modern life demands, moreover, that our personal links receive repeated affirmation. The close-knit small social worlds that we create, like islands in the sea of our mass society, are essential to our well-being, but they are achieved by means of considerable, reiterative labour. The mobile or cell phone fills just such a purpose: people anxiously keep in touch with intimates as though each separation, each outing, means a foray into an alien jungle. Most cell-phone calls perform obsessive, minute-by-minute maintaining of contact with home base: "I am just approaching the parking lot." "I'm in the bus now." And so forth.

Just thinking about what to give one's relatives and friends and then finding the proper article requires ongoing effort. The Winnipeg Ritual Cycle Study, conducted by David Cheal in the 1980s, set out to discover how people nowadays managed to cement relationships. One woman explained that gift decisions are made "usually by thinking, or watching and then seeing what they need." And another, "First of all, when I'm with them I listen to them, to the kinds of things they are doing and needing. For instance, I know my sister is travelling next year, so my gifts for Christmas will be in connection with travel—a trip book and a wallet for my sister, a trip book for her husband."[11] Gift-giving forces one to pay attention to others and to keep on doing so; gifts are repeatedly given to the same people.[12] We might notice in addition that, as usual, it is women whose task it normally is to maintain links, through "keeping in touch," alertness to wants, and appropriate gift-giving. And the sister got more than her husband did: women not only work harder on gift-giving but also tend to receive more presents than men do. Money will not normally do as a gift. Money gifts are "lazy."[13] What is needed is an object chosen with care: "Money is kind of cold. It's spent usually on nothing in particular, and when it's gone the memory's gone. Whereas if you give a gift—like even a book, or a dish, or a picture or anything—you've got something material to remember that person by."[14]

In our society, the necessities of life are nearly always supplied by means other than gift-giving, so that the sphere of the gift is left free, as it were, to concentrate on sentiment and on personal relationships alone. We give mostly as individuals, to other people one by one, each of them with unique circumstances and preferences that the giver tries to take into account. Finding the right gift for each person—who is likely to be someone who can afford to go out and buy what she wants when she wants it—requires "going shopping," armed with detailed knowledge as well as inventiveness and imagination: we have to be able to put ourselves in another person's shoes, to envision what the world looks like to her, before we hunt down what we think is the perfect gift, but which is nevertheless something she has not already bought for herself.

When we give something, we are "saying" what it is that we imagine the receiver wants and likes. In our consumer society we are taught to think of things as defining us: the watch (or "timepiece" if it is expensive enough), which can intimate that the wearer is by nature elegantly streamlined, for example, or tough, or sufficiently high-flying to need instruments for navigation through his complex world; the perfume (does she like being—or do I want her to be—defined as sexy, refined, exotic, mysterious?); the car (you are what you drive). These three objects in particular are advertised with zeal during the Christmas season because they are gifts many of us believe to be image creators and image projectors. They are model performers of the identificatory and prestige-enhancing roles of property.[15] It is difficult to remain unsnagged by desires for an advantageous image, especially if one can create that image merely by holding up, as it were, the right objects for inspection and approval by others.

When shopping for gifts, we often fall back more lazily, and more cheaply of course, upon items whose interest can be guaranteed to be strong but temporary: on clothing and other items that are "in" this year; on boxes of chocolates because they are usually liked and soon eaten, so we can give another one later; on clothes for children, who constantly need new garments as they grow.

On some occasions we deliberately give presents that will not last, as when we offer cut (not potted) flowers on Valentine's Day because the giver does not want to risk looking more than momentarily infatuated. A guest arriving for dinner should not bring too large or too enduring a gift (a standing lamp, say, or a statuette). It might appear to mean that the gift represented by the dinner invitation has been more than "given back" already. It might pre-empt a return invitation, that further underlining of a friendly relationship.[16]

The giving of presents is most often confined to one's own small group of family or intimates, in which case the to-and-fro of gifts is simply repeated confirmation of existing links. Such confinement amounts to social closure: those on the outside have small chance of getting into the giving group. Reciprocal giving, however, can also be used to forge links between disparate groups within a society; destroy generalized social reciprocity and society falls apart.

Anthropologists have demonstrated this principle through examining the universal human taboo on incest, which is related to demands in human groups for reciprocity. Now, incest may certainly have painful physical consequences: it raises sharply the possibility of genetic defects recurring in offspring. But this fact is only one facet—the physical—of the customary human repression of incest. The other facets are social, beginning with the cruelty, selfishness, and psychological damage involved in incest, particularly with a child. And then, from an abstract and structural point of view, if people within a family produce offspring by each other, they will make no alliances with other families in that society. Families are groups with clear boundaries; if they were to fail to interact with other such bounded groupings, society as a whole would disintegrate.

This potential societal problem is solved by sons, daughters, sisters, and brothers marrying *out*—that is, young people accepting without question the rule that one weds people with different lineages from one's own. In doing so they create bonds linking the tight, self-evidently solidary family groups. An often-cited aphorism of the Arapesh people vividly expresses the feeling that it is better to exchange and interrelate than to maintain self-sufficiency: "Your own mother, your own sister, your own pigs, your own yams that you have piled up, you may not eat. Other people's mothers, other people's sisters, other people's pigs, other people's yams that they have piled up, you may eat."[17] Women, we notice, are to be exchanged—"eaten"—just as pigs and yams are. Men are not mentioned. They are the agents, whereas women can be thought of as items to be exchanged.

All over the world, women tend to be seen as links between families. Indeed, a woman marrying may herself be treated like a gift from one family (represented by her father) to another. With the other term of the "tie," her husband, she will produce children who are embodiments of a permanent bonding. The prohibition of incest further rests upon a usually unspoken agreement, which the Arapesh made explicit: it forces *every* family to give and to receive women. The ruling males of each family say, in effect, "I will give up my daughter or my sister—but only on condition that my neighbour does the same."[18]

When it comes to celebrating the creation of the mighty bond between families that is a wedding, the relatives and everybody else who witness it participate in a feast and usually contribute presents as well: things the new family will need to found its "house," but also things that ritually echo the "gift-giving" that is being accomplished at a deeper level. In Britain today, weddings among families of Pakistani origin usually entail prodigal spending—this among people who are normally careful, even frugal, about money.[19] Gift-giving in India and Pakistan, because of the caste system, tends to flow "upward," to the highest castes. A family that gives a wife to another family counts as *lower* than the bridegroom's family, who are wife-takers and therefore higher. This is the case even if the wife is of a higher caste than the bridegroom.

The bride's family present jewellery and other precious gifts along with their sister and daughter. In doing this, they can catch up somewhat—though never totally—with the status of the family of wife-takers. These gifts express a fundamental contradiction within this culture: people are ranked, superior to inferior, but they also aspire to equality. The bride's dowry, a gift that cannot be returned, denies the inferiority by creating a permanent debt on the side of the bridegroom's family. But the wife's family nevertheless keep on giving. They repeatedly hold large dinner parties for the wife-takers, and continue to give them obligatory gifts. Pakistanis say that the burden on the girl's family never ends—even if they can ill afford it.

In British Pakistani society, as in other societies, a daughter is a person who will marry out; she will leave her "natal" family and join her family "of procreation." At the wedding ceremony the bride, like all South Asian brides, is regarded as "a wonderful, marvellous gift." *Ti praya than* is a Muslim proverb: "A daughter is a gift belonging to another." She appears adorned with precious jewellery—that is, magnificently wrapped, as befits a gift. "But an undecorated bride, by contrast, without a shimmering silk outfit or golden jewellery, is a sad sight, a shame to her family." In traditional Indian and Pakistani marriages, neither the bride nor the groom is free to choose. The match is arranged by the two families concerned: the link is more important than any romance could be. The husband is not allowed to set eyes on his wife before the wedding. At a climactic and highly emotional moment in the ceremony, he lifts the veil covering her face and beholds her for the first time: the receiver opens his gift.

Traditional Western weddings also involve dressing up the bride. She wears white, a sign of purity, and her head, though not her face, is covered by an archaic veil to go with her full-length dress. She trails a long train that may be carried by children, both train and little ones symbols of her future productivity and fertility. The bride's father "gives her away." A shared feast celebrates the new consolidation of society, while witnesses—relatives and friends—contribute gifts.

The binding link, meanwhile, has been ritually expressed by the exchange of vows and the mutual gift of golden wedding rings. The bride may already have received a jewelled "engagement" ring, the giving and acceptance of which was the first movement in a ritual that is completed when confirmation is added to the engagement ring in the form of the simple wedding band. Neither of these two presents in itself imposes an obligation; they are symbolic objects expressing previous agreements freely made by the people giving and accepting them. A marriage not entered into freely, in the Christian tradition, for instance, is no marriage. Nowadays the groom often receives a wedding band (though not an engagement ring) from his wife: he too accepts a gift that symbolizes and makes public his commitment. Wedding rings will henceforth be worn permanently, as symbols of consent and promises made, of destinies undertaken, of the eternal give-and-take that is marriage.

C. A Gift Must Be Freely Given

Although there are many occasions when we feel obliged to give, we persist in believing that giving should be a voluntary act; a gift is the opposite of an exaction. It is a ritual sign of affection and respect, freely offered by the giver. Receiving the gift and making some return for it accept the link proposed; the second and third parts of the ritual belong to the receiver. The virtue in gift-giving is not only freely practised, but is twofold; some of it is the giver's virtue, and some the receiver's.

The freedoms we require in the giving and receiving of gifts are of various sorts. Politeness enjoins principles of behaviour on these occasions—but these are pressures, not obligations, and they often exist precisely to ensure that the exchange of gifts may continue to be intentionally free and in action unhampered. Since one of the chief purposes of gifts is to forge or confirm links, it is normally advisable when a gift is proffered to continue the ritual by accepting it, even if we do not want the object. For we ought to presume that the giver's intentions are good: "It's the thought that counts." This assertion is one of the ways in which we try to play down attachment to things in themselves, as we have seen other societies also striving to do.

We ought, we feel, to "look beyond" the object given, and prefer to think of the giver's benevolence and generosity.

In O. Henry's short story "The Gift of the Magi," the advantages in possessing things are shatteringly erased from the picture, leaving behind only the givers and their relationship in love. A young wife cuts off and sells her long, brown, "rippling and shining" hair in order to buy her husband a chain for his proudest possession, a gold watch "that had been his father's and his grandfather's." He, meanwhile, sells his watch to buy her a set of tortoiseshell combs with jewelled rims, "just the shade to wear in the beautiful vanished hair." In the end all these "two foolish children" have left is each other and the presents that each received, now useless yet all the more significant for that: each has proof now of the perfection of the other's love. O. Henry thrusts home the message: "But in a last word to the wise of these days let it be said that of all who give gifts these two were the wisest."

Our culture avoids ritual gift-giving practices that dictate what shall be given; it leaves givers free to choose what to offer. There are inappropriate gifts, to be sure, and a pursuit of the typical in objects such as Valentine gifts and cards, but there are no prescriptions. A forced and prescribed gift, especially if given without hope of any return, is taken to be nothing more than tribute offered to power, much as a vanquished city is made to hand over its treasures to the conqueror. Tribute, being unfree, is not what we mean by a gift.

And as for making some return when given a present, our culture provides no enforcement there either. The trope of the so-called Indian giver was developed from stories told of "cultures of the Gift," where both giving and returning were obligatory: an "Indian giver" is a person who shockingly asks for his gift back if he should get no return. The rule he breaks (A gift, once given, is no longer the giver's; he has no power over it. If he gets anything back, it must be something else, not what he gave) is there to protect the freedom of the receiver to return—or not to do so. In our culture, once a gift is given, it belongs entirely to the receiver. The giver may have desires as to what should be done with it, but her wishes have no force; the new owner is now responsible, which means he is free to do what he likes with what once was "her" gift. He might take her wishes into account—indeed, he ought to do so if her wishes are wise, for by doing so he can demonstrate gratitude. But if he does, that is his virtue. It is not the giver's right.

A gift that is a link, meanwhile, keeps the voluntary aspect of the gift; it cannot, therefore, be binding, even though it is a "link" and so might be taken to share in the metaphor of chains. The fact of having received a gift does not entail (although it may awaken a desire for) a commitment to the giver. Those who receive donations from the distant rich often feel they have been made to accept an inferior status, that the act of giving which is supposed to create relationship has in fact denied it to them. They do nevertheless have a weapon at their disposal: they can refuse the gratitude that only they can give; their hearts might not "go out" in return. An obvious answer to the question "Why give back?" is simply "Because people want to." The question "Why do they want to?" will lead us further than the mere "Why do they?"

"Oh, you shouldn't have . . ." people sometimes say on opening a present. This response seems to mean that there might have been a felt obligation in the mind of the giver, of which the receiver now absolves her. But this sentence, incomplete as it is, is not about obligation. It is about excessive giving: the speaker is expressing concern at the amount of care or money expended. "You shouldn't have . . ." is in no sense a reproach; there is no question of turning down the gift, or of any ingratitude for it. The receiver's protest at the giver's excessive generosity is a form of thanks for clear signs of caring. What is being said is that "the links of friendship are so strong between us that we don't require presents to strengthen them. There was no need to take so much trouble, to pay so much on my account." The words are comparable to the Japanese expression "I am so sorry," in that attention is deliberately turned away from the present itself and from the recipient, and directed to the giver. And the giver immediately gives a deprecating reply: "Oh, it was nothing." "It was my pleasure." That is, "I enjoyed doing this for you—it was in no sense a nuisance, no pain involved." The phrases also imply, "I would not have done it out of anything but free choice, springing from my affection for you."

The freedoms that in our eyes are conditions of the gift are not negated by the fact that gifts usually bring pleasure and often bring profit in their train. Any desire that gifts should be "pure," that there should be no taint whatever of a reward because that might involve self-interest on the part of the giver, is entirely academic and secular. All of the great world religions promise that good will come of giving, and not only in the world to come. "Give, and gifts will be given to you," Jesus said. "Good measure, pressed down, shaken together, and running over, will be poured into your lap; for whatever measure you deal out to others will be dealt to you in return."[20] We should not calculate returns from specific gifts, but giving in general will bear a harvest, not a dearth.

D. A Gift Is Not a Commodity

The word *commodification* seems to have entered the English language in the mid-1970s; *to commodify* first appeared in the 1980s. Many European languages still lack single words to express either the noun or the verb. Commodifying means turning something that is not by nature commercial into something that can be bought and sold. The new word has arrived because this modern activity's power is now evident to all of us: we feel that commercialization of the world—turning whatever we can into things for sale, or commodities—is spreading to an unacceptable, even an alarming, extent. Sex is far from being the only thing not by nature commercial that can be prostituted (from Latin, "stood up for [sale]").

The history of the word *economy* is equally revealing of a significant change in the structure of modern Western lives. *Economy* means, from the

Greek, "the management (*nomos*) of the household (*oikos*)": *oikonomia*. For millennia people's work was accomplished largely at home, in their *oikos*, and until the mid-twentieth century the household produced much of what families needed: we made our own soap, butter, candles, clothes. Many of us until quite recently grew vegetables, preserved food for the winter, kept chickens, even made our own houses and furniture, while the rich among us stabled their own horses.

In the course of the nineteenth century more and more of us moved into cities and became dependent on being able to buy food instead of raising it. We began to have to work for others in order to get the money for food, and for the things we now had to buy because we were so busy working that we had no time to make them. In any case machines often made them better and certainly made them faster than we could. We became dependent on electricity, on water supplies to the cities, on drainage, and on steam-driven and then motorized transport. All these services had become convenient—but also, in the new context, necessary.

The words *at work* now designated not merely an activity, but a place. And this place was not at home. "Work" was elsewhere; getting to work required transport. *Economy,* the word for "management of the household," now meant "management of all commercial transactions, everywhere." "Everywhere" included households, of course, because people live at home and give birth to future workers who then purchase the things "the economy" supplies. We are the ones accustomed to buying—the "customers." But in a strong new sense, the household was no longer the economy. "Work" meant what one did outside of the household, for pay; "house work" was therefore something other than "work," and pay did not apply. The effect on women's "place," as it was called, is well known.

The great differentiation between "home" and "work" had many other consequences. One of them was that economic and social relationships became increasingly distinct categories. And since the economy now included everything impersonally bought and sold, the household, the site of "privacy," was obviously the primary place for what was personal. Friends and relatives were the people one invited into the small social worlds where gifts were exchanged, very often in one another's homes.

In opposition to the invading force of cold, calculating, purely material Commodity relations now stood the ideal of the Gift, freely offered by the giver, unearned by the recipient, warmly expressive of love, tending to arouse gratitude, generative of return gifts, creative of a cycle, a dance, of reciprocal affections. Markets are about quantifiable results; gifts are concerned with people's feelings and intentions. Commodities earn profits; gifts, express-ing and encouraging personal relationship, give increase. One of the great Opposites constitutive of our culture,[21] that of Commerce versus Gift-Giving, stood forth with clarity; the battle was joined.

But by now, almost all manufactured objects were made outside the home. Gifts had to be bought, like everything else: gifts cost money. One riposte to the ubiquity of monetary cost, as we have seen, was the symbolic designation of bought things as gifts, by means of our manner of presenting them, the occasions of their offering, our addition of wrappings to dress them up, our insistence on freedom in giving, getting, and returning.

Commerce, of course, fought back. Those on the side of Business claim that, actually, it is commerce that is free, whereas gift-giving is full of obliga-tions. (It is worth noting here that denying that gifts are freely given performs useful service in the interests of Commerce.) Nobody is forced to buy from anyone in particular (even though buying is a general condition of modern living): if a buyer does not like a deal, she can simply go somewhere else and get what she wants at the price she wants it, from a business competitor. Buyers and sellers submit to contracts—which are protective devices, freeing us, by their very impersonality and their subjection to law, from the tyrannies of personal influence.

The Gift replies: we are human beings, not commodities. We are persons, and not faceless, unconnected, identical monads that "add up," like the coins, banknotes, and numbers that "economics" adores. Each of us is unique. We are embedded in personal relationships, and we find these, rather than money, enriching. Gift-giving is directed to what really counts for us. And money cannot buy it.

The world of commerce responds by stealing ideas from the realm of the gift—by seeing what is thought of as considerate and "warm," and then copying it. For example, many business people have learned to be excruciatingly polite, just as manners outside of business seem to have relaxed almost into non-existence: business understands the lubricating effect of politeness. People involved in business transactions commonly exchange gifts—in wrappings, of course. Feasts are given by the firm, Christmas cards sent, unrequested discounts offered, and "specials" made available for "good" or "favoured" customers who, it is hoped, will be so pleasantly surprised and so grateful that they will carry on buying.

A strong opposition between Commerce and Gift does not necessarily operate in other cultures. In Japan, for example, there is no culturally induced feeling that "the economy" is distinctively impersonal. "Work" is a major site for the elaboration of friendships. Bosses are traditionally supposed to be paternally benevolent, and the company is considered a protective, loyal, familial unit.[22] But Japanese business giving, as a one-way flow of gifts "upward," openly expresses rank; it is a custom that is perfectly acceptable in Japan. In our culture, even our business gifts never display their prices on the packages, which is common Japanese practice: different conceptual categories produce different customs.

In the multitudes of small social realms of gift-giving in the West, it is true that we are not "free" of other people but conditioned by their presence, responsible for them, dependent on them; we are capable of feeling indebted to those who help us. In the world of commerce and commodities, by contrast, we are categorized as *autonomous*—literally, from the Greek, "a law unto ourselves"—meaning that we are free to buy whatever we like. But this claim for commercial freedom quickly displays its own limits. People wander "freely" in the bright world of commodities only if they have money to spend; most of us have to work to get this money, and nobody even tries to suggest that freedom rules the world of work.

Our very selves have changed, we have been told, from "gift" selves to "commodity" selves.[23] We are now equal, identical, separate, free—that is, no longer controlled as we were in the past by the harness that relationship requires. Most of us would not find this description accurate, at least to the extent that we actually long for personal authenticity, as we do for relationship and even for commitment, no matter how hard these may be for our modern "selves" to achieve. Most of us recognize that it is precisely within a network of relationships that we experience depth, and indeed the very desire to give, receive, and return. We have noted the importance we attach to feeling free when we engage in "the dance of the Three Graces." Sociologists, however, tend to discount this claim of freedom, dismissing it as dishonest, as at best "popular ideology"[24] that serves to obscure what they believe to be the facts: an endless reduction in our minds of everything to our own self-interest, and an equally endless desire in all of us for commodities.

Recently a new model has been discerned, which introduces its own opposition (or rather, another version of an old one): that between the consumers and the producers of merchandise.[25] The meeting place of these two contrasting worlds is the Market. The consumer's preferences rule; producers today must submit to volatile expressions of individual self-interest in consumers. Since all of us—even "producers"—consume, this respect for the consumer is irresistibly attractive, and even taken to be proof that it is "the Market" that makes us equal. Commerce among strangers lightens social ties and renders them non-durable; it weakens, devalues, and renders obscure the world of the gift. The Market assures us in addition that it does not impose: the client is king. We all act in our own self-interest—which, many believe, ends up benefiting us all. There is only one condition for all these benefits to be ours: we must accept the commodification of everything. The far more ancient model of community, with its means of expression, the Gift that strengthens links, makes itself felt especially in times of crisis, when people in extremity sometimes rediscover solidarity. But on the whole, the world of the gift is either submerged or taken for granted.

E. Show Deference, Then Give Back Something Different

Gift-giving dislikes direct exchange and avoids equivalence. In this it differentiates itself again from commerce, in which a participant finds out the price of an object, collects the precise sum required, pays it, receives written proof that he has done so, and leaves with his new possession: equivalence having been achieved, the transaction is over. But the aim of giving a present is the continuance of the ritual—the acceptance, then the giving of another gift in return. The meaning is a relationship ongoing.

The sociologist Pierre Bourdieu claims that gifts, if we are honest, can be distinguished invariably from commodities in only two ways. Gifts exchanged are always different, and people usually defer the return of a gift: there is "difference" and there is "deferral."[26] To Bourdieu's two ways we should add a third, namely a difference in status: there is "deference." In our culture this deference must be demonstrated towards the giver by the one receiving the present. Later she will return the gift and so recover her status: the first giver will then "bow" to her. Gift-giving creates alternating superiors and inferiors. We shall look again later at modern people's revulsion at accepting lower status, however temporarily. But we might remember from the beginning that deference is a kind of difference.

A gift returned should be something of approximately the same value as the present received—but it had better be something different. This precept echoes, but is not the same thing as, the rule of manners that it is extremely rude to refuse a gift, and therewith an offer of friendship, by giving it back.[27] To seek for something exactly resembling what was given—a small pink jug for an identical small pink jug, say—and give that back would be less emotionally devastating than to refuse the gift in the first place, but this too is "not done." An identical gift could look mockingly parodic and therefore spiteful; it would certainly make the recipient of such a gift wonder what was going on. For this implicit rule is so rarely broken that there are no customary strategies for responding to its infraction.

Money is less satisfactory than are objects for the give-and-take of gifts; for one thing, price is all that money is. Money is "cold," therefore, and "when it's gone the memory's gone," said the woman in Winnipeg to David Cheal.[28] Banknotes, furthermore, being mere signs of amounts, are all "the same"; they lack individuality and the identity required by even the most predetermined gift. When the Maring of Papua New Guinea first encountered money, they incorporated it into their reciprocal exchanges—but first wrote the giver's name or cryptic signs on the banknotes so that they could avoid using the same ones when returning money gifts.[29]

Giving like for like seems to cancel the gift, and with it the personal link that a gift may create and sustain. (A couple giving each other almost identical wedding rings means the exact opposite. Wedding rings, however, are not gifts so much as symbols of promise.) It is always possible, as well, to change the unspoken rule of difference, provided that both partners understand and agree. In 1972 American sociologists observed children during school break exchanging identical cookies from their lunch boxes. They had asked their mothers to give them exchangeable items such as these cookies, so that they could use them to make friends in the schoolyard.[30] Some would not classify these cookies as gifts because they were identical, and because they were exchanged without a wait between transactions: this was swapping, therefore, and not gift-giving. We should realize, however, that children are normally unable to provide gifts that are different, and in any case people do not swap identical objects. These children understood perfectly, I would say, that it was the meaning, not the cookies, that counted. They might even have found the similarity of goods expressive of affinity between the partners. Always, with the giving of presents, the intentions and understandings of the people giving and receiving matter more than the gifts.

There is, however, a haunting similarity between the offering of favours and the inflicting of harm, in that in both cases a response is elicited: on the one hand returning the gift, on the other striking back. It seems likely that we all know at some level that gift-and-return is the exact opposite of offence and counter-offence. Gifting must always have been a substitute for fighting. This understanding explains the ceremonial and public nature of the handing over of offerings, and some of their obligatory weight, in the so-called societies of the Gift. People say, by means of objects presented, "We—as a group—recognize your group. In other words, we are prepared to trust you, enter into relationship with you." In such a first move there is a kind of challenge: "Give back, or we must come to blows: you must show us you want to be friends and not enemies, and the way to do that is to hand over to us something in return."[31]

Revenge, unlike gift-giving, loves imitation in the thing "given back," which is as often as possible a part of what is called "satisfaction": if you carry off our daughters, you had better start protecting your own. A man or woman inflicting vengeance longs to make the enemy feel what he or she felt in being wronged: nothing is so naturally satisfying as a riposte that is a mirror image of the original offence. To avenge oneself is to equalize, which is why vengeance often portrays itself as justice. (The second of Bourdieu's characteristics of the gift—deferral—is often characteristic of vengeance too, as we shall see later.)

Gifting behaviour, on the other hand, does not seek equality but rather *equilibrium over time,* as the gifting ritual—including waiting before returning—is repeatedly performed. Neutrality, a form of equilibrium, has been thrown out by the first gift. And the giver in our culture, where the ideal is that it is better to give than to receive, has immediately a higher status: equality has gone, together with neutrality. Part of the purpose of returning something is certainly to redress the balance somewhat. But what happens is that the return giver immediately causes a new imbalance, where the first giver now "owes something" to the second.

A first giver, we saw, remains superior because his action was more spontaneous than a response can ever be. It enters an empty field, as it were: when responses arise, the first gift has always already occurred. A return gift is given partly because one does not want to appear to sponge on another. Sometimes a receiver even gives back a somewhat costlier gift than she was given (in other words, the difference always courted reappears), so that her gift, in its excess, becomes more like a first offering. All freely given presents characteristically strive to be "more than expected," to be "something extra." Givers like to surprise. And returners of gifts try to do likewise. But surprise, of course, requires difference—something new.

Giving something different is dissimilar in meaning from the practice of "giving more in return" in societies where gifts are compulsory, where what is to be given is often predetermined, and where the continuity striven for is that of keeping obligations in force. An example can be found in a reciprocal practice reported from India and Pakistan: "On the occasion of a marriage, departing guests are given gifts of sweets. In weighing them out, the hostess may say, 'these five are yours,' meaning 'these are a repayment for what you formerly gave me,' and she then adds an extra measure, saying, 'These are mine.' On the next occasion, she will receive back [the extra measure of sweets] along with an additional measure which she later returns, and so on."[32] In other cases, such as the potlatch, "giving more" is itself an obligation and part of the battle for honour—to be more generous, therefore "larger," than the previous giver.

In a system where free giving is important, the second gift is a new gift: it is the giver's decision, his choice—and this includes his choice of what thing he shall give in return. Copying the gift he received would be inappropriate, he knows, because the other person is unique, as he is, with her own tastes and needs: differences among persons, we feel, require differences among gifts. Meanwhile, the second giver wants not so much to draw equal to the first as to carry out the next step in the ritual, the retracing of the link, in order to endorse the relationship. Deference, too, takes turns. As in a game of see-saw, one partner rises as the other falls, and the pleasure of the game depends on keeping the beam in motion by each person springing upward in turn: should the ritual come to a "horizontal" rest in equality, the ongoing expressions of relationship would stall.

When the law of revenge rules among us, there is no forgiveness for shame endured. Here humility is no virtue: where we make "size" everything, deliberately to "reduce" oneself is to behave shamefully. Thus there is an obligation, underpinned by honour, to return injury for injury, "tit for tat." In honour systems, vengeance "cannot but" occur; freedom not to take one's honour back is out of the question for an honourable man. He takes revenge in order to be "quits." The word comes from Latin *quietus,* "calm," because now things are equal; the avenged one can at last relax. Of course, the one who has "paid" will probably (his own honour now requiring appeasement) have a different vision of the future in mind.

Reciprocity is a sort of ebbing and flowing, like the sea: *re*-ci (receding) and *pro*-ci (moving forward). Reciprocity is in itself amoral—mere movement to and fro. It can be deadly—or life-giving. It can be compulsory—or freely undertaken and continued. A giving–receiving–returning circle can be vicious—or virtuous. Either way, reciprocity encourages continuity in the same kind of activity. One of the reasons for the back-and-forth, the swinging pendulum of giving and returning, is a desire for continuity: a relationship expressed by an alternating disequilibrium is far harder to break off than is one that dispenses with give-and-take. Alternating obligations to vengeance are also extremely difficult to bring to an end. It is possible—though difficult—to escape such a trap if one who suffers injury manages to find it in himself to refuse vengeance in return. Just as refusing to return an overture or a confirmation of friendship can break a relationship, refusing to pay back an injury can break a cycle of violence.

The lowest and most terrible level of reciprocity is that of total chaos and civil war, a generalized outbreak of what René Girard calls "mimetic violence," all against all and gang against gang, each one imitating everybody else and no holds barred, in omnipresent rage and hatred. The second level is war: us against them. War can bring unity within a society, expelling disorder beyond its borders. The third level is talion, or revenge limited by law to strict retaliation: "life for life, eye for eye, tooth for tooth, hand for hand, foot for foot"—and no more.[33] Next and higher comes the Silver Rule: "Do to no one what you would not want done to you."[34] The Golden Rule makes the Silver Rule positive: "Do to others as you would have them do to you."[35] The highest level is "When people hurt you, your return shall be to continue loving them."[36] Modern precepts of tolerance rest on the Silver Rule, which can—though with difficulty—receive legal support. Laws lay down in advance what cannot be done, or what can be done only under certain conditions; they cannot inspire either intention or will. The Golden Rule (which is beyond law) is the one germane to gift-giving. One can make the first move and create new possibilities, but one cannot control what happens thereafter. A giver can hope for, but never expect, let alone demand, a response. The final rule—"Love your enemies"[37]—goes beyond reciprocity altogether.

F. A Receiver Must Wait Before Giving in Return

A considerable part of what is given with a gift is the time spent in reflecting, remembering, planning, shopping, choosing, wrapping. At Christmas wrapped presents will pile up, people dutifully leaving them unopened, even when they lie in full view in all their enticing mystery, until the agreed-upon moment arrives and the decorated parcels are compelled to give up their secrets. Even during the ceremony of present-opening, ritual delays may be built in, serving to enhance the surprise and emotion of the event. In our household, the gift-opening drama is interminably stretched out as the youngest child, with eyes closed, grabs a gift at random, reads if she can the card attached, and takes the parcel to the person addressed, who then opens it, exclaims at the contents, holds the object up to be seen, and hands it round to be admired by everybody else. The giver meanwhile makes a commentary on his gift; he might tell where he managed to find it, or describe how the idea came to him. Then it is the turn of the next present—audience assured—and then the others, one by one.

All of this drama takes time and effort to be performed properly. Since gift-giving is ritual, it uses some of the sovereign means by which ritual and drama create their effects, namely time, timing, and tempo. Gift-giving is meant to enact—give embodied form to—what otherwise might be unseen and unappreciated sentiments and social links. Needless to say, human beings are capable of pretending that their sentiments are warm and loving when really they are not. Drama includes acting, after all, and acting is behaving *as if* what is expressed is real.

Occasions designated for gift-giving for all by all involved, such as Christmas, are unusual in that everybody waits for the moment, and then gives and receives *at once*. Normally there is, between giving and returning gifts, a time lapse—Bourdieu's "deferral." Jeffrey Fadiman gives a striking example of the operation of "deferral" in a society where a gift or favour must be repaid in the future—when convenient to all sides. "While conducting business on Mt. Kenya in the 1970s," he writes, "I visited a notable local dignitary. On completing our agenda, he stopped my rush to leave by presenting me with a live and angry hen. Surprised, I stammered shaky 'thank-yous', then walked down the mountain with my kicking, struggling bird. Having discharged my obligation—at least in Western terms—by thanking him, I cooked the hen, completed my business, eventually left Kenya, and forgot the incident.

"Years later, I returned on different business. It was a revelation. People up and down the mountain called out to one another that I had come back to 'return the dignitary's hen.' To them, the relationship that had sprung up between us had remained unchanged throughout the years. Having received a favor, I had now come back to renew the relationship by returning it. I had, of course, no such intention. Having forgotten the hen incident, I was also unaware of its importance to others. Embarrassed, I slipped into a market and bought a larger hen, then climbed to his homestead to present it. Again I erred, deciding to apologize in Western fashion for delaying my return. 'How can a hen be late?' he replied. 'Due to the bird, we have *uthoni* [obligations, thus a relationship]. That is what sweetens life. What else was the hen for but to bring you here again?'" The author, writing for American business people worried about what to do when foreigners seem to be offering bribes, concludes: "Western interest lies in doing business; non-Western, in forming bonds so that business can begin. Westerners seek to discharge obligations; non-Westerners, to create them. Our focus is on producing short-term profit; theirs, on generating future favors."[38]

We think of a gift as being in a different category from that of a commodity. And despite the commodification of our world, we still understand the logic that underpins the Gift. For us too the time lapse between gift and return is normally important. In our culture, to wait too long before giving back or at least making a return signal is wrong, because the delay makes the giver wonder unhappily whether the recipient is forgetful, indifferent, or even hostile to his overture of friendship. The people of Mount Kenya appear to have had a firmer faith in other people's continuing goodwill: for us, a hen may certainly be too late.

But it is also rude to return a gift too promptly; it is even incorrect to telephone and thank the host immediately after a dinner party, or to ask her back too soon. For one thing, to do so is to ignore the categorical difference between gift and commodity. Instant return has a whiff of payment about it, of reluctance to accept a moral debt, of being anxious to discharge an obligation, of hoping to avoid a relationship by immediately turning the other's gift into a thing of the past. One is supposed to savour the gift, think about it, spend time remembering the person who gave it.

There are ruminations, as well, when somebody is resentful enough to long for revenge. This revelling in thoughts of vengeance makes revenge-seeking structurally similar (because diametrically opposite) to the behaviour of people deepening their relationship while taking time to consider how to return favours and presents. The avenger thinks long and hard, enjoys imagining what she might do to equalize, looks forward to the day when her vengeance will be complete: "Vengeance," it is said, "is a dish that is best eaten cold."

The North American businessman's story is unusual in that the people never saw him between visits. Usually, in societies such as the one he describes, everybody lives reasonably close by. And while a gift is still unreciprocated—during the period of deferral—partners are likely, and even expected, to stay in touch with one another. In Mende, Papua New Guinea, people enter into more or less permanent giving partnerships in a relationship called *twem*, "delayed gift-exchange between individuals" or *samting ikam igo* in Melanesian pidgin: "Recipients ought to visit to eat and talk with their donors from time to time, and if they both live in the same community, they ought occasionally to chop firewood or do other favors for them. Donors are also expected to visit the people to whom they gave valuables. They are also expected to help their recipients; failure to do so has a bearing on the latter's obligation to repay the debt." The other side of the coin is that either partner's avoidance of the other may be taken as a sign of an intention to default: "Two teen-aged men ... admitted that they often borrowed from 'old women' in the community and then worked hard to avoid them, running off in the opposite direction whenever they heard one of the women coming towards them on village paths." There is a material dimension to *twem*. But "*twem* is more than its material transactions."[39]

"Do good to your friends and harm to your enemies" was a favourite maxim in ancient Greece. Another fundamental reason suggested for a time lapse between gifts would take seriously the corollary of this adage: one should never harm a benefactor.[40] It follows that time spent under obligation to a giver is time during which enmity with that person ought to be unthinkable. We have already seen that giving must often have replaced war. The "obligation time" was a time of trust—the longer the time, the greater the confidence shown. Then, when the return was finally made, it was often more than the original gift. Aristotle says that the purpose of this increase is to turn the first giver into a debtor.[41] And ever since Mauss,[42] anthropologists have been tempted to see this extra amount as a form of "interest" paid for the time waited.

In our own culture, gift-giving by taking turns, described earlier as an alternating disequilibrium and an equilibrium established over time, is an uncertain business and, I have argued, must remain so in order to protect the freedom of the participants. It expresses the difference between gifts, on the one hand, and commodities, contracts, and the paying of interest on time "taken," on the other. Normally, with us as with the people of Mende or those of Mount Kenya, time lapses after the giving of a gift. Only the receiver can bring the break to an end, when she decides to make a return. Contract specifies duration (we accept in advance a date by which payment must be made), but the Gift does not. The receiver, meanwhile, not being forgetful, feels indebted to the giver. The amount given back might be more than the original gift, but that is neither a stipulation nor a form of interest. It is much more likely to be an attempt to make the return as little like an obligation or a payment as possible.

In Japan, as we have seen, everyone is taught to feel endlessly, and mostly happily, indebted to specific other people and also to all Japanese, both living and dead: a "gift-debt" is a small, concrete instance of a vastly extended network of indebtedness. We too know the feeling of indebtedness. We feel it individually, and most especially when someone has done us a great favour. Having accepted such a gift, we then (if we are grateful) spend time waiting and watching for a chance to do something or give something in return.

This is the time of "obligation" pointed out so triumphantly by Mauss and his followers. The waiting period has often been seen, moreover, as itself an onerous kind of "payment," as though a giver thirsted for some sort of revenge for having given. According to this account, the recipient must give the donor time to savour the obligation owed him. "Overmuch eagerness to discharge an obligation is a kind of ingratitude," says La Rochefoucauld:[43] "giving the benefactor time" is in itself a part-payment in return. An obligation is thought of as a weight or load that must be carried for a decent length of time before it is laid down or "discharged." The giver meanwhile enjoys his superiority, and his knowledge that future benefits will be his.

Another interpretation is to see the waiting period as a time for the receiver to spend appreciating the gift, and for strengthening the link traced, by thinking about it. A gift that is a concrete object can be looked at, reflected upon; it should make you turn about in your mind the giving of the thing you are contemplating and, most importantly, its giver.

Bourdieu would say that someone placed under an obligation through receiving a gift was being given time to deceive herself. Thanks to the time lapse, givers and receivers never become totally aware of the way in which reciprocity invariably forces them to keep on playing the gifting game; they therefore suppose that they are being generous and grateful, spontaneous and free. But the gift is there for a purpose: it was given out of the self-interest of the donor. To imagine anything else is to disguise the truth from ourselves. That is why, Bourdieu says, we are not supposed to give back too soon: we would be revealing our awareness that the donor gave out of self-interest: "To betray one's haste to be free of an obligation one has incurred . . . is to denounce the initial gift retrospectively as motivated by the intention of obliging one."[44] In a peasant culture, Bourdieu writes elsewhere, a man feels he can afford to "be generous" with the time taken waiting, knowing as he does that the "crop" sown by means of his gifts will eventually be his: "In a world in which time is so plentiful and goods are so scarce, his best and indeed only course is to spend his time without counting it, to squander the one thing which exists in abundance."[45]

But for us, time is precisely what is scarce: time plays a role as omnipresent, as constraining, and as exigent as reputation plays in a culture built on concepts of honour and shame. Deliberately to squander time, or to spend it remembering somebody else, is for us a wanton refusal to be "reasonable," which is to calculate our own self-interest. Buying gifts takes time, and so does wrapping them. It is also hard work to pay attention to what others might want to receive as a gift. One has to think and shop in advance of giving. As the Canadian woman explained to David Cheal, gift decisions are made "usually by thinking, or watching and then seeing what they need."[46] Even taking time to remember the giver before doing something in return is for us a kind of gift—but not because the giver wants us to suffer indebtedness for as long as possible. "Spending" time and "taking" time for other people must be considered a costly gift in our society where, under the pressing and invasive rule of commodities, we are capable of pronouncing that "Time is money."

PART III

∞

Meaning

11

Votive Offerings

Things are easier to describe and discuss than are feelings, virtues and vices, thoughts, or intentions. They are *objects,* a word which means literally "things thrown down in front of us": we can inspect them, all of us considering them together. Things in themselves—without meanings attached to them—are, in the end, essentially opaque: we can describe them, calculate their properties, measure them, count them, but we can never "understand" them. Objects never enter into or issue from our minds; only ideas can do that. When thinking about ritual objects such as gifts, we have to remember the opacity of things, and also the fact that we have saddled them with meanings. We let thoughts and feelings "ride" them while we perform the ritual. Gift-objects are a kind of shorthand for matters of great complexity. We often use things in this way—consciously or unconsciously—to represent what we find difficult to say or to discuss, matters that are often far more important to us than are the things in themselves. In ritual action we handle objects, move around them, lift them up, pass them to each other, direct our united attention to them, think about what they are "saying."

The meanings with which we invest objects-turned-into-gifts depend upon an enormous number of factors, including context and culture, feelings, thoughts, memories—yes, and also conventional obligations and perhaps deliberate designs upon other people's benevolence. This is the first paradox that modern people have to grasp, unaccustomed as we have become to understanding what ritual is (even though we practise many rituals daily). An object that is part of a ritual is both itself *and* something that carries meanings. And in ritual, persons and meanings often matter more than objects do.

This last point becomes simpler if we consider favours rather than gifts. An old woman living alone in the country needs a draining ditch dug so that her dirt road will not flood in winter. Her neighbours pitch in one day and dig the ditch. The woman meanwhile prepares lunch for them to enjoy when the work is done. This too is "gift-giving." The neighbours did not help her in order to get lunch. The lunch is in no way "payment" for the digging. The question that seems harder to answer than "Why make lunch?" becomes "Why did the neighbours give their time and effort in the first place?" The woman does not feel "put down" by the favour done, although everybody knows she could not have dug the ditch herself, or paid to have it done professionally. What she does feel is grateful. She then thinks of what she *can* do and makes lunch. The neighbours do get lunch out of their morning's work—and knew they would get it. That they foresaw lunch does not mean that they dug the ditch to get lunch. Or that they were not giving when they helped out.

Gifts are often understood to be *only* objects—commodities, things desired by receivers of them. If that is all they are, then a person finding her desire for one of these things suddenly satisfied might simply take the object of her desire and start thinking about what else she wants. There is indeed no reason to give anything back, if the object itself is the only consideration. But this is not normally what happens. She thinks, instead, about the person who gave her the gift and why he did so, tries to find out what he would like, goes to look for it (or, in the case of lunch, to make it), and gives him that, if she can. Commodities—or efforts—are important in both gift and counter-gift, but they are not the point of either transaction.

Gifts and favours are neither simple nor clear. Contracts are clear, but in our culture gifts are "the opposite" of contracts. They are not spelled out, not laid down. There are always mixed motives for their giving, an array of emotions involved, satisfaction in the fact of bestowing as well as in receiving, desire to please for reasons worthy and unworthy, a felt need that something should be done in return. A debt is created, a sense when one has received a favour that "now it's my turn," and a feeling that giving back is justice: "It's only fair." There are, it is true, social conventions that pressure people to return favours: other people might be watching, judging, criticizing. But most receivers of gifts and favours, in our culture, would answer Mauss's question "Why give back?" by saying, "We give back because we feel grateful."

We would *not* normally say, "Because society demands it" or "Because reciprocity is a norm" or "Because I have to think of my prestige." Naturally, our not saying these things does not mean that they are false. There is some truth in each of these sociological answers to Mauss's question. But we might at least consider what most of us think of as the main reason. (In his famous book Mauss pays no attention whatever to gratitude.) And needless to say, "We give back because we are grateful" raises this question: "What is gratitude?"

To answer it, we might begin by looking at votive offerings, which are among the oldest surviving signs of human feelings of thankfulness. They and the practices surrounding them still continue today. Votives are concrete objects, solidified recognitions of favours received, and manifestations of gratitude.

∞

Statuettes of human beings and animals and models of other objects have been found associated with temples and shrines in archaeological digs all over the world. They are known, at least in historical times, to have been offered by worshippers to divinities in gratitude for favours received. They may be magnificent works of art (such as the life-sized bronze Charioteer of Delphi, offered to Apollo after a victory in the Pythian Games in 474 BC), and they may be created out of precious materials, like the jewelled votive crowns of the Visigothic kings of Spain.[1] But most of them are small, made of common inexpensive substances, and often summary and crude in execution. In the Middle East and the Mediterranean regions in particular, thousands of the humbler objects have come to light. Temple staff must have had to clear them out from time to time, in order to make room for more offerings that kept arriving. They were often, apparently, protected from destruction by some kind of taboo and were in addition rarely of value to robbers, which explains why so many of the small and simple ones have survived. Modern searchers occasionally come upon caches of them, collected in large numbers and set aside or buried.

The custom of making votive offerings to the gods may have begun during the Upper Paleolithic era, before 9000 BC.[2] Because of the lack of written explanations, it is uncertain what they meant to their earliest creators. From the beginning votive offerings were totally differentiated from an equally ancient custom in which animals (including, originally, human beings) and vegetable offerings were sacrificed to honour the gods. Votive figurines placed in shrines were specifically not destroyed: they were meant to go on standing there.

Votives continued to be produced and offered in shrines throughout the ages of Sumer, Akkad, and Babylon, ancient Egypt and Persia, the Minoans and Greeks, Etruscans, Iberians, and Romans. Christians took up the practice, adapting it, as people always do, to their own beliefs; and in Greece and Italy, Spain and Latin America, especially in Orthodox and Roman Catholic churches, it continues today. The ancient Chinese made magnificent votive offerings. The conquistadores of Spain, whose Iberian and Roman ancestors had practised the custom, brought it with them to South America—to find that it already existed among the populations they encountered there.

Because these carved and moulded objects were made from durable materials—clay and bone, wood and metal and stone—they have survived. But perishable things must also have been left in shrines for the gods, "sacrificed" in the sense of being forgone by human beings in order to give the gods a share of them. For seven thousand years at least, ever since the agricultural revolution began in the Middle East and human beings started to produce food for themselves instead of relying on hunting animals or collecting edible vegetation in the wild, people would deliberately set aside a small part of the crops they had raised—"first-fruits"—and take them to the temples as offerings. They would then celebrate the harvest with a thanksgiving festival.[3]

There is speculation that the reason for offering first-fruits was to maintain a taboo on beginning to gather in the crop before it was fully grown: only when the gods had been honoured with offerings of mature plants was consumption allowed. But the people who offer first-fruits have always thought of them as indispensable for the future fertility of their land. Greeks called first-fruits *aparchai,* "beginnings," and habitually began their meals, in the same spirit as that of the sacrifice of the first-fruits, by offering bits of meat and pouring out some of their wine for the gods as signs of respect and mindfulness. The customary offering of first-fruits created and continued a relationship with the divine and with other human beings in the celebration of common beliefs, ethical principles, and rituals. And this piety was thought to be needed if people were to keep up and benefit from the cultivation of the land. Nature and the gods gave their gifts, and human beings did well to appreciate them, "give back" a mindful share of them, and so ensure that plenty would continue. Ungrateful farmers were likely, in the end, to be bad farmers. Ungrateful eaters were likely to be as thoughtless in other matters as they were about their good fortune in having access to a supply of food.

Thanksgiving at harvest time is a widespread custom still. It is a joyful recognition of being "blessed"—a notion we shall look at again—by abundance of food. After the crops have been brought in, people sit down together to feast, to enjoy the "first-fruits" of their labours. They may also bring to churches and temples offerings of food from the harvest, remembering that their own good management is not all there is to take into account. The aspect of "first-fruits" that means "beginnings" also has its place in modern harvest festivals: Thanksgiving in North America, for example, is a feast of initiation into winter, a celebration of riches gathered in and confidence because we are well prepared for the cold months ahead.

Votive offerings, on the other hand, were figurines and other objects left for the gods as the fulfillment of vows (*vota* in Latin). People prayed to a god for help, promising to give something to the deity should their request be granted. Such gifts are now known as votives or ex-votos: they are kept promises, vows fulfilled. There is reciprocity involved and—shockingly to many—a sort of bargaining with the supernatural. In modern Mexico ex-votos are known as *milagros*, "miracles." The English word *miracle* and the Spanish one are rooted in the ideas of "looking at something in wonder" (from *mirare*, as in "admire"), and of being made joyful thereby. The English word *smile* has the same Indo-European root as *milagro*.[4]

Chosen statues of saints in certain Catholic churches in Mexico today are decked, festooned, even covered all over with *milagros*. In Italy galleries adjoining churches are sometimes set aside for pictures and thank-offerings that cover the walls. In nineteenth-century Europe one practice was, and sometimes still is, to hang up marble tablets with written thanks engraved on them. In Hispanic cultures, people buy *milagros* or sometimes have them especially made and bring them—sometimes long distances, for the practice and the vow can include a pilgrimage—to the church. They present these articles to express gratitude—long lasting, since such objects endure—for the granting of a specific favour. The person making the offering is called in Italian the *graziato* or *graziata*, "one who has received grace." The gracious favour asked for and received could be recovery from an illness, getting a job, having a baby, finding the down payment for a house, escaping without injury from an accident.

The object brought by the *graziato* is offered either in simple thanks, or in fulfillment of a vow made when he was anxious or suffering and praying for release or for something intensely desired. (There is in these cultures no censoriousness about a thing being offered to God; the thing does not preclude, and may intensify, prayers of thanksgiving.) Creativity is expended in deciding what object would best represent both the original need and the answered petition. It might be a depiction of oneself praying, made perhaps of pressed tin (most *milagros* are produced in large quantities and cost little). The kneeling figure would most probably be a generic, often sexually inexplicit "grateful person" who represents the *graziato*. Candles left burning in churches similarly represent people who have visited, and their prayers. Rosaries—solidified prayers, very personal possessions, both colourful and easily hung up—are common offerings. One might present a model or a sign representing what has been achieved (a car that is finally one's proud possession, a truck representing work as a truck driver). An ex-voto can show or embody in some way the danger that was averted or overcome: a picture of the *graziato* falling down stairs or out of a tree or into the sea; flames enveloping a house; a liquor bottle for a recovering alcoholic; a model of a jail ora pair of tiny handcuffs; and often real crutches offered up in memory of the suffering now ended.

Ex-votos are always meant to be highly specific, even if they are offered anonymously. They are created to look as realistic as possible. If a particular place is depicted in a votive picture—often a narrative depiction of the moment of danger—other people who know the place must be able to recognize it. In many cases, explicit information is supplied by attaching to votives notes and descriptions: names and dates, and narrations of what happened when the person was saved. Where there are no inscriptions, the exact meaning of a votive offering may be ambiguous to an onlooker, much as the most ancient votive offerings are for us today: does a model of a lit cigarette mean that somebody has succeeded in giving up smoking, or is it offered in gratitude because a tobacco business has been successfully launched? Does a model boat mean a successful fishing season, a longed-for fishing craft that has finally become the *graziato*'s own, or his safe return, despite storm or accident, to harbour? One thing is certain, however: gratitude for a great favour is being expressed.

Because so many prayers are for recovery from ill health, favourite motifs in Spain and Latin America—they have been common for three thousand years in the Mediterranean region—are human body parts. These tend nowadays to be stamped and cut out of tin or modelled in wax: legs, arms, heads, eyes, breasts, kidneys, lungs. People offer them in thanks for pain and sickness having passed from these limbs or organs in particular. Body-part *milagros* are small and therefore take up little space on an image already hung about and encrusted with *milagros;* they are cheap and anonymous, but still specific. Modern votives rarely show diseased bodies: we see photographs of healthy people (photographs are perfect for ex-votos because of their specificity), and body-part *milagros* too are almost invariably whole and well. Their point is to show the happy result of recovery and not, as in pictures portraying accidents, what the person was saved from. *Milagros* may be offered in petition rather than in gratitude, but these, in Christian cultures, are a small minority of cases. Almost always they do not represent a wish but rather celebrate the granting of one, and simultaneously fulfill a promise: the offering of the *milagro* itself, together with the trouble of procuring it and the journey to the shrine to carry out the vow.

In pre-Christian times, offerings in temples were often also propitiatory—that is, they were made and offered as a precaution, or to appease an angry god. They could also be concrete payments for crimes committed. In ancient Athens, for example, each of the political leaders called archons swore on taking office to dedicate a golden statue if he ever broke his statutory oaths. In the course of the immemorial history of first-fruits and votive offerings, we can be certain that they were often intended to extort favours by means of magic, or to satisfy a deity's demand for tribute. It is impossible, of course, to know exactly what people who made offerings meant by them unless they tell us. But Christian practice is to try to limit them to a thanking function.

Vast numbers of votive offerings have been found at ancient Greek sites. These finds, and copious descriptions by the Greeks themselves of lost examples of historical interest, make their practice of offering votives among the best recorded in the world. A modern archaeologist describes the seat of Apollo's oracle at Delphi as the expression of two cardinal emotions: anxiety and gratitude. In his estimation, it was anxiety that gave rise to the oracle itself, while "gratitude . . . covered the site with treasuries and statues and other offerings."[5]

Those who survived shipwreck customarily dedicated in Greek temples the clothes they wore during the escape. People also offered other personal possessions, representing many different reasons to be grateful: weapons by soldiers; animal skulls and skins and antlers by hunters; mirrors and jewellery and loom weights by women; masks worn in winning plays; sports para-phernalia, such as balls and quoits; and also prizes won in the games, such as a tripod, a crown, a vase. An object could be offered purely because it was astonishing and unnerving, so that people thought the gods had better look after it: the stone swallowed by Kronos who mistook it for the baby Zeus, the cursed necklace of Eriphyle, the wings of Daedalus, a meteorite, or a mammoth's bones. Items from war booty were also offered up, occasionally because they were amazing, like the throne of Xerxes, but most commonly as a kind of first-fruits from the "crop" of what had been seized, and as thank-offerings for winning. Votive offerings in Christian shrines today can include famous objects as well as precious personal possessions: a handsome motorbike helmet offered as a gift in gratitude for escape from an accident; a favourite piece of jewellery offered in joy for safe childbirth or for the recovery from sickness of oneself or another; the bullet that nearly killed Pope John Paul II, now set in the crown of the Virgin's statue at Fatima. Votive offerings are by no means always examples of simple or "popular" piety. People have vowed and then built whole temples, churches, chapels, hospitals, and monasteries out of gratitude for blessings received.[6]

The bronze figure of Saint Michael atop the Mausoleum of Hadrian, renamed the Castel Sant'Angelo after him, portrays in thanksgiving a vision reported by Pope Gregory the Great: he saw the Archangel sheathing a sword and thereby announcing that the plague was over—a release for which the entire city of Rome had been praying.[7] Artists such as Van Dyck and Mantegna (who designed a votive church in Mantua and supplied a great votive tableau for the altar inside it) painted magnificent votive pictures.[8]

Depicted as a detail in the bottom right-hand corner of Titian's painting for his own tomb is a votive tablet of himself and his son praying.[9] Raphael's *Virgin of Foligno* is said to have been offered by the donor (depicted in the painting) in thanksgiving for his house having escaped serious damage after it was struck by lightning; the house is visible in the background. Saints Jerome, John the Baptist, and Francis accompany him, as he kneels and thanks the Virgin and Child, who appear above "robed in the sun" and accompanied by a host of angels.[10] A small angel stands among the saints below, bearing a board that might have described the saving event, but whose inscription has not survived. (Not all scholars agree with this interpretation of the picture; the inscription would have made the meaning clear.)[11] The austerely intellectual French artist Philippe de Champaigne painted a votive picture in 1662 of two nuns, one of them his daughter, after her miraculous recovery from paralysis. He included on the painting, now in the Louvre, an inscription recording both the event and the sisters' prayers for her.

Votive offerings, of whatever date and from whatever society or social class, speak vividly, from as far back as it is possible to reach in time, about the complex human emotion of thankfulness. Even when the reasons for their offering seem to diverge from what we now mean by gratitude, they help us to understand our own categories better and why we have them. For example, the very existence of votives tells us what we still know: people feel that saying "thank you" is not enough, and that doing something proves that one's gratitude is truly meant. Votive offerings are presents, given in response to generosity received. They are, however, different in two important ways from gifts as discussed in Part Two of this book: they are not offered to people but to supernatural beings, and they are the concrete fulfillment of vows. In Roman legal terminology, *do ut des* ("I give so that you might give in return") expresses the pressure to reciprocate. An ex-voto employs the opposite strategy: "If you give, then I undertake to give such-and-such in return."

People who offer ex-votos feel they have been favoured by an unseen power, a supernatural being with whom they have had direct contact. They have usually *asked* for help, and their prayer has been heard and granted. Not content with thanking their benefactor, they feel a great desire to express their gratitude in a concrete manner. They felt this from the beginning, even as they prayed for help: in specifying their return gift, they *promised* gratitude. For them, giving something back is essential to the expression of gratitude itself. And their need has been great: nobody offers an ex-voto for a trivial matter, such as opening the window or passing the butter.

The benefactor is powerful—more so than any living human being could be—and the grateful one feels very small in comparison. Because of this difference, the receiver has not found it difficult to ask. Requesting a favour among human beings is the action of one who is "lower" than the one who can give. That is why one shows respect through deference both when asking and when thanking, and also why modern people often find it difficult to do either: in our culture, a sting automatically accompanies any revelation of a lack of self-sufficiency. To understand the operation of gratitude in any given instance, we must first clearly perceive the distance between giver and receiver, the crucial distinction between a favour given between or among equals and one that travels downward, to be returned (if it can be returned) by being sent back upward.

The supernatural being is always free not to give: that is what makes a *graziato* feel so grateful, even beyond the promise made. The ingenious custom of votive offering grants the suppliant on her side freedom as well, in that it was she who decided to make a vow in the first place, and that vow is conditional: should there be no acceding to her request, she does not have to give the divine helper the ex-voto. A bargain has been struck, although bargaining breaks the normal rules of gift-giving. But this agreement with a supernatural power is needed in order to create a limited and temporary rapprochement between the two hugely distant sides. The achievement of closeness is also why a *graziata* feels grateful: her ex-voto will celebrate a relationship made concrete in the giving and returning of gifts. The question "Why give back?" is answered in advance: one gives back because one has promised to do so. There is certainly an "obligation to return," but it rests on the *graziata*'s own prior, non-obligatory vow, which she *wants* now, in her gratitude, to carry out.

The person offering an ex-voto does not do it at home, in privacy, but travels to the shrine to make his gift. His relatively small status makes this "only proper"—you would go to the palace to give to a king, not expect him to come to you—but that is not the only reason. An ex-voto is a very public gift. It stands in the shrine or decorates the image for all other worshippers to see. It lasts, so that not only the benefactor who is thanked but also other people will continue to see it long after the person who has offered thanks has departed. It may even be meant in part to signal to those others, expecting them to reflect on the offering, interpret it, appreciate it, at any rate *notice* and react to it.

Incidentally, to make a votive offering is to tell other people that one has received a wonderful benefit. An ex-voto therefore encourages—is meant to encourage—other people with problems similar to one's own. It says, demonstratively because it is an image and a public one, "Look what has happened to me!" And it adds, "Something like this could happen to you." Notably, the miracles referred to by votives almost never happen in church. The story and the *milagro* are *brought to* a church, and there they are told and displayed, to be made known to others. Gratitude concerns things that happened—stories told and remembered. Another message of an ex-voto is "God can work anywhere, anytime." It is felt too that goodness and happiness, given the way the world goes, ought to be shown to exist as vividly as do evil and suffering.

One of the gifts being rendered to the benefactor is the actual publicity of this thanking. If there are many *milagros* offered, many candles burning, many photographs or tablets saying "*Merci,*" they amount to collective praise. *To magnify* is to praise; the word means literally "to make great." A large number of grateful offerings is a highly effective attestation of the benefactor's greatness, and a reason for other *graziati* to join in praising the gracious giver. The offerings add to songs and words of praise a chorus of concrete proofs of gratitude. Praise may or may not include gratitude. Being grateful, however, is impossible without at least some impulse to praise.

Votive offerings may be made collectively, but the vast majority are presented individually. A multiplicity of small votive offerings clustered at a shrine presents a powerful sight because these gifts have nearly always been brought by individuals, at their own personal trouble and expense. They amount to a powerful testimony, freely offered. For despite the offering of vows, freedom is essential to the custom: it is the one who prays who decides to make the vow, in private. She also decides, of course consulting custom in the process, what the ex-voto shall be. The grateful usually bring votives to the church wrapped up, and uncover and place them when and where they want to do so.

There is nothing official about *milagros* offered in churches. The Catholic Church makes no rulings about votives, performs no rituals supporting them. It permits them to be offered according to folk tradition, merely watching over the practice in case votive behaviour becomes too bizarre. To many people unaccustomed to such traditions, the Church seems astonishingly tolerant of them, though it has often denounced them.[12] A typical priestly response, made to Eileen Oktavec at San Xavier Mission near Tucson, Arizona, in the 1980s, was, "At shrines like San Xavier you tend to see more popular expressions of people's faith than that which comes out of the institutional Church. It's a very meaningful kind of practice for the people because it flows from their life experience . . . So you let it happen and even encourage it. The popular faith and the official Church go hand in hand, and one enriches the other." Another priest gave this reply to a question about what the Church thinks of votive offerings: "The position of our theologians would be that the action of having milagros made and giving them out of a motive of piety would be sacred; the material objects themselves would not."[13]

When there are too many votives in a church, the parish cleaning lady will probably remove them, as her predecessors have done from time immemorial, to make room for more. Depending on decisions made locally, they will be discarded, kept in storage, or (occasionally) buried. There is no taboo, but there is respect. Oktavec records, for example, an occasion when a church melted down its votive offerings and used their metal to cast a large bell.[14] A decision taken to throw out old *milagros* must involve making a hard and conscious distinction between an object and its meaning. This is precisely what people do who say, "It's the thought that counts": gratitude is always about intentions, although it is often expressed through concrete things such as gifts. One cleaning woman and her husband decided to save some *milagros* she found ready to be thrown out. Together they made a red velvet backing, set the *milagros* out on it, and returned them to the church. "It touched us," she explained. "You touched each one and thought of the person who brought it."[15]

In Christian churches, ex-votos are rarely offered to God; there is something obstinately and inescapably human about them and the reciprocity they entail. They go instead in vast numbers to the Virgin Mary, and to saints who are famous for their advocacy with God. Votives, in other words, belong to that part of the spectrum of Christianity that sees saints as anxious, and able, to help the living. People understand them to be mediators between the faithful and God, as approachable because human like ourselves, as part of what is known as "the communion of saints"—that is, all of humanity, living and dead together, ready to lend one another a helping hand.

In Islam, as it is practised in Iran, saints and votives offered to them play a similarly important role, though for different cultural reasons. In an article describing the sociological structure in Iran of public and private spheres of life, Anne Betteridge[16] explains that making and fulfilling vows to saints is experienced as extremely intimate and emotionally satisfying behaviour. It is utterly different from the obligatory gifting that takes place among human beings in the public sphere, where everyone knows what should be given, in which circumstances, and how much it should cost. There is, in Iranian public giving, no need to wrap presents; there is no surprise involved. In this culture people closely guard their personal feelings, Betteridge explains, and certainly neither involve nor reveal these feelings when doing the polite thing by handing over a gift. It is perfectly permissible, for example, on receiving a conventionally obligatory present, to give it away immediately to somebody else.

In Iran people often apologize, as they do in Japan, for the worthlessness of their gift, even if it cost a lot. Betteridge mentions no gratitude for gifts, apart from her initial puzzlement at never being thanked for her own presents. In a footnote, however, she describes an occasion when gifts were offered "in a Western manner" during a visit to a couple who had moved into a new house. These presents—apparently deliberately "Western" objects such as a thermometer mounted on a key-shaped piece of gilded wood—were, exotically, wrapped and later opened in front of everybody. And "the recipient in each case felt obliged to make effusive expressions of gratitude, which were not always convincing."

Votive offerings and prayers to saints, on the other hand, involve highly individualized behaviour, nothing to do with the public sphere of obligatory formalities. Iranians report the relief they feel in relating to saints. These invisible friends are trustworthy confidants, never unfairly critical or judgmental, always intent on goodness and understanding; they never take advantage of what one tells them. Relationships with God and the saints are on the one hand intensely familiar—one uses the informal "you" to both—and on the other utterly unequal. Because of the power differential, favours can be explicitly asked for. A bargain is struck—to give a specific object, known as a *nazri*, if one's prayer is answered—but there is nothing either conventional or obligatory in making such a vow. As Betteridge explains, "One is on one's own with God and the saints, out from under the weight of social obligations and family pressures; there self-expression is given free rein." The *nazri* celebrates both the achievement of the desire and the existence of a close, intimate, private relationship with the saint, whose consideration has been demonstrated through granting the favour. Again gratitude is not mentioned, but the combination of intimacy, love, and relief that the *nazri* expresses holds much in common with gratitude.

Among Mexican Christians, the statues of saints are sometimes treated with signs of love that can be deeply shocking to people on the lookout for idolatry. Images may be bathed and dressed in specially made cloth garments (as ancient Athenians used to do to the statue of their goddess[17]). There are often practical reasons for such care. At Magdalena de Kino in Sonora, for example, people line up to caress and kiss the recumbent statue of San Francisco Xavier and gently cradle his head,[18] attentions which after a while dirty the image; moreover, the real cloth robes he wears are all the better for pinning *milagros* on, and sometimes the clothing wears out. People may on occasion attach a *milagro* to a statue even when their prayers have not been answered, believing that the saint might need reminding: he or she is not God, after all, but merely human, and saints, like us, can forget.[19] All these actions—indeed the entire practice of votive giving—can be easy to dismiss as "indecorous, base, and superstitious" in the words of Saint Charles Borromeo.[20]

And then, suddenly, a worshipper speaks with another voice entirely. "For the last week he [the saint] had a white blanket trimmed with gold that someone made," explained a member of the Feast Committee for Saint Francis Xavier, to Eileen Oktavec in 1993. "But so many people came last night and touched it that it got dirty, so we changed it. I brought over a Pendleton blanket that's very special to me, but a lot of the elders didn't like it because it was too heavy for him in this heat . . ." She then added, "We treat the saint just like he was one of us. We treat the statues as though they were alive, although we know they're not."[21] The saint is a distant figure—powerful, and now with God. Yet he is "just like one of us," and people feel free to express their gratitude for his help—indeed, for his very existence, his having led such a heroic life—in concrete ways, as explicitly and as warmly as they can. For them, the statue is not alive, and they know it, but the saint is in heaven, and he will appreciate the expression of their love for him. They grant themselves the means to prove their love, both emotionally and in concrete acts. Deep gratitude is a powerful emotion, which always seeks to be expressed in action.

Meanwhile, there have been many spiritual benefits from the faith of the devout and from their visiting the shrine. They have witnessed the faith of others, heard their stories, seen the large and famous church and the other interesting sights; the handicapped and the sick have got away from their confinement at home, as have their families. They have been accompanied on their journey by others who have themselves concretely manifested their caring by bringing them, helping them, and looking after them. All sorts of people were there, and the camaraderie and communion have been restorative in themselves. Awareness has been raised of the sufferings of others, contacts have been made, there have been meals in common, and fascinating conversations—to say nothing of the amazing behaviour of people at the shrine, to remember and think about. Votive offerings in shrines perform in a kind of drama, with antecedent hope and gratitude for its theme. A participating audience is part of the play. Gratitude is a matter that concerns two players only, one gracious, one *graziato,* and a thing or a favour given. But onlookers count as well. Onlookers applaud gratitude, encourage it, and are outraged by its opposite. Gratitude is intensely private, yet all of society has an interest in promoting it.

And there is more. The saint, as these people are well aware, is only human. He might need reminding that he has been asked a favour; he—that is, his statue—needs to look nice and clean; he deserves to be kept comfortable. Therefore, "although many pilgrims go away uncured ... people know that the saint is only an intermediary, so they usually do not blame him if their prayers go unanswered." The saint has tried, and God has decided not to intervene. *Si Dios no quiere, el santo no puede.* (If God doesn't want it, the saint can do nothing.) "Most people do not blame God for not answering their prayers," says Eileen Oktavec, "because they trust his judgment."[22]

Those with the greatest faith offer *milagros* without having gained their request. They are thankful anyway. One woman had made a vow for her husband's recovery, but he died. "I promised the milagro while he still lived," she said, "but even though he died, I'll bring it."[23]

Unpacking "Gratitude"

My father was a wandering Aramaean. He went down into Egypt to find refuge there, few in numbers; but there he became a nation, great, mighty, and strong. The Egyptians ill-treated us, they gave us no peace and inflicted harsh slavery on us. But we called on Yahweh the God of our fathers. Yahweh heard our voice and saw our misery, our toil, and our oppression; and Yahweh brought us out of Egypt with mighty hand and outstretched arm, with great terror, and with signs and wonders. He brought us here, and gave us this land, a land flowing with milk and honey."[1]

These were the words that an ancient Israelite was expected to say as he offered the first-fruits of his crops, having brought them to Yahweh's temple in Jerusalem. Jews did not, of course, make votive representations of themselves, or carved, painted, or moulded references to fulfilled desires of their own: all image-making was forbidden by the Second of the Ten Commandments.[2] But they did make vows when asking divine favour, and kept them, immolating animals and making offerings of vegetable food. Just as other peoples did, they took first-fruits from their crops and herds and "gave them back"—in their case, to Yahweh. First-born children were offered in the temple, then "bought back" with money: they too were a sort of first-fruits for Yahweh. First-fruits became for the Jews an occasion for remembering that the one God they worshipped had made them out of dust and placed them on the earth with its animals and plants in the first place; the fruit of their labours depended always upon the First Giver.

But with this ritual recital of the Israelite's history of his tribe, something extraordinary has happened to the custom of offering first-fruits, thousands of years old as it was when these particular accompanying words were pre-scribed.[3] First-fruits were no longer a celebration simply of the vegetation cycle—though they remained that—and certainly not of its divinities. The Israelite, offering his first-fruits, told a story. It was about the god Yahweh's care for his people, whom the worshipper sees as the collective hero of a lengthy narrative, represented by this summary recital. The cyclic movement of time—the yearly, eternal return of the seasons—has opened out and made room for the unfolding of a "historical" narrative; cyclic time has become linear. Human beings, their struggles and decisions, take centre stage. It was a totally new way of conceiving human life.[4]

Another level of thinking was reached in the elaboration of the belief that there was one infinite God, and one alone, who was beyond human imagining in his power and extent, and who had brought everything into existence. Eternal, invisible, and almighty, God nevertheless cared, not only in general for the things he had created, but for human beings in particular. Furthermore, the theme of the Israelite's story was liberation, with the help of God, from oppression: time as linear, as a "journey," could conceivably mean not merely progression but progress. Human intentionality was essential to this process. And there is a sense in which repeated recognizing and thanking by means of telling the story not only accompanied but contributed to the gradual dawning of monotheism itself.[5]

Telling the story of how Israel cried out and was heard was a way of praising God. In modern English we might say that the liturgical action, of making offerings to God while praising him in this manner, thanked God every time it was performed. What became in Israel the best way of praising God—that is, telling the story of his blessings—operated a transformation in Israel's view of human nature and of God. This transformation in turn was to influence greatly the formation of the worldview and attitudes of Western civilization. Certainly, praise, narrative, and remembering remain for us today an essential part of anything that could be called gratitude.

In the Hebrew Bible, however, people did not "thank" God, but rather *praised* him as they remembered his kindness to them. This was no doubt in large part because "gratitude" in these texts is nearly always offered to God, not human beings. No people had ever conceived of a god as great as this; praise was obviously what was due to his infinite magnificence. One's manner of thanking depends, as I have mentioned, largely on the perceived distance between the benefactor and the one favoured.

We shall see later—we have indeed noticed already—how words are culturally determined. If, in English, we start from a modern European concept called (from Latin) "gratitude" or (from German) "thanks," we must not be surprised to find that people whose culture and history are different—who have neither Germanic nor Roman roots—will speak a language that lacks that highly specific noun. Context—and culture creates context—matters intensely to all meaning. Each culture, each language, naturally has its own words—especially words denoting emotions—that others have to work hard to grasp in all their complexity. People of all languages and cultures, if they take the trouble, can certainly come to understand what "gratitude"—or any other culture-specific category—means. Our concepts can be explained to others, and they can explain theirs to us.[6] And learning about how other people think, and why, always illuminates our own presuppositions.

Our own culture, and therefore our words, have a history, one large element of which is the Hebrew Old Testament. There is in fact no one word in biblical Hebrew that corresponds in all respects to English *gratitude*.[7] Translations of the Bible into English, however, often render the Hebrew word for "praise," *todah,* as "thanksgiving" or "gratitude," and in modern Hebrew *todah* has come to mean, with lexical precision, "thank you."[8] In the Old Testament *todah* is in the first place the name of one of three related

kinds of offering made in the Jerusalem temple.⁹ The other two were the
votive offerings (*nedah*) in fulfillment of a vow should prayers be answered,
and *nedabah,* an offering made without a preceding vow. *Todah* involved sac-
rificing an animal and making an offering of bread that was burned on the
altar with the victim. *Todah* meant praise, through remembering. But *todah*
was to begin with an action performed, an action that was accompanied by a
song of praise. One "did" *todah.*

Other people would be invited to witness the sacrifice and to become the
chorus singing God's praise.¹⁰ Such songs are among the 150 Old Testament
psalms that have come down to us. The following example proclaims what
God has done; like the other surviving psalms, it has been repeated down the
centuries by people applying its sentiments to occasions in their own lives:

> You have turned my mourning into dancing,
> you have stripped off my sackcloth and wrapped me in gladness;
> and now my heart, silent no longer, will play you music;
> Yahweh, my God, I will praise you for ever.¹¹

Many psalms end with a climax like this one. After the opening acclamations,
the misery suffered may be described, this being the main, central portion of
the song. Then suddenly—without warning, as if after a miracle—the psalm
changes direction completely and ends with a radiant cry of praise, because
God has intervened and darkness is dispelled. Three aspects of "gratitude" are
discernible here. There is recognition of a favour received; a powerful sense
of contrast and relief ("in the evening a time of tears, in the morning shouts
of joy!" cries the psalmist); and an insistence ("silent no longer") on voicing
aloud and so letting other people know what the psalmist has experienced.
The inviting of others to witness the praise offers them a chance to rejoice
with their friend. It is also an offering to God of public recognition—analo-
gous, at a politeness level, to gifts being displayed in one's house so that other
people can see them.

The word for "offering," *minha,* literally means "gift." So the sacrifice is meant to "give back" something to God. The song of praise is in itself a return gift. In the psalm just quoted, the singer begs God not to let him die. He then adds that his death would not be in God's interest:

Can the dust praise you or proclaim your faithfulness?

"Giving back" is normal in the circumstances, and temple ritual has explicitly provided the means of making some return. God is expected to be pleased, despite the offerer's reminding God that he too has something to offer, namely doing public *todah.*

"What return can I make to Yahweh for all his goodness to me?" asks the singer of another psalm. He knows what the ritual prescribes:

I will offer libations . . .
I will pay what I vowed to Yahweh;
may his whole nation be present when I do so!
I will offer you the *todah* sacrifice . . .
I will pay what I vowed . . . [12]

Yet it is perfectly well understood that "giving" to God is impossible: everything that exists belongs to God already, since he has brought it into being. What God really wants is the one thing he has deprived himself of the right to force from us—namely, a human person's desire to change his ways and choose righteousness:

Sacrifice gives you no pleasure,
were I to offer holocaust, you would not have it.
My sacrifice is this broken spirit.
You will not scorn this crushed and broken heart. [13]

Next, God wants people to remember. And then, people should never exult in pride over the good things they enjoy, to the neglect of law and under the illusion that they themselves are the ultimate source of their prosperity: "Take care you do not forget Yahweh your God, neglecting his commandments and customs and laws which I lay on you today. When you have eaten and had all you want, when you have built fine houses to live in, when you have seen your flocks and herds increase, your silver and gold abound and all your possessions grow great, do not become proud of heart. Do not then forget Yahweh your God, who brought you out of the land of Egypt, out of the house of slavery: who guided you through this vast and dreadful wilderness, a land of fiery serpents, scorpions, thirst; who in this waterless place brought you water from the hardest rock; who in this wilderness fed you with manna that your fathers had not known, to humble you and test you and so make your future the happier. Beware of saying in your heart, 'My own strength and the might of my own hand won this power for me.' Remember Yahweh your God."[14]

A word and a concept specific to Hebrew is "blessing," *barak*. A modern commentator says it means "praise, accompanied by strong sentiments of respect and gratitude."[15] (We might recall incidentally that the etymological root of English *bless* is *bleed;* to "bless" was, in pre-Christian Britain, to "sanctify with the blood of sacrifice.") It is, according to Anna Wierzbicka, characteristic of Jewish culture that good and bad feelings are generally expressed by means of good and bad wishes.[16] The extraordinary thing about *barak,* and therefore blessing, is that it works both ways: Yahweh blesses us (as in Psalm 113B/115:12–13) and we bless Yahweh (as in Psalm 112/113:2). The use of one word (*blessing,* or *benediction* from Latin) for two different actions depending on the status of the one who is blessing, was imported into European languages along with the Old Testament practice of verbal blessing.

Yahweh's blessings perform actions: when he blesses crops, for example, they grow (Psalm 106/107:38). And among human beings, where fathers are very powerful, they may be thought capable of either giving or withholding their blessing, with important consequences for the lives of their offspring. When people bless God, on the other hand, they are above all praising him. But they may also feel amazement, love, remembrance—all of them aspects of "gratitude." Saying "Bless you!" to another human being properly means "May God bless you (that is, give you good things)." In modern English this expression is very close to a thanking formula. It is a wish, which may be deeply emotional, for the prosperity of a giver.

The English term *gratitude* comes from Latin *gratia,* which derives from Indo-European and then Sanskrit *gurtih* and *gurtah*—"praise." The etymologists tell us once again that the Vedas, the four holy books of Hinduism (compilations made from 1800 BC onward), have no word meaning "gratitude." Praise was offered together with sacrifices because of favours received from the gods—and these words and actions were intended to achieve further gifts. Praise constrained the addressee—powerful person or god—to give, the mighty to the lowly. Georges Dumézil, the investigator of Indo-European social organization, suggests that the Latin juridical phrase *do ut des* ("I give so that you might give in return") might be converted into *laudo ut des* to describe the Vedic strategy "I praise in order that you might give."[17] A powerful motif of favours accompanies the ritual sacrifice and prayer—favour felt and bestowed by the deity, and favour received and felt and hoped for again by the devotee.

The Latin language separated out praise from gratitude. It has two entirely different words, *laus* (praise) and *gratia* (gratitude)[18], despite the original root meaning of *gratia* having been "praise." This distinction marks a change, and a divergence from the usage of many other languages. Latin marked gratitude off as a concept and a feeling in its own right. And many European languages inherit this configuration.

But Latin *gratia* remained something one did (*agere*), had (*habere*), brought and gave (*ferre*). There was no verb; *gratitude* was (and remains in English) a noun that can become an adjective or an adverb, but never a verb. It was our

Germanic roots that supplied English with the verb *to thank*. In religious terminology there remains the phrase *acción de gracias* and its equivalents in Latin
languages other than Spanish: it means all the actions, including religious
ritual and the objects prescribed by ritual, that add up to a human demonstration of gratefulness to God. The modern North American festival called
Thanksgiving refers to all the actions, the things eaten, given, and shared, as
well as the thoughts and words that make up this ritual celebration. Thanks
are plural.

The first recorded instance of gratitude spoken as opposed to "done" in
Latin is in Virgil's *Aeneid* (ca. 20 BC)[19], and even there it occurs together with
a desire to do something in return for the favour that has aroused gratitude.
The interaction is notably not between worshipper and god but between
two human beings of equal status. Camilla offers to fight Aeneas, and Turnus,
in awe at her generosity and bravery, replies: "O maiden, glory of Italy, what
thanks shall I try to utter or return?"[20] Virgil brings out here a distinction
between two parts of the operation of thanking: there is *saying* you are grateful, and there is proving it in action. The two are of necessity separated in
time, unlike the *todah* sacrifice or the Vedic ceremony, which were each of
them accompanied simultaneously by a song of praise. Religious ritual con-
flates saying and doing thanks; human interaction has usually to occur in two
separate moments.

The word used by Virgil and translated above as "thanks" means partly
gratitude and partly something given—partly words of thanks for a favour
received, and partly a favour that should later be done in return by the grateful receiver. The Latin adverb *gratis,* originally *gratiis* ("with thanks"), means
"for free." It arose from the distinction between saying thanks and returning
a favour: something is done *gratis* when the only return required is saying
"thank you." The utterance might be merely polite or heartfelt—it depends
entirely on the response of the thanker.

Having isolated the idea of gratitude and concentrated it on favours,
the Romans went on to elaborate the rules governing favours and gifts and

everything to do with returning them. These were rules for the behaviour of people towards one another, rather than rules for the performance of religious ritual. This is not to say that other societies had no such rules—we have seen at length that they always have—but that the Romans defined gratitude in the context of the mechanisms of giving. The most exhaustive work on this subject remains Seneca's seven books *De Beneficiis,* "On Favors." In these books and in other writings he enumerates the types of benefactions, and explains how to give them, receive them, and return them. He raises and discusses every conceivable ethical problem that might arise. For example: Is it shameful to be outdone in an exchange of gifts? May I remind somebody obliged to me of his debt of gratitude? Can a benefaction be taken back? Do involuntary benefactions entail obligations? Can good intentions be a sufficient return?

Seneca goes much further than working out the laws of concrete giving; his text reaches on occasion the highest levels of morality. We should, says Seneca, imitate the gods, who give even to the ungrateful. A good man who loses by giving always gives again (although he is more careful the next time). The giver ought to forget how much he has given—but the receiver should remember, and want to give back even more than he received. And Seneca says he felt it necessary to write on this subject, for giving and receiving were "the chief bond of human society."[21]

Ancient Greek contributed another whole dimension of what we call "gratitude" to Roman *gratia.* The Greek word we translate as "gratitude," *charis,*[22] meant first of all "loveliness" and was derived from *chairein,* "to be delighted." It was characteristic of Greek culture to prime the aesthetic—to find the cause of joy in beauty. *Charis* meant also, as *gratia* did, a sense of being favoured: to "know *charis*" or "feel *charis*" we may safely translate "be grateful." Yet where we would say "Thank you" in ordinary discourse, and Romans would say "*Gratias,*" Greeks said "Beautifully done!" or "I applaud you!" or "I praise you!" (For "No, thank you" they would answer, "It's going beautifully," as we might refuse a drink by saying, "I'm fine, thanks.")[23] It is interesting that praise could be uttered instead of gratitude in the ancient Mediterranean region, not only in the lofty contexts of religious ceremony—such as we have considered in part because of the nature of the texts that have come down to us—but even as the small coin of conversation among human equals.

We have met *charis* before, in the three beautiful female dancers, the *Charites,* whom the Romans adopted and named *Gratiae,* and we call the Graces. They were, in the beginning, fertility goddesses, and only later became embodiments of the felicities of gift-giving, and reciprocity in general as foundational for the functioning of the State. *Charis,* being an emotion, was felt by the individual, but it also had a social dimension. The State always longed to appropriate its individually felt intensity.

Greek *charis* had an important erotic charge, as pleasure that both provoked a response and arose from response. Sex that was freely shared rather than forced, the immensely heightened pleasure that comes from mutual delight, was governed by *charis* and experienced as a divine gift from the gods. But there was another side to sexual *charis:* the male lover of a boy considered himself the boy's benefactor. If no *charis* was forthcoming—if the boy was unwilling and satisfaction of the lover's desire disappointed—he was considered to be ungrateful, and retaliation was in order. Revenge, in the Greek view of things, had its own pleasures—its *charis.*[24] In many a love song, down almost to modern times, resentful lovers have denounced the beloved who refused favour as "ungrateful." The French troubadours' "*belle dame sans merci*" was a woman without mercy, but the word *merci,* at the time, was in the process of changing in meaning from "mercy" to "gratefulness."[25]

When early Greek poets spoke of *charis,* they saw it as a kind of glow, consequent on success. It was bestowed, for example, by the *charis*-like goddess Niké ("Victory") upon a winning athlete: a radiance, as he stood forth in triumph before the admiring crowd.[26] *Charis* imagery is of light, and gleaming, and gladness (the word *glad* originally meant "bright").[27] It came as the final touch, a flourish that is expressed by the conventions of applause, something not only delightful but extra; a modern writer calls it "the icing on the cake."[28] The ancient Greek athlete's prize, a crown of leaves placed on his head before the watching crowds, embodied it.

Other images for *charis* were jewellery and gleaming unguents: things, typically shiny things, added to the person of the one being honoured, expressing the marvel of others at his enviable beauty and triumph, and embodying his prestige.[29] We could compare medals for the winners of sports today: bronze, silver, gold, hung round their necks in honour of degrees not only of prowess but of something approaching *charis*. The witnessing and transported crowd is essential to the glory and the glamour. The modern idea of *glamour*, meaning "allure," derives from the powers of magic charms: objects or incantations that bestow an uncanny force or attractiveness.[30]

Charis was a stunning moment of divine favour—which in human beings passed quickly. One seized it on the wing: in the wise, an awareness of the frailty of good fortune was supposed to increase the pleasure of *charis*. Poetry of great quality, however, such as an ode by Pindar honouring a victor in the Games, could immortalize such a moment and help others—even people yet unborn—to behold it. The poet praised the winner even as he strove to account for the *charis* that the gods had lavished on this particular being.

The delight of *charis,* its character as something shared, held in common with Roman *gratia* the notion of favour. Both the Greek *Charites* and the *Gratiae* at Rome were pressed into service to the State as embodiments of the useful social virtues of reciprocity. But *gratia* also took on board the glamour of *charis*:[31] Romans frequently admired and then borrowed Greek ideas in this fashion. From them we inherit the words *grace* and *gracefulness,* meaning elegant loveliness allied with charm. Gratitude is a form of happiness—including the pleasures of interaction and the enjoyment of benevolence—which is felt by both bestower and receiver.

The Christian contribution, the concept of divine grace, reaches us as the translation into Latin (*grace*) of the Greek word *charis* in the New Testament. For the expression of this new religious idea, we reach back to the Old Testament and also into the meanings of Roman *gratia,* with consideration, of course, for the Greek connotations of *charis*. Christian *charis* includes the Jewish practice and meaning of blessing, experience of the mercy and continuing care of the one God of Israel for human beings, praise for the amazing goodness and might of God, the delight and surprise of Greek *charis,* the thankfulness for favours of Roman *gratia*. This last was made prominent for Christians because of their belief that God had come to live among human beings, had made himself their brother in Jesus, and so given human beings a new, previously unheard-of intimacy with himself. This closeness makes it possible not only to praise but also to thank God.[32] Grace is believed to be unmerited (the irruption of Jesus into human history is read as both a once-for-all and an ongoing grace) and given *gratis*. But gratitude will make those who receive grace and accept it long to give something back, and they have been told how to do so: at God's request we should give back to God by loving other people and giving to them. Ideally, one will not expect a return from them; a gift to another person is at the deepest level a response to grace, which is a gift already received. The Christian notion of grace has in its turn influenced the concept of gratitude, greatly increasing its scope and its emotional charge.

Old English, the Germanic root of our language, added one more important dimension, the specific designation of something already very much present in grace. German *danken* ("to thank") is related to *denken* (English "to think").[33] "Thank" and "think" are one: a person given what he or she wants does not just grab the thing that satisfies, but takes the trouble to think about who gave it and what this giving means. Gratitude is not only an emotion, but also a matter of thought—a form of awareness. It arises from realizing what has been done for us by others, from appreciating their kindness and our good fortune, and also from contemplating and reacting in awe to such things as the wonder of life and even the marvel that is our own consciousness.

In French, "gratitude" is *reconnaissance,* re-cognition, ac-knowledgement: the thoughtful dimension of gratitude is stressed in these Latin-based and

Middle English words. The other French term for it is *remerciement,* from *merci,* "thank you."[34] These words come ultimately from the same root as that for *commerce, merchant,* and *market:* they are about knowing the cost of something, its price. They recognize the value of what has been given. A similar idea is to be found in *appreciation,* from Latin *pretium,* price. Another aspect of *merci* meant "pity": kindness or compassion shown to a person who has no right or ability to demand it. *Merci* and *remerciement,* despite their origins, are not about obligations either to pay up or to repay, but rather about understanding, thinking, thinking back or remembering, and appreciating. None of these can be forced from anyone, so that *remercier* keeps the freedom required for the expression of gratitude, *gratis.* Being thankful is impossible without mindfulness, recollection, and recognition. And we are reminded again of the ancient Jewish idea of story and memory, *todah.*

13

The Fourth Law of Nature

Yet another meaning once fitted perfectly into the configuration of ideas that make up gratitude, and that was loyalty. People are loyal because they are conscious of what they owe others—not all others, but those to whom they recognize a special allegiance. In both these ways gratitude resembles loyalty: in its awareness (one is grateful because one *thinks*) and in its partiality. For gratitude is in the main a response felt and granted to previous, equally conscious and deliberate, givers. But despite the overlap, we should be unwilling today to confuse loyalty with thankfulness. Loyalty (as its root in French *loi,* "law," suggests) is nowadays taken to be a commitment—something prior to benefactions and responses to them, not a bond created out of them. Loyalty, like law, keeps on working even when our feelings and wills have to be constrained to conform to it. Gratitude, on the other hand, is something that must be felt: a person is not grateful unless she *feels* grateful. The matter of feeling—emotion—will be the subject of the next part of this book. But it is interesting to consider briefly how, in certain social contexts in our own past, people exalted loyalty to the point where it almost crowded out the idea of gratitude. At the same time, gratitude was reduced to its external signs. For "giving back," in and of itself, was what counted as loyalty; one's feelings were almost irrelevant.

When the Roman Empire broke down in Europe and barbarian hordes poured into its lands, the basic needs of self-protection and survival demanded a substitute for the declining authority of the Roman government. People turned to the patronage of men of military might, surrendering their independence in return for security. Each group took formal pledges of loyalty and service,[1] swearing to be reliable liegemen, retainers, and fighters for their lord, in order to present a united front against possible military attacks. There was mutual need and mutual advantage; the lord dispensed *largesse* at the beginning and continued to do so. "Freedom" meant freedom from fear, or at least a hope of armed support. Ancient writers describe the pattern—and we can recognize it today. A chief must show his liberality, and the followers expect it: "They are always making demands on the generosity of their chief," writes Tacitus of the Teutonic bands called *comitati*. "They ask for a coveted war-horse or a spear stained with the blood of a defeated enemy. Their meals, for which plentiful if homely fare is provided, count in lieu of pay. The wherewithal for this openhandedness comes from war and plunder."[2]

In the epic poem *Beowulf* (eighth to tenth centuries AD), the young warrior "by his goodness, by generous gifts of property while he is subject to his father . . . prepares for his old age. He will then have people anxious to serve him; when war comes he will have supporters."[3] There is no mention of "gratitude" here, but loyalty is certainly founded on gifts, together with an unqualified duty to return favours: an obligatory reciprocity. Geoffrey of Monmouth (twelfth century) tells us that as soon as Arthur became king of Britain, he "observed the normal custom" of handing out generous gifts to many.[4] The result was that "such a great crowd of soldiers flocked to him that he came to an end of what he had to distribute." Geoffrey rams home the lesson: "The man to whom open-handedness and bravery both come naturally may indeed find himself momentarily in need—but poverty will never harass him for long." Others will feel obligated to come to the aid of their previous benefactor in his need. The original gifts, in these instances, are what people nowadays might call "an investment": the eventual return was not therefore what we would call "gratitude"—and it is not called "gratitude" in these texts. It was an expression of loyalty, and it had quasi-legal status: if receivers of such "gifts" tried to get out of repaying their debt when the time came, their behaviour was deemed outrageous and punished accordingly. Out of gifts and their consequent obligations feudal lords gave birth to loyalty, binding their vassals to themselves, no matter what.

A model for absolutely reliable loyalty has always been to hand: that of the indissoluble and unconditional bonds that unite parents and children. In the passage from *Beowulf,* the young warrior prepared for his "old age" when he distributed largesse, presumably because, like a father, he would eventually be able to rely on his vassals to help him in his need as though they were his sons. In early medieval Europe, however, the feudal bond, vassal to lord, was often made out to be even stronger than family ties; it was loyalty to a personal benefactor and therefore tighter than allegiances to distant king and impersonal country. Strengthened over the years by favours and counter-favours, the bond was underwritten by a feeling of horror and revulsion at treason (from French *trahison,* "betrayal," literally "handing over" to an enemy). A common man, however, who by definition did not belong to the circles of lords and noble vassals, was known as a mere "churl" (*ceorl*), from Old Norman and German *Karl,* "man." He was supposed to be obedient to his betters, but was not bound by the rules of vassalage. In aristocratic eyes he was boorish and often surly as well—churlish, in short. He could not be counted on to be "honourable" or to act out of unconditional loyalty.

It should be remembered that alongside this feudal system there existed an entirely different attitude towards human life and relationships. The Christian Gospel gives full recognition to the coercive nexus that reciprocity can become. But it unties the knot, for those who wish to have it untied, by separating material self-interest from spiritual well-being, and giving priority to the latter: the kingdom of God is not "of this world," and "you cannot serve both God and money."[5] Moral principles are to prime loyalty-no-matter-what. Eventually, the slow evolution of centralized government, legal safeguards and other conditions of impartial justice, some reduction of the gap in power between the powerful and the lowly, and the growth of a commercial rather than a warlike economy softened and changed the social system. A first stage was the creation of medieval chivalry, which kept the ideas of loyalty and largesse, but added to these the obligations of a knight towards his God, his religion, his lady, the oppressed, and the defenceless. The assumption remained that a prince (now no longer a mere local warlord) bestowed benefits on his subjects, who therefore owed him loyalty in return. The fear and loathing of disloyalty remained, but began to translate into something less fierce, something underwritten more by goodwill and a grateful disposition than by sheer obligation.

What also filled the space left by the decline of quasi-contractual obligations between lord and noble liegeman was the existing notion of "honour." This was a quality that a nobleman knew he possessed, because of who he was and because other people kept honouring him for it. It was up to him to protect and if possible enhance it, not diminish or "stain" it. This he did in part for the benefit of his family, for a family's honour was invested in that of each of its kin; one shameful member could reduce the honour of all, just as a family member with a great reputation gave credit to all the others. And honour works best among equals: an honour code is something held in common among the honourable. Those outside the charmed circle of the honourable are by definition strangers to it, and excluded thereby.

If sufficient conviction were planted in a man, he himself could be counted on to try, of his own free will, to do what was honourable: an honour system can be an admirably effective force, motivating each honourable man from within. "*Noblesse oblige*" meant that a nobleman "could not but" do deeds of loyalty and valour, because of the honour he was born to. He would never be a traitor to his friends, refuse to return a benefit, or fail to avenge an insult, on pain of losing his honour. The revulsion his fellows felt for behaviour that contravened the honour code was normally sufficient punishment for any lapse, and extremely useful for keeping honourable people in line. For honour, which is believed in such a system to be innate, is maintained by reputation, the opinion of others; it follows that, especially where people are defined by the honour granted them, any humiliation caused by the contempt of others can be unbearable. But Christianity and its teachings were set aside whenever people insisted on their honour as something at once innate, exclusive to a superior inner circle, and dependent on reputation, at the opposite pole from humility, to be upheld "no matter what," an attack on which was a motive of vengeance.

A further breakthrough, religious this time and with broader influence than aristocratic honour codes, was made during the course of the twelfth and thirteenth centuries. It began with and was accompanied by a new fascination in European literature with the subject of gratitude in itself, above and beyond the rules of gift-giving. Society was changing. The new interest in and reverence paid to gratitude were signs of a corresponding need for a relationship-encouraging force that could hold society together. The "explosion of gratitude" that is said to have characterized thirteenth-century Europe[6] was not merely, or even mainly, intellectual. One powerful example among many is to be seen at Laon in France, where the cathedral was completed in 1205. Sixteen huge stone oxen still stand looking out across the town from the top of the church towers. They were placed there by the congregation in grateful memory of the animals that dragged the stones up the steep hill to build the church.[7]

The word *gratitudo* appeared for the first time shortly before 1270. It was formed from Latin *gratia,* in the context of medieval scholasticism. The new word is more abstract and carefully defined, more theoretical than *gratia* in the sense of "gratitude." It usefully distinguished, for the purposes of academic discussion, human gratitude from *gratia* meaning "divine grace." It took a while for *gratitude*, from the Latin, to become everyday usage. In English, the ordinary term was the Germanic *thank.* Julian of Norwich (ca. 1342–post 1413), for instance, for whom "gratitude" was of profound importance, uses always the nouns *thanke* and *thankyng,* and the verb *thankyn,* but never *grati-tude* or *being grateful.*

The churchman Thomas Aquinas, in the *Summa Theologica* (1266–1273), written in Latin, carefully discusses gratitude within the Christian tradition, using the new word *gratitudo* often.[8] He pays due attention to Aristotle and Seneca, and sees gratitude as very different from obligatory loyalties such as those of feudal vassalage. Gratitude is a virtue distinct in itself, though of lesser significance than religion (the worship of God), or filial piety, or respect for our superiors; it is about thankfulness to our benefactors. Gratitude is important—indeed, it may be limitless—but that is because it flows from love; love must be there first. Moreover, gratitude, like love, must be given of one's own free will (*sponte*).

Dante, although of the generation after Aquinas, sounds far more "feu-dal." In the bottommost circle of hell, Dante saw the giant Satan standing buried to his chest in ice. Flapping from the necks of his three joined heads (a grotesque perversion of the Trinity) are six huge bat wings, replacing the six glorious pinions with which he once flew as an angel; they cre-ate a downward blast of freezing wind. In each of his three mouths Satan grinds a sinner between his teeth, most horribly Judas Iscariot (whose head is forever inside the monster's maw), who handed over to the torturers his friend, benefactor, and Master—his God. Second in heinousness is Brutus, filially impious as well as a traitor and killer of his benefactor: he sided with Pompey, who was responsible for the death of his father, and he murdered Caesar, who had pardoned him after defeating him. And third is Cassius, who also received pardon from Caesar and then killed him. Brutus and Cassius dangle upside down from two of the mouths of Satan. The three sinners are especially wicked because of the trust their lords had placed in them, and the benefits their lords had given them. Dante never gives abstract names for their crimes, but demands that we remember what they did as he places them in the jaws of the greatest traitor of all, Satan, who rebelled against God in the beginning.[9]

One of the changes that had come about since feudal times was a restored emphasis on filial piety, most especially, of course, the duty of sons and daughters towards fathers and mothers. This requirement "went without saying"—it was nothing less than *natural*. (We note that Thomas Aquinas himself rates it higher than gratitude, and higher even than reverence for superiors.) In late-thirteenth-century England, a person who showed benevolence and due reverence to another was said to be "kynde." This word came to translate *gratus,* "grateful" in Latin. It was an enormous tribute to the idea of gratitude, for *kynde* was a word that derived from *kin*. Gratitude as *kyndenesse* was behaviour believed to be in accordance with nature; it mirrored, at least in part, the unique and unconditional reverence that was filial piety.

The English poet William Langland, in *The Vision of Piers Plowman* (1362), has his protagonist Will ask the equally allegorical figure of Wit the question that interested the poet most: "'What kynnes thyng is Kynde?' quod I, 'kanstow me telle?'" ("'What kind of thing is Kynde,' quoth I, 'can you tell me?'") And he learns that *kynde* means "compassionate," "natural or innate," "that which pertains to one's kin," "that which pertains to God [whom Langland calls "Kynde"]," and "grateful."[10] "Kyndeness," sometimes called "naturesse," is said in the poem to help form community, and to cement existing relationships both social and economic.[11] Gratitude enhanced social cohesion and harmony, while ingratitude menaced both; gratitude was natural and ingratitude monstrous. The theme was durable, and lost nothing in intensity for more than two hundred years. William Bullein devoted a whole chapter to ingratitude in his *Bulwarke of Defence against all Sicknesse* (1579), and there he speaks of an evil "to bee numbred among the synnes Mortall, whych is an euyll moste intollerable and moste odious of all unto a good Nature, whych is called Ingratitude, churlishnes, or unkyndeness."[12]

William Shakespeare often unwrapped the sunny, unquestionably virtuous, ordinary significance of *kindness* to reveal the word's original anchoring in the sacred, primeval ground of kinship—and its extensions to include duties to benefactors, lords, and kings. Antony wrings the hearts of his hearers

when he describes how the "honourable" Brutus joined the other tyranni-
cides in stabbing Caesar, his friend as well as his benefactor:

> Judge, O you gods, how dearly Caesar loved him!
> This was the most unkindest cut of all;
> For when the noble Caesar saw him stab,
> Ingratitude, more strong than traitors' arms,
> Quite vanquished him: then burst his mighty heart . . .
> O, what a fall was there, my countrymen!
> Then I, and you, and all of us fell down,
> Whilst bloody Treason flourished over us.[13]

Antony has succeeded in making ingratitude and treason one. The citizens
weep and shudder as Dante did when he saw Brutus hanging by the feet
from Satan's jaws.

In *King Lear* (1605), Shakespeare stares with horror into ingratitude's cold
and baleful eye. Gratitude—above all "kindness" to a father, a king, a benefactor—founds the very dispositions of the just, of those respectful of divine and
natural order. But in this play we watch the virtuous being mocked, tortured,
killed by people who "like rats" have bitten through the "holy cords" of
filial and married love to free themselves in order to further their personal
worldly interests and their lusts.[14] Lear learns to repent of his own "unkindness," which at the beginning of the play disinherited his daughter Cordelia,
who had spoken truly to him and who remained faithful even when she had
no cause to be grateful. He is forced to suffer "sharp-toothed unkindness, like
a vulture" eating his heart, and in his agony he curses Goneril, hoping she
will one day feel

> How sharper than a serpent's tooth it is
> To have a thankless child.[15]

Ingratitude has fangs that tear at human hearts and rip apart the fabric of family and society. The "dues" of gratitude, meanwhile, Lear hopes for from Goneril and Regan and does not get: not even respect for the very ties of kinship, let alone the so-called obligation to return a benefit.[16] Lear thought he could rely on family bonds to make Goneril and Regan, now in possession of his riches, continue to show the love and reverence due to him as their father. But his daughters live in a world where children will show "filial piety" only when their father has benefits to bestow: "Fathers that wear rags," sings the Fool,

Do make their children blind,
But fathers that bear bags
Shall see their children kind.[17]

Gratitude can be smothered and thrown overboard; it can cease to be considered "natural."

When the villain Edmund first appears on stage in this play, he announces that "Nature" is his goddess, and therefore he refuses to "stand in the plague of custom."[18] His "Nature" is a world of self-interest and force, blind to the transcendent; gratitude has no place in it. Edmund is "churlish" because he is a bastard (a "natural" child). Despite his noble appearance and his attractiveness to women, he feels excluded, by the pure chance of birth, not only from the advantages of his society but also from its ideals; he sees nothing to be grateful for. He is determined therefore to subvert the system and win. "All with me's meet that I can fashion fit," he says,[19] meaning, "I consider anything just that serves my own interests." In modern terms, he believes neither in religion nor in human laws, ideals, or relationships. He succumbs to no pity, feels no remorse, and cannot see what makes a human being greater than the undeniable fact that he is at bottom what Lear describes as "such a poor, bare, forked animal."[20] Edmund believes, therefore, that he is free to decide, using his quick intelligence, whom and how to swindle, manipulate, deceive, and betray. He is an individualist, ungrateful and alone.

Thomas Hobbes was seventeen years old when *King Lear* was first performed. His philosophical treatise *Leviathan* presents us with a worldview that could scarcely be more different from Shakespeare's—although Shakespeare obviously knew men who thought like Hobbes. And it is Hobbes, not Shakespeare, whom many people today consider "modern."[21] For Hobbes, human beings by nature thirst for power and are disposed to violence. We all have three main desires, he writes: for Gain, for Safety, and for Reputation. These three keep us perpetually prone to fight one another in "a warre of every man against every man." Unless we can be restrained from doing so by "a common Power to keep [us] all in awe," we shall inevitably find ourselves living lives "solitary, poore, nasty, brutish, and short."[22] Transcendence, for Hobbes, amounts to a social agreement to hand over the monopoly of force, and with it our own power, to a sovereign. This person may continue in power even if all his subjects want to depose him. It is impossible for him to be accused of injustice by his subjects, since they have themselves agreed to grant his actions absolute authority.

We are brought to capitulate so totally because, in the interest of self-preservation, we must do whatever it takes to seek peace, contract for peace, and perform justly the contracts we have made. Hobbes calls these necessities the first three Laws of Nature. Human beings have one thing in common: their desire for self-preservation. A Law of Nature, therefore, is what conduces to survival. Since they have been arrived at by reason, however, such laws are contrary to our natural passions, and they need artificial power to enforce them. Reason tells us, further, "that every man, ought to endeavour Peace, as farre as he has hope of obtaining it; and when he cannot obtain it, that he may seek, and use, all helps, and advantages of Warre."

Peace can be achieved if we can be made to enter into contracts and keep them. But living in society also involves giving to others: Hobbes realizes that contracts cannot cover everything. "First gifts" are made by choice, so

Hobbes calls the action of giving first "Grace." He says that we give in order to gain friendships and obtain other people's services (including their protection). Other motives are to gain "the reputation of Charity, or Magnanimity," to deliver our minds from "the pain of compassion," or to give "in hope of reward in heaven."[23] In other words, we give in order to get—and especially for Gain, Security/Comfort, and Reputation. If we did not get anything out of it, we would stop giving: "For no man giveth, but with intention of Good to himselfe."

Hobbes draws up, in all, eighteen Laws of Nature. The Fourth of these is gratitude—very high on the list. The Law is formulated thus: "That a man which receiveth Benefit from another of meer Grace, Endeavour that he which giveth it, have no reasonable cause to repent him of his good will."[24] A gift, for Hobbes, is a reward given in advance, "to encourage, or enable men to do [the bestower] service."[25] And in the same manner that injustice destroys the keeping of contracts, ingratitude ends gift-giving. Nothing is said of feelings: the Laws of Nature, being founded on Reason, are the opposite of emotion. Gratitude is doing what the giver "of meer Grace"—who had no obligation to give—wants you to do.

Where people had traditionally accepted that law depended on morality, Hobbes proposes that morality rests on law. Morality is not something one *believes* in; it is merely useful for our comfortable survival, and so should be enforced. The gift ends up neither free nor the expression of relationship among equals. Gratitude is action performed out of simple calculation. The awareness that is essential to it has become merely an astute consciousness of where our own material self-interest lies. Hobbes—who for Shakespeare was anticipated by Edmund in *King Lear*—ushered in the world of the Utilitarians and the modern Social Darwinians. It is a vision that in our own day has become all too familiar.

14

After All

One Saturday morning in June 2002, Ángela packed her eighty-six-year-old mother María into a taxi with her belongings and took her to her sister Rosa's place in the Catalan village of Santa Margarida i els Monjos. Rosa was not at home, but her husband was. Ángela hurried the old lady into the house despite the husband's efforts to stop her, then left so quickly that she forgot to unload María's possessions from the taxi. The husband frantically telephoned his wife, who was away in Valencia, but the fact was that he was now stuck with his mother-in-law.

At this point a granddaughter, Ana, and her boyfriend entered the story. They were prevailed upon to drive the girl's grandmother back to Ángela's apartment building. Nobody was at home, so they left the old lady standing on the pavement in front of the doorway to await Ángela's return, or for a neighbour to take her inside. Ana came back later and the grandmother was still there. At the trial the court was subsequently told, in Ana's defence, that she took the trouble to go away, find, and bring her grandmother a chair "of the sort she liked." She sat María in it on the pavement and left. Later still, the police passed by and found the grandmother abandoned on the sidewalk in her chair.

They made enquiries. María was the mother of eleven surviving children, ten of whom lived nearby; she had fifty grandchildren. The family had put her in an old age home when she began to suffer from dementia, but so many of them refused to pay their portions of the fees that she had to leave. All of her descendants then fought to avoid taking her in. All María had to her name were her sixty-one children and grandchildren and the belongings Ángela had forgotten in the taxi: a grandson explained to the press, using extremely coarse language, that he could not see why he should be expected to look after somebody who was leaving him no inheritance. Five months later the family was ordered to pay costs and a two thousand euro fine, plus one thousand euros to the old woman. María, however, died of "*demencia senil*" and "*abandono familiar*" shortly after the sentence was handed down.[1]

From one point of view this story is an all-too-imaginable modern *fait divers;* from another it is the tragedy of *King Lear,* without a Cordelia.[2] In the play King Lear casts off his loving daughter, but then has to suffer the cruelty of her false and grasping older sisters. Shakespeare would have understood all too well the sentiments of María's grandson. He knew about children who can't wait to get their hands on their parents' money, considering the cash their right and therefore feeling no gratitude when they get it, and abusing their parents when they have no money left to give. Regan's icy retort to her father is one of the play's most horrifying moments:

LEAR: I gave you all—
REGAN: And in good time you gave it![3]

For Shakespeare, filial ingratitude discloses itself as an incestuous monster, a family eating itself alive. He did not have to explain his revulsion; expressing it vividly was enough:

Filial ingratitude!
Is it not as this mouth should tear this hand
For lifting food to it?[4]

Even now, when family feeling has lost much of its power to haunt us and make us tremble, every one of us knows exactly what Shakespeare meant. Yet the truth is that filial gratitude—like gratitude of any sort—can be forced from no one; if any compulsion occurs, it is no longer gratitude. Gratitude is morally fundamental yet cannot be coerced: that is at least in part why people have tended to hedge it about with reverence and (when it is missing) outrage.

The hierarchical traditions of China and Japan modelled the power and authority of elders in the state on the self-evident prerogatives of fathers and grandfathers in the family. Modern Japan in particular has successfully maintained reverence for elderly parents and grandparents.[5] The traditional Chinese way was to render filial piety (*xiào* in Mandarin) so unquestioning and so unquestioned that it took precedence when any other good conflicted with it. It was "the trunk of the tree" upon which all other virtues depended; after all, every child learns how to behave from its parents and within the context of the family. The duties of *xiào* included, apart from filial support for parents in old age, never rebelling against one's elders, always being courteous to them, providing the family with male heirs, brothers not fighting, adult sons advising their parents with wisdom while always concealing their elders' mistakes, displaying sorrow for their sickness and death, respectfully burying them, and carrying out the prescribed sacrifices after their deaths. People's feelings were of secondary importance to proper actions, clearly enunciated and laid out as visibly as possible: other people would be watching.[6]

In ancient Athens a man accused of neglecting his parents could be debarred from holding public office.[7] In ancient Israel a son who cursed or struck his father or his mother could be executed.[8] In our own day a case of neglect of a parent can conceivably be brought before the law: the Catalan police took exception to an old woman's children depositing her on the sidewalk. We should note, however, that in this case the problem had become so virulent that it broke out and manifested itself in public. Families usually keep their vices private—that is, successfully concealed. This is one of the reasons why modern laws cannot enforce filial piety.

When Plato as an old man came to compose his *Laws*, he was able freely to think up appropriate punishments for behaviour he loathed. His protagonist, the Athenian, goes so far as to compare aged parents kept safely in one's house to the statues of protecting deities, able to bring good upon the family; he approves greatly of the supernatural powers his culture vested in parents, like gods, to bless or curse. He imagines laws by which anyone neglectful of parents should be reported to the State's "guardians of wedlock." The difficulty of revealing iniquities that occur in secret behind family walls is cleverly addressed: any slave who brings to light neglect of the elderly will instantly be granted freedom. Those discovered to have been filially neglectful shall be whipped and imprisoned—a son if under thirty and a daughter if under forty. If people older than these abuse their parents, a hundred and one of the oldest citizens in the state will be called together to judge them and have them punished, no doubt in a manner ingeniously fitting the crime.[9]

Two hundred years later the Greek historian Polybius commented that other people could be counted on to be furious at filial abuse "because they will look to the future, and reflect that every one of them will one day be in a similar situation."[10] They will shame the neglectful, just as they habitually honour the brave with their praise. Greek and Roman sources speak rarely of how children actually feel towards their parents. Offspring are quite simply obliged, by taboo and by honour sanctioned by shame, to look after their progenitors.

In Latin, filial duty was not in fact called *gratia* (gratitude), but *pietas*. The word meant correctly manifested respect towards one's country, and to one's parents and other kin.[11] The great hero Aeneas, whose epic adjective was *pius*, not only founded Rome, but also bore his father (who carried in his arms the city's household gods) on his back, and held his small son's hand as the family fled from burning Troy. The image of this threesome—the wife and mother Creüsa followed behind but was lost despite her husband's frantic search for her—was an ideal picture of the perfect Roman family's dutiful male line.[12] *Pietas* was personified as a goddess and given a temple in Rome. Her attribute was a stork, because this bird always helped its old parents.

When elderly storks lost their feathers and their power to fly, their offspring covered them with their own plumage and fed them. The young also carried their parents about on their own wings, and solicitously exercised their stiff and feeble legs.[13]

The Greeks and Romans felt that filial piety was prior to and greater than any entirely voluntary thankfulness for the benevolence of parents. Duties to parents, for the Greeks, were part of what was called "unwritten" law, and as such exerted unspeakable power. Mothers in particular, if they suffered violence from their children, were avenged by the Erinyes, or Furies, goddesses of Vengeance and of Kin. In Rome murdering one's parents was at least by convention so horrendous a deed as to be unthinkable:[14] it was what the Oceanian Tonga have taught us to call a taboo.

People have usually been convinced that parents love their children "by nature," and desire their welfare even above their own. Human babies need long nurturing; nature has seen to that. Eventually, usually after many years, parents become themselves dependent, and everything was (and still is) done to make their children, "by nature," look after them in their turn. The principle is that if parents have been less than sufficiently benevolent (which might make a child ungrateful), filial piety still demands care for them in their old age. After all, sages would remind people, babies need not "give first" in order to receive parental attention—yet they once were given it. Parents were always "first givers," holding the higher moral ground that, as we have seen, belongs in Western cultures to those who give first. Aristotle says that no son can ever honour his parents as they deserve: children remain their parents' debtors for life.[15]

Remarkably, even today, an adult who dislikes his old parents might still believe that he should help them. He does not let his own parents drop in order to look after other old people—other people's parents—instead. He could start recalling instances, even isolated ones, of help his parents gave him in childhood. But what is likely to occur to him first is what the French call *l'évidence,* a fact that cannot be gainsaid: "After all, they are my parents."

By the first century, Romans, despite their ancient *pietas,* felt free to ask themselves why this statement of fact ("after all, they are my parents") should issue in an obligation;[16] it was the concept of gratitude in the sense of reciprocity for benefits that enabled them to argue about the otherwise unspeakable. Sons give many things to fathers, it was said, but a father gives only one thing, the son's existence—and even there he was merely enjoying himself at the time.[17] A man, other sons complained, has children for his own benefit, not theirs. He enjoys many advantages in having a son: he keeps the law (Romans had by law to procreate if they could), receives respect, continues his house and family, basks in his son's fame should the son achieve any. Such a son, however, could apparently claim that his father had contributed merely his bodily self ("you gave me only what I have in common with flies and worms": a modern son would have spoken of genes). Anything the son accomplished thereafter he had to manage on his own. Why, then, should the son feel constrained to help his old father? So the arguments went, and Seneca takes the trouble to answer them. He points out, at some length, that parents give not only life, but also nurture, upbringing, and education. Therefore, children *do* owe them gratitude.

In modern times, ever since the thinking of men like Hobbes broke with existing tradition, filial responsibility has become a conundrum—in some circles, a philosophical chestnut. For example, the Old Testament commandment "Honour thy father and thy mother," has been dismissed by some as an illusion because it takes its source in religion, which, they argue, promotes blind obedience to divine authority.[18] There are no obvious grounds, say others, for asserting that filial obligations exist.[19] A child has not given her consent to be born—indeed, nobody even consulted her—and "it is difficult to believe that one has any moral duty to show gratitude [to parents] for benefits one has not requested."[20] And the same author adds, "It is hard to make sense of the claim that bringing a child into the world benefits that child." Gratitude for having been born is illogical because "if no person is brought into existence, then no person exists to endure the relatively worse state of nonexistence."[21]

Moreover, some now argue, not only does a child not choose to be born, but she might well, given the choice, not have wanted *this* upbringing by *these* parents, so why should she be grateful? Would she not be justified in paying them back in kind, making them as uncomfortable now as she remembers they once made her? Gratitude *might* be fitting where a parent has been outstandingly gifted at child rearing, or has made exceptional sacrifices on behalf of her young. But gratitude, strictly speaking, is not owing for what is done for us out of duty; nor is it due to someone who is merely filling a role. Parents are obviously obliged to take care of their children; but if they do only what parents are supposed to do, and are not perceived by their offspring as having shown excellence, then gratitude is not required. In any case, why should any repayment of our parents consist of care for them in their old age? Why not find out how much they have spent on us, and as soon as we are in a position to pay them back, give them the money?[22]

A modern person often feels that friendship is the only morally and logically acceptable model for loving human relationships. Friends are people one *likes,* whom one *chooses.* Now, it is possible to like one's parents, and anyone who does so will want to help them in old age because they are friends. If, however, parents have by their behaviour forfeited this friendship, then they should have no claims on us. Often parents and children find they have little in common, or end up having little in common, apart from their biological origins. Friendships, even close ones, can break up if they are no longer working—for example, if one person thinks the other is no longer an asset. Fathers and mothers are well advised to make sure that their children never see them as no longer measuring up, because the children might decide that friendship with their parents is over.[23] It has been asserted, moreover, that "younger persons can gain few advantages by fulfilling duties of justice to older individuals . . . Nothing that we do now will affect the benefits that members of older generations have conferred already. In particular, disenfranchising older persons from a share of social resources will not cause those benefits to be taken from us."[24]

The ancient idea that parents "by nature" love and take care of their children has been given a new slant. One consequence of the discovery of our genetic makeup has been the conclusion reached by many that we exist merely in order to hand on our genes. Parents who love and care for their children, therefore, are only acting in accordance with nature: they are preserving their own genes. The next step is to realize that, once old, they have already handed on their genes: they are no longer genetically significant, quite apart from their offering "few advantages" to children who now look after them. Why not learn from nature's practical habit of disposing of the redundant and the spent?

Of course, children do not have it all their own way. Adults, after all, can choose whether or not to procreate, whereas children have no choice whether or not to be born. Parents today are "increasingly able to control the timing and circumstances of reproduction and the gender and health of offspring . . . By contrast, children are obviously not free to select the parents who will bear them."[25] In ancient Greece and Rome, a father had the right to determine whether any child of his would live. If he decided against permitting the infant's life, she was exposed. Not receiving nurture from her mother—the next step in parental giving—she would die, unless somebody found the child and decided to take her home and adopt her.[26] *Not* having been exposed as a baby was therefore grounds for gratitude to a father, who had kindly consented to the child's survival. Not having been aborted might perhaps be expected to arouse a similarly grateful response in a child today.

Hobbes thought that children had better help their old parents, or people would simply stop procreating and humanity would eventually die out: "Nor would there be any reason, why any man should desire to have children, or take the care to nourish, and instruct them, if they [*sic*] were afterwards to have no other benefit from them, than from other men."[27] His reasoning here resembles his "Fourth Law of Nature," where gratitude prevents the giving and the return of benefits from dying out. However, no parent can be sure that his or her children will understand and carry out their part of the Hobbesian bargain. They might not, for example, see why they should put the continued existence of the human race before their own immediate convenience.

Families are about continuity; children are the future. The virtues implied in filial gratitude rebuke the short-sightedness of much of what modern people take for wisdom: self-enclosed individualism, materialism, greed, living for one's own immediate self-interest. A widely distributed folktale, "The Man, His Son, and the Mat," related from Europe to China, tells of an old man dying, and his son deciding to wrap the body for burial in a filthy old straw mat. The son's little boy, having fetched the mat, cuts it in half first, saying, "I could use this myself." The miserly father of the child, delighted by his son's frugality, asks what the boy will use it for. His son replies, "Your body will need a piece of matting when you die." Children can see through the wickedness and injustice of the older generation. Someone who makes short shrift of his parents will teach his children cruelty, which they will later inflict on him. A pitiless insistence on utilitarian calculations might be valued in the marketplace, but it can only cause misery in the family.

Others argue that begetting a child is not an act of benevolence—and therefore deserves no gratitude—because a benefit must be (a) intentionally offered, and (b) given to a specific person. A parent might want to be benevolent towards *a* baby, but a parent remains necessarily unacquainted with the child before it has been born, so he or she cannot have meant to benefit *this* baby: "After all, had conception been postponed a month it would have been a different child."[28] Samuel Beckett expresses the difficulty succinctly when Hamm in *Endgame* expostulates before his parent, the "accursed progenitor" now crouching in his ashcan:

HAMM: Scoundrel! Why did you engender me?
NAGG [Hamm's father]: I didn't know.
HAMM: What? What didn't you know?
NAGG: That it'd be you.[29]

The problems of how to behave towards the old have exercised humanity ever since we reached the stage where people survived long enough to *be* old—that is, weak and dependent on others, somewhat as children must in early life depend on parents. But we have our own particular difficulties in this regard. First, more people in the rich cultures of west and east live to old age, older in some cases than people previously imagined possible. At least for the present, there are more old people than the young feel it is fair to ask them to cope with, and most of us have much smaller families than we once had, so there are fewer kin to bear each family's responsibilities.

The family, in an individualistic culture, is exceptional in important ways—rather as gift-giving is different from commerce. Relationships between children and parents stand in contradiction to our modern rejections of hierarchy. Children are physically dependent on—unequal to—parents for many years. They have to be protected, fed, looked after, and taught the principles of moral behaviour. It is a protracted, patience-demanding process, and parents have to learn to give up their own liberties and let go of many pleasures in life in order to "bring their children up," as we put it. True, it is exciting and rewarding to watch a baby grow in vigour and understanding. It is sad, on the other hand, to see an adult deteriorate mentally and physically with age. Just as young parents once had to learn new degrees of selflessness when they had children, a whole new level of understanding and generosity must be discovered by the middle-aged as they watch their previously powerful, dependable parents slowly decline and become needy.

These asymmetries of relation have to coexist today with the achievement of a degree of egalitarianism within the family that was almost unheard of in the past. Gone is the early Roman *patria potestas*—the father's omnipotence in his family[30]—and almost all of its later, attenuated versions. Nowadays, grown children can get out from under both parents' authority to an unprecedented extent; they can earn their own livings and turn down parental advice about how they should live their lives. Adult children, as they follow their careers in an increasingly mobile society, often move away from where their parents live, so that links between older and younger generations of a family may insensibly weaken.

It has long been understood that a parent may disqualify himself for his children's gratitude: "Tell me," says Seneca, "are not some fathers so harsh and so wicked that it is right and proper to turn away from them and disown them?" He goes on, "It is just as if someone should lend me money, and then set fire to my house. The loan has been balanced by my loss. Having made him no return, yet I owe him nothing." Seneca carefully makes the point that there *had been* benefits before the harshness and wickedness made themselves felt, or the child would not have survived infancy. He should therefore not take revenge upon his terrible parent. Withholding his gratitude (that is, not giving in return for the original benefit) is enough.[31]

In a modern setting, a grown child may well feel justifiable resentment towards parents who failed her when she was young. For example, her elders might have condemned disobedience or disagreement as constituting "ingratitude" and then used the fact of their past aid to control the child's life rather as a feudal lord expected loyalty from vassals to whom he once had given gifts. It would be difficult, indeed, to make sacrifices in order to look after parents who have done their utmost (even if they have failed) to destroy one's freedom to live life the way one believes to be right. We see it as a child's duty, in fact, to break free of truly unreasonable parental controls; cultural norms that render escape impossible we consider to be unjust. Conversely, parents, in our culture, cannot be blamed for their children's failure to live as they should. Yet many adults who hold grievances against their parents still feel they have a duty (no more, but also no less) to provide care for their parents in old age.

Another intractable affront that the family represents for many today is that it often seems inimical to choice. Modern people tend to have difficulty understanding that unquestionable relationship is the way the family benefits us, despite our just aspirations to freedom and individuality. Each of us longs for unconditional acceptance. We also gain from the security of family ties that by definition cannot be broken on a whim, no matter how much we want to be free to choose or discard our associations with other people. The trick is to love these family members whom we have not chosen—and even to recognize, while keeping our good humour, our own characteristics in relatives we may dislike.

Parental care is essential for the survival of a human baby, but of course the family's usefulness does not end there. Many parents go far beyond the demands of "duty" to share and play with, teach, encourage, and give pleasure to their children. They often help them out financially if they can, many years after their offspring have attained adulthood, and take every chance to offer them what they have to give. After the years of nurturing and education, long after grown children have left home, the family's presence continues to loom large in most people's lives. Family members help one another through hard times; they provide for one another dependable support and advice and company. They share memories; each helps create the identity of each, even as all of them join together in weaving a family's narrative.

The emotional depth and the profound and lifelong influence, happy or the reverse, of family relations—especially those between parents and children—are given more recognition now than they have ever received in history. And it has repeatedly been observed in the modern West that when people grow old, it is the family that almost invariably provides their principal emotional support. After childhood is over, a long period of time normally passes before children may be called upon to look after their old parents. Yet dutiful children are expected, if possible, to stay connected, and certainly to remember. Memory is part of gratitude, as it is part of civilization.

We might imagine that old parents would think of what they have given and perhaps suffered on behalf of their offspring down the years, that they would simply accept help from them now, as repayment for then. But apparently this is seldom the case. Research into the behaviour and responses of elderly, dependent people[32] has shown that most of them are not happy just to receive; they still want to be able to give back benefits to those who help them. This longing to be able to reciprocate is a matter largely of security, of a desire to maintain relationships in a stage of life when many of their friends have died or live apart from them. And give-and-take, as we have seen, is not only equalizing, but also an insurance that the relationship will continue.

In addition our culture places powerful value on independence, in and of itself. Our manners, for example, often require us to prove to others that we are in no need of their assistance. At table we are expected to sit up straight, handle our knives and forks with aplomb, never to lean, slump, support ourselves on our elbows (we may be allowed to place elbows on the table provided we demonstrate that we do not *need* to do so), yawn, or fall asleep. Keeping all this up says: "Don't worry about *me*—I can take care of myself, *thank* you very much!" In part our behaviour expresses an enculturated agreement that other people want, above all, not to be inconvenienced by the incompetent or the feeble. When the courteous armour of self-sufficiency falls away from people in their old age, they can therefore feel very vulnerable and insecure. Old people often go to considerable lengths, which uncomprehending offspring may find strange and irritating, to prove that they have some power left: something they can give—or withhold.

Research has confirmed that elderly parents rarely think of their children as "owing" them anything. What they have done, most of them feel, they did out of love. Vladimir Jankélévitch, in his *Traité des Vertus (Treatise on the Virtues)*, called this the "infinite, inexhaustible gift of parental love," where "even thinking of return is dishonouring."[33] Children often say they are helping parents "because they helped me." Their parents do not see it that way. They want not a "return" for what they did for their children, but relationship in love. They are, we are told, often reluctant to accept help—indeed, they are likely to refuse it, or not ask for it. They are terrified of being a burden to their children: they want above all to keep on giving, to keep relationships active.

What they did for their children from the beginning was not done as "favours" (which might perhaps be reciprocated), but just as—what? A Gospel parable tells us of Christ saying at the end of time to those at his right hand, "You have my Father's blessing; come, enter and possess the kingdom that has been ready for you since the world was made. For when I was hungry, you gave me food; when thirsty, you gave me drink; when I was a stranger you took me into your home; when naked you clothed me; when I was ill you came to my help, when in prison you visited me." The reaction of the people invited into heaven for these reasons is sheer amazement. They do not realize, understandably, that they have helped God. But it is likely also that they simply cannot recall having done any of these things.[34] People who help others and expect nothing in return do so because there is a need to be filled and they fill it; they are quite capable, despite what economists and social scientists would have us believe, of not nursing expectations of "getting something back." The parable almost sounds inspired by the ordinary self-forgetfulness of parental caring. Your child has a runny nose—so you wipe it. The child screams—so you comfort her. These are the actions of love, and they are not done in order to receive rewards, either now or later. Elderly parents want something of the same kind of unconditional concern from their children. Family relations are a matter of sharing and old intimacy. They are also a complex mixture—hard as we have worked to separate them into different categories—of duty and affection.

Historically speaking, state government in the West has sought to lessen the suffering of the poor by attempting to make use of the goodwill of children to support their impoverished parents. Laws have been passed, duties of children spelled out.[35] But the State and the law can neither offer love nor demand that people shall love. Responsible citizens can, however, ensure that no old parents need feel they are a financial burden on their children, or fear that having physical needs looked after is contingent on their children's affection or lack of it—on their decisions whether to help or not. It is entirely possible, though rarely put into practice, for a well-run State to give, in addition to adequate pensions, material and practical help to old people *as citizens,* as their right.[36] If that right were recognized, adults would then, as a society, contribute towards the material well-being of all old people, including those who have no families to support them, and including themselves later. Occasions for shame and resentment would be removed, and society would receive much greater cohesion and goodwill between generations.

The rest—the love and attention, the time taken talking, reminiscing, telephoning, writing, the actual caring—can never be legislated. Yet consideration and emotional support are perhaps what old people long for most. Children can give their parents that affectionate care, as only they can give it; it is their virtue to give it, just as it is the parents' virtue not only to look after their children when young but to keep being concerned about them as they grow up and start families of their own. The children's reasons should include gratitude where appropriate, but their motivations are likely to extend much further.

Parental love for children leaves "duty" far behind: anything approaching good child rearing has to be founded on love. It is true that obligation plays a part, and that children are nothing if not demanding. Old people can also require extra comprehension from their children, in their impatience at the loss of their capability and authority, and their anxiety as they realize their weakness and watch death approaching. An old parent arrives, after a long journey with its epic narrative, at a stage in life when justice and respect from others are necessary and good, but love is better still, after all.

15

Tipping

Gratitude can be a long-cultivated disposition to remember what one owes to the loving care of someone as important in one's life as a parent. At the other end of the spectrum it can characterize a quick response to one small favour from a person quite unknown. Tipping is an example of the second "pole" of grateful behaviour, but this does not make it a transparently simple act.

If you give a tip for service received, and do so not merely because tipping is a convention, then the tip is an expression of gratitude and as such freely given. The gratitude is for the willing, energetic, and efficacious way in which a service has been performed. It might be possible to oblige someone else to perform an action, but no one can command the spirit in which it is done: gratitude is therefore in order, although it cannot be demanded. Gratitude is a response to goodwill that cannot be exacted; there is freedom on both sides. A tip is called a "gratuity"—something freely given. *Gratuity* derives from Latin *gratis,* but also from the root of both words, which is *gratus,* "grateful"—so closely connected are the ideas of gratitude and freedom.[1] Thankfulness is especially felt where service has gone beyond duty. Doing more than one has to is a gift;[2] giving money one is not required to give, as in the case of a tip, is a gift in return.

This commonly accepted account of what happens when a gratuity is handed over is roundly rejected by those economists and sociologists who dislike any explanation that involves gratitude, freedom, or "altruism," because their model insists that human beings—despite any protests to the contrary—act only for motives of self-interest. The fact that the amount of a tip is not—or should not be—laid down in advance is all the freedom they will admit, although the reason for this provision must then be accounted for. A typical sociological definition of a tip is that it, "like the gift, is given under voluntary guise, but in fact under a constraining normative framework in situations where the mutual obligations are not exactly specified."[3] Sociological researchers certainly pay sufficient attention to tipping behaviour to alert us to the extent to which this custom, "like the gift," transgresses the conventions of modernity; for them, tipping is a pervasive enigma. And certainly the naive account I gave at the beginning of this chapter requires further inspection.

To begin with, tipping is not egalitarian behaviour, apart from the freedom (should one admit that there is freedom) on both sides. For example, passing a tip to someone—as opposed to leaving one behind, on a restaurant table, for instance—is often an almost furtive movement, hand to hand. This approach is partly to spare the receiver's feelings: as we have noted, in our culture to give is higher than to receive, and therefore, openly receiving a tip, no matter how much the money is appreciated, is having one's lower status displayed. The receiver, on his side, may not look at the money in his hand, at least not in the presence of the giver: he usually likes appearing not to care and certainly not to have been longing for a tip.

In many languages a tip is called by a term that can be perceived as demeaning. It is a pittance, just enough for a drink: *pourboire, Trinkgelt, propina.* A tip is a small reward, which implies that the service too was small. The English word *tip* is sometimes said to stand for "To Insure Promptness." In fact, *to tip* is sixteenth- and seventeenth-century canting slang for "to hand over," and this sense also came to be applied to "tips" as secret information or private warnings: a tip is a personal and private thing, one on one.[4] But the false etymology reminds us that a tip can be given in advance, to encourage lively service later: in these cases a very thin line—or none—might separate a tip from a bribe. The tip's smallness helps protect it from shading over into bribery. In fiercely egalitarian regimes tipping is regarded as an insult. A Western journalist who remembered the early days after the Communist Revolution in Russia was struck by the fact that "the waiters and hotel servants had organized and refused tips. On the walls of restaurants they put up signs which read, 'No tips taken here,' or 'Just because a man has to make a living waiting on tables, is no reason to insult him by offering him a tip.'"[5]

One study of modern tipping enumerates thirty-three occupations where tips are usually given. These include facial beauticians, fishing boat crews, gas station attendants, golf caddies, tour guides, hairstylists, chambermaids, concierges, doormen, parking valets, hotel transportation pickup service drivers, taxi and limo drivers, locker room attendants, manicurists, masseuses/masseurs, pool attendants, waiters, bootblacks, porters, and ushers.[6] These people are not normally thought of as occupying positions of superior status, or as uniquely gifted experts in a job requiring high qualifications. People who tip them have been served by them, in a direct sense in which receiver is easily thought of as "higher" than giver. In cases of clear hierarchy, it will be noticed that, for a "high-up," giving a tip is high, and receiving a service is also high.

But inequality of status is not the only factor. The services supplied by the people listed in the study are personal, requiring direct and intimate contact with the client and the client's possessions, even involving touching the client's body; there is often total though brief dependence upon the server. A hairdresser wields scissors around your ears and face, while decisively affecting your appearance for weeks subsequent to his or her ministrations. A manicurist also uses cutting implements, on your fingers. Pool attendants and fishing boat crews could conceivably hold your life in their hands, while bad will in a facial beautician might easily ruin your day. Car valets and porters have access to expensive possessions—your car, your luggage. Chambermaids have an angle on your habits in the bedroom and bathroom. All of these people are in a position to know things about you close up. Yet we place ourselves in their hands and can only hope that they will not abuse our trust. One of the triggers of gratitude is relief. Imagination is involved, and realization: a comparison between what has been given, and what could have been withheld or gone wrong; things could have been worse.

The kinds of people we normally tip have a lot in common with professionals in the strict sense, those prestige-laced grandees in the social scale of modern life. Professionals are people to whom we give official, direct access to ourselves at our most vulnerable and who are entrusted with our secrets— who are able, therefore, to do us grievous personal and sometimes bodily damage. Our attitude towards them is one of respect and even fear. We often give them very large salaries as well, and can only hope they will do their duty. We cannot force them to have goodwill or indeed to pay sufficient attention to our case. The four original professions are the priesthood, the law, medicine, and university professorship.[7] Other groups try to emulate these four since the rewards are high. Some, such as architects and engineers, convince us that we need them, even though we know full well that any mistakes they make could spoil our cities or cause catastrophe. Professionals, like people we reward with tips, can be dangerous; we are relieved—grateful—when they help rather than injure us.[8] Professionals have in consequence to be "qualified." We regulate them with ferocity, and force them to spend long years getting their degrees, practising, proving themselves, and generally being initiated before they are deemed worthy to join the ranks of the professionals. They are clever; they know things we do not know. We are forced to admit this and to realize that we cannot wring from them either competence or dedication: there is no "equality" between professionals and the rest of us.

Tips are supposed to be given *in addition* to a salary, and only as a token of a customer's satisfaction. (Relief, the negative aspect of such gratitude, is not openly expressed: of course it might reveal the tip-giver's weakness, or it might insult the server.) The customer pays the tip to the server "one on one": the employer should have nothing to do with it. Neither customer nor server hides this action from the employer: this is another way in which tipping differs from bribery. Indeed, the employer frequently uses the tipping custom for his or her own ends. Waiters often depend heavily on gratuities, unpredictable as they are, to make up unconscionably meagre wages. The amount a customer should tip the waiter may be shamelessly stated on a restaurant bill. (It is said that waiters for their part have been known to pursue angrily into the street customers who "stiff," or fail to leave a tip.) Or "service charges" are added, a percentage of the amount owed. In this manner employers compel waiters to use their only power, their personal contact with diners, to make clients spend more and so benefit from the percentage of a larger bill themselves. A service charge, being utterly unfree, is in no sense a gratuity, but merely an addition to the bill. Where tips are part of a worker's salary, there may also be tax evasion: because they are gifts, tips are unofficial and therefore unaccountable.

Personal contact is what may or may not give rise to gratuities for a service worker. Social scientists have found that restaurants make ideal laboratories for showing how tips—apparently freely given—are in fact deliberately coaxed out of unsuspecting customers. All kinds of ingenious experiments have been contrived whereby servers, secretly directed and monitored by the scientists, have elicited tips from diners.[9] A waiter may introduce himself or herself by name while taking special care to look attractive (for example, wearing a handsome waistcoat, or a flower in her hair), keeping up a kindly expression and a carefully modulated voice, smiling often and broadly, touching clients on the shoulder and even on the palm of the hand, and otherwise making "verbal and nonverbal signals" of personal friendliness. It can be profitable, if a waiter scents the possibility of a large tip, to make a number of "non–task-related" trips to and from the table; frequently asking whether everyone is enjoying their meal is one way of doing this. Some waiters go so far as to squat down beside diners in order to advise them and listen to their wishes, so displaying energy and youth, intimacy, deference, and perhaps a satisfying inferiority.

Waiters may handwrite the word *thank you* on the backs of bills before giving them to customers "back-side up so that the first thing the diners will see is the server's expression of gratitude." This is apparently a common practice, and sometimes embellished by the addition of a quick drawing of a round smiling face. Experimenters tried the writing of *thank you* plus the waiter's first name—which had, of course, been provided during the introduction phase of the operation—but customers, oddly, did not give more money as a result. In other instances, however, we are told that "expressing gratitude to targets can increase actors' influence over them. [*Influence* here means the kind of allure that might elicit bigger tips from 'targets.'] Gratitude is likely to increase actors' likeability and appearance of friendliness." The waiter's presence gains "increased salience," which raises the amount she is given.[10] In these experiments, some clients received these attentions, others did not, and the sizes of tips were correlated. The results establish, of course, that personal contact and perceived goodwill are what tipping is about. People apparently now reject the Jeeves model in waitering, which was once considered real excellence: swift, efficient, able to anticipate a diner's least requirement, but unobtrusive, the server's mien deliberately impassive. A strenuous attempt to achieve personal contact would definitely have been frowned upon—and considered abject in the waiter.

Waiters have always known that it matters, as far as tipping is concerned, who the client is. Men tip more generously than women do, especially if they are trying to impress; not only are tables with children hard work, but parents tend to tip less. Women and parents can be unimpressed by serving since they do so much of it themselves, and also usually have less money to spend than single men or men on dates. The size of a dining party apparently affects gratuities more than proportionately, and alcohol consumption increases generosity. People who are frequent patrons of a restaurant, however, are unpredictable tippers: either they give a comparatively large tip because they "expect future interaction," or they give less for the same reason. It is clear from the research that waiters use intricate skills and sharp judgment about what makes people give, in order to survive in the métier.[11]

A gratuity is a small monetary present. It is disqualified, however, as a gift on three counts. First, it is usually given immediately after the service has been done: the time lapse said to be essential to the gift is missing. Second, a tip is money. And third, a gratuity ends the transaction: there will be no equalizing by means of reciprocity, no friendship instituted.

The lack of a waiting period between service and tip arises from the practical fact that the client will soon leave. Most people tipped will never be seen again by the giver—and immediately the idea that a tip might be a gift receives a setback. Gift and return gift, as we saw, travel the invisible trajectory formed by bonds linking people, creating and strengthening ties of friendship. The time taken between receiving and returning is time to reflect, to appreciate, to think of something one wants to give back. To give a tip immediately after service makes this "return" resemble payment.

The same is true of the nature of the gratuity: money. Cash is payment, cold, abstract, impersonal, and often considered, therefore, inherently unfriendly. It is the stuff of contracts, not a meaningful, carefully chosen expression of thoughtfulness and esteem; money is not a "proper" gift. There is, of course, no time to go away and buy a gift, and even if there were, the attendant is usually only a slight acquaintance, and the giver cannot know what gift-object might please her. Money is what the server wants, anyway; and money is necessarily what is given because there is no time, and no tie.

Finally, a tip is not a gift in that it ends a relationship. There may be gratitude, but like the acquaintance it is ephemeral and without fruit; it resembles somewhat the English custom we looked at earlier, where saying "Thank you" can mean "Good-bye." Canny waiters may give clients a subliminal nudge towards producing more money by performing some sort of rudimentary "personalizing" action. But the last thing a tipper is likely to want, in fact, is a real, ongoing relationship with the server—and vice versa. The waiter will not make a return gift; the client will leave and forget the waiter's existence. Tipping, then, can be mere automatic convention, or something close to a bribe, or a form of payment and as such a semi-contractual matter, or a sign of superiority—all of these being satisfactory explanations for economics and social science. But there remains the possibility of freely given, not duty-bound, effort on one side, and the free expression of gratitude for it on the other.

A special kind of tip, one that maintains a continuing relationship, is the regular annual Christmas gift, or bonus, which could be classified in part as the "To Insure Promptness" type. By means of these presents the giver keeps and encourages personal contact with often-encountered service providers, such as postal workers, who are acquaintances but rarely friends. In rural France members of the fire brigade, in full uniform, arrive every year bearing the gift of an irresistibly picturesque calendar for the coming year, depicting the fire brigade. They expect a solid sum of money and a lengthy conversation with the inhabitants of the house: the fire fighters are very knowledgeable about what goes on and who everybody is. (The round of visits, and the conversation-period, are on company time.) Gratuity-givers are happy to know personally the people upon whose benevolence much could depend, at any moment. The object given, a calendar, is a lasting and concrete reminder of the time ahead, during which services might be needed.

The more each person thinks a relationship with a server might be too equal to give rise to a tip, the more embarrassed either party, or both, will feel. A tour guide, for example, who has pointed out in minute detail the capitals in a Romanesque cloister and explained their meanings, is someone whose superior knowledge often makes a tourist feel uncomfortable about giving her a tip: he often tries to give it unobtrusively, with perhaps a complicit smile, to show he has been listening, and as though "we two" were the ones in the group best able to appreciate the art. On other occasions it is hard to know whether or not to give a tip at all—in case one might offend either by giving or by omitting to give—and how much a tip should be. In the modern West, knowledge of this kind is not very often a *sine qua non* for daily existence, with rules accordingly clear and unequivocal, as is the case in many closer-knit and hierarchical societies that are less pressured and overshadowed by market exchange. Yet we apparently do feel we ought to try, despite the clumsiness and the anxiety. We know that gratefulness, where felt, should be expressed, in this case through giving a gratuity. (And some of us might reflect that even where services have not been very successful, any effort shown is still a matter for gratitude.)

A different explanation for tipping is that it performs what some psychologically inclined researchers may call "an ego massage" for the giver. The tip dispenser, from this point of view, is forced to give by the pressure of social norms, but persuades himself that he is giving as an individual and exercising free will. He partakes for a brief moment in the power (disguised as freedom and generosity) that used to be wielded by an aristocrat, and derives pleasure from seeing the gratitude he appears to evoke in one lower than he is. If he is a rich tourist in a foreign land, he enjoys flexing his monetary muscle—when he is not feeling guilty for being so rich and experiencing various inner compulsions, therefore, to tip more heavily than necessary.[12] Status and force, once again, cover the field as the explanations offered.

The tipping custom and its puzzles have nevertheless laid bare for us the impossibility of discussing gifts and gratitude without considering their constant dialogue with notions of freedom and obligation, equality and rank—the subject of the next section.

16

Freedom and Equality

Social custom in our culture allows a return giver two clear freedoms: choice as to what to give back, and when to give it. (There are inappropriate or disproportionate gifts, to be sure, and occasions, like Christmas and weddings, when on a definite date gifts are "in order" for all involved.) And also, a receiver may decide not to give back, or indeed fail to feel grateful at all—and the first giver cannot demand a response, even though she is likely to desire one. She will be thought extremely rude if she disobeys this rarely spoken rule. Gratitude cannot be exacted; otherwise, it would cease to be gratis.

There are conventions and sometimes social pressures to encourage gratitude, and even to punish its opposite, but no laws are allowed to govern it. The word *convention* literally means "a coming together" (as in a business convention). People have "come together" in agreement that it is right and just to reciprocate a favour by doing a good deed in return, and that a thinking person who is open to others and wants to live according to moral principles will feel grateful for a benefit done. They also realize that giving and returning link people in relationship. Conventions, since they are human agreements, are always liable to change. The one that expects gratitude has lasted, which does not mean it could never be jettisoned. In "individualistic" societies the convention is extensible enough to permit its own flouting, for the prior understanding is that gratitude must be free.

Immanuel Kant (1724–1804), for whom gratitude means primarily "giving something back," differentiates gratitude from justice. It is important for him to do this, because of the element of freedom in gratitude that has to be taken into account. Kant calls justice a "perfect" duty, something that requires only the right sorts of action. It is something peremptorily clear, with no loopholes. A just man, for example, does his duty by keeping a promise. Beneficence, on the other hand, Kant sees as an "imperfect" duty, by which he means an action depending on a person's adherence to a moral maxim, such as (for gratitude) "Help prior benefactors when the opportunity presents itself, because they once helped you." Just how one should follow the accepted maxim—in this case what one should do, and when, to help or give back to a benefactor—is left to the discretion of the person seeking to carry out the maxim.

Kant says that a perfect duty like justice always primes an imperfect one like gratitude. For example, if I owe George gratitude and kill George's enemy in order to do him a favour, the wrongness of the killing (refraining from killing being a perfect duty) is not diminished by gratitude defined as doing a benefit in return (an imperfect duty). But, thinks Kant, gratitude can encounter perfect opportunities for "giving back," and then the virtuous person owing gratitude cannot desist from making a return—provided that a perfect duty is not violated in doing so. That "cannot desist" makes gratitude a *narrow* imperfect duty, unlike *wide* imperfect duties that permit more latitude in that they can sometimes be set aside, even though they can never be forgotten. Kant insists that the priority of the "first giver" never ends: gratitude to this person, as to one's parents, is for life and is owed even to deceased ancestors. Gratitude is a "holy" duty: one cannot transgress it without giving a scandalous example to others, and it can never be completely discharged.[1]

Certain freedoms (what, where, when, as well as cost left unspecified) are insisted upon in egalitarian societies, in which hierarchical structures, although they continue to exist, are supposed to be constantly questioned, controlled, limited, and even liable to discouragement; people are usually prevailed upon at least to dissimulate such "structures" during daily converse.

Where people live in hierarchically organized societies, as we have seen, what gifts should be given to whom and when, as well as what they should cost, are matters often laid down clearly in advance. People externalize "gratitude," especially emphasizing gesture and posture, even enacting a ritualized drama that is designed to be legible to other people as well as to the one being revered for generosity. One example is that of the Tamil population of South India. Arjun Appadurai writes that it is difficult, though not impossible, for a Tamil to say "thank you." *Nanri,* literally "good thing," is the closest equivalent, and the word's use as an approximation to *thank you* is very recent.[2] Tamils traditionally make obligatory demonstrations of appreciation, however, that are non-verbal and at the same time underline the lower rank of the performer. Such actions typically include "the touching of the feet of the superior, the lowered or averted eyes, the use of honorific titles and respectful terms of address, the bodily postures of dependence, the tones of deference." People of high rank are expected to give generously, and those of low rank literally bow down in appreciation and in open acknowledgement of their immutable status.

Next, the receiver must praise the giver. Praise of the benefactor is performed in this society whenever there is permanent hierarchical ranking, lower to higher. It is important in such a case that the giver himself be praised, and not the things he has given or his acts of generosity. On the other hand, where Tamils are in a temporary relationship of inequality, then praising is for the gift, not the giver. One permanently inferior praises the donor because he has no right to have preferences regarding what he is given (and indeed, the gifts are likely to be prescribed by custom): "Thus if a farm laborer presumed to praise the thickness of the cloth given to him at the time of harvest, or the sweetness of the rice given to him at a ceremony by his patron, he would be seen as acting insubordinately." However, the labourer could quite properly praise the patron himself. Appadurai explains how various the meanings can be when people are close enough in rank to praise the gifts themselves: there may be authentic or merely formulaic praise, and laudatory comments can even constitute disparagement of the gift. The practised people listening know how to analyze and interpret "a very delicate series of tonal, lexical, and nonverbal cues." Praising a gift can actually become, through its manner, an appraisal of its quality—and a criticism of its giver.

The writer concludes, "Since gratitude is culturally constructed [among Tamils] not as a matter of inner states but of various kinds of return, they are obliged to take the forms of return (both verbal and nonverbal) very seriously." In the West morality and etiquette are two very different matters. But in societies like the Tamil one, Appadurai says, "morality and etiquette are inextricably linked." Feeling is not the point: action is. Response is externalized, for all to see: it is important to note that the presence of other people watching and judging is frequently mentioned. The action of praising and the exigencies of gift-giving are openly subject to rules (although the rules can be subverted through the manner of their application); ranking must be expressed in the process. There are degrees of hierarchical distance, and those are dramatized as well.

Traditional Japanese, as we have seen, strictly codify gifts—not only what is given to whom and when, but also how much a gift costs. Displaying the price on a gift is often perfectly correct behaviour. Rank is expressed through gift-and-return. "Gratitude," and the relationship expressed and created through it, *is* giving a gift or a favour in return. "Higher" people, according to a recent description,[3] give more—and get more in return. Sons, for example, both give and get more than their sisters do. "Higher" people guard jealously their right to give more, since it is an expression of their rank; it is perceived as an insult, for example, when at a gathering to offer a larger gift than the one given by the most important person present. (Such a miscalculation can, indeed, constitute a gaffe in our own society: it could, for example, make the giver's own gift look like a reproach to those who have not given more.) The politely deprecatory attitude of the Japanese may lead them to protest, when offering a return gift (what we might comparably call "a token of my gratitude"), that it is *soshima,* literally "trifling gift, inferior goods."

When writing thank-you notes, they are known to use the word *osoreirimasu,* "to be overcome with shame" for having received:[4] we meet again the shrinking, the apologetic bowing to the other, the attitude that makes the Japanese say "I'm so sorry" when they receive favours. Hierarchy and obligation are the structural principles.[5]

Aristotle describes the man of honour in his own society as one "large of soul," *megalopsychos.* This man, Aristotle says, "is fond of conferring benefits, but ashamed to receive them, because the former is a mark of superiority and the latter of inferiority." The shame of this man is not like the pain expressed by Japanese delicacy in consideration of how one's very existence can obligate another to give. "He returns with interest a service done to him," Aristotle explains, "because this will put the original benefactor into his debt in turn."[6] The response to receiving a favour is giving something back. The motivation is status, the desire—indeed the necessity, if he is to continue being a Big Man—is to be "on top." The Large-Souled Man is so sensitive, so protective of his reputation as "the best," that he will not even attend social occasions where other people take the first place.

He is admirable for not being entirely given over to material possessions, even though a *megalopsychos* is normally rich, for this is part of his being "big."[7] Honour is what counts—in this case, keeping others in his debt, while he owes nothing to anyone. There is no sense in which freedom governs the giving and receiving of gifts; and there is an iron link between obligation and lower status. Obligation is therefore tolerable for the Big Man only when it shackles someone other than himself. Receiving a gift is receiving an imposition that must be "discharged." If someone should dare to become a "first giver" to a *megalopsychos,* it is therefore a presumption and a cause for resentment in him. Aristotle goes on to describe the Big Man as remembering favours he has done, but not favours he has received.[8] He does not speak of "gratitude" (*charis*) here—and no wonder. In a different work, however, Aristotle does mention gift-giving that is free because not meant to receive a return.[9]

Modern societies such as our own have undergone a change since Aristotle, from the "honour and shame" society of the ancient Greeks to the "guilt culture" fostered by Christianity. Where honour and shame are guiding and controlling principles, one's honour, and its opposite, shame, are constituted by the judgment of other people, for these others have to do the honouring. After all it is they who, in the end, allot his imposing "size" to an honourable man. They need information with which to make up their minds about whether he deserves this admiration. Honour accordingly requires enactment: physical demonstrations of intentions and attitudes, not only from the vulgar, but also from the honoured few.[10] It is often part of a receiver's "return gift" to tell everyone about what the generous giver has done. Letting others know means that honour will come from many more people than from the beneficiary alone. Honour is "added to" a person as an admission, by others, of his "largeness." It is a socially determined, external phenomenon.

In a "guilt culture," on the other hand, guilt may be defined as the fact of having committed an offence—as culpability and therefore liability to a penalty. As such it may be punished by society. But guilt is also thought of as a feeling within the offender. A person may feel guilty even if other people are not aware of what she has done. Guilt in a wrongdoer can be removed by being forgiven, but first it must be felt and the wrongdoing admitted by the malefactor herself; out of that guilty feeling will arise a need to apologize and to make reparations where possible. What the word *gratitude* means in our culture resembles our concept of guilt in that it is something felt; the feeling gives rise to expression in some form of appropriate action. It follows that apology, for us, is not as different from thanking as it at first appears.

It is reasonable to claim that this internalization of morality came to us in large part through Christianity. Gratitude, like guilt and forgiveness, is a key concept in the Christian worldview. What has occurred in addition to undermine the glories of strutting is the arrival of the Christian virtue of humility. It was impossible—it would indeed have been incomprehensible, a contradiction in terms—to ask Aristotle's Big Man to be humble. Honour is about Size, its difficult procurement, and its protection from reduction, which is the withdrawal, by other people, of their esteem. The chief virtues of honour are courage (for the winning of honour) and pride. This kind of pride, of the type we used to call "vainglory," becomes a vice in the Christian view. Pride still means, as Aristotle would agree, "a proper sense of what is becoming to oneself." But humility adds a readiness to admit one's own faults and to let others have "space"; an ideal of equality is difficult to imagine without it. Christians do not find humility degrading: their ideal heroes or saints think of themselves as "small" rather than "large." In the Gospels, Jesus performs miracles and immediately commands people not to rush off and tell everybody about them. The point is surely the new refusal of the Big Man ideal: what has been done and its consequences are important; praise that merely inflates honour is not. A Christian's identity should not be defined by the opinions of other people. And there is great emphasis placed on the equality of all human beings before God.

What is important here is to recognize that humility is an essential component of thankfulness. (It is notable that Aristotle's famous list of the virtues does not include gratitude.) Grateful people are not affronted by the idea of admitting that somebody else has done them a favour, or of accepting an indebtedness to them, even should that debt turn out to be unrequitable. They are unlikely to suffer, as a recipient of favour, from a feeling that they are "one down." And they are actually pleased to receive a benefit (another part of gratitude is pleasure), even if a thing given should not be to their taste, or a service less than magnificently performed. "It is the mark of a happy disposition to see good rather than evil," writes Thomas Aquinas. "Wherefore, if someone has conferred a favour, not as he ought to have conferred it, the recipient should not for that reason withhold his thanks." There is no question of debt-paying being allowed to replace moral principle, Aquinas continues: one should never repay a benefit by helping another to do something wrong, "because this would be repaying not good but evil."[11] It is the person giving who ought to be the focus, his goodwill that is appreciated. And not only "first gifts" but benefits bestowed in return should be true gifts—that is, freely given.

People often fail, of course, to live up to these ideals. But they know very well what they are. Gift-giving rules deemed "enigmatic" by social scientists can usually be explained quite simply through reference to these principles. Refusing to let people ask for their gifts back if they do not get the return they expected; not allowing anyone the right to enforced or legally backed "gratitude" (meaning "a return gift") as recompense for a favour; claiming paradoxically that giving is better than receiving;[12] persisting in calling a tip a "gratuity"; refusing to accept the expression of a receiver's gratitude ("Not at all—don't mention it—it's nothing"); even refusing to explain exactly why it is that we give back—all these are human strategies that have evolved to protect freedom and equality in giving.

It is true that people break the rules while pretending to keep them, manipulate them in the course of power games, use gifts to put other people down, or deliberately prevent relationship from developing out of giving and receiving. Thomas Hobbes, who apparently thought of himself as a Christian, writes that "benefits oblige; and obligation is thraldome, and unrequitable obligation, perpetuall thraldome, which is to ones equall, hatefull." And he goes on to say that we love being obliged to a superior "because the obligation is no new depression":[13] we are all used to being "depressed," meaning "lowered," by receiving benefits from our betters and then being forced to return them. (We must recall that Hobbes believed that all men were equal by "naturall condition," but that we have had to give up our equality and embrace hierarchy for security reasons.) It is fashionable, as we have seen, to deny the very possibility that anybody could give anything for a reason that is not entirely a matter of his or her own self-interest. But none of the phenomena listed changes the ideal; the breaking of rules does not prove that there are none.

Gift-giving, we saw earlier, is part of a process; one is asking to be mystified by it if one moment in the process is isolated and then relentlessly examined in

its singular state, unconnected with any of the rest. We likened the gift-giving process to the pleasures of playing see-saw: first I go down, then I go up.
The humility of gratitude is the sinking of the see-saw: it is giving the other
person his or her "due," not because I am obliged to grovel, but because I am
genuinely impressed, touched, surprised, pleased—in a word, grateful. Later,
should I be willing, I shall give in my turn—and I shall then occupy the
"higher" place and receive the other person's acknowledgement, her gratitude.
She will "bow" to me, and ours being an ongoing relationship, it will soon
be my turn to bow to her again: the strategy of giving and receiving and
giving back encourages a relationship to last. On the other hand, a see-saw
that maintains equality through constant horizontality is an immobile plank,
a pointless bore for both partners.

Our culture is not very rich in non-verbal signs, but like all human beings,
we accompany our speech with gestures, in many situations that include the
giving and receiving of gifts and favours. It is worth pausing to consider the
gestures that express the humility that is part of gratitude, and the use of
similar actions to mean something very different.

17

Gestures

"Minding one's P's and Q's" means being adept and punctilious about one's behaviour, especially when dealing with other people. At least six explanations are given for this expression. First, in the old days when printers set up type by hand, it was easy to reach for the wrong one of the two letters, especially because the boxes containing p's and q's stood side by side, as these letters stand in the alphabet. Second, the two letters look very similar anyway, so that learners of the alphabet should note their differences. Third, pints and quarts of beer in pubs used to be written up as "p's" and "q's," and customers were wise to keep an eye on the considerable difference in their quantities. Fourth, the expression has a French origin, *pieds* and *queues* ("feet" and "wigs tied back in a bunch at the nape of the neck"): dancing masters warned their pupils to give heed to their feet while executing steps, and prevent their wigs from falling off when they bowed low. Fifth, and alternatively, French women at court were urged to watch their feet so as to avoid tearing and entanglements when wearing a train (*queue*). All of these explanations stress attention and awareness. But most of us today, I think, take most naturally to the sixth explanation: P's and Q's are Pleases and Thank*you*s. We know that those who wish to live in ease and friendship with their fellows will be competent practitioners in the arts of observing ("minding"), asking, and thanking. (The sense, however, that this is what we are being exhorted to do by the maxim probably also means that we are in danger of forgetting to obey it.)

Gratitude, like petitioning, has to do with the principle in our culture that receivers and, of course, askers too are normally "lower" than are givers, even when givers insist that the reverse is true. Receivers and petitioners show deference, therefore, in speech—and also through gesture and body postures. In Dante's *Inferno,* at the bottommost circle of hell, the ungrateful are punished by being eternally frozen in the postures of deference they had failed to perform during their lifetimes: trapped rigid in enveloping ice, they stand erect or upside down, lie prone, or bow face to feet.[1]

Non-verbal submissiveness is commonly found among animals: cringing and crouching (hanging back and sinking to the ground) are common, as are mechanisms such as the cock's lowering his crest, showing that he has laid aside his belligerence and hopes his antagonist will feel it unnecessary to attack. These actions make the animal smaller. They also inhibit its rage and combativeness, and physically display the fact that this inhibition has taken place. A normally voracious fish floats head down and tail up before a cleaner wrasse, demonstrating its non-aggressive state as it prepares to enter the remarkable "cleaning" symbiosis. But the observing scientist who exclaims that the fish was "just begging to be cleaned"[2] must merely have been trying to entertain her television audience. A human bow is a very different thing from that of a fish. An instinctual component remains, but the act is in the main intentional: a performance that is learned, then deliberately polished and perfected through the medium of culture. A bow may be a social obligation, or a cold formality, or sincere and highly emotional, or filled with complex suggestiveness, or used as a disguise for countless seething thoughts, or slyly manipulative. It may also be merely culturally inappropriate.

Lower than a bow and much more intense, prostration is a gesture accepting a great difference in status between the superior, who is usually standing or sitting at the time, and the one at her feet. *Prostration* means lying on the ground before someone, literally or figuratively "kissing the dust" and perhaps kissing her feet, sometimes three times, as well. The word can be used for lying full length or for kneeling and then bringing one's head to the ground; in the latter case the bowing action can be performed several times. Prostration almost never occurs in public in modern Western cultures. An exception is the intense moment of consecration to God of priests and nuns and bishops in Catholic professions or ordination services: lying face down and at full length before the altar, and in the presence of the congregation, means total dedication and humility in people proclaiming their desire to serve others rather than be served. The word *humility* comes from *humus,* earth. When people prostrate themselves, they take the etymology literally and lie level with the earth, sit on the ground, or touch the earth with their heads, and so express their lowliness. Orthodox Christians bend forward and touch the ground with the right hand in ritual prayer; otherwise, prostrations (to God alone) are purely personal Christian practice. Islamic ritual prayer involves repeated prostrations in the direction of Mecca (*sujud*), but only before God.[3]

Prostration before human beings is recorded in the Bible; in the main this action signifies profound gratitude. Joseph presents his sons to his father Jacob to bless, and then falls to the ground to thank his father.[4] Ruth prostrates herself when she thanks Boaz for taking her under his protection.[5] The Shulamite woman, whose son was brought to life by Elisha, falls at Gehazi's feet.[6] In the New Testament Jesus heals ten lepers, but only one comes back to thank him, falling at his feet to do so.[7]

In all these cases the gesture demonstrates awe and wonder—the benefactor is in two instances a miracle worker—in addition to gratitude. Elsewhere, however, a great favour between friends results in prostration. Jonathan loves David, but his father King Saul hates David and wants to kill him. Jonathan, in opposition to his father and his king, saves his friend's life. And David "fell with his face to the ground and bowed down three times. Then they kissed each other and both shed many tears."[8] A friend—not a subordinate—

who is intensely grateful deliberately lowers himself, in this way honouring the benefactor in a physical action that displays the strength of his personal emotions. Kissing and weeping express love, gratitude, relief, and amazement at the power of love.

Among the Gonja people of northern Ghana, greeting is traditionally used for thanking.[9] This is a society that places great store by rank. A song they often sing points out that "the arm-pit is not higher than the shoulder"—in other words, precedence is birth-given and natural, and to challenge it unthinkable. "Greeting" starts a conversation, defines and affirms status, and can be used when entering upon the manipulation of a relationship with an end in view. One phrase this society uses for "thank you" is "*Ansa ni kushung!*," "Greetings for your work!" But it is more common to say when thanking, "*Me choro,*" "I greet you!" Every day family members greet by saying these words, a junior member of the family having to approach a senior (never the other way round) and crouch at his open door to do it. Twice a week the community's elders have to greet and thank the chiefs. They remove their hats and lie down on their left sides, left arms extended. (This is the male's mode of self-abasement: the female's is to lie down on the right side, right arm extended.) People hesitate to withhold greeting-and-thanking from a superior, even if he is a political opponent. On a famous occasion during the nineteenth century, a chief summoned his rivals to greet him, and provided only a sea of mud as space for their prostrations. His guests did not demur. Only later did they rebel against the man who had humiliated them.

Thanking on less formal occasions may be accompanied among the Gonja by more ordinary gestures of deference: removing the hat, crouching, kneeling, gently clapping hands. Thanking may also be expressed after a lapse of time through return gifts, or actions to please the benefactor, or visits that include the self-lowering that is expressed in physical greeting-and-thanking. The non-verbal expression of respect and deference is in itself a gift to a man's honour. If anyone wants to receive favours from another, he has to visit him and perform greeting-and-thanking many times before making his desire known: relationship is required before giving can begin. At a funeral wake people dance and play musical instruments for those who attend. Afterwards the men of the deceased's family go round to each household whose men had given money and joined in the dancing and gratify them by "greeting" them. This ritual brings the funeral to an official end and thanks others for their help.[10] It is instructive to hear that among the neighbouring LoDagaa, a society very different because not hierarchically organized, no abasement gestures are customary, and there are no rules about who is to approach whom. The LoDagaa people also deny that they would prostrate themselves before anyone.

In Classical Greece prostration (*proskynesis*) before human beings was habitually condemned as barbarian practice, behaviour typical of slavish races ruled by kings. However, the institution of suppliancy (*hiketeia*) in Greece laid down a gestural ritual, performed as an immensely emotional drama, which recurs many times in Greek epic and in Attic theatre.[11] A suppliant, having ostentatiously disarmed himself, could make his plea to a standing figure by kneeling and flinging his arms round the mighty one's legs at knee level, sometimes kissing his knees as well. The knees, in ancient Greece, were strategic points of both weakness and power in the human body: they were sites of the life force. Often the subject of vivid attention in Greek sculpture, they represented the energy of the human form.[12]

The suppliant would hang on; he was miming aggression even as he inverted it by abject self-abasement. He "attacked" the future benefactor at his most vulnerable points, refusing to let go or to leave. Paradoxically, all this was in its way a gift of honour to the honourable. The honoured man was at once grateful, in his fashion, and appalled. He was caught: he could do no other than raise his suppliant, first physically and then by granting the request, being obliged, and often pressured by the presence of expectant and judg-mental onlookers, to break the unbearable tension, redeem the intolerable shame of his "aggressor" and restore the honour—the human dignity—that had been deliberately forgone in the dramatization of needy wretchedness.

Suppliancy was an extreme measure, but as long as honour could be counted on to motivate the "victim" of the assault, it worked.

Homer's *Iliad* begins with one such scene and ends with another. In the first of these, Thetis, the mother of Achilles, goes to Zeus to beg for the restoration of her son's diminished honour. She crouches before the enthroned god, touching his knees with her left hand and holding his chin in her right. Zeus nods and gives Thetis what she wants.[13] At the end of the *Iliad,* Priam, the king of the doomed city of Troy, comes to beg Achilles for the body of Hektor, so that he might bury his heroic son. Achilles has killed Hektor, in the wrath—for honour lost and in vengeance for his friend's death—that is the poet's theme. Homer describes how Priam walks wholly unexpectedly into the tent of Achilles, falls to his knees, and clasps the young man's knees: "He kissed the dread murderous hands that had killed so many of his sons."[14] This act, which breaks in one stroke the mighty laws of honour, of blood pollution, and of vengeance for kin murder, is the shattering emotional climax of the entire epic.

After a horrified silence, during which Achilles allows the appearance of his enemy, Priam, to call to his mind his own dead father, the hero breaks the suppliant's hold: he gently pushes Priam away from him. (Respect, as we saw earlier, requires distance: it is standing back so as, in the literal meaning of the word, to *look* at the other.) Both men together then succumb to their endless grief over the deaths of a father, a son, a friend. Priam lies at Achilles' feet, no longer holding on to him, and "the house was filled with their lamentation." Achilles finally raises Priam to a standing position, then invites him to sit down. Priam refuses, and by this limit placed on his generosity, Achilles is pushed almost over the edge, back into his anger: he is tempted to sin against suppliancy and treat his suppliant as the enemy that normally he is.

But Priam sits; Achilles takes the ransom given for the body of Hektor and himself lifts the corpse onto the wagon Priam has brought. The two men then share a meal, famished as they are: for many days they have not been able to eat for grief. All the meanings implicit in a meal eaten together are included in this action: balance and common humanity (for everyone, Homer tells us, even mothers whose children have been murdered, must in the end take food), relationship and agreement, a re-established equality, and resignation and communion in the face of relentless Fate. Now the two men find it possible to appreciate one another: "Priam marvelled at the beauty of Achilles for he was as a god to see, and Achilles marvelled at Priam as he listened to him and looked upon his noble presence." There will be ten days' truce to bury Hektor. And then the fighting and the killing will begin again. All listeners to the *Iliad* knew that it remained—it was Fate—for both Achilles and Priam to die, and Troy to go down in flames.

Suppliancy was a device that could act as a safety valve to an honour-and-shame culture, and to its related vengeance system. By turning the conventional world upside down for a moment, it could bring about a truce to enmity. Through a formal ritual that relied on the intense emotions and the motivating power that honour itself supplied to a hierarchical structure, it occasionally allowed the weak in their extremity to prevail over the powerful, a crying need to be supplied, transcendence to arise. Suppliancy constrained the powerful to give to the weak in return for the suppliant's two gifts: the first of his own honour, of which he divested himself in order to hand it over, thereby increasing the honour of his future benefactor; and the second of letting go once his point had been made. The powerful one had seen, understood, and now was grateful to be released, while the suppliant mercifully agreed to become an honourable human being once more. The supplicated opened his hand, and gave.

The Chinese *k'o-t'ou*, (literally "knock head") known in English as "kowtow," involved kneeling, lowering one's head to the ground before one being honoured, and bumping it three times. The rationale was that "when a person so abases himself before another as to rub his head in the dust, the person receiving the honor is bound to save the kowtower's face, that is, restore his human dignity by showing great favor or kindness."[15] Reasoning similar to this is often found in societies based on the principles of honour. The practice was adopted in Japan between AD 700 and 900. In 1192 it became official court etiquette.[16] Until 1868, one kowtowed to the emperor, to court officials, to the shogun, to government ministers. For kowtowing, like suppliancy except that it was common rather than extraordinary, helped underwrite prestige in the powerful and hierarchy in general; it came eventually to amount merely to a mark of respect. Failure to kowtow, however, when superiors required it, could mean death. People still kowtowed on very formal occasions in Japan until 1945. But today bowing has taken its place, the shift in manners constituting an intentional expression of the changes that have taken place in Japanese society. Bowing is in no way demeaning. It is a sign of polite consideration for other people, nothing more—and nothing less.

There are different kinds of bow in Japan. A light one is used by superiors to inferiors, or for casual occasions among equals: greetings, farewells, as signals to draw attention, to ask questions, to indicate that one has understood directions, and to accompany many other strategies of daily converse. A medium bow is for extremely polite, formal occasions and for inferiors to superiors. A deep bow is kept for expressing strong emotions: great sincerity, respect, sorrow, and (crudely to use a Western word) gratitude. The Japanese have begun to adopt the Western habit of hand-shaking—in addition to light bowing—for everyday occasions. They point out, however, that a quick bow is in fact easier and much more convenient than is shaking hands.

Japanese children start learning non-verbal expressions of apology (which, as we saw, commonly takes the place of our thanking) at the age of eighteen months.[17] They rub each other's heads (Japanese children are taught to be comforted by this gesture) and also bow, though only when prompted to do so. At two to three years of age they apologize spontaneously, provided that they are absolutely sure they are to blame. (The article chronicling this behaviour does not speak of thanks.) The word the children use for "sorry" is first *gomen* and then, at as young as three, the more formal *gomennasai:* the complex "public" term, *sumimasen,* is introduced later. By three and a half, Japanese children apologize without having to be prompted. They appear to say they are sorry not only when they know they have done something to make life difficult, but also because they realize that other people like to receive an apology, and that a continued good relationship with them depends on it. In other words, they know that apology not only repairs but also enhances a relationship. They are also fully cognizant that words are not enough: one has to make restitution; one has to give something back.

In our own culture bowing gradually replaced kneeling. In the Middle Ages men knelt on two knees to God and on one to their superiors; women knelt on both knees to both God and human beings. Ceremonial kneeling to other people was known in the sixteenth century as a *courtesy,* which was behaviour refined enough to be the habit of courtiers. *Bowing* (the word rhymed with *rowing*) meant gracefully lowering the body by bending one or both knees.[18]

By the nineteenth century the bow (now rhyming with *bough*) came to require rigid knees and bending the torso forward from the waist only. "Courtesying," shortened to "curtsying," now meant lowering the body by bending both knees—with adjustments contributed by the feet—and simultaneously increasing one's width by spreading one's skirts. This gesture became the female equivalent of a bow. A curtsy is an unstable posture that needs to be learned through practice because it is a movement difficult to achieve with poise and dignity. It has been suggested that curtsying is inherently more submissive than bowing because it lowers the whole body.[19]

Respect is an attitude, provided that it is reinforced by emotion, that lies very close to gratitude and may overlap with it. Many of the gestures expressing gratefulness also show respect. For us, respect is formally expressed by stiffening as opposed to relaxing one's posture, which is why people rise from their seats when a superior person enters the room. But physically lowering oneself remains appropriate. Men, for example, should they be wearing hats, must still take their headgear off and bow slightly. Curtsying has almost disappeared in recent times: modern women's clothing would in itself have seen to this. The bow has now been reduced mostly to a nod, an inclination of the head alone; its use is extremely common, and women nod as well as men. Nodding is a signal of agreement and encouragement.[20] It is also used for recognition and acknowledgement; as such, it is employed when thanking and may suffice for the purpose.

Bowing and nodding have the advantage that they can be done while sitting or kneeling, and do not require moving towards the object of one's esteem, as hand-shaking does. Bowing can therefore be frequently performed during the constant give-and-take during meals in Japan, where bowing is the norm.[21] On arriving as a guest, a traditional Japanese gentleman in 1908 would bow low, one hand holding his knee; to express his emotion he might simultaneously suck his breath rapidly and audibly in through his teeth. A woman would fall to her knees, her head almost touching the floor.[22] The Chinese Li Chi (first century BC) pronounces that: "Guest and host bow on the guest's arrival, as the cup is washed, when the cup is received, when it is presented in return, when the drinking is over. This prevents quarrels . . . Every act of courtesy requires a bow."[23]

It has often been the custom that hosts expressed their esteem by passing delicacies to certain guests, who were bound to accept and eat them. In eighteenth-century France Jean-Baptiste de La Salle writes, "One must receive with thanks whatever one is presented: this is done by bringing the plate towards one's mouth as if to kiss it, and at the same time making a polite bow ['une honnête inclination']."[24] The Li Chi advises the guest to whom a piece of fruit was offered as a token of esteem to show appreciation by bowing first, eating the fruit, and then sucking the pip clean and slipping it down the front of his robe, to show that he was not throwing any of the gift away.

Gesturing, of course, is done mainly with the hands. In Mediterranean cultures people famously feel incapable of talking without accompanying their words—or even replacing them—with hand movements, and various head and body movements as well. Arabic gestures are generally confined to the hands. Out of 247 Arab gestures catalogued in one study, 66 of them are confined to the right hand, with an additional 75 involving the right hand

and some part of the body; where both hands are used, the right is privileged. Indeed, the left hand in this culture is inappropriate for communicating feelings.[25] Arabs gesturing in order to express gratitude will use the right hand almost without exception: thanking must convey sincerity.

Kissing among Arabs is offered as a sign of loyalty and status, lower to higher. People of inferior standing may express extreme respect by kissing a superior on the forehead, nose, feet, right shoulder, or right hand. A plea for mercy once involved kissing a dignitary's right hand or foot. Gratefulness is expressed to another by kissing the back of the right hand, then raising it with the palm up. When the eyes are also raised, this gesture expresses thanks in the name of Allah. In the give-and-take of small intimacies such as someone's lighting another's cigarette, the receiver touches the back of the benefactor's hand with the tips of his right fingers, then places them on his forehead in a sort of salute, and bows the head slightly forward. When the palm of the right hand is placed on the chest, sometimes with the head bowed and the eyes closed, a person is expressing thanks—a matter of the heart.[26]

In our culture, one clear demonstration of gratitude used to be clasping one's hands together, raising them, and even moving them both back and forth, to express emotion and possibly to draw attention to the action. This was so insistent a gesture that it came to be suspected of insincerity or even thought worthy of ridicule, particularly if another extravagant movement was added to it: "You have given me life, Madam, said I, clasping my uplifted hands together, and falling on one knee."[27]

A widespread stricture is that one should not, when being given something directly by another person, simply hold out one hand. Even in our own culture we tend to compensate for the minimalism of this gesture by adding words of thanks, bowing slightly, smiling, and so on. (The rules do not apply in very intimate circumstances, or if people are concentrating on working together.) When a person receives Communion in the hand in Catholic churches today, the correct way is to hold out *both* hands, open right palm up and cradled in left, to show reverence and gratitude. In Mediterranean

countries, thrusting out one hand to receive something without any mollifying word or sign such as a bow is the behaviour either of the arrogant, or of
beggars of the "shameless" type: taking without thanking is offensive, almost
aggressive, behaviour. In similar fashion, Africans were shocked by the habit
of northern European colonials, who habitually took things in one hand. For
the Zulus, receiving in one hand was a rude suggestion that the host's generosity was small. A Malawian riddle, collected in 1939, asks what this object
might be:

RIDDLE: Even the *Mzungu* (European) respects this. What is it?
ANSWER: A peanut.
(Even a European takes it in both hands to shell it.)[28]

In Burmese myth, *lapet,* or tea salad, a plant eaten in the sealing of all bar-
gains, was a gift originally given in gratitude for saving the life of a drowning
boy. But the tiny tea salad seed was taken by each of two planters in only one
hand—and therefore they remained poor, despite the riches the plant would
otherwise have brought them. The plant's name, derived from *let-tit-pet,* "one
hand," reminds all those entering into exchange relationships to remember
respect and gratitude.[29]

It is speaking one's thanks that is most common in modern Western
cultures, and we have seen that we are not, on the whole and at least for
the time being, parsimonious about offering this simple form of respect.
We do occasionally bow and nod our thankfulness as well. On emotionally
charged occasions among intimates, we hug and may also kiss one another
to express gratitude. And we shake hands, in a physical embodiment of the
mutual appreciation that links two persons. This gesture has since Classical
times symbolized honour, solemn alliance, the forming of a contract, and
confidence generally between the two people performing the action. Using
the right hand for it is sometimes said to have arisen as a "disarming" gesture:
showing that one had no intention of seizing a weapon. In Europe people

used to kiss each other formally in public far more than they do now. (It was always a practice liable to be condemned for reasons of health or purity: ancient Egyptians, Herodotus tells us, used to refuse to kiss Greeks on the mouth because they thought Greek food unclean.)[30] During the nineteenth century in northern Europe, public kissing began to be discouraged. People stood back from one other, and started shaking hands if they wished to make their point about connectedness.

Hand-shaking still accompanies meetings and leave-takings, congratulations, and also formal thanking. It is an egalitarian gesture, carried out by women and men; though formal, it is also intimate, since it involves direct contact with another's clasping hand. Importantly for the expression of gratitude, the action requires two persons to perform it and is limited entirely to these two. The French are particularly punctilious about shaking hands, insisting, for example, that every time someone joins a group or leaves it he or she should shake hands with every single person present. Kissing—or miming doing so—on both cheeks has been maintained in Latin countries generally. North Americans and northern Europeans have recently taken up polite kissing again, using the Latin manner of doing it, after more than a century of normally refraining from the practice.

Applause achieved by striking our hands together means in our culture appreciation and agreement; it is a reward, granted by the group, for a performance they admire. The word comes from the Latin *plaudere,* "to beat," with an attempt (the Latin vowels rhyme with *pow!*) to imitate the sound of loud clapping; *clap* is a similarly echoic word. *To explode* originally meant "to make someone leave by loudly clapping the hands"; we still speak of an idea being exploded. *Plausible*, which meant at first "worthy of applause," came to signify "specious, ingratiating, and (merely) fair-spoken." (Only very recently the word has come mainly to mean "possibly acceptable to the intelligence.")

In Spain people often clap their hands at a funeral, which can be quite shocking for Anglo-Saxons, who take clapping, as in the Bible, to be a sign of delight, or at least of pleasure. The Spanish, however, are showing respect—which almost certainly includes gratitude—towards the deceased person and their togetherness in grief at this death. An audience in a theatre unites itself in one group with an artist, whether actor or musician, by applauding at the end of a work. In our culture art, despite the high prices it may fetch, is carefully distinguished from commerce. The artist—a "gifted" human being—has "given of himself" in any dramatic performance and is pleased if the audience members—the receivers of his gift—do the same in return at the end of the work. This they do by applauding, and on occasion standing up for an "ovation" (from Latin *ovare,* "to utter cries of joy"),[31] shouting and stamping and begging for more.

Speech givers often elicit applause deliberately.[32] To do this, they make signs, understood semi-subliminally by the audience, that they are saying something that everybody should think admirable, and therefore they expect applause; the audience, surprisingly often, complies, thus showing that "we all agree." For applause gathers a group together; a speaker angling for applause says "we," and so claims to be the spokesperson for everybody present. The word for an oratorical sign that the audience should now applaud is a *claptrap;* advance information is supplied to warn the audience that it is about to be swept up into applause. So cliché-ridden are these devices that *claptrap* is now synonymous with a series of worthless though rousing remarks. Modern examples of claptraps in the original sense, found, for example, in political speeches, are the mention of predictable, obviously desirable goals such as "peace," assurances that things are getting better, expressions of relief that obstacles have been overcome, and expressions of gratitude towards people—they must be *named* people—who have helped in an enterprise.

A speaker prepares for applause by the way she phrases sentences, or by making a pause for clapping before she introduces a new subject, or both. Given the right signals and timing, a supportive audience will clap almost automatically. A practised speaker can evoke applause at the end of every paragraph delivered. An audience in the swing of things will quite commonly start to clap before a speaker's applause-readying sentence is complete. When she has successfully provoked applause, the speaker may give a fond look around at the listeners, waiting for the applause to die down. People apparently tend to desist from clapping for a group of people who are thanked by name at the end of as opposed to during a speech: such a peroration is presumably too long and dull to arouse applause. In any case the audience is gathering itself to applaud the performer standing before it. Applause resembles thanks in being directed to specific persons who are, if possible, present on the occasion. Like thanks, in formal circumstances clapping is dutifully supplied at moments, even "set-up" moments, that seem because of the conventional rhythms of speech to require its interjection. Applause also declares a link, as we have seen, between performer and audience.

Being a kind of praise and often a form of gratitude as well, applause puts on a pedestal the person being applauded, and those thus raised tend to respond with grateful nods and bows. Nowadays theatrical performers often "equalize" at the end of the show by clapping the audience in return, showing gratitude and appreciation to the people for coming and for being responsive. Finally, applause marks the end of proceedings in much the same way that thanking closes a conversation. At a recent theatrical performance in London the audience was explicitly forbidden to applaud, "because the situation depicted in the play was still going on."[33]

18

Memory and Narrative

When the modern philosopher Martin Heidegger ruminates on what exactly we mean by "think," "thinking," and "thought,"[1] he reaches, as he often does, into the etymology of words. In German, *denken,* "to think," is related to *danken,* "to thank." Memory is a kind of thinking: *Gedächtnis,* from the past participle of the verb *denken.* Most moving and most revelatory to him, however, is the Old English noun for thinking: *thonc* or *thanc.* The *thanc* meant not "a notion," but what it is that gives rise to what we now call "thoughts." The *thanc* was "the gathered, all-gathering, thinking that recalls." It was the human being's disposition, our "heart's core."

Truth, for Heidegger, is not correctness, but rather what is otherwise hidden from us but now revealed—through thinking. The etymology of the Greek word for truth, *aletheia,* is "not being the victim of oblivion, *lethe.*" (Lethe was the river in the underworld that caused those who drank from it to forget.) Thinking and philosophy have the task of revealing. Real thinking takes place in the *thanc,* and it is what makes us human: the more thoughtless we are, the less human.

The assumption is that something exists which is to be "dis-covered," something that needs to be revealed in order to be known. Thinking, however, is not questing by nature, but rather receptive. It "receives a call" from the nature of things, and it responds to that call. Thinking, then, is grateful in its essence: it receives and responds. German famously uses the words *es gibt* ("it gives") for English "there is" and "there are." (We ourselves talk of what we call a "received" supposition as "a given.") Being, then, is not a thing but an event. It is an event that mere beings forget. And human beings are called to recollect this event of the gift of Being. Thinking, says Heidegger, cannot force the gift of the call, from What Is, to think. We do not think by willing. All we can do is prepare ourselves so that we can hear the call when it comes, listen and attend to "the given," accept it, and respond. The overcoming of forgetting is what the *thanc* in its thinking is called to do.

"Both memory and thanks," writes Heidegger, "move and have their being in the *thanc*." By "memory" he means "a constant abiding with something," not only what has passed but what is present and leading to the future. "Memory" is a form of awareness; it is attention paid; it is faithfulness. (A faithful person, we say in English as in German, is "true.") Like thinking, remembering is a grateful action. It is not only recollection, but also "an unrelinquishing and unrelenting retention" in the *thanc*.

"In giving thanks," Heidegger continues, "the heart gives thought to what it has and what it is."[2] The supreme thanks would be thinking—remembering the gift of our being. And utter thanklessness would be thoughtlessness. Heidegger wonders which came first—thinking, or thanking? Both involve memory. Yet thanks, like verbal thanking or a return gift or a votive offering, is something that one gives. "Pure thanks," says Heidegger, "is not giving back. It is simply thinking. . . . This thinking . . . does not need to repay, nor be deserved, in order to give thanks. Such thanks is not a recompense; but it remains an offering."

In ancient Greek, *charis* meant, at first, only "favour." This word later came to mean "gratitude,"[3] and when it did, the expression we would translate as "I am grateful" was most frequently "I know *charis*" or "I have *charis*": that is, "I know the favour [which I have received]" or "I have the favour and I know it."[4] Gratitude was something one *knew*. It involved the thought that the benefactor was the source of favour, and this thought was deemed to require declaration on the spot: "I know *charis.*" In Indian Buddhism the tradition lists *krtajna* and *krtavedana* as the nearest thing to "gratitude"; these words mean literally "the act of being aware of what has been done (*krta*) for me." Repaying the kindness will be the next step—but the terms limit themselves to the awareness.[5]

Gratitude on the practical level depends on the use of one's reason; there is an appropriateness about it. A modern ethicist has pointed out that if you helped someone not knowing that she was a previous benefactor, you would not have helped her out of gratitude. He concludes that gratitude must involve benefiting others *discriminately.*[6] This is in a sense correct: we do try, out of gratitude, to find ways of helping specifically those who have helped us; gratitude is personal. Yet it is a mistake to limit gratitude to a strictly targeted reciprocity; one could give, for example, to one person out of gratitude to someone else. If gratitude is in part *knowing*, it has far greater scope and depth than precise reciprocity allows, as Heidegger's approach has already demonstrated.

The declaration of one's gratitude—having the favour, knowing it, and saying so—takes place out of a recognition that a benefactor's thoughts, intentions, and efforts cannot, in fact, be repaid like a debt. Indeed, they cannot be "repaid" at all; they can only be *acknowledged.* The word *acknowledgement* entails knowing, as does the Latin-derived term *recognition.* This acknowledging and recognizing are what the French most commonly take to mean gratitude itself: *reconnaissance.*[7] Recognizing by means of saying one is grateful actually constitutes, in some circumstances, a return gift.[8]

Seneca counsels the use of reason in giving: "No gift can be a benefit unless it is given with reason, since every virtuous act is accompanied by reason." We should therefore consider, he says, when to give, to whom, and how and why. The person chosen should be one who is worthy of receiving, one who will be grateful: the likelihood that he will make a return, however, should not be a criterion. "It often happens that the grateful man is one who is not likely to make a return, while the ungrateful man is one who has done so." Seneca does lend support, however, to the Latin adage that "a farmer does not commit his seeds to sand."[9] Seneca's noble approach to giving and thanking, at least in this part of his Book Four, is close to the ideal found in the Christian Gospels, where giving should indeed require thinking, but not figuring out one's own advantage. Yet in the Gospels, God himself fails to heed the proverb about not bothering to sow seed in sand: in the parable of the Sower, the seed that is God's Word falls (is given) everywhere, in the same way that the sun shines "indiscriminately," on the just and the unjust alike.[10] Thinking takes place when human beings imitate God in their giving, but thinking does not select the receiver on the grounds of her moral worthiness, or because she is likely to "give back"—or, indeed, be grateful.

The thinking that ought to go on in the process of both giving and being grateful is encouraged by social customs. These include leaving what to give up to the giver, who has therefore to ponder what gift might please this particular beneficiary; and the injunction to wait a while before thanking a host for hospitality or before making a return gift. Gratitude can actually be evoked by reflection. This is the reason why we sometimes ask people to stand for two minutes in silence, on Armistice Day, for example. The commemoration of the fallen in the First World War, which has taken place at the eleventh hour of the eleventh day of the eleventh month of every year since 1918, changed its name in 1946 to Remembrance Day, to include a memorial of the dead in the Second World War as well. Taking time out to pay attention and to remember is meant at least in part to invite people to make the further step (in liberty, because gratitude is *gratis*) of being grateful to those who "gave their lives," as we say, for their country's cause and protection.

When the early sociologist Georg Simmel turns his mind to the two questions perhaps most fundamental to sociology—"How and why do societies change?" and "What is it that enables them to stay the same, even as they change?"—he chooses Faithfulness and Gratitude as two significant and related strategies that human groups employ to achieve stability.[11] Faithfulness for Simmel is keeping commitments, while gratitude "establishes the bond of interaction." Both are necessary for society because they supplement the legal order. (We might now add that they help fill in the huge gaps in human well-being that "the market" cannot satisfy.) Gratitude and faithfulness assure continuance, especially needed in an individualistic society. "If every grateful action," Simmel writes, "which lingers on from good turns received in the past, were suddenly eliminated, society (at least as we know it) would break apart." He insists on the "atmosphere of obligation" with which social pressure surrounds thanksgiving, and on gratitude's creation of "microscopic but infinitely tough threads" that bind society together: "Gratitude is perhaps the only feeling which, under all circumstances, can be morally demanded and rendered . . . [It] seems to reside in a point in us which we do not allow to change. . . . Gratitude, as it were, is the moral memory of mankind."

Given the extraordinary importance to society of gratitude in Simmel's view, and the fundamental role for our very humanity that Heidegger attributes to thanking, it is remarkable how often, in cynical witticisms, we hear the complaint that true gratitude is seldom to be found—that an injury is nursed for years, for example, but a benefit is soon forgotten.[12] Seneca even says that it is unkind to be angry with someone who has not remembered the kindnesses one has done him in the past, because such forgetfulness is "a universal failing," and you are probably guilty of it yourself.[13] "The memory is a very frail vessel," he adds. And when it founders, gratitude sinks with it.

Seneca advises, therefore, giving someone a durable gift, "for they are few indeed who are so grateful that they think of what they have received even if they do not see it." We have noted how hard it is for a child to remember to say "thank you" for a gift when it is no longer in her arms to remind her. Favours that are not concrete presents are easy to forget. Good manners, Seneca continues, demand that we never remind people of what we have done for them, for that might seem to be asking for something in return. But an object is capable of reviving the memory that is fading: "I shall be more willing to give wrought than coined silver; more willing to give statues than clothing or something that will wear out after brief usage. Few there are whose gratitude survives longer than the object given . . ."[14] It is notable that even in Seneca's day money could be thought of as not memorable enough to constitute a personal gift. It cannot adorn anything or be displayed; it will soon be spent and forgotten; it is simply not interesting enough, in and of itself. Rena Lederman describes how shells among the Mende people of Papua New Guinea constitute "mnemonic records." People say that they make a distribution of riches "big," as money cannot, for money can neither adorn nor be displayed. And furthermore, "with shells people have more to talk and argue about."[15]

An important feature of gratitude is its ability to bind a person into memory and into a rich story of interrelationship. Being part of a story is essential to human personhood. A person (as opposed to an "individual") is inextricable from interrelationship with others; one is a character in one's own story, as well as in the stories of other people. "Man is in his actions and practice, as well as in his fictions, essentially a story-telling animal," writes Alasdair MacIntyre, adding that "I can only answer the question 'What am I to do?' if I can answer the prior question 'Of what story or stories do I find myself a part?'"[16] One could also say that decisions can arise out of what stories one wants to enact. And James Alison reminds us that "someone without a memory not only does not know what happened in the past, but quite literally does not know who he or she is: that is what happens in grave cases of amnesia."[17]

Memory creates narrative, but narrative can also ensure the durability of memory. And a tale can last and achieve constant retelling through social custom: impressive stories are told beautifully and repeated, and they may be deliberately attached to physical, durable objects. Ancient Spartan soldiers would sacrifice to the Muses, the goddesses of memory and poetry, before they went into battle, in their determination to do deeds worthy of being remembered in song for generations.[18] Athletic victories won twenty-five centuries ago in Greece are still recalled because poets of the quality of Pindar wrote odes of praise for the victors, not only celebrating their triumphs but also adorning their family histories with erudite and striking mythological exempla; the glory of winning was turned into mystical song and remains available for contemplation today.

In Greek epic, funeral games were celebrated for dead heroes: the prizes won in the games[19] would be handed down through generations in the victors' families with the stories of their winning attached to them, the objects themselves remaining as reminders and as evocations of each family's noble past. (The custom persists in the display of sporting trophies on modern family mantelpieces.) The tomb of the dead man was erected as a monument when the games were over. The one for the dead Achilles was itself remembered in epic song:

> And then we, the sacred army of Argive spearmen, heaped
> a great and excellent funeral mound up over Achilles' bones
> on a strand jutting forward on the broad Hellespont,
> so that it might be seen far over the ocean by men,
> both those who are born now and those who shall be hereafter.
> . . . You were very dear to the gods.
> So you did not lose your name even when you died, Achilles.
> There should be noble renown for you always among men.[20]

In modern times we have war memorials to honour those fallen in battle. But in the context of our very different society, such monuments are liable to elicit reactions quite dissimilar from the admiration offered to the splendour of Achilles. In Britain for example, monuments raised after the First World War remember ordinary soldiers, not men of "renown"; they refer to "everyman" killed in battle.[21] The ideal figures depicted on war memorials were taken to be those who had *volunteered* to fight, those who first responded to the call to arms, and who, as it turned out, died in the greatest numbers. The act of having freely chosen to enlist made gratitude to them a natural response. These young men (and women, because for the first time in history ordinary non-combatants, including women, were commemorated by war memorials) were understood to have died saving their country from even worse horrors than the war had spawned. People felt, and were encouraged to feel, that it was incumbent on the survivors to ensure that these sacrifices, these gifts of their lives, had not been offered in vain.[22]

But the latter half of the twentieth century has taught us a very different attitude to war: we are capable far more easily of regarding the lives of our war dead as pitifully wasted. We feel horrified at their loss, and guilty. In the Second World War there was conscription; the huge numbers of soldiers were not a professional fighting class and were not, on the whole, volunteers. Non-combatant citizens—people like ourselves—died as horribly as soldiers did and in even greater numbers. Gratitude is a response to the behaviour of others, not ourselves.

More recently, we have taken to erecting walls of names of the dead— all of them grouped together and not only those from a specific town. (It was after the First World War that it became common practice to list alphabetically on local war memorials the names of all soldiers who had died. Meanwhile the people who erected the monuments, who in the past always expected to be named on them, began to receive no mention; artists signed their work discreetly or not at all.) We feel that we owe it to the dead that they should not remain anonymous, that we should pay personal attention to each one of them, regardless of class or rank. Here we might locate an element of gratitude, although we often say we are grateful for the lives of the fallen rather than for their deaths; gratitude is always an intensely specific and personal matter. A relatively new practice is to recite all the names of the dead—both combatant and non-combatant victims, from all over—aloud, one name after the other, the very time needed to say all the names being a reminder of the extent of our loss. Reading the names unites the living in sympathy. The idealists among us try to feel too that we can most appropriately "give something back" to the dead by preventing war in the future, that in this way we can try to give meaning to these otherwise senseless deaths.

Gratitude is always profoundly meaningful; it springs from meaning and also creates it. The solid monuments (the root of this word is *mind;* a monument is literally "something that calls to mind") are there to keep all of us thinking and remembering. Gratitude is about making the past continue to affect the present.

It may also reach into the future. People who leave money to others when they die normally give because they are gratefully mindful of their friends, and of course without any hope that they will receive a "return," other than the thought that their inheritors might perhaps feel grateful for having been remembered in the giver's will. Leaving money to members of one's family may be different, where people think of themselves less as individuals than as parts of a family, to the fortunes of which they must make their contribution. It is certainly true that estate decisions about who shall receive what do exert power beyond the grave.[23]

Psychologists have located a thought-pattern that they name "generativity." It occurs in highly successful middle-aged or older people who have usually maintained a lifelong habit of gratitude. They remember the opportunities and advantages they enjoyed earlier in life, and in gratitude to everyone who ever helped them and in a desire to help others less fortunate, they endow scholarships, build libraries, pay for research projects, provide sports stadia, and so on. In return, it is true, they enhance their already glowing reputations. Many of them insist on having their names attached to their gifts to the public—but others are modest about receiving acknowledgements or may even ask for their gifts to remain anonymous. They provide material for discussion among social scientists reluctant to admit instances of "altruism." "High generativity" is said to derive from "a commitment story"—an instance, perhaps, of what Simmel calls "faithfulness"—that ends up inspiring the powerful to help others.[24]

Much of the meaningfulness inherent in gratitude flows from this linkage of past to present to future. A complete sequence of actions and characters, people giving objects or doing favours, receiving, being grateful, and giving again forms the backbone of many stories and subplots, which people remember and tell, handing them on to one another and to their children. We have looked already at *todah,* the grateful memory-and-praise of Judaism, the refusal, over thousands of years, ever to forget God's favours to his people.

Gratitude stories, however, may be about *forgetting* as well as remembering—forgetting, that is, as virtue in the giver. One must give and forget—or, better, give without pausing to calculate. One thinks, but not about one's own advantage. Folklore, which may be defined as "the traditional stories and wisdom of the people," agrees with the message of the Gospel parable of the Good Samaritan who—in contrast to the pure and the haughty, those mindful of the risk to themselves and their reputations—forgets his status as a member of a despised minority, and helps the wounded man *because he has been hurt;* the Samaritan is simply "moved to compassion." He never wonders what could be in it for him, or takes into account his own loss of time and money, or stops to remember the hurt he has endured through being classified as excluded.[25]

The Tale of the Kind and the Unkind Girls has been collected by folklorists in hundreds of versions from northern Europe through Russia to India, and from Japan, Africa, and Jamaica.[26] It is a story about a good girl who, in the course of a perilous journey, wins gold. When she returns home with her reward, the bad girl sets off to do the same, but comes home having received only toads or snakes. A common episode in the story concerns the encounters the first girl makes on her journey. First, an apple tree begs to have its abundant ripe fruit picked. Despite the urgency of her quest, the girl stops, shakes the tree, collects the harvest in bags, and then goes on. Next she meets an oven, crying out to have some perfectly baked hot loaves removed from its interior. She turns aside and performs the service. Then a cow, with a pail hanging from her horns in the Scandinavian versions, says she needs milking because her udder is full. The girl pauses in her journey and complies.

When the Kind Girl has completed her adventures, she returns home with her prize: a scuffed old box, which she preferred, on being given the choice, to a showy and pretentious one. The old witch or ogre or some other monstrous being, enraged because the girl did not prefer the pretty box as expected, tears after her. When the cow, the oven, and the tree are asked if they have seen the fleeing girl, they steadfastly do not reveal that she has passed by or where she is. When the Kind Girl opens the box at home and finds gold in it, the Unkind Girl decides to set out to acquire gold for herself. But intent on achieving her end, she ignores the cries of the tree, the oven, and the cow; later, she chooses the glittering box. She too is pursued, and in some versions beaten or killed, unaided by the creatures she failed to help. In any event her box contains everything nasty, and no gold.

An important principle demonstrated by the story is that one ought naturally to do what needs doing. Ripe fruit on trees, bread baked to perfection, a cow's udder ready for milking are matters that will not wait. They need to be attended to at once, just as the Good Samaritan attended at once to the needs of the man beaten up by robbers—even if these urgencies do not appear to be part of the narrative of one's own life, and even if one is very busy. Ignoring the right moment—missing what Greek philosophers called the *kairos*[27]—by disregarding pain and allowing spoilage and waste is, in folklore, a criminal lapse. Ignoring is wicked, but doing the right thing is not on that account a matter for self-congratulation either. One acts because something needs doing and then one forgets about it. A grateful person remembers and steps in to help a benefactor when an opportunity arises—but the memory associated with gratitude is a virtue not of the giver but of one who has received. The tale tells us that *giving without any desire for a return gift* is what in fact rewards the giver. A gift has to "disappear" completely before it will bear fruit. Calculation of one's own advantage is fatal. "Returns" are always unexpected—out of the giver's control entirely.

An ancient device for producing an ethical effect by means of a story is to tell of animals behaving extraordinarily well; this tactic delivers a heavy rebuke to wicked human beings. Animals, for instance, are grateful; they remember favours done. As late as the nineteenth century Mark Twain uses

the technique in an adage: "If you pick up a starving dog and make him pros-
perous, he will not bite you. This is the principal difference between a dog
and a man."[28] Often in folktales we hear of the weak, against all odds, aiding
the strong out of a sense of gratitude. In one of Aesop's fables, for example,
a lion saves the life of a menaced mouse, knowing the creature's frailty and
uselessness. Later the lion is caught in a net and the mouse, remembering, returns the favour by chewing a way out for the lion. Dolphins always
fascinated ancient Greek seafarers because of their intelligence and their
habit of playing around boats. Koiranos of Paros once, standing at a dockside,
saw some dolphins caught in a fisherman's net, bought them, and set them
free. He was later almost drowned in a shipwreck, but a school of dolphins
rescued and carried him to shore on their backs. Years after, when Koiranos
died and was cremated on the seashore, the dolphins gathered in the water
near the beach to attend his funeral; only when the fire was quenched did
they swim away.[29]

The earliest trace of the folktale of "Androcles and the Lion" has been
found in Aulus Gellius (ca. AD 180). Aelian (second to third century) retells
the story, he says, to show that "memory is an attribute even of animals."[30] In
his version Androcles, the slave of a Roman senator, commits some offence
and flees to save his life, to the desert in Libya, where he takes shelter in a
cavern. His refuge turns out to be the lair of a lion, who returns from hunting
to find the terrified man cowering in its cave. But far from attacking him, the
lion whimpers and holds out its paw; it has been pierced by a stake. Androcles
draws out the stake, and the lion prostrates itself before its benefactor. The
two become friends and henceforth live together, sharing their meals—raw
for the lion and cooked for the man.

After three years, Androcles' hair grows long in the wilderness and he
develops an itch. He leaves his refuge to remedy his discomfort, but is caught,
bound, and shipped off to Rome, where he is condemned to be eaten alive by
wild beasts before the crowds in the Circus Maximus. When the lion that is
to devour him is released into the arena, it approaches Androcles but, "letting

its whole body sink down, threw itself at his feet." Androcles, in his turn recognizes this lion as his Libyan friend and "table companion," flings his arms
around it, to the amazement of the spectators. They think that Androcles
must be a magician, and a leopard is let loose to kill him. The lion (proving
thereby that its power was in no way weakened by its devotion to Androcles)
tears the leopard to pieces. At this point questions are asked, and when the
spectators hear the story, they "shout aloud that both man and lion must be
set free."[31]

Part of this story, which no doubt had many variants,[32] was told of Saint
Gerasimus of Lycia in Asia Minor, who founded a monastery near Jericho;
he died in AD 475. Here the wounded and healed lion became "tamer than
a domestic animal" and was set to look after the monastery's water-carrying
donkey while it was at pasture. One day a caravan of merchants stole the
donkey. The lion returned to the monastery, dejected. On being questioned,
it could only look back silently and miserably over its shoulder at Gerasimus.
"Thou hast eaten him," scolded the abbot. "Blessed be God! But henceforth
thou must do what the donkey did." And the lion had to carry water for
the community. One day the thieves passed by again, accompanied by the
donkey. The lion frightened them off and returned in triumph to the monastery, leading the donkey by the reins held in its mouth, and three camels
in addition, bringing up the rear. The grateful and forgiving lion, christened
Jordan, refused to eat when Gerasimus died, but lay down on his master's
grave and beat its head upon the earth, roaring. After a few days Jordan
himself was dead.[33]

The tale was adopted for the hagiography of Saint Jerome, whose name
was spelled Geronimus (easily confused with Gerasimus), and who also lived
for a while in the desert of the Holy Land. The lion became Jerome's attribute.
Christian themes easily attached themselves to the story of the Grateful Lion.
The encounter in the wild, for example, was popular in Christian myths,
where the Desert Outside, a liminal space, is often a place of epiphany. The
lion, its paw pierced, was taken to be a figure of Christ (who is often symbol-

ized by a lion in Christian art), hidden within the needy; Jesus had said that anyone who helped "the least of his brethren" did so him.[34] Gratitude could, in the Christian dispensation, be felt by God towards human beings.[35]

Isaiah's vision of the Peaceable Kingdom, where "the wolf lives with the lamb, the panther lies down with the kid, calf and lion cub feed together, and a little child shall lead them,"[36] was drawn into a new view of heroic behaviour. Where Homer's lion—roaring, eyes glaring, lashing its ribs with its tail—had been a simile for the wrath of Achilles and the terror he inspired,[37] these Christian lions were proofs of a saintly hero's gentleness. Friendship with a lion had become a sign of special grace made manifest in the generous and wise.[38]

There were several further examples in medieval epic of saints accompanied by lions. One of these joined his paws together, "*piez joinz,*" for his master, the hero Yvain, as a vassal pressed his palms together between the hands of his lord to express his fealty.[39] In some of these stories the acquisition of a tamed and grateful lion marks a new stage in the hero's progressive redemption. Perceval, in the epic poem *La Queste del Saint Graal,* sees a serpent carrying a lion cub in its mouth, with the cub's "crying and roaring" parent following behind. Perceval rescues the cub. The lion takes its baby home and returns to spend the night with Perceval, serving him as his pillow. Perceval dreams of two women, one riding a serpent and the other a lion. He recognizes the lion maiden as "the New Law": he has made his soul's choice by "choosing the lion's side" over that of the serpent.[40]

In many stories in the Western tradition, episodes of thankfulness signify the possibility, or the beginning, of redemption for the person able to feel grateful. In Dostoyevsky's *The Brothers Karamazov,* Dmitry is a violent and sensual man who in the end is sentenced to twenty years of hard labour for murdering his father—a crime he did not commit. There are intimations in the novel that Dmitry will be saved by being sprung from prison in Siberia. But twice he shows gratitude, and these moments are far more important for his soul than any plan of escape could be. In the first, Dmitry has just had a powerful dream that awakens pity in him for suffering children. Then he hears his lover Grushenka promising never to leave him, and her words awaken him from his dream. A detail shakes him to the depths of his soul: somebody—who it was he never knows—had shown compassion for him by putting a pillow under his head while he was asleep: "'Who put a pillow under my head? Who was that kind person?' he exclaimed with a kind of ecstatic, grateful emotion and in a voice that almost wept, as though God only knew what boon had been accorded him." Dmitry's life, in this moment, has changed. But gratitude was something he already understood, as we find out later, during his trial. There the old German doctor Herzenstube remembers giving a pound of nuts to Dmitry when he was a deprived and abused child. And twenty-three years later Dmitry had come to thank the doctor for this small gift, which had meant so much to him and which he had never forgotten.[41] The effect of these two tiny incidents on the reader is all Dostoyevsky offers of comfort and hope for Dmitry's ultimate destiny. But it is enough.

Our personalities, then, are embedded in a web of memories, to the point where to be deprived of memory is to lose one's identity. Gratitude is deliberate memory, and expression of it a proof of openness to others. And being able to be grateful is an early sign of the possibility of deliverance when we have lost our way, when our very identity is under threat: gratitude points forward. *The Man Without a Past* (2003), by the Finnish filmmaker Aki Kaurismäki, is about a man so badly injured in a beating that he loses his memory. The film recounts his recovery and eventual salvation; a new and finer identity will be his. His redemption, however, is implicit from the beginning. For when he regains consciousness but not his memory, in the house of people who, he realizes, have taken him in and looked after him without knowing who he is any more than he knows himself, the first words he utters—and they are his first words in the film—are "Thank you."

Ten lepers were once healed by Jesus,[42] who sent them to the priests (whose job it was to pronounce a leper "cleansed" and so no longer posing a danger of infection to others). On the way there—and not before—they all find they have been cured. Only one of them, however, remembers to whom he owes his amazing recovery. This man "turned back praising God aloud. He threw himself down at Jesus' feet and thanked him." And he is a Samaritan, an outsider. "Were not all ten cleansed? The other nine, where are they?" asks Jesus. The words are not merely a reproach for ingratitude to himself; they express concern for the spiritual infirmity that afflicts the other nine men. Jubilant over their regained health as they are, in their thanklessness and thoughtlessness they are lost. And the man who remembers and is grateful is not only cured, but also saved.

PART IV

∞

Feeling

19

Emotions

Gratitude longs to communicate itself. We want people who have helped us, encouraged us, or given us excellent advice to know that we are conscious of what they have done, and how much their generosity, their expertise, or their very presence have meant to us. And so we externalize what we feel in actions, words, and gestures. We have so far been looking at these manifestations and what they signify. Most people today, however, think of gratitude as a feeling or a thought, something that goes on in the mind and the heart of a person who has received a favour and recognized another person's benevolence towards him or her. It is worth stepping back, therefore, to look at what emotions are, or are said to be. This consideration will involve us in the strange history of intellectual attitudes towards human feelings, a history that is at present particularly conflicted and confused.

∞

In Australia some years ago a baby was abducted, and for two days intensive searches were carried out by the police; media coverage of the hunt was intense. Finally the baby was found and returned to his mother, who had thought she might never see him again. The report on ABC television described the mother as "emotional": "The baby was reunited with his emotional mother." To a watching Polish immigrant to Australia, this was one of those moments, familiar to all who leave their countries of origin to live in a place with a culture different from their own, where the visitor is brought face to face with the extent of her foreignness. A single word can open up vistas of strangeness, even a sense that one is not merely displaced but utterly bewildered. Emotional! This mother was described as *emotional* when she saw her child again!

Anna Wierzbicka, scholar of meanings in language, is able to explain.[1] Anglo-Saxon culture, she says, demands that people spend enormous amounts of effort on repressing the display of emotions in public; we think of ourselves as "breaking down" when we begin to sob in front of other people. There is a great deal of variation among cultures in such matters, as there is, for example, in the maintenance of physical distance between people talking to each other. In comparison with the Japanese, Anglo-Saxons in general and North Americans in particular have been shown to encourage physical expressiveness: people touch each other in ordinary converse twice as much as Japanese do. But "from a Polish perspective, Anglo-Saxon culture in general (including American culture) seems as restrained in physical expressiveness as Japanese culture seems to Americans."[2]

An emotion, Polish *uczucie,* is for Poles a thoroughly good thing, a powerful reaction worth communicating to others. People who experience strong emotions are thought of as deep, rich, warm, admirably human beings. They are therefore allowed to express their emotions with a readiness that surprises and even shocks Anglo-Saxons when they encounter it. Russians are similar in this regard, as reading Russian novels quickly makes plain to us. "The cultural ideal of 'composure' as a person's 'normal state,'" writes Wierzbicka, "is alien to mainstream Russian culture."[3] In other words, in Poland people display emotionality over far smaller events than something like recovering a lost child; a Pole is stunned by the poverty of the term *emotional* when used in such a case. In the Australian context, the mother was permitted this emotionalism because of the enormity of her suffering; to have shown her emotions in public was a measure of what she must have gone through. Wierzbicka points out further that in Australian culture it is usually "quite all right to swear, that is to show 'strong,' 'masculine' feelings. What is not all right is to show, without restraint, 'weak,' 'soft,' 'feminine' emotions, such as tenderness."

The amount and kind of demonstrative emotional behaviour that is allowed and encouraged is an important characteristic of every culture. Another is the actual isolating and naming of separate emotions. William James wrote long ago that "we know from introspection that, on the one hand, we are capable of a great variety of feelings, and on the other, that these feelings are not clearly separated from one another and can not be counted."[4] But as we have seen in the case of "gratitude," different cultures "cut up" this continuum differently, and proceed to give names in their own languages to the segments they have themselves delimited; some of the continuum quite often escapes naming altogether. Anthropologists are able only roughly to count the terms denoting emotional feelings in any given language because people rarely think of emotions as a cut-and-dried affair. But it has been said that the Chewong of Malaya have only eight words denoting emotions, the Malays about 230, the Taiwanese 750. English, according to this particular account, has 400.[5] To make matters even more complicated, many cultures do not make the distinctions we are used to between body and mind, or emotion and cognition.

A linguistic term, aided by many kinds of cultural insistence, gives what modern scholars call "salience" to an emotion in a given society. One can nonetheless feel something for which one's culture has given no name, or grasp an "emotion concept" without ever having experienced it. Considerable sympathy and sensitivity on both sides of a relationship are needed to convey feelings that one's own language has not designated with a simple term—but it can be done. And my language may have a name for something your language groups quite differently and your culture stresses more—or less—than mine. It is now known, adds Wierzbicka, that *no* emotions are lexically recognized as distinct and identifiable in all languages—not even fear, anger, and disgust, which many scientific experts have defined as basic to the human psyche. For in every case, cultural models influence the emotions of individuals.[6] We have seen already that *gratitude* is a term rooted in Western European culture and given "salience" by its Christian history; it is a complex emotion that puts together feelings and reactions that other cultures keep separate, downplay, or reserve for occasions uniquely provided by their own social systems.

Wierzbicka gives several examples of distinctive terms for emotions that are impossible to translate directly into English.[7] Japanese *amae,* for instance, is, to be crudely brief, a feeling of "helplessness and the desire to be loved." Its adjective *amai,* meaning "sweet," is used to describe both the taste of certain foods and some human relations. The overriding metaphor is that of a baby's relationship to its mother. The verb *amaeru* is both "to be dependent on another" and "to behave self-indulgently, presuming on some special relationship."[8] *Liget,* for the Ilongot of the Philippines, is "energy, anger, passion"—whether it be felt in killing, in alertness, or in physical effort. It is a will to compete and to triumph, in fierceness and masculine force: male babies are a product of *liget,* concentrated in sperm. Chili peppers possess *liget,* as do liquor, storms, and fire. *Liget* is born out of envy, out of the clash of things and people; it provides the energy, for example, to stay awake all night or to work extremely hard. But it can also lead to "sporadic bursts of basket-slashing, knife-waving violence."[9]

The people who live on the Ifaluk atoll in Micronesia have a word, *fago,* that is clearly a version of "love"—but "sadness" is essential to it, while sexual attraction and continuing personal intimacy are not. *Fago* in Ifaluk is triggered by illness in another, a departure from the island, or lack of food: the one who has *fago* gives food, cries, or speaks kindly to the person suffering (*fago* is "a sadness that activates"). A woman heard her younger brother singing as he fished from his canoe in the lagoon; she said she had "a bit of *fago* for him" because, although he was at present happy, she imagined that something bad might conceivably happen to him. We ourselves know this feeling, but we do not have a specific name for it; we are assured that "compassion" and "feeling protective" do not capture it. *Fago* can also be a sort of admiration, aroused by another's exemplary behaviour: "You *fago* someone because they do not misbehave. You *fago* them because they are calm and socially intelligent." And *fago* is an emotion that can be called upon to prevent violence.[10]

Clearly emotions are to an important degree *social* matters: they usually arise from our relationships with others, and the culture we live in names them, elicits them, and limits or encourages their expression. Yet *emotions* (we should be aware that this is a term that arises out of our own culture) take place in the individual. The word itself implies that they are *movements,* and they are commonly experienced physically by the person undergoing them. While they are in motion and we are "moved," and also as we move out of calm into emotion (the word means literally "motion *out of,*" Latin *e-*), our hearts pound and our facial muscles move; we may also breathe heavily, heat up, redden, sweat, weep, and make energetic gestures. All of these activities, and especially our facial expressions, see to it that we communicate our emotions to other people watching. One can manage to control one's appearance in order to dissimulate one's feelings, but it normally requires a struggle, unless we have previously spent a lot of effort acquiring this skill. It is difficult to describe emotions, but consciousness that others feel them too enables us to speak of them in metaphors that we can expect others to understand. And simultaneously, the metaphors say a lot about cultural expectations: we often feel what we are "supposed to" feel (we have to learn, for example, to respond to insults with anger)[11], and we can *recognize* emotions we have heard about before, when we ourselves experience them for the first time.

The English language, for example, through common expressions provides us with a graphic model of how emotion works.[12] According to this model we picture ourselves as containers full of liquid, which is cool and calm when we are not "emotional." Because emotionality in our culture is frowned on and demonstrating it believed to be a sign of weakness, "cool" people are thought admirable: they are sure of themselves, calm, and therefore inscrutable to others; their containers are not easily "upset." "Cool" people do not get "all steamed up," but are "laid back"—that is, horizontal and relaxed rather than rigid and aroused or "worked up." For the fluid in the container can heat up, and when it does, it becomes agitated and rises, like milk boiling. Then we "lose our cool," become "hot and bothered," "lose our tempers." (Another of our metaphorical models is about ourselves as composed of parts that can become disconnected under stress. We should in difficult circumstances "pull ourselves together," not "fall apart." Our "tempers" belong to another and related metaphor, that of "balance." "Temper," like "cool," ensures calm; it should be "kept" and not "lost.")

We do not, the container model says, give rise to the emotional heat that is the opposite of cool: we *undergo* it, as liquid does in a pot placed over a flame. We do not normally put the pot—that is ourselves—on the fire. Something else does it for us or to us. An event outside ourselves occurs and sets off an emotion. Inside the container steam builds up. We can try to "keep the lid on," but it is difficult to do so, and control is likely to become impossible; trying to achieve control might even make matters worse. Unless we "let off steam," the container may actually "blow up," and the hot liquid could pour out and injure other people and ourselves. Notice again that we do not deliberately hurt people; the emotion does it because it has become agitated beyond endurance. Our model says that we are not responsible for our emotions, or for the consequences should we become overwhelmed by them, for at the height of an emotional episode a person is irrational. She cannot see the world as it really is, and is likely to do things she normally would not, because she is temporarily overwhelmed by a force stronger than she is. Once we have "blown our tops," however, we can be expected to calm down again. For emotions do not last. They rise like waves; they crash, and they recede.

Anger, obviously, is the prototype of this language-based, fatalistic folk model. There is a fatal chain of events as well as a fatal cause. Anger numbers all the links in this chain; other emotions may follow it only in part. The stages are as follows: calm—cause—emotion—attempt at control—loss of control—action—return to calm. The action that becomes emotion's goal

may be known to be morally wrong, which is why there is an attempt at control. Here culture can help. In our case (for it is an Anglo-Saxon model that
is being described) it can forbid the display of too much emotion through
the exertion of social pressure. For we are aware that physical expression of
an emotion can "turn up the heat" on the emotion itself. One is therefore
supposed to require special indulgence from others before one may "become
emotional." Without it one is likely to encounter alarm and strong disapproval from the outset of the episode: other people will try to put out the
flames and limit the damage.

We are repeatedly warned that emotionality is irrational, and our culture
clearly privileges the rational. We feel that when emotion is allowed free rein,
it is as though a force, an opponent more powerful than we are, is "aroused."
It takes over and drags us down. There is some metaphorical illogicality here,
since boiling fluid rises. But another of our general metaphorical models tells
us that rationality is "up"—that is, bright, sunny, calm, and clear—whereas
irrationality is dark, swirling, obscure, and "down." Within the emotive sphere
we do have "positive" emotions such as happiness, which make us feel "up";
miserable emotions are merely "negative," and "down." But miserable emotions are what we usually mean when we describe emotions in general, for
"affection" or "happiness" are normally, like rationality, calm states, and emotion means, precisely because literally, agitation.

Emotions in this model are "the opposite" of thoughts. Reason, for
example, is free, while emotion is something that happens to us: we merely
"endure" emotional turmoil. Thinking is intentional and can range widely,
in the end reaching previously unplanned conclusions. But people "in the
grip" of emotions (the metaphor suggests that emotions may behave like
wild animals or demonic beings) are essentially passive. The word *emotion* is
quite new; it was used in its modern, psychological sense for the first time
in the mid-seventeenth century.[13] Before that, people spoke of their "passions." Passions, like appetites, were animal, sensual, involuntary, visceral. But
in human beings there were other, higher categories: those of the moral

sentiments and rational affections, where feelings were not dissociated from will and cognition.

The original meaning of *passion* was "suffering."[14] And "to suffer" is "to endure" before it refers to pain felt. *Passion* began to mean "strong emotion" and "love" at the beginning of the thirteenth century, "enthusiasm" or "zeal" from the early sixteenth century, and "violent love" later in the same century. The essential points about passion were its intensity, one's passivity when undergoing it, and—later—one's inability to resist it. When the word *emotion* first appeared in English in the 1660s, the emphasis was simply on the change that takes place in someone experiencing emotion, from calm to "being moved" (still passive voice: something else moves me).

Emotion has remained a more neutral and distanced, a more "scientific" term than *passion*. But this "scientific" limitation of the term to signify "change" laid it open to the acquisition of a purely physical significance. In fact, the English word *emotion* refers to three things: feeling and thinking as well as the commonly experienced bodily accompaniments to a person's emotions. The word *emotion* can refer to "anger" or "fear" or "love"—but we do not say "an emotion of hunger" or "an emotion of heartburn," because a purely bodily sensation is not enough to make up an emotion. The German word *Gefühle* (from *fühlen,* "to feel") means "thought-related feelings," and no bodily disturbances at all. And our word *sentiment,* from French *sentiment,* is similar.[15]

The concept of "emotion" as a version of "passion" inherits the ancient belief, as old as Plato, that passion is not usually a good thing because it is opposed to reason. Descartes, for example, differentiated mind from body, assigning reason to the mind and passions to the body. (It is worth noting that *reason* was singular, but *passions* plural, befitting both their manifold nature and their ability to tear things apart.) Passions, for Descartes, were able to undermine thought, and therefore human beings could not be held to account for their feelings. (The latter idea is still taken by many to be simple common sense.) Spinoza, and he was not alone in this, thought emotions were marks of human servitude, while intellect was the expression of human freedom. (We recall that our folk model still says much the same thing.) Max Weber's idea that the increasing rationalization of the world meant the decreasing significance of emotion in human conduct has been accused of being responsible for the expulsion of the study of emotion from sociology.[16] Marcel Mauss himself admired "the Gift" as a strategy to create cooperation and not violence, and therefore, above all, as eminently reasonable—despite the intense emotions invested in the objects exchanged by "the peoples of the Gift."[17] It has been suggested that Mauss was fascinated by "the spirit of the Gift" not only because it explained why gifts were later returned, but also because it injected an emotional charge into the process which the very reasonableness of gift-giving and reciprocation threatened to efface.[18]

Emotions and passions, then, have for many centuries been seen in our culture as part of our "lower" selves. They could be enjoyable and enriching, but usually they were deeply inadvisable; anyone aspiring to be a sage fought to overcome their power over him. The list of Seven Deadly Sins included several bad emotions, such as envy, anger, and hate. Women, unfortunately, were emotional creatures; men's role was to be reasonable and (therefore) in control. It is no wonder then that "passions" remained under-represented in writings on virtue. Theatrical performance revelled in the passions, of course; much was done to categorize them and to conventionalize gestures capable of letting the audience know how the figures on stage were supposed to be feeling. And in the eighteenth century, the new art form of the novel gave permission to an author to describe what was going on inside the hearts as well as the minds of his imagined characters.

During the course of the nineteenth century, French scientists started to look anew at the bodily reactions that accompany emotional episodes in human beings. These were, after all, observable and eventually measurable phenomena: manageable as a subject for natural science. In 1873 Charles Darwin gathered this material together and, including his own observations, wrote *The Expression of the Emotions in Man and Animals*, with illustrations, showing how similar human beings are to animals in the expression of emotion.[19] People had always insisted on how different they were from beasts. Now the page turned: the theory of evolution made us more and more fascinated by the extent to which we are no different from animals.

Darwin's book shows how much of animal behaviour is explicable if we understand the Principle of Antithesis. A hostile dog, for example, stands rigid, its tail erect, with bristling fur, ears pricked and directed forwards, and staring eyes. An affectionate dog, therefore, sinks downward, lowers its tail and wags it from side to side, its hair lies flat, ears are drawn back and down; the eyelids meanwhile are elongated through the movement of the ears, so that there is no stare. The first stance shows readiness to attack, while the second gives assurance, in its submissiveness, of a desire to please and to show pleasure; its body uses signals opposite to those of hostility to demonstrate its lack of aggressive intent.

A second special interest of Darwin's was the direct connection between mind and body that expressiveness demonstrates. Human blushing is a particularly striking example, where self-consciousness and embarrassment—entirely social, interactional reactions—actually cause the colour of our faces to change. And there is nothing we can do to stifle a blush once it gets under way: a third interest of Darwin's was the automatic, uncontrollable nature of bodily reactions to strong feelings in the mind. Our hearts thud under the onslaught of emotion, we tremble with fear, our bodies jerk convulsively when we suffer pain. Darwin speculated on the usefulness for our survival of the quasi-automatic bodily manifestations of rage: the creature collects itself for attack, energy floods in to back up the need for a powerful response, while the signs given out—the whole figure rising up in what we call a "towering" rage, bared teeth, roaring, and so forth, serve to terrify the object of fury. A human being can "control himself" even in the grip of rage. Nevertheless, Darwin noted, he cannot still his pounding heart.

Some very powerful emotions show no outward signs. Envy and jealousy are examples of these, although what we commonly call the "sour" facial expression of an envious or jealous person is likely to betray a decidedly uncheerful state of mind. The reason, Darwin said, is that these feelings typically lead to no immediate action. Expressive emotions such as fear or disgust usually issue in sudden physical movements, which incidentally serve to warn watching others of danger. They are not only violent but short-lived: after the action is over, they die down. In human beings, emotions are either conventional and artificial—or they are innate and universal. Darwin added that the second kind "alone deserve to rank as true expressions."

"No emotion is stronger than maternal love," Darwin wrote—and yet a mother may not show it by any outward sign, apart from a gentle smile and tender eyes produced by the pleasure of loving, and slight caressing movements resulting from the common desire to touch a beloved person. Since her love does not habitually lead to decisive action, there is no bodily expression that specifically expresses it. Darwin noticed too that while emotions give rise to gestures and facial movements, "the free expression by outward signs of an emotion intensifies it."

The biological approach to the emotions is perhaps most ambitiously represented today by Paul Ekman and his associates; it is, of course, deeply indebted to Darwin.[20] It maintains a special fascination with involuntary changes in expression and physiology—what happens to us "independent of the will," as Darwin put it. It restricts itself to the "innate or universal" feelings because of their bodily manifestations, and rejects from consideration any emotion that is not physically uncontrollable. The ancient ideas are maintained that emotions are changes that are irrational, passively undergone, irresistible, and essentially "animal." A modern scientist allows himself no opinion as to whether or not they are morally desirable; they just "are."

The patterns of activity in the autonomic nervous system have been shown to be distinctive for the emotions of anger, fear, disgust, and sadness. These four, Ekman has said, are the fundamental emotions, the ones with survival value because they automatically prepare the organism for dealing quickly with threatening situations. For example, blood goes to the hands in anger, and this encourages fighting to ensue. Fear is expressed by screaming, pallor of the face and a look of terror, flight or the freezing of movement, perhaps fainting. Disgust produces both avoidance—a physical drawing back—where there is a possibility of poisoning, and a very specific facial expression that warns other people not to try the disgusting food. Ekman did not describe the immediate practical applications of "sadness." It is even more noteworthy that none of his four fundamental emotions can be called pleasurable.

The differences among the various emotions is a source of intense interest to these scientists, as is their enumeration.[21] Ekman takes those on his expanded list to be universal because biological; they are, he claims, in no way cultural constructions: social learning merely provides "amplification and detailing" but essentially changes nothing important about them. Every true emotion must have seven characteristics: automatic appraisal of a stimulus, non-cultural and non-individual elements in the contexts in which they occur, presence in other primates, quick onset, brief duration, unbidden occurrence, and distinctive physiology. For him, the emotions thus defined are (in the alphabetical order in which he lists them) amusement, anger, awe, contempt, contentment, disgust, embarrassment, excitement, fear, guilt, interest, pride in achievement, relief, sadness, satisfaction, sensory pleasure, and shame. He allows, he says, for no "nonbasic" emotions; he assures us that there is no convincing evidence that any emotions are unique to human beings. He ignores the profoundly social and cultural context necessary for feelings of embarrassment and shame. We notice that neither love nor gratitude are mentioned.

Part of the definition of an emotion, for Ekman and his colleagues, is that it lasts only minutes or seconds. If there appears to be any duration, that is because a series of short-lived emotions has occurred. Some of them cause signals to be provided for the construal of others; these are universally found in anger, fear, disgust, sadness, contempt, and embarrassment. The "positive"

emotions, which are amusement, contentment, excitement, pride in achievement, relief, satisfaction, and sensory pleasure, "all share a single signal—a
particular type of smile."[22]

It is not surprising that there is now an ongoing reaction against this
reductionist view of human beings as mechanical information processors,
with emotions that are built-in, hard-wired reactions, every one of them
simple and clear-cut, like a series of discrete blocks, immune to thought and
fundamentally inaccessible to the methods of cultural analysis.[23] Since the
early 1970s the study of human emotions from many different points of view
has become more and more voluminous—a flood that shows no signs of
abating. For there is an enormous field here that is, from the scientific point
of view, still largely unexplored. The disciplines of sociology, anthropology,
psychology, history—even archaeology[24]—have trained their attention on
the subject of the emotions, the scope of research extending far beyond the
measurement of neural responses.

In the multi-ethnic societies of the present, cultural differences have
become impossible to overlook. Typical questions raised are these: Is it possible really to sympathize with what other people feel, if we have not experienced what they have known? How are emotions manipulated by political
structures? Are they inevitably marked by the power relations so beloved
of social science? The importance of emotions has never been more highly
appreciated. "Emotions matter because if we did not have them nothing
else would matter," writes one scientist.[25] Most people no longer claim that
emotions are utterly automatic or irrational; many accept that they arise
out of conscious social understandings and in interactive relationships. Some
claim that emotions are to a large extent intentional, that they can be deliberately used by those who feel them in order to influence the outcome of
events,[26] while others are certain that "no genuine expression of emotion
takes place as a means to some further end."[27] We can speak of emotional
meaning, appropriate emotions, emotional intelligence. Nowadays it is readily admitted in the psychological and neurological literature that thoughts are

essential to emotions, and vice versa. The hunt is on, we are told, to find out what the conditions are that cause thinking to drive emotions, or emotions to drive thoughts.

Anthropologists remind us that in some cultures, for example in Samoa, "there is not much talk of feelings as origins of behaviour," or that in China people speak of the body rather than the mind, and discuss their emotions relatively seldom.[28] Anthropologists in particular have recently learned to question themselves, to wonder how much we project our ideas onto others when we "study" them. When therefore we are surprised by the Samoans or the Chinese, we now know that we should go on to ask why it is that we are so interested: why are *we* different from them? A scholar like Anna Wierzbicka can wonder, when confronted with a list of "fundamental emotions," how it is that "fear," "shyness," "anger," "contempt," and the rest are "all so neatly identified by means of English words." How recognizable, in fact, are any of these concepts to the people whose behaviour is being analyzed with reference to them—whose languages often do not have terms that directly translate these words? She points out that, after all, "the feelings identified in English by means of the words *disgust, distaste, revulsion,* and *repulsion* are different feelings and they cannot all correspond to the same discrete fundamental human emotion."[29]

We saw earlier how gift-giving has been forced, by our culture's privileging of commercialism, into a "private" sphere; it is said that there is now a corresponding split between emotion (at home) and practical interest (at work).[30] Social structure has itself been seen to have implications for people's emotions. We looked earlier at the importance of hierarchy and egalitarianism for the possibility of what we mean by "gratitude." For some scholars it is the individual's position in society (factors such as gender, age, or status) that gives rise to his or her emotions, so that it is impossible, without political and social theory, to understand another person's emotions, emerging as they do from lived but in many ways pre-structured experience. It has even been suggested that a young ethnographer, with necessarily limited life experience, is ill equipped to engage in the cross-cultural investigation of emotion.[31] A lot of research has been conducted into the ways in which children are taught emotional competence within their culture. People have to *learn* what is considered dangerous, what is worth having or disadvantageous to lose, what risks are worth taking, and so forth. All of these preordained cultural decisions necessarily have a direct bearing on how people feel. And conversely, people's emotional responses can be clues to a foreign scholar's understanding of how a society operates, or point to areas in which it is changing.

Moods very recently have begun to attract attention as *lasting* phenomena, even though they are subtly "emotional."[32] A mood can last all day, or even for several days. Some people nurse them, others throw them off quickly or without difficulty; it depends on the individual personality. Moods also fluctuate in intensity and are less accessible than emotions are to conscious awareness. They have been defined as "intermediate terrain between emotions and affective traits [of personality]."[33] They are a sort of soup of comparatively low-level, pervasive feelings that have their effects on our thinking, our perceptions of other people, and our ability to cope with stress. Out of a mood, an emotion easily gathers, and can also erupt and then subside "back into" the mood.

For example, the desires involved in our emotions are quite often not satisfied.[34] When this happens, there may be a kind of residue that settles into or mingles with a mood of resentment; it is a survival in a noxious form of our badly dissolved frustration. (The chemical metaphors are perhaps a new folk model in the making.) The leftover angry emotion may, eventually, simply dissipate. But if it does not, it lies ready and waiting for an opportunity to release itself. Suddenly, and "without warning," anger can reignite, in totally different circumstances and often for entirely new "reasons." Is this outburst a different emotion, a repetition, or the survival of an old one, thanks to the fertile ambience of a waxing and waning mood? An emotion is often described these days as an "episode" that can create a mood, while a mood can give rise to an "emotion episode."[35] In short, mood analysis enables scientists both to keep their insistence that emotions are by definition short-lived, and to allow for the possibility that they could last, either as potentialities or as nebulous feelings, hanging about and liable to solidify at any moment into "emotion episodes," should the appropriate events occur to activate them.

Another recent development among psychologists is a decision to concentrate—at last!—on the "positive" emotions of amusement, contentment, satisfaction, pleasure, and the rest. People want well-being, scientists realize, but the profession has been fixated on mental illness since its beginnings—that is, for far too long. In any case, more people want to be happy than are actually mentally ill: an enormous potential clientele has been passed over. The "positive" emotions, with their single expression, the sincere smile, have never before been thought worthy of much scientific study. They are not histrionic enough, far too calm (we have seen that the very definition of an emotion was "agitation"), too "dependent on the will," and in addition seem to be, once they are achieved, about staying the same rather than changing. They have tended to be lumped together under one "positive" heading, and tagged on, as it were, to the highly differentiated, sudden, and rampant emotions such as rage, fear, and disgust. In any case, what is so often taken to be the final arbiter, the body's autonomic system, produces no distinctive patterns for any of the "positive" emotions. Even the silent sin of envy has received more attention than has something like "joy," presumably because it falls in with the interests of social science: it venomously compares statuses and wishes to alter them to the envious one's advantage. But now psychologists swept up into the new movement have started to offer a growing public what it cannot but wish for: optimism that can be learned, "positive outlooks" through rising above depressing thoughts, and, finally, the achievement of "authentic happiness."[36]

Meanwhile, study of the corporal manifestations of emotion continues. It has been shown that the heart is essential to the emotions, as folk wisdom has always said it was. The heart, "a sensory organ and an information encoding and processing center that works together with the brain and the nervous system," not only registers emotions, but actually helps to generate them.[37] It can "learn, remember, and make functional decisions" independently of the brain lodged in our skulls.[38] As the word *emotion* has already suggested, we are dealing with changes. The interesting new information is that the heart changes its rhythms, often without any alteration in the amount of heart-rate variability.

What happens, we are told, is that the human body creates, in the normal course of living, a kind of background set of familiar patterns, built up, maintained, and developed by experience. Digestive and respiratory rhythms, heart rhythms, recurring muscular tensions—all are monitored by the individual's brain, which becomes accustomed to this pattern. An important factor is also a person's habitual facial expressions—the kind of thing that produces, over a lifetime, what common sense calls the "character" that other people respond to in a human face.[39] The heart transmits this complex backdrop of rhythmic patterning to the brain and to the rest of the body. When an emotion occurs, the heart reacts—very strongly in some instances—so that we feel its throbbing and hammering. Something has happened to disturb the pattern, something "extra-ordinary."

We are often advised, as a folk remedy for emotional agitation, to take a few deep breaths before we speak or act, for example, in anger. This is a wise idea, for what we are doing is regularizing our heart's rhythmic activity by means of our breathing—and thereby calming down our emotional turmoil. For the body registers emotion, but also to a degree creates it; the heart influences the brain. Scientists now understand that it is not the heart's rate or amount of pumping that matters so much as its rhythmic *pattern*. Anger, for example, produces in the heart a disordered rhythm as well as a quickening heartbeat. Awe and appreciation, on the other hand, give a highly ordered, smooth heart rhythm. A present happening is always registered in comparison with the backdrop tapestry of familiar norms in this particular human being; "now" is compared and contrasted with "usually." (It follows, of course, that an emotion that becomes habitual may make its contribution to the tapestry of the familiar.) In addition, studies have proven that emotional processes operate much faster than thoughts do. They may even, at times, bypass "linear mind reasoning" entirely. And increased coherence in the heart's rhythms actually improves our ability to think. It is not enough, therefore, to think sensitively; we must also feel wisely. And the more we do the latter, scientists are telling us (as writers on virtue have told us for centuries), the easier it becomes.

As we "pre-analytical" human beings have always known, we never feel so alive as when we are experiencing emotion—even when the feelings are painful. For when we are moved, we are fully involved with what is going on around us; we are not merely watching, but also taking part. In consequence, people have always sought out emotional experience. When we want to supplement or to illuminate what we get of it in everyday life, we turn to art: to stories and songs, dance, poetry, or movies. We know perfectly well that our bodies register and even encourage and prolong emotion: a lump in the throat, a clenched fist, laughter, or tears. Common sense tells us that we do not shut off our thinking capabilities in order to experience emotion. And few of us would want to think only coldly and at a distance, without feeling anything; we have only to watch the ecstatic expressions on the face of a violin player or a pianist to be aware of the complex interconnections that can occur between mental concentration and feeling. We have always suspected too that people can "feel something going on" before they have thought it through, or even started to think about it at all: we call this "intuition." Feeling not only gives us the energy to think, but also helps to provide the necessary persistence and the power to focus our attention—even as it can perturb or inflame our thoughts. Emotion is specific and vivid, wild, grave, and voluptuous, as well as an incitement to the imagination; it can fairly be described as the colour of thought.

20

Feeling Grateful

Gratitude is a feeling that depends on thinking: it is ignited in the receiver's heart not only by another's kind action but also by his or her own attention, awareness, understanding, reflection, and openness to seeing and accepting the goodness of somebody else. When the receiver becomes in turn a giver, this feeling of gratitude develops into a pivot between the first favour and the next; it begins as a reaction and a recognition, and then—after further reflection—turns into a motivator. The fact that gratitude is an emotion helps it to motivate. In conjunction with thinking, it produces a decision. This operation might be mysterious,[1] but the word *gratitude* does not refer only to the action of "giving something back" in itself. Giving back is *showing* gratitude for the benefactor to see and perhaps for others to see as well; the "real" gratitude, the motive for returning a favour, lies hidden in the heart, and therefore requires verbal expression as well as an appropriate externalization in action.

That is not how people have always seen gratitude. In the past, and still sometimes today, people have thought of gratitude as above all an action (returning a favour) that is not only virtuous in itself, but also valuable to society. It is therefore "called for" in a beneficiary: the obligation was likely to be supported by the approval of other people, or their censure in the case of a failure to do the right thing and reciprocate. "There is no duty more indispensable than that of returning a kindness," writes Cicero in a book whose title means "On Duties," and in a later chapter he adds, "All men detest one forgetful of a benefit."[2] He says nothing about what emotion the person returning a kindness might experience, although he does not deny either that a receiver ought to feel something for his benefactor. The emphasis, however, is squarely on the need to respond by returning the kindness. Seneca is capable of seeing a spontaneously grateful reaction to a favour as a feeling, but even for him what the receiver owes is uppermost in his mind: "He who receives a benefit gratefully (*grate*) repays the first instalment on his debt."[3] Good people did the right thing; how they felt about it was on the whole beside the point. We have seen that in some cases, such as feudal regimes, "gratitude" meaning "returning a benefit" was more strictly obligatory still.

This was certainly not the Judeo-Christian tradition in its essence. There, what people feel, what their dispositions are, and what they intend are of prime importance. This does not mean that action will not occur. On the contrary, right feeling must lead to virtuous action: "by their fruits you shall know them."[4] Thomas Aquinas writes in the thirteenth century that gratitude was more about feeling than action—even though recompense was wherever possible the expression of gratitude, for "repaying favours is a part of justice." Where gratitude is appropriate, a poor person is as capable of virtue as a rich one. She can at least thank the giver and honour him, even if she cannot "give back" an equivalent gift or favour. In every case it is the disposition that matters, and therefore the freedom to give and to give back is essential.[5] Amount, in and of itself, is never the point: the desperately poor widow's two small coins are "more" than all the gifts out of the superfluity of the rich.[6] It is the widow's generous intentions that count.

Philosophers of a utilitarian bent have usually taken gratitude to be a convenient producer of profit in the shape of an exchange of goods. The receiver's duty to give back is what encourages potential givers to be benevolent in the first place; they will not give unless they can be sure they will get something out of it. "Of all Voluntary Acts, the Object is to every man his own Good," writes Hobbes; "of which if men see they shall be frustrated, there will be no beginning of benevolence, or trust; nor consequently of mutuall help; nor of reconciliation of one man to another; and therefore they are to remain still in the condition of *War*."[7] Without gratitude-as-reciprocation, society will eventually descend into chaos and violence. "Gratitude," meaning the return of a gift or favour, was therefore, as we have already seen, what Hobbes calls "The Fourth Law of Nature."

Jean-Jacques Rousseau is often admired for pointing out that "gratitude is a duty which ought to be paid, but not a right to be exacted."[8] The context of this remark is a passage about obedience to one's father: "By the law of nature, the father is the child's master no longer than his help is necessary; . . . from that time they are both equal, the son being perfectly independent of the father, and owing him only respect and not obedience." Rousseau sees the crucial distinction between the role of the grateful person and that of the one deserving gratitude. He also understands that gratitude can be offered only in freedom. Yet he still takes "gratitude" to mean a dutiful action rather than a feeling.

Adam Smith, father of modern economics, also wrote a book on moral sentiments, by which he meant feelings resulting from imaginative thought.[9] In it, he turned away from the prevailing belief that duty and reason are all that count when it comes to virtue, and thereby made an important step towards the validation of the emotions that arrived soon after, with the Romantic movement. But he kept Cicero's connection between what one should do and what we imagine other people will think and say if we fail to come up to scratch. Smith, indeed, elevated human sensitivity to the opinions of others into a total explanation of how and why morality works. He was modern in his insistence on delving into the individual's apprehensions of reality. But for Smith "gratitude" almost always meant "reward"—and this, significantly, needs to be explained in modern discussions of his book. Other people "show gratitude" when we behave well—that is, they reward us with their approbation, and they punish us with "resentment" when we are bad. His view is therefore heavily relativist: everything depends on what a particular society deems "proper."

The ancient "shame culture" component of this view of morality is evident. But so is the new emphasis on how people—even those merely watching a transaction—feel.

In the realm of politeness, it is still the case today that a receiver who does not *feel* gratitude should nevertheless thank the giver verbally and later provide a favour or a gift in return. Politeness is "shame culture"; it cares about social propriety before it cares about sincerity, or even morality. A known thief, provided he is clean, properly dressed, a skilled conversationalist, and mannerly, is far more likely to be invited to a polite dinner party than is a filthy, ragged, inarticulate beggar who is innocent of any crime. For it is manner and appearances that normally count before morals or feelings, among people who practise a preferential option for gentility. Making a social gaffe— eating with one's mouth open, bringing up the wrong subjects in conversation, being smelly—is likely to be unforgivable, essentially because morality is not the criterion: manners are. And a judgment based on shame is without redress: people with poor manners will find themselves definitively excluded from polite society, not asked back if they were ever asked in the first place.

What one does rather than what one feels is what matters where politeness is the point. A polite person can therefore *say* "thank you" and not mean it—she may even go through dissembling motions, looking as though she feels grateful. Such behaviour is much less offensive than making no response at all; it can indeed be a form of respect offered to the goodwill of others, where we really cannot summon up an emotional reaction to it. But still, given the basic suppositions of our "guilt" culture, expressing gratitude that is not meant and returning a favour entirely out of duty may be polite, but they do not constitute gratitude. "Not every person who fulfils the duties of gratitude," wrote La Rochefoucauld, "can flatter himself on that account that he is grateful."[10]

Politeness rules have their own wisdom. For example, in the course of polite human interaction, ordering and asking are essentially discourteous acts: one imposes or interrupts in order to perform them. They therefore need to be hedged in polite conversation ("Would you mind very much if I asked you to close the window?"): as a general rule, the longer one takes to say something, the politer. Thanking a person for doing the favour requested ("Thanks," the shortest and simplest response, is casual and therefore intimate) serves to repair the tiny rift or imbalance that has been created by asking. There is rarely any feeling involved, yet repeatedly being "rude" and then not smoothing things out, by apologizing if necessary, can lead to serious—that is, emotional—annoyance, and even an eventual breakdown of relations.[11] It is usually advisable to behave politely simply to avoid the unpleasantness that is likely to ensue otherwise.

The reasoning behind the rule is that saying "thank you" and "giving back" are, even today, social acts with desirable consequences that include goodwill and the cohesion of the group. *Not* thanking and *not* giving in return, especially after receiving a considerable favour, can cut links, discourage giving, and hurt feelings. They also scandalize onlookers: society strives to see to it that while not showing gratitude is a game that might be tempting, it is seldom worth the candle. Society can, of course, reward and punish only gratitude and ingratitude that are *shown,* for feelings lie out of sight unless they are expressed; what onlookers see, name, and judge is most obviously what is given, what is said, what is done. Society also lays down rules of politeness, as we have seen, for how to show one's gratitude, especially in public. Thanking has to be appropriate to the services given. A simple hug or even a nod and murmured thanks might be enough, while sending a large bouquet of flowers could be insufficient: politeness rules are acutely conscious of demonstrations that are either overdone or inadequate. It depends on what has been given or done, how much it cost the giver, how much it means to the recipient, and what the relationships are between the people concerned.

But despite the advisability of proportion and of *savoir faire* generally, ordinary modern people persist in thinking that the emotional component of thankfulness is what gratitude "really" is. "Giving back," in this view, should result from the primary facts, which are the understanding and the emotion arising from it. Without this motivation, the actions of saying "thank you" and returning a favour (which the opposite camp considers to be the whole point) seem merely conventional at best, and certainly not genuine gratitude. This belief prevails in part because, in a society where social pressures are relatively weak, emotion is expected to take up the slack: it has to provide an internalized motivation for reciprocity, in the form of grateful feelings. Freedom and individualism, as we saw, are linked to the likelihood of people feeling what we mean by "gratitude." Deeper down, we adhere to an ancient tradition of insistence on motivation and on what we really feel. Saint Paul writes that it is possible to give away all I have to feed the poor, or to be burned alive for my beliefs—but if these things are not done out of love, they are worthless.[12]

Feelings, attitudes, and motives matter at least as much as actions do; indeed where gratitude is involved, they often matter more. It is possible for someone to be deeply grateful and yet not reciprocate because there is no opportunity or no means to do so. Even showing gratitude by saying we are thankful can be trumped by sufficient proof of emotion, provided that it is sincere. Emily Dickinson says that a person can feel so grateful that she is unable to speak; she weeps instead, and her tears, insisting on being shed, are a purer expression of her soul's gratitude than any words—or deeds—could be:

> To try to speak, and miss the way
> And ask it of the Tears,
> Is Gratitude's sweet poverty,
> The Tatters that he wears—

> A better Coat if he possessed
> Would help him to conceal,
> Not subjugate, the Mutineer
> Whose title is "the Soul."[13]

The demand for feeling is, of course, a demand for sincerity. "Action can be coerced," wrote Erving Goffman, "but a coerced show of feeling is only a show"[14]—and a "show," which in highly regulated and formal societies may be enough, is not sufficient at all in a society such as our own, which prizes the egalitarian, the spontaneous, the casual.[15] And sincerity cannot be forced: the soul is a "Mutineer" and will not be subjugated. Gratitude in particular makes, as we have seen, a particular claim to be given *gratis:* it insists that a giver who does not receive thanks from a receiver has no right to demand it. One reason for this insistence on freedom is that feelings cannot be produced to order, and it is real (not pretended) feeling that counts. (It is interesting that certain muscles of the face that we employ whenever we make a genuine smile are impossible to move by direct intention alone. An actor can produce a genuine smile—but only if she first and wholly enters the part she is playing.)

A person might recognize another's benevolence and be truly grateful for that, even if the gift itself does not particularly please. It is possible also to feel grateful for benevolence in and of itself, without a specific manifestation of it; this is common between close friends, who can rest upon the history of their loving relations. For somehow one has to have been convinced that the benevolence is there. It is hard to take seriously a claim that someone is either grateful or loving when there is no action to show it. That is one practical reason why people show their love by acts of kindness and "prove" their gratitude, if they can, by doing something in return. But our definition of "gratitude" is still not merely the action, but the emotion and the thought that give rise to it.

We should not be too quick, however, to think that where the other point of view—the privileging of action—prevails, people ignore feeling altogether. Emotions are felt by the individual, and the social fabric may count, quite simply, for more. Indeed, the feeling component of gratitude, especially in stories (where readers and audiences "look on" rather than take part in the action), seems often to have been understated because it was so obvious, and even because it was so deeply felt. The audience is left to divine the feelings from their results: it is a powerful literary device for tapping into the readers' and the listeners' own emotions. Homer's *Iliad,* for example, begins with the anger of Achilles over his slighted honour, and his determination to force the other Greeks to recognize his worth. His mother, the goddess Thetis, implores Zeus on his behalf to let the Trojans prevail in the war until the Greeks are forced to beg the insulted and sulking Achilles to come back and fight. After all, Thetis reminds Zeus, her son is fated to die young; he deserves this honour.

The demand is outrageously partial: the mother has only her son's interests at heart and cares nothing for the sufferings her request entails for the rest of the Greek army. Why then does Zeus bow his head and agree to intervene, permitting all the carnage that ensues? Why do gods and men accept his decision without a murmur, when they are so quick to complain on other, less egregious occasions of the gods' meddling on behalf of their human sons and favourites? The answer is that Zeus is deeply grateful to Thetis, to the point where he cannot refuse her request. Homer's audience knew the story, and the poet needed only to mention the facts obliquely in order to move listeners deeply; modern people have to be reminded of the background.

Both Zeus and Poseidon were in love with Thetis, longed to marry her, were rivals for her hand. But Themis, goddess of prophecy, revealed that Thetis was fated to give birth to a son greater than his father. She advised that Thetis should marry a mortal instead of one of the greatest of the gods, so that her son—greater than his father—would, however heroic, merely die as mortals do. Thetis obeyed, married the mortal Peleus, and gave birth to Achilles. In agreeing to do this Thetis had averted the downfall of Zeus and with that the overthrow of the cosmos. Homer mentions this story only a few times. Zeus is never made to express his feelings. Homer expects us, however, both to know Zeus's reasons and to imagine how he felt. How could Zeus refuse the request of this goddess whom he loved, who had saved his life, who had rescued the universe? Zeus's gratitude for the selfless sacrifice of Thetis, who nevertheless so intensely loved her human, brilliant, and doomed son, broods over the entire *Iliad*.[16]

The folktales of the Grateful Lion, the Grateful Dolphins, or the Kind and the Unkind Girls similarly say nothing about what the protagonists feel: the characters show the depth of their gratitude through their actions. This is an aspect of the genres of folktale and myth—and it is still a powerful narrative method, even in the novel, which permits an author to tell us directly what is going on in the minds of the characters. Novelists today are aware that it is usually wiser, more vivid, more concrete, more provocative of the reader's engagement to *show* how their characters feel through an external economy of gestures, actions, and speech, than to keep the readers passive by telling them what exactly those feelings are. When we are leading our own lives, however, we cease to be watchers; we are subjects and agents, responding with feeling to external events. As far as gratitude is concerned, the "drama" of the return gift is our own to perform, and it springs from the emotion we feel in response to another's goodness.

We saw that scientists, even social scientists, have not, until recently, paid much attention to studying the emotions. But even after the rise of an intense academic interest in the emotions, gratitude has taken extra decades to be considered worthy of investigation. That is because, given the scientific definition of an emotion, gratitude has difficulty fulfilling the conditions required. For example, thankfulness might be profoundly felt, but it is rarely a turbulent emotion—and as we have seen, emotions are defined as agitation. We are told that the autonomic nervous system shows no distinctive patterns of activity for it, although researchers repeatedly and understandably complain that it is difficult to precipitate gratitude in a laboratory setting in order to measure it. Perversely for an emotion, furthermore, gratitude is supposed to last. "I'll never forget your kindness," grateful people say and mean it, unaware that scientists believe emotions must always be sudden, involuntary, and short-lived. And then gratitude necessarily arises out of relationships with other people. Worse, it requires reflection and intentionality: it is not, therefore, a purely physical, automatic arousal. Expressing thanks is often simply a matter of etiquette—that is, it can depend entirely on will and habit, and require no emotion at all. Gratitude, complex and multilayered, reaches deeply into culture and social life, with characteristics such as "appropriateness" attached to it. And finally, gratitude has not counted as an emotion because, unlike rage or terror, disgust or contempt, it is said to lack a facial expression of its own.

But grateful people do in fact look grateful; their facial expressions often change in the course of the realizations involved in thankfulness. A person conscious of having received a great favour typically becomes silent, her features still. Should her benefactor be present, she looks into his eyes and often smiles: pleasure is an essential component of gratitude.[17] The receiver may embrace the giver and may also, as in Emily Dickinson's poem, be moved to tears. There could be a surprised reaction before the features grow still: surprise and relief are major triggers of grateful emotions. Thankful people typically experience the favour offered by the giver as unexpected, undeserved, or both.

Silence is for thought: the grateful receiver realizes the extent of the favour, the cost to the giver, the value of this goodness to herself. There will also be trust involved, and openness in the expression of her face, as she freely accepts indebtedness, while perhaps already making a resolution to give something in return when an opportunity arises. In our culture, deliberately looking into another's eyes is a powerful expression of connectedness: gratitude's most important component is relationship accepted with joy. And finally, the grateful person says "thank you" and may add an expression of "warm"—that is, genuinely felt—appreciation.

Careful experimenting has been deemed necessary to establish that people are more likely to thank others who help them when eye contact occurs between them. Psychology students at the University of Bristol stood guard, unbeknownst to passersby, at swing doors in the library. As somebody passed through, an experimenter would rush forward and hold the door open for him. Two experiments involved a researcher going in the same direction as the passer-through, and two required an approach to the passer-through from the opposite direction. It was found that a person going through swing doors behind somebody moving in the same direction (that is, the experimenter in front was walking with his back to the innocent "participant") would very rarely say "thank you" for having the door held open for him; he did say "thank you" if the person in front turned round as he held the door open, or if he was approaching from the opposite side and looked into the "participant's" eyes. On all occasions where eye contact took place, the participant thanked his thoughtful benefactor. The thanks grew more emphatic the more effort was spent by increasingly effusive door-openers—provided they looked into the eyes of their beneficiaries. (An observer stood unobtrusively by the wall in front of the door opening, to watch the lips of the passer-through and to take notes.) It was proven in this manner that people thank when eye contact is made, but usually say nothing at all when presented only with the back of a helper's head.[18]

Humility is often a prerequisite for the joy of gratitude, since the receiver temporarily accepts the lower place. We recall Emily Dickinson's picture of gratitude as "himself" poor and wearing tatters; that is because a deeply grateful person typically feels unable to respond adequately to extraordinary goodness in another. Facial expressions arising from thankfulness are in some cultures augmented—or replaced—by external gestures expressing humility, in the actual lowering of the body. Nodding the head, an abbreviation of bowing movements, is for us a gesture of acknowledgement, and is often part of our demonstrating thankfulness. When we shake hands as a formal gesture of gratitude, it is a symbol of admiration, benevolence, and gratitude on both sides, through a dramatization of connectedness in the clasping of hands. The giver of an honour feels grateful to the one honoured for what she has achieved, and the receiver for her part feels grateful for the honour.

The heart, as we saw, has been scientifically proven to be important for the feeling of emotions, just as non-scientists have always claimed. People say in English that they speak and relate most sincerely and most directly "heart to heart"; that is, they communicate what is interior to them with each other in total openness and trust. The heart is thought of as "central" to a person, although this organ lies in fact high up in the body and usually to the left within the human chest. It is also imagined as "deep" within and as such as the seat of who we most genuinely are. We should perhaps be grateful to our culture for continually suggesting to us that at our core (the word is from the Latin for "heart") we are loving and benevolent. When we express thanks, we want to assure others that we are "warm" and sincere. We therefore say that our gratitude is "heartfelt" or, more extravagantly, that we are thankful "from the bottom of our hearts."

Gratitude, as a feeling, is something interior to the person, yet it has exterior manifestations and consequences. Parents teach their children gratitude—first to show it, then to feel it. We saw how the day that a child spontaneously feels grateful and says so is a momentous sign of his or her development, both personal and social. It is likely that this step will be preceded by another: *not* feeling grateful but realizing that "gratitude," in the circumstances, is "called for," and supplying the correct demonstrations. Feeling grateful is in fact a *further* stage; being polite, although cerebral, complicated, and "proper," actually occupies a more primitive level than that of true gratitude. Once children have experienced real gratitude, they no longer need to be prompted (or at least not often) to feel that they owe something in return to people who have been kind to them. This "unnatural," entirely taught attainment, the ability to feel indebted-because-grateful, has often been attacked by those who believe that it is forced on people by society and the social system: it is debunked as an imposition, a compulsion, a cunning social manoeuvre that is covered over and flattered by a pretense named "gratitude." But it is a mistake always to suspect mere benightedness in people who say they feel sincerely grateful and who insist that they give back freely.

For there is a distinction between gratitude and contractual indebtedness, and the difference between them lies precisely in areas of feeling and of freedom. To begin with, gratitude involves no prescribed contract, to be strictly fulfilled by a certain date, appropriately under pain of legal sanction. With a

FEELING GRATEFUL ✦ 283

contract, everything is agreed in advance. This is impossible with gratitude, where the future remains undetermined. When someone owes a contractual debt, he need feel no desire to be either generous or especially kindly disposed towards the person to whom he is indebted. Indeed, until he has paid up, he is likely to want to avoid his creditor. Someone grateful, on the other hand, wants to continue the relationship initiated by the giver of a favour, and seeks ways of helping her in some manner, undefined and freely chosen, on some future occasion still to be discovered. There is a creative element in gratitude, as there is in giving, which is excluded by contracts and debts.

A promise, like a contract, must be fulfilled. A sincerely grateful response, on the other hand, like the part of a gift that is not purely conventional, is freely given; as an emotion, it is spontaneously felt. An ancient and widely told folktale, "The Grateful Dead," plays with the difference between contract and gratitude. The story has many variants,[19] but in essence it goes like this: A man finds a corpse lying beside the road unburied, and despite great cost to himself manages to bury it. The ghost of the dead man appears to him, thanks him profusely, and promises to help him make his fortune, on condition that he, the Grateful Dead, will get half of everything gained. The man agrees. After many adventures together, the man finds what he really wants in life: a beautiful woman whom he wants to marry. But when the hero, with the help of his sidekick, has met and obtained the consent of his beloved, the Grateful Dead demands the fulfillment of the bargain: the man must now divide his wife in two. He is horrified, but realizes that a promise is a promise. He draws his sword and is about to cut the sleeping woman in half, when the ghost stops him, says he merely wanted to test the man's constancy, and disappears.

Gratitude, unlike contractual obligation, is freely given and so escapes from necessity. It transcends Fate. The story says that "promises must be kept"; circumstances offer no extenuation. Fate cares nothing for how well-meaning someone is when he makes a decision that will later prove to have been disastrous. It actually thrives on such fiendish traps—and they can certainly inspire wonderful stories. A contract is a contract and "half" means "half": cut the woman in half, then![20] In the end—at least in this version—the Grateful Dead is only a tease. He admires the hero's decision to do his duty despite his feelings. We might consider the ghost to have been truly grateful because he lets the hero off his contract even though, given the story's deference to precision, he need not have done so.

21

Learning and Lasting

Gratitude always has a giving side and a receiving side: at least two people then, their personalities, and their stories; two gifts (or one, which must then confront a crying gap); either sincere inner feeling exteriorized by physical action, or the ritual expression of regard together with the enactment of emotion not actually felt; inner freedom combined with social pressure to "behave"; either a self-induced or a socially demanded sense of obligation, or both—even though gratitude must be spontaneously felt in order to count as gratitude; an intricately structured communication of intentions, attitudes, and feelings first on one side, then on the other; thought and emotion interacting and then inspiring action; on either side a powerful narrativity and memory of the past, invoked even as a new incident occurs to ensure the continuation of the narrative—and then, in addition, the negotiation of a whole network of considerations that prescribe how an act of thanking and giving back is to be done, which every one of us has had to learn in order to make our way within our own particular social world. Gratitude is a complicated business indeed.

Interpersonal relationships in all their complexity are, after all, what engender human emotions, and very particularly gratitude. And being thankful itself can be thought of as a compound emotion. According to a recent example of cognitive analysis, gratitude combines admiration ("approving of someone else's praiseworthy action") and joy ("being pleased about a desirable event").[1] The adjectives *praiseworthy* and *desirable* are wisely mentioned here, for gratitude involves moral judgment and appreciation as well; it is about what another's action means, and how it affects oneself. Gratitude, according to this study, is likely to be intensified by its double source, and therefore felt more powerfully than either of its constituent elements, so that gratitude is a stronger emotion than admiration, just as remorse is sharper than one of its components, distress. Thinking, as we have seen, is capable of heightening the emotion still further.

During any episode of receiving-and-feeling-grateful, changes and developments occur. It all begins, often, with surprise or relief resulting from the giver's action, and pleasure almost immediately follows. The receiver then turns towards the other, the benefactor. She imagines what the giver means by his action, what made him give in this way. She is moved by the thought that she herself is the object of his benevolence. Wonder at the present happy surprise can give rise to a new understanding of the relationship and a new view of this giver, or confirm an already strong admiration for the giver's goodness; in gratitude, love can be kindled or intensified, knowledge achieved or deepened. Grateful emotion finds physical expression—not perhaps as dramatic or as unique as the reactions accompanying fear, anger, or disgust, but often visible nonetheless; grateful people are, for example, sometimes moved to tears. Culturally determined words and appropriate actions—thanks and hugs, for example—must follow immediately. Then comes reflection on the future: How should she respond? What can she herself do later, to give him a pleasant surprise too and a token of her own love?

At every step, the sequence could break down. The service could be unwanted, badly timed, or done without grace. The receiver of it could fail to be either surprised or pleased. She may even feel that she deserves it and wonder why she did not receive it sooner. She could be annoyed if she wanted no intervention—or none from this particular giver. She might be pleased at the favour but ignore the giver, forgetting about him altogether in her satisfaction at getting what she needed or desired. Being aware that gifts make links, she might resent the very idea of a link being made. A failure, for whatever reason, to consider the other person would prevent the flow of kindly thoughts about him from occurring. There would be no love, no increase of understanding, and finally no possibility of wanting to make a return. The fact that emotions cannot be exacted makes it imperative that gratitude occur in freedom. Should the giver insist on a return gift, he destroys not only gratitude but the very definition of what he handed over: whatever it was, it was not a gift. Emotions must arise spontaneously. And yet Georg Simmel wrote that "gratitude is perhaps the only feeling which, under all circumstances, can be morally demanded and rendered."[2] And Simmel is right.

The reason has to do with the bridges between one stage and the next, in the very summary sequence sketched out above. Why feel surprise? Why relief? Why pleasure? Why should a receiver, having got what she wanted, turn to the one who gave it, in wonder, admiration, or love? And then—to repeat Mauss's question—"Why give back?" Human beings think; and thankfulness is both deeply emotional and a form of thought. Since it is not a purely natural and automatic response, gratitude has to be taught—first that it exists and is possible, then how to recognize it and the occasions for it, and finally that one is capable of it oneself. One day a person feels it, and henceforth knows what it is, from within and not merely from observation. Being disposed to be grateful may now, if she practises it, become part of what we call her "character." Gratitude arises from a specific circumstance—being given a gift or done a favour—but depends less upon that than on the receiver's whole life, her character, upbringing, maturity, experience, relationships with others, and also on her ideals, including her idea of the sort of person she is or would like to be. One can see the mighty influences of "culture" in all this: gratitude is taught within the context of a specific culture, and is usually carried out through the medium of a manners system. We have already seen that the notion of "gratitude" is culturally delimited and named. Gratitude is not a knee-jerk reaction; it does not cause automatic withdrawal like disgust or vastly heightened physical energy like anger. It does produce a response, undetermined in its nature but very specific in its reason—which always goes beyond the gift to the giver.

A feeling of gratitude, as we noted, often begins with surprise. It might seem that surprise is something wholly involuntary: many of the seekers for the "fundamental"—that is, the automatic—emotions have included "surprise" among them, along with rage, disgust, and the rest. In one sense, being startled is a wholly physical reaction. But surprise may also be a consequence of intelligence, and this is where gratitude begins. It is possible to cultivate in oneself a capacity for surprise.[3] This readiness demands attention—the sheer noticing of what is going on. Out of a habit of paying attention develops the ability to discern revealing juxtapositions and incongruities: surprise often causes people to laugh. A similar attainment is that of being able to "tell the difference." Gratitude has a great deal to do with imagining what it would be like if things were different.[4] Somebody, or some institution, gives a student money that frees her to pursue knowledge that interests her rather than spend her time working on what does not. She knows perfectly well—she can picture it—what the year would have been like without this grant of money. It is precisely the comparison between what might have been and what now is that makes her grateful. Not having expected the grant, which renders the change more sudden and surprising to her, is likely to make her more grateful still.

A grateful person does not, as we put it, "take things for granted." The phrase refers to a wholly ungrateful taking of matters as "given"—and therefore uninteresting. The French say we take something "as having been acquired," *pour acquis*. This means that we cease to think about this thing ("I already have that," "Been there, done that")—and turn to the next. "Taking for granted" is about benefiting from advantages or riches or other people *without a thought,* leaning on what we have but forgetting about it and looking elsewhere; "taking for granted" is often an aspect of greed. Gratitude turns down this option. It remembers, thinks, takes an interest, compares, perceives reasons to be surprised, and agrees to be pleased with what has been given. In a further, even more thoughtful step it looks beyond the granted to the giver. All these reactions, which demand liveliness, awareness, and practice, can be taught and learned, even though they cannot be enforced.

The elderly mother of a friend of mine was eligible for a Canada Pension, and every month she received it. Every month she forgot about it, and had also ceased to remember why such a sum of money should ever arrive in an envelope with her name on it. The result was that every single month she was thrilled and amazed at the generosity of the unknown people who had sent her a cheque; she would ask her children who they could possibly be and why they had favoured her in this way. Her gratitude and her pleasure were unfailingly ignited by her surprise—and were also the result of a lifelong habit of being grateful to the giver for whatever she received.

When people, by convention, wrap presents, they are doing so in part to provoke surprise as a possible precursor to gratitude when the receiver opens the gift and discovers what is inside. Surprise is so important to the drama of opening a present that if it is not felt, the receiver out of politeness often feigns it. Such surprise need not be provoked entirely by the gift; it should derive at least as much from the action of giving and its reasons. Pleased surprise is indeed part of "giving back"; it gives pleasure to the giver. Being surprised excludes both taking for granted and the deadening effects of what some psychologists call "habituation." Experiencing a happy surprise, like gratitude itself, is an emotion that awakens thought and pleasure; in this it is the opposite of feeling bored.

Another convention is that return for a gift should normally not take place at once; it should occur only after an appropriate lapse of time. This gap helps to make the gift's return into something that might not have happened; it could therefore be a surprise, or even cause relief, when it does. In any event, the time that passes between gift and return is time for the receiver to remember and remain grateful. A gift may not be returned for many years, perhaps because there has been no opportune moment for the response to occur—and yet the receiver remains faithful to the memory of the favour. When finally the right occasion arrives, the once-receiver turns into a giver, and the happiness of the original giver is great, as he discovers the persistence of the new giver's memory and therefore the depth of his gratitude.

Marie Joseph Gilbert de La Fayette was a French nobleman who supported North American aspirations to freedom and played an active part in the American War of Independence. Nearly a century and a half later, on the Fourth of July 1917, just after the United States entered the First World War, Colonel Charles Stanton made his way to the Marquis's tomb in the cemetery of Picpus in Paris, stood before it, and cried, "La Fayette, we're here!" ("*La Fayette nous voici!*")—a declaration that has remained a fresh and grateful memory (gratitude, that is, for gratitude) in France ever since. Gratitude and its repeated manifestations, including the between-times during which people remember, easily weave themselves into the narrative of two lives—or of two countries.

A further reason for gratitude is often found in cases when the giver comes to believe that his gift is not going to receive any acknowledgement, when he has begun to believe that the other does not care. Should a return gift in fact materialize, he feels grateful to have not been forgotten, for a relationship not broken off, or even out of relief that he need not feel hurt anymore.

After this point, gratitude is more and more the result of the receiver's will. There is an imaginative and comprehending phase, a realization that he is the object of affection, and he allows himself to be moved and pleased at this. Here, perhaps, we might begin to be mystified. For now the receiver ceases to regard himself and the gift that corresponds (or might not correspond) to his needs and tastes, but turns to the other in love and happiness.

The way I have stated this shows joy issuing from gratitude. A well-known psychological theory puts a capacity for enjoyment first, and sees gratitude as its consequence. The psychoanalyst Melanie Klein (1882–1960), who seeks to derive most of human behaviour from the infant's experiences of breast-feeding, thinks that a baby who is satisfied in his suckling is on the way to becoming a grateful adult.[5] He "internalizes the good primal object," by which she means that he accepts the breast as a secure source of satisfaction. Because—and not unless—this has been achieved, he is able in later life to overcome envy and greed and replace them with gratitude.[6]

Klein has some terrifying pages on the hatred of an unsatisfied infant for his mother's breasts: he feels, according to Klein, that a breast that does not give him his milk has spitefully kept gratification to itself, and he longs to spoil the breast and make his mother pay. Should the baby not get what he wants, he becomes not only insatiable when he grows up but even liable to confuse good and evil. A child that has learned enjoyment, on the other hand, will find in himself when he is an adult an ability to devote himself to other people and to social causes. Klein, in short, makes satisfaction at the breast as an infant determine the adult's ability to enjoy, and this capacity provides the likelihood of his being able to be grateful. Gratitude in turn, she says, enables the adult to lead a serene life, and also to recover relatively easily from adversity: he will remember the pleasures of the past and enjoy what the present has to give. Blaming everything on breast-feeding, or crediting everything to it, can seem nowadays to be reductive and even absurd. But Klein's insistence on the connection between first being able to enjoy and then finding thankfulness easy is worth pondering.

The further steps taken in the course of what psychologists call an "episode" of gratitude show how emotion and thought are inextricably intertwined. The social aspects of gratitude—the understanding of relationship, the seeing of oneself as part of a social matrix, the reliance on conventions learned and practised because they make life so much easier and pleasanter when the rules are kept—are folded into the emotional, inner responses "demanded and rendered," as Simmel puts it. Someone who thinks he can properly interact with other people, while feeling nothing, is quite simply mistaken. Those who have to deal with him, who themselves are "demanding and rendering," are extremely skillful and sensitive when it comes to the emotions; they can tell. They will not let going through the motions without any feeling pass without indignation and dislike. An egalitarian society is in its way more pitiless than a hierarchical one: there are more judges, for one thing, they see you closer up, and they can be extremely strict. It is actually impolite, in our culture, to be coldly correct: the casual in human relations is not only accepted but often demanded. And it is extremely difficult to pretend when there are relatively few rules behind which to hide.

Gratitude comes out of something that has already happened; and as an emotion it cannot be a calculated pretense. For both reasons it is reprehensible, in our culture where feeling thankful *is* gratitude, for an appearance of thankfulness to be pressed into use in order to get something out of other people in the future. We have already seen that a genuine gift—and gratitude is a gift and a response to a gift—cannot be given in order to force a return. And people are grateful almost to the exact extent that a return was not the reason for the gift.

But we can learn to control our own emotions.[7] First, we should not let them get "out of hand"—the old metaphor of passions as the wild animals in us, needing to be "reined in" by our conscious selves, the "drivers" of the "chariots" of our souls.[8] We can learn to replace turbulent passions with peaceful emotions. Sincerity is again key: emotions, including peaceful emotions, have to be real, not feigned. The new psychophysiologists, researching the interactions between our hearts and our emotions, have shown that emotional processes operate much faster than thoughts. But, they have discovered, human beings can deliberately—that is, mindfully—intervene and influence the turmoil in their own breasts. They can take the time needed to step back in their own minds from the stressful situation, take deep breaths, consciously focus upon their hearts, and bring to bear their capacity for impersonal appreciation. This "self-generation of positive emotions" increases heart-rhythm coherence, and the regularity rediscovered calms body and mind. It is a habit that can be taught and practised.[9]

The claim has been that gratitude involves thought, yet we now seem to be saying that the thought has to be of the right kind. This is because gratitude is not only thoughtful and emotional but also moral. As Simmel said, it is *morally* demanded and rendered. After all, even emotions can be right or wrong: I would be wrong to be sorry if my rival recovered from an illness, for instance, but right to be sorry for another's suffering, including that of my rival. Given that emotions cannot be coerced, and given also that they are so closely involved with moral action, human beings are educated, or teach themselves, to have the right emotions. They can learn at the very least to be able to tell when they are themselves at fault in their feelings. Emotions, indeed, in their directness, are useful for learning about ourselves; they can reveal to us what it is, deep down, that we value. I might, for example, feel perfectly calm when told that a planned holiday will not take place—but furious merely because I missed meeting somebody recently. I might learn to my surprise from my own reactions that I was not particularly looking forward to the journey, and that I badly wanted to see that person. I can now start asking myself why.

We all recognize gratitude as a moral matter when, as bystanders, we deplore somebody else's ingratitude to another. He has not failed in a duty, unless further factors create a duty, so he cannot be punished or even held to account for his lapse—its source lying in the emotions, after all. We might nevertheless feel free to reproach him, and try to make him reconsider all the factors in his situation. Failure to *feel* grateful is not a dereliction of duty but a moral flaw, and as such related to a person's character in general. A duty, in contrast, is something "due," a clear obligation, a rule that can be "broken." It refers to what is to be done more than to the person doing it. It has little to do with feelings. Gratitude does entail an obligation, which is anterior both to feeling thankful for a particular favour and to the action of returning a benefit: it consists of a responsibility to cultivate in oneself a disposition to be grateful.

So gratitude depends upon education, and specifically education of the character, as parents acknowledge when they spend so much effort teaching it to their children. There is a good deal to be learned about gratitude that goes way beyond manners. Construing a gift includes, first, understanding at least at an unconscious level what gifts are, even though their meaning and operations are complex and far from obvious. Second, it includes judging what people's motives in giving are or could be. Finally, it includes all that is involved in fathoming people and interacting with them. We can learn habitually to remember benefits we have received, and to pay attention to the narrative of our life and how it is unfolding. People are often advised by therapists and other guides to keep diaries, list their advantages in life, think of ten things from the day to be grateful for before falling asleep, and so on. The reason why such methodical disciplines can be useful is that they invite and remind people to remember the good things in their lives—memory being the indispensable precursor of gratitude. Human beings, unlike animals, can deliberately decide to recall events in the past, and they can teach themselves to do so often. This ability can cause us a great deal of suffering—or happiness. People can also "reframe" events—that is, find a good light in which to see them—and learn to emphasize what has been gained rather than what has been lost. Even though it might not be easy, people can practise precipitating feelings of gratitude in their lives. Eventually gratitude becomes "second nature": something that becomes normal, but for which we ourselves are responsible.

The *expression* of gratitude is, we have seen, part of the return "owed" to the giver. In busy modern lives people often forget to thank benefactors, especially for long-standing benefits they have received. After too much time has gone by, they commonly feel it is too late to say thanks. But so important is the expression of gratitude, not only to the giver of the favour but to the receiver as well, that another therapeutic scenario has been devised which deliberately reopens the way to thanking. This is done primarily for the good of *the thanker*. The original giver is left to feel what he may; he might squirm with embarrassment, but he is just as likely to be surprised and grateful for being thanked, even after a long delay.

Practitioners of the new Positive Psychology thoroughly understand the need to show gratitude openly, if at all possible in the presence of the giver.

People who are working on being happy rather than the reverse are urged to try, early on in the process, not only to feel grateful often, but to express their gratitude directly to someone to whom it is owed. Choose one person in your life who has helped you in the past (they are told). Try not to think of the possibility of future gain—the kind of motivation that cynics and scientists have so often accused the grateful of always really harbouring. Write down on a piece of paper just what you are so grateful for. Spend time doing this: several weeks may be needed. (Gratitude requires thought, reflection, memory, time taken.)

Next, make an appointment to see this person. It must be a meeting face to face: a letter or a phone call are to such a degree a second-best option that they will not suffice. Do not tell the person why you are coming to see him or her. Laminate your sheet of paper: it will be a gift and should be something that lasts. You must, soon after your arrival, get out your laminated sheet and read it aloud "slowly, with expression, and *with eye contact* [my italics]." This is part of the facial movement that gratitude itself "naturally" provokes in our culture, and in our culture it both expresses and produces relatedness. Then give the other person time to react. And take further time to discuss. We are told that it is usual on these occasions, when there are often other people present as well, to see "literally not a dry eye in the room."[10]

Some scientists argue that by definition emotions do not last. One suggestion has been, however, that some emotions do, and that we might save the idea of sudden and short-term emotions, biologically determined for the survival of the fittest, by calling lasting feelings "sentiments." Emotions would be "organic" and sentiments "processed."[11] Alternatively, we can keep the short duration of emotions and admit that people might have ongoing dispositions to feel them. Fear is easily triggered in a "fearful" person; that does not mean the person lives in unrelieved fear. I can say, "I have loved him for thirty years" and mean it, even though I have not thought only of him all my life: what I am saying is that my love has been an important background to everything I have thought or done, that it has always been there, "on the back burner," ready to be turned to and called upon. Gratitude, similarly, is easily felt by people for whom thankfulness has become part of their emotional landscape, their "repertoire." An emotion often felt in its turn reacts upon and strengthens the disposition to feel it again.

The links created by gratitude are highly specific in respect of persons, despite the freedom allowed as to feelings and as to the actions chosen to express gratitude. The fact that one is grateful to a person makes gratitude last much longer than the time taken for the simple handing over of a gift in return; giving-and-returning may be over, but true gratitude remains. Gratitude from this point of view resembles loyalty. It is also like loyalty in that a proof of its reality is that it lasts; they are both forms of faithfulness. For both, dispositions of openness to and a readiness to oblige a specific person or group are essential: the disposition may be more important even than the actions arising out of it. Gratitude, indeed, frequently makes us disposed to reciprocate even if we cannot find a way of doing so.

About two-thirds through Charles Dickens's *Great Expectations* (1861),[12] the novel's 23-year-old hero, Pip, hears a footstep on the stairs late at night, and a big man with long iron-grey locks appears, holding out both his hands and apparently pleased to see him. Pip invites him in, not without resentment because this unknown man seems to expect him to respond. After some time contemplating him—the man holds both hands out again—Pip realizes that this is none other than the escaped convict he had met among the tombs as a child, whom he had hidden and fed and whose presence he had kept secret until the man succeeded in getting away.

Pip now gives the man his hands and submits to having them kissed: "You acted noble, my boy . . . And I have never forgot it!" Pip pushes the old man away to avoid an embrace, and says primly, "If you are grateful . . . I hope you have shown your gratitude by mending your way of life. If you have come here to thank me, it was not necessary." The man's eyes fill with tears. He holds Pip's hand as he tells the story of his life as a sheep farmer in Australia, how he had worked hard and done "wonderful well." In deep embarrassment, and longing for the man to go away, Pip returns the two pound notes that the man, whose name is Magwitch, had given him in return, all those years ago. Magwitch burns the notes and drops the ashes into the drinks tray.

It is Pip's turn to tell how *he* has done. He relates how fortune has favoured him: he has been chosen to succeed to property, although he does not yet know what or by whom. Magwitch lets Pip know that he is aware of everything that has happened, down to the smallest details. Then Pip realizes that it is to Magwitch the convict, this vulgar, rough man, that he owes his fortune. Pip almost faints; the man catches him and lays him on the sofa, goes down on one knee beside him and puts his face up close to Pip's. "It's me wot has done it," declares the convict. It was he who had "made Pip a gentleman," working and saving for him, thinking of him with gratitude for sixteen years. "Do I tell it fur you to feel a obligation?" cries the man. "Not a bit."

Pip feels no gratitude whatever, only abhorrence and dread. He loathes the very idea that he has been beholden to a man like Abel Magwitch. He shrinks from the man (who keeps kissing his hands), and his blood runs cold. Pip learns next that Magwitch has risked his life to see Pip, for if caught he will be executed. He trusts Pip not to turn him in to the police. Pip hates the man. If only he loved him, he realizes, "his preservation would then have naturally and tenderly addressed my heart." He gives the man a meal and a bed: Magwitch again takes both Pip's hands in his and says "good night," leaving Pip, alone at last, to brood on his own faithlessness to Joe, on the fact that Estella was *not* designed for him—the rich "gentleman" Pip—by Miss Havisham, and on the convict's promise to make Estella his "if money can buy."

Pip now truly begins to learn who he is and what mistakes he has made. He tries to help Magwitch escape. But Magwitch is wounded in a fight with a man who betrays him, and is caught by the police. Pip has come far enough at this point to find his repugnance for Magwitch gone: "In the hunted, wounded, shackled creature who held my hand in his I only saw a man who had meant to be my benefactor, and who had felt affectionately, gratefully and generously towards me with great constancy through a series of years. I only saw in him a much better man than I had been to Joe." Pip refuses to pretend that he does not know Magwitch, and faithfully stands beside him in the dock, holding Magwitch's hand, when the sentence is delivered. He visits him in prison, and places both his hands on the old man's chest when Magwitch dies. He goes to thank Joe and Biddy for everything they did for him. He begs forgiveness for his ingratitude to them, and vows to work and repay all the money Joe had spent on paying off his debts. "Don't think," says Pip, "that if I could repay it a thousand times over, I suppose I could cancel a farthing of the debt I owe you, or that I would do so if I could!"

Dickens tells here a tale of redemption through the medium of gratitude, learned and lasting. He does it with gestures, chiefly the clasping of hands, the sign of commitment and connectedness—so horrifying to someone who wants no connection, but a pledge of relationship when accepted on both sides. Gratitude is like an emotional and willing hand-clasp in friendship. Truth is a mighty part of gratitude, and so is justice. Even they are not enough, however. There remains the willingness to see and understand, and the freely taken step of accepting one's own commitment for the future. Pip "gives back" and is therefore saved. He will go away and work hard for eleven years, remaining grateful all that time to Joe and Biddy, and only then will return to see them and to meet their child, to whom they will give his name, Pip.

Gratitude will have deepened and strengthened Pip's friendship with Joe and Biddy: that will be his reward. He needed—just as much as Oedipus did, or Achilles—to find out who he was and what he really cared about. For Pip, it is gratitude that reveals and underpins both discoveries. Suffering and loss will have to be undergone, but they are worth the price. The "great expectations" of the novel's title become deeply ironic, but in another sense they are very real, should the reader understand what it is that Dickens believes to be genuinely important. Pip says he expects always to remain, and wants to remain, obligated to his benefactors, even after he has repaid the last farthing. He accepts, of his own free will, the endlessness of his debt. He is indeed *happy* to be obliged to them. "Happy to be obliged" is friendship.

PART V

∞

Rejecting

22

The Marble-Hearted Fiend

It is difficult for modern people to sympathize, let alone agree, with what was once a common precept and often taken for granted in our own culture: that ingratitude is the most terrible of all sins. Distasteful, hurtful, selfish, a vice—ingratitude is for us all these things. But we do not ordinarily think it the most heinous crime of all, worse, for example, than murder or hatred or robbery. Yet Kant as late as 1797 called it "the essence of vileness and wickedness," a horror so evil that it was almost unimaginable to normal human beings. Long before Kant, a medieval Latin adage declared, *Ingratitudo peccatum maximum,* "Ingratitude is the greatest sin of all."[1] The idea was expressed in English by John Lydgate in 1439:

> For of al vicis, shortli to conclude,
> Werst of alle is ingratitude.[2]

Something has dramatically, and fairly recently, changed in our attitude towards ungratefulness, and it is worth considering both sides of the question. What made ingratitude so wicked from the Middle Ages on, and why did outrage at lapses in gratefulness grow to a climax during the Renaissance? The section after this one will address the second question: What has reduced in passion (though not removed) our reactions to ingratitude today?

The loathing of ingratitude had historical roots in feudal and tribal social rules. Later it came to depend on a vivid realization of gratitude's importance for coherence in society—and of ingratitude's corresponding destructiveness. And eventually people began to understand that the responsibility for encouraging gratitude in everyday human relationships fell squarely on the shoulders of every individual person. Gratitude had to be taught by fathers and mothers to children—but could not be enforced by law. Therefore a perceived rise in ungrateful behaviour was not only a terrifying threat to society as a whole; it was also something that only the moral outrage of people witnessing ingratitude could address. What we often hear is that outrage in full throttle.

We have already seen how loyalty, as the binding force of benefactions from a lord and the duty of a vassal to "give" in return, helped to hold feudal hierarchies together. People talked then of loyalty and of fealty (allegiance or fidelity) rather than of *gratitudo,* which was a word created during the thirteenth century out of the earlier Latin term *gratia.* The arrival of the word *gratitudo* was a small sign of the dawning of profound social changes. Feudal practice was gradually being replaced by centralized government, codified law, and the spread of commerce; society was of necessity coming to depend on new kinds of ties to keep it together. Gratitude became during this later period the subject of a good deal of engrossing discussion: in any culture, as we saw, words for emotions both stress and define, when definition is felt to be necessary, segments of the continuum of human feelings. *Gratitude* emerged partly as a replacement for feudal loyalty, adding increasingly strong doses of freedom and equality while attenuating—though keeping—notions of moral obligation and faithfulness.

Ingratitude too was a newly formed word. The concept obviously resembled treachery against those to whom loyalty was owed, and accordingly it inherited feudal vituperations against breaking faith with one's lord. But *treachery* is all action, frequently political action, and involves hypocrisy and cunning; it is a word cognate with *trickery,* from French *tricher,* "to cheat." "Ingratitude," however, was from the beginning less political, more personal than full-blown treachery; it was a vice very often committed and suffered at the level of everyday life. It meant being unkind to *anyone* who has treated us well, not helping him if we can do so—especially if he is in need—and failing to respect him. It also included the feelings and attitudes that result in failure to do a good deed when it is one's "turn" to perform one. People continued habitually to speak of gratitude and ingratitude as things done rather than thoughts or emotions, but the implication of internalized personal feeling had become stronger than it was in either feudal loyalty or treason. Now the very emphasis on the personal was what made ingratitude base.

Thomas Aquinas, writing in the thirteenth century within the tradition that produced the term *gratitudo,* says that this virtue has more to do with feelings than with deeds or words, although one must always thank a bene-factor and give back when one can; even the poorest person can at least thank and honour the giver. Aquinas, referring carefully to Seneca, writes that there are three degrees of gratitude and three corresponding levels of ingratitude.[3] The first and highest level of gratitude is the recognition of a grateful receiver, who turns his attention to the giver and accepts the favour given, together with the obligation—indeed the desire—to respond that it creates. The prior *disposition* to be grateful is important here: a person is not ungrateful if he is unaware of a favour and fails to repay it, but is *predisposed to do so if he knows.* The lowest degree of ingratitude, corresponding to the highest of gratitude, begins with not recognizing the reception of a favour, "whether by forget-ting it or in any other way." The forgetfulness here is not what Aquinas calls "a natural defect," a lapse of memory, but rather the deliberate ignoring of a favour or the refusal to admit that a benefit has been given. This becomes a mortal sin if inward contempt motivates it, or if something necessary to the benefactor's welfare that could be given to him is deliberately withheld. It amounts to thinking of a kindness with loathing, and returning evil for good. Aquinas is no doubt recalling here accusations of this kind of wickedness in the Old Testament Psalms, and the execration in the New Testament of what is called "the sin against the Holy Spirit."[4]

The second level of gratitude is saying "thank you": the verbal expression of felt appreciation. Ingratitude's second degree, accordingly, is declining to indicate that a favour has been received. This can be twisted into actually finding fault with benefits given ("looking a gift horse in the mouth"). The third degree of gratitude is giving something back, "at a suitable place and time, according to one's means." And correspondingly, the third (and least serious) level of ingratitude is failure, where it is possible, to return a favour. Aquinas treats ingratitude with moderation, however, and also puts gratitude and ingratitude "in their place," declining to see them as either the highest virtue or the lowest vice. For him, love is the highest and the central virtue; gratitude is an aspect and a result of love.[5] Ingratitude is blackest when it not only falls short of love, but actually destroys the habit of loving.

Five centuries later, Immanuel Kant (for whom gratitude still is not a feeling but a dutiful and appropriate action) speaks of a kind of ingratitude that is a fault so grave, it is almost incredible that anyone would commit it.[6] For him, the three most horrific vices are inhuman when unalloyed. These are (sheer) ingratitude, (all-consuming) envy, and (utter) malice. Other wickednesses Kant thinks are human because "indirect": he takes it for granted that the human mind has no immediate inclination to wickedness. For Kant, therefore, the kind of ingratitude that issues from pride or selfishness is "human," and so is ungratefulness resulting from a lack of understanding. Not so when someone is guilty of the vilest ingratitude, where a man "cannot bear his benefactor and becomes his enemy." The other two worst vices, envy (wanting to be the only happy person) and malice (directly desiring the misfortune of another), are private or at least localized sins. Treating one's benefactor, knowing he is a benefactor, as one's enemy is worst of all because this is an evil that most obviously produces society-wide effects. "Such ingratitude is of the devil," writes Kant. ". . . If such conduct were the rule it would cause untold harm. Men would then be afraid to do good to anyone lest they should receive evil in return for their good. They would become misanthropic, haters of men."[7] As Hobbes has put it, this kind of ingratitude might bring to an end all peaceful human interaction and unleash uncontrollable violence (Hobbes's "*Warre*") upon humankind.

The word *gratitudo,* once coined, included a reference to the sentiments that a person will, out of his virtue and therefore "naturally," feel. It continued, of course, to refer to an appropriate or proper action, what society deemed suitable because it fitted into conventions and social norms. Ingratitude was therefore an anti-social vice and, as the opposite of the "normal" virtue of gratitude, "unnatural." Ingratitude, adding to disloyalty and faithlessness a disregard for someone's love shown in acts of kindness, came to seem not only improper but immensely cruel, and as such the behaviour of a beast, not a man. In English speech, "kindness" and "unkindness" kept, into the seventeenth century, the connection with "kin" that we examined earlier: ingratitude as "unkindness" could feel close to filial impiety, so deeply unnatural was it.

Other people were responsible for making these judgments and for denouncing ingratitude as abnormal. Before the triumph of modern individualism people were interdependent to an extent that we can barely imagine today. In cities and towns they resided—as we would see it—in such close quarters as to live "on top of each other." They often knew one another from childhood, watched each other, judged each other, kept one another in order, and punished misdemeanours through social strategies, such as destroying reputations and casting the reprobate out of the group, so essential to anyone's well-being. It was the group's duty to prevent or at least discourage ingratitude in particular. For gratitude was a virtue that, despite what was agreed to be its vital importance for the functioning of society, the law could not enforce. We have seen that "gratitude"—even where it is thought of as primarily action, a "return"—should be given as a gift is given, gratis. And the more gratitude is acknowledged to be something felt, the less it can be thought obligatory. Legal support for gratitude would destroy its essence. And therefore legal enforcement is not allowed to punish ingratitude.[8] Even in modern society, therefore, the opinions of other people often step in and exert on the seriously ungrateful the pressure that is social disapproval.

But a longing for the law to punish the ungrateful frequently recurs in human history. Ancient Romans appear occasionally to have found it irresistible, once a slave had been freed, to try to claw back some of that freedom by demanding favours from him. Should he fail to comply, the ex-slave was deemed "ungrateful" for the freedom he had been given.[9] Attempts were apparently made to pronounce a freed slave's "ingratitude" punishable by law, the ultimate application of which would mean that he could be re-enslaved. If they were in fact made, these attempts ultimately failed; we have no proof that the emancipation of a slave was ever revoked for ingratitude. Some scholars believe, however, that Seneca wrote *De Beneficiis* in order to warn the Emperor Nero not to commit the error of making "gratitude" legally enforceable.[10]

But when people discussed the necessity of upholding gratitude in society, and insisted that gratitude was obligation, they habitually pointed to passages in ancient literature to show that there had indeed existed nations that punished ingratitude through recourse to the law.[11] Jonathan Swift satirizes this reliance on the practice of "some other Countries" when he makes the Lilliputians in *Gulliver's Travels* consider ingratitude a capital offence: "Ingratitude is among them a capital Crime, as we read it to have been in some other Countries: For they reason thus; that whoever makes ill Returns to his Benefactor, must needs be a common Enemy to the rest of Mankind, from whom he hath received no Obligation; and therefore such a Man is not fit to live."[12]

Ancient Greeks enjoyed describing oddities in the behaviour of foreigners partly for their amusement value, but also as a means of defining what Greek culture was not, and occasionally to show how Greeks could learn from others to behave better. Xenophon describes the ways of the Persians in his day, the fourth century BC, marvelling at many of their fine social rules. The elite core of one hundred thousand men who lived in the royal palace of Cyrus were, for example, never allowed to spit, blow their noses, or show the slightest inclination to fart. They were never seen leaving a group in order to urinate.[13] Xenophon attributes this superhuman bodily control to Persian abstemiousness from drink, and to the fact that they worked and therefore sweated so much. Their upbringing was rigorous and, he says, "began at the beginning."

Boys accepted for education in the royal palace were taught immunity to any temptation to commit improper or immoral acts. "The boys go to school and spend their time in learning justice," writes Xenophon, the implication being that whereas elite Persian boys studied justice, Greeks learned merely to read and write. " . . . As a matter of course," he goes on, "boys . . . bring charges against one another, just as men do, of theft, robbery, assault, cheating, slander, and other things that naturally come up; and when they discover anyone committing any of these crimes, they punish him, and they punish also anyone whom they find accusing another falsely." And there follows a passage that has been endlessly quoted down the centuries as fundamental for thinking about ingratitude, and especially for suggesting that ingratitude should be punished by law. We notice again that "gratitude" here means mainly a duty to "give something back":

And they bring one another to trial also charged with an offence
for which people hate one another most but go to law least, namely,
that of ingratitude (*acharistias*); and if they know that any one is
able to return a favour and fails to do so, they punish him, and
severely. For they think that the ungrateful are likely to be most
neglectful of their duty toward their gods, their parents, their
country, and their friends; for it seems that shamelessness goes hand
in hand with ingratitude; and it is that, we know, which leads the
way to every moral wrong.[14]

Xenophon gives away in this last sentence the didactic purpose—for his Greek readership, since Persians would be unlikely to read his account—of his description of the perfect Persian upbringing. He has thought about ingratitude, and he wishes, as many have done since, that people would bring their children up to appreciate the damage that ingratitude can cause. Among the Persians gratitude was a matter of upbringing, in this case apparently by means of the "trials" staged in the palace school. However, unlike theft, robbery, assault, and so on, strictures on ingratitude were not codified as law. This was by no means clear when the many subsequent quotations of Xenophon on this subject begin with "And they bring one another to trial . . ." "They" were children, but the truncated passage sounds as though adult Persian society functioned in this way. People felt free then to wish that their own society would take ingratitude seriously enough to punish it by law (which might in fact have been Xenophon's wish).

Ingratitude, Xenophon believes, is the companion of shamelessness, by which he means that ungrateful people are capable of caring nothing for the opinions of outraged others. Honour and shame are opposites that support each other. The true enemy of shame is not honour but shamelessness, which is both a refusal to keep the rules of honour and a resistance to the pressures of shame; it is the ultimate falling-off in an honour culture, and, as Xenophon perceives, "leads the way to every moral wrong." If in an honour culture people cease to care about reputation, then important moral matters that cannot be regulated by law are left with nothing to maintain them. Ingratitude is one of these ungovernable matters; in conjunction with shamelessness it can also lead to the dismantling of an honour system. For if gratitude helps knit society together, ingratitude will prevent relationship from forming and break the links already in place.

Xenophon's point that ungrateful people are likely to go on to commit many other crimes against gods, parents, country, and friends was also to have a long history; it is one of the pillars, constantly referred to, that support the idea that ingratitude is part of every sin—and that ingratitude itself implies every other wickedness. Seneca was to say that ingratitude is worse than murder, tyranny, adultery, robbery, sacrilege, or betrayal, "unless it be that all these spring from ingratitude, without which hardly any sin has grown to great size."[15] The suggestion is that every crime, in its general denial of the necessity of obeying rules of behaviour, involves a breaking away from society. But ingratitude is the worst sin because, as a movement of sheer rejection, it accompanies the preliminary fracture, and then goes on to encourage further breakage. A maxim of Publilius Syrus became, in sixteenth-century English, "We have named all the naughtiness that can be objected when we have termed a man unthankful."[16]

Blanket denunciations of ingratitude as a force for disintegration in any social system also found support in what Aquinas and others saw as gratitude's first requirement, which is remembrance: no memory, no gratitude. Readiness to feel gratitude will, in turn, encourage remembrance, while those disposed to be ungrateful will forget what they owe to others. In the Old Testament, memory and praise are the components of what we call "thanksgiving." Memory links the present to the past, and the deliberate recall and recounting of past benefits is itself a form of gratitude. Civilization, and culture generally, require memory and tradition. The latter (literally, from the Latin, "a handing on") means a kind of gift, from what has been learned through experience, from the past to the present. The society that now accepts the gift is therefore "grateful" to the past. And rejecting the past may be considered an act of "ingratitude."

People have always thought of the capacity for deliberate recall as a distinctively human trait: refusing to remember kindness, therefore, is not only a sign of contempt to a giver and of a general desire to subvert social norms, but also a falling-back of humanity into what is animal—that is, lower—in us. In human beings with their memory and their innate intelligence, ingratitude was perceived as inhuman and unnatural; it has often been said to make human beings resemble rocks or animals. In Shakespeare's *King Lear,* for example, Goneril and Regan are called "tigers, not daughters."[17] Virgil's Dido excoriates the faithlessness of Aeneas with a similar thought:

False one! no goddess was your mother,
Nor was it Dardanus who founded your line,
The flinty rocks of jagged Caucasus begot you!
Hyrcanian tigresses did give you suck![18]

A modern African proverb asserts that "the gratitude of a donkey is a breaking of wind."[19] It means that to expect gratitude from people who are unaware that gratitude exists—whose humanity simply cannot be appealed to—is to court disappointment, and worse. For "natural" though gratitude is in human beings, thanklessness is in a sense more "natural" still. Ingratitude is "lower" and therefore more fundamental in us, whereas gratitude is "higher": we have to strive to learn what it is, to feel it, and to act on it. Some have thought that, despite the word's being formed as a negation of *gratitude*, it was ingratitude that came, and always must come, first because it is easiest and most basic. Ingratitude is unmindful, closed, and essentially inert; it shares some of the characteristics of stone. The worst kind of ingratitude adds to unreachable indifference, immobile as death, the horror of a lively and intentional cruelty. When King Lear cries, "Ingratitude, thou marble-hearted fiend!"[20] the contradictoriness of the image turns ingratitude into a monster of inexorable evil, at once cold and furious, filled with intentional malevolence and yet unmoved. It is a beast with a heart of stone.

Shakespeare, indeed, often chose to hold ingratitude up for scrutiny on stage. For this is, to begin with, a peculiarly dramatic vice. We have noted the importance of other people—onlookers—as judges and potential victims of ingratitude's danger and its nastiness; in the theatre we may all of us take on this witnessing and feeling role. In *King Lear*, Shakespeare sets ingratitude and filial impiety side by side and in interaction. In *Timon of Athens* he shows a man generous to the point of folly, exploited and ruined by ungrateful "friends" until he becomes a misanthrope, a hater of humanity. Macbeth is not only a treacherous regicide but the murderer of his loving benefactor. Coriolanus is a hero, but—although his first word in the play, ironically enough, is "Thanks"—he is also a man obsessive about his honour, in the manner of Aristotle's *megalopsychos* or large-souled man: he refuses to accept benefits, and when a favour is nevertheless done him, forgets about it; he treats a kindness as though it were unkindness. Rome is ungrateful to him—but he is himself ungrateful to Rome.[21]

But Shakespeare's horror at ingratitude cannot be accounted for merely in terms of dramatic potential. For him, ingratitude issued both in personal cruelties of all kinds and in the general rupture of the ties that create and support human relationship. In a paroxysm of suffering, King Lear calls upon the raging storm winds to "strike flat the thick rotundity of the world" which gave birth to "ingrateful man": the world's end, suggested by the storm, seems to Lear in his extremity to be no more terrible than the perniciousness of his two thankless daughters. Indeed, human ingratitude is actually worse than anything the savage elements can inflict:

> I tax not you, you elements, with unkindness.
> I never gave you kingdom, call'd you children,
> You owe me no subscription. Then let fall
> Your horrible pleasure![22]

The cosmos, even in its destructiveness, is innocent. It is human beings who are capable of specifically directed, deliberate cruelty, even to parents and to those who have shown them kindness.

Shakespeare inherited the classical and medieval loathing of ingratitude as treason and as faithlessness, as the source of every kind of wickedness. Yet his hatred of ingratitude—wounding, pitiless, ugly, and inhuman—is so intense that we sense in it not only anger but also a measure of fear. He seems to have had a premonition that the new imperial and commercial era was bringing with it vastly increased and uncontrolled greed and selfishness, which relied on wanton heedlessness of the traditional virtues of community and personal interrelationship. The old certainties embodied by hierarchy and obligations were also breaking down. At the moment of transition in which he lived, all the modern vices—greed, heedlessness, selfishness, refusal either to respect or to remember—readily seemed to be caught up, instanced, and rooted in ungratefulness.

He portrays ingratitude as a monster, with cannibal proclivities exhibited when family members "devour" each other, or when we see a city "like an unnatural dam . . . eat up her own."[23] For ingratitude tears society apart in order to feed the voraciousness of those "on the make." A monster—the word derives from Latin *moneo*, "I point out" or "I warn"—is a creature that mixes species which evolution has carefully separated out, and is therefore unnatural. It crosses categories, making "sameness" into "otherness," for example, when it turns people's fellows into their fodder as cannibals do; it arouses horror and fear in us, and rises up as a warning that things are going terrifyingly wrong.

Ingratitude in Shakespeare is a motiveless iniquity. Why are Goneril and Regan, unlike Cordelia, ungrateful? Why is Iago full of envy and hatred? There are no "explanations."[24] It is foolish, however, to deny the existence of such evil in human beings, monstrous—another meaning of which is "unbelievable"—as it is. Lear is foolish for trusting that his daughters will return his goodness to them; Prospero thought his brother would not harm him; Timon gave to unworthy people who later on abused him. Gratitude, on the other hand, requires all that is highest in human beings. From the receiver, it calls for recognition, memory, intelligence, consideration, and justice. From the giver, when generosity is met with ingratitude, it requires forbearance, acceptance, and refusal to turn sour, no matter how hurt he might feel. If memory, justice, forgiveness, and the rest are expressive of human nature at its best, then so is gratitude. If not, then ingratitude is "natural," and all that we should expect.

23

We Are Not Grateful

"I don't need to be grateful: I can buy whatever I want." The person who said this to me in a comfortable tone felt cozy because she was what is called "well off." She felt comfortable also because her estate is easily perceived as ideal: it fulfills the ambitions and receives the rewards of much of our ambient culture. It was nevertheless shocking to hear her thought put into words: such a sentiment normally remains unsaid. The words are simple, but their implications broad.

The speaker may have disliked the possibility of having to feel grateful in part because a receiver is for the time being "lower" than a giver, and she wanted never to occupy that place, even temporarily. She assumed that people give in order to get. She knew the further rule of manners, according to which people who receive gifts are supposed to thank and if possible give something back: they have to display, even if they do not feel, "gratitude." And so for her, a situation requiring gratitude was merely an imposition that those who can do so strive to escape.

She probably understood that links to the giver would be created thereby. But she wanted no relationship with another person unless she chose it herself, and unless it remained under the thumb of her inclinations: she wanted free choice, no commitments, no hint of an obligation, no ties. Having plenty of money meant being able to choose "gifts" to give to herself, whenever she wanted them—not having to accept other people's choices and timing. The woman felt free, liberated by her money. It not only cosseted but insulated and protected her from having to please anybody in order to get anything.

Not lacking anything herself meant not having to give. This thoroughly modern person felt lucky because she had the means to live in a kind of impermeable pod, mixing with her kind but as little as possible responsible for or concerned by other people, self-sufficient herself and expecting others to be so too. When individualism rejects giving, receiving, and gratitude as burdens to be avoided, it ends up further subjecting the weak: it ensures that those who have, keep, and those who have not, never get. Finally, this person assumed that she wanted and needed nothing that could not be bought.

Her assumptions conform to modern commodity culture as a coin fits into a slot machine. Modernity has produced her and is set up to accommodate her. Yet the woman's airy claim, even before its implications are spread out for inspection, will be found lamentable—or so I believe—even if we do not become sufficiently angry to accuse her of being a marble-hearted fiend. If we are honest enough, we might also see her reactions as options deliberately to turn down precisely because we are easily tempted and infected by them ourselves.

Modernity, in the West, is prone to begrudge gratitude and to indulge its opposite. As we have seen, it is commonly taken for granted today that human life is driven solely by selfish, instrumental, and financial calculations. Students of the life sciences often appear to confirm that, given our genetic constitution, we are incapable of any motivation other than self-interest; they take "gratitude" in particular to mean "giving back," and when we produce this response, it is because our genes have programmed behaviour in us that turns out in the long term to be materially advantageous to the group. The bias of the social sciences—sociology, economics, anthropology—is in general towards seeing gift-giving and gratitude as either lies or illusions that serve to maintain systemic social inequalities. A cynical but common view holds that gratitude pretends there is freedom where there is really only obligation; that it is about unequal status and not respect between equals; that where gratitude appears to be felt and therefore spontaneous, it is actually forced upon people by social pressures to conform. The cruder assertions of modernity also devalue memory, both historical and personal. And gratitude withers when memory declines.

The limitations of seeing human existence in terms of self-interest and status, and any distaste we might feel for the extreme individualism of the woman who was glad to live without gratitude, should not tempt us to reject individualism altogether. We have fought for more than two thousand years to achieve it, and its benefits are manifest. It is good, for example, to take responsibility for our own behaviour and not permit ourselves to blame our failings on others, to make decisions according to our own consciences, to take initiatives, feel free to disagree, make improvements in our lives, and strive for personal authenticity while allowing other people equal freedom to do the same. The point is that the freedom and equality that are, as we have seen, conditions for gratitude are also ideals without which individualism itself would die. Four basic goals and demands condition one another, in a constellation specific to our society: freedom, equality, individualism, and giving-and-gratitude. If one of these falls away, the rest become difficult to achieve and quite soon impossible to maintain.

Freedom and equality need each other and also provide correctives to each other. (Freedom without equality, for example, would give all support to the fox in the chicken coop. Equality without freedom is thraldom, like being a battery hen.) Equality and freedom produce and require individualism. The "odd man out," a kind of fourth dimension to all the rest, is giving-and-gratitude, which supports community and solidarity, the absolutely necessary opposite of the independence and self-sufficiency that make up individualism. The world of commodities and cash, then, has an opposite—both a corrective and a supplement—which is essential to our well-being and in fact holds society together; it is the underappreciated but vital and persistent world of gifts and gratitude.

Gratitude cannot be a mere duty-to-return. It was to begin with (the word's roots, as we have seen, are symptomatic of this) a free though deeply desired response (free in the grateful, desired by the giver and by society both). In our own history "gratitude" became a duty whenever and to the extent that inequality constrained it. Where people were required to return favours given, their feelings were irrelevant. Indeed, where "gifts" are obligatory, it is almost impossible to feel moved by them; receivers who then "give back" must do so according to rules, not feelings. In Western cultures today most people take gratitude to be something felt before it is something done: the motivation for a grateful act must be a grateful *feeling*. That is because of freedom, individualism, and equality, in combination. Where obligation is weakened, emotion "has to" provide an internalized motivation to respond. But emotions cannot be felt to order.

As an emotion, gratitude means being genuinely moved by another person's kindness in giving. Manipulating a mere appearance of gratitude—hoping, for instance, that by showing thankfulness one might get more—already enters the sphere of ingratitude. In *The Devil's Dictionary*,[1] Ambrose Bierce defines *gratitude* as "A sentiment lying midway between a benefit received and a benefit expected." The Devil has removed people entirely from his definition. He mentions only a disembodied and unspecified sentiment, a lack of freedom, and benefits (things or actions): some *thing* is *expected*. He has given a definition not of *gratitude* but of calculating greed, which as a response to kindness presupposes ingratitude.

Gratitude, like giving, is about regard and respect. (Both words literally mean "looking at" with the prefix *re-*, and we may remember the expression of gratitude, which includes looking into the giver's eyes.) *Regard* is kindly and affectionate, with a measure of admiration in it; *respect* is a less emotional term, a matter of deference, which requires distance and restraint. *Respect* in particular is immensely important in our multicultural world because of its apparently simple neutrality, as a sheer granting of space. It can express a difference in status (one "looks up" to somebody one respects), but its deference can also be what is due to equals.

A grateful receiver freely accepts the lower place, even as the giver proves his reverence for her by giving. We have seen what happens where receiving is presumed to be "higher" than giving: gift-giving soon becomes obligatory and may turn into tribute. "Giving back" may still be called "gratitude," but with the falling away of the feeling component, the action quickly becomes ceremonial, and in our culture may degenerate into being either mechanical or resentful. Where either giver or receiver utterly refuses deference, there can be no gratitude in that party to the transaction.

Strong egalitarianism easily refuses deference, and where it does so it must threaten the existence of gratitude. The French philosopher Alain Finkielkraut in his book *Ingratitude* makes the accusation that "modern people respect everything so as to have nothing left to admire."[2] He means that they level everything, accept it all, but do not feel actual esteem for what they "respect." Admiration[3] is an emotional response; it implies a readiness to be affected. Finkielkraut suggests that egalitarian modern people provide respect because they would prefer not to admire, just as they would prefer not to be grateful: they feel that both gratitude and admiration allot somebody else a higher place.

Ingratitude, on the other hand, is disregard—paying no attention and so slighting—and disrespect. It rejects, disparages, or ignores gifts and favours. More importantly, it rejects the person giving them. It can also despise and reject what has come to us from the past: social arrangements, moral beliefs and attitudes, and artistic and other concrete achievements. Modernity is partly founded on a series of political revolutions. When people decide to rise up and change the way society is run, they necessarily "turn down" and usually show disrespect for their past. Edmund Burke—who loathed everything about the French Revolution, "institutes, digest, code, novels, text, gloss, [and] comment"—wrote with utter contempt that "ingratitude to benefactors is the first of revolutionary virtues."[4] Revolutionaries themselves, of course, would deny that there had been any benefaction. Gratitude recalls goodness, and revolutionaries execrate what they remember. When people hate and then overthrow their rulers, they are apt to erase the rulers' names from inscriptions and topple statues set up to commemorate these detested figures, in a paroxysm of *damnatio memoriae*, "condemnation of memory."[5]

Ingratitude arises from *not wanting*. And not wanting can be an entirely good thing and a correct response. It all depends on what is given and the intentions of the giver. Both gratitude and its opposite are the results of judgment: we have always to ask what it is we are grateful for and why, and often whether rejection is not the better course. Not wanting something immoral, for example, is not ingratitude. Gratitude is not owed when the person offering a gift is not being benevolent, if the favour costs the giver nothing at all, or if it is the action of a person who is inappropriately interfering. People disposed to gratitude will, however, consider the intentions of the meddler and might—for thankfulness is in the gift of the receiver—feel grateful to him for meaning well, even if they are ungrateful for his ministrations.

The prerogative of a receiver is to refuse to be grateful for an untimely or merely self-serving offer of a "gift." When the Earl of Chesterfield recommended Samuel Johnson's English Dictionary, having for seven years remained deaf to Johnson's pleas for assistance, Johnson was famously not grateful. "Seven years, My Lord, have now past," Johnson wrote to the Earl, "since I waited in your outward Rooms or was repulsed from your Door, during which time I have been pushing on my work through difficulties of which It is useless to complain, and have brought it at last to the verge of Publication without one Act of assistance, one word of encouragement or one smile of favour. Such treatment I did not expect, for I never had a Patron before."

But now the dictionary was done, and the help had become irrelevant: "Is not a Patron, My Lord, one who looks with unconcern on a Man struggling for Life in the water and when he has reached ground encumbers him with help. The notice which you have been pleased to take of my Labours, had it been early, had been kind; but it has been delayed till I am indifferent and cannot enjoy it, till I am solitary and cannot impart it, till I am known and do not want it.

"I hope it is no very cynical asperity not to confess obligation where no benefit has been received, or to be unwilling that the Public should consider me as owing that to a Patron, which Providence has enabled me to do for myself."[6]

We applaud Johnson's brilliant expression of ingratitude when gratitude was not due. But we also object to ingratitude where we judge that gratitude is called for. Accusing someone of being ungrateful is invariably a powerful reproach, in part because ingratitude means so very many things. Inequality, lack of freedom, calculation, refusal to remember, lack of consideration: ingratitude in our society is as implicated in all these as gratitude is in their opposites. Ingratitude in a modern context not only arises from inequality, but can also create it: where gratitude is in order, ingratitude typically involves contempt and lack of both respect and regard for a giver; these are attitudes that see another person as less worthy—lower—than we are.

And people who feel they are being put down by a gift will not be grateful either. The modern poor may justifiably resent gifts given in a manner that denies all possibility of a relationship between giver and recipient, and that demands expressions of gratitude-as-deference precisely because receivers lack the power to equalize by giving back. "Charity" (meaning "giving out of caring") that deliberately avoids, with distaste, the people it purports to be helping is not charity. Receivers of unloving alms quickly see through the gifts to the givers and note their preference for the kind of distance that underlines inequality. Gratitude must be freely given; it cannot be demanded, but it can legitimately be withheld.

Writing with a rare honesty and out of practical "hands on" experience, Michael Stein describes working in various soup kitchens, where he received no pay and was under no obligation to serve. His article is called "Gratitude and Attitude."[7] Street slang calls disrespect, arrogance, defiance, resentment, lack of cooperation, or sullenness towards other people "attitude." (Emotions, in the normal sense of the term, are rarely either simple or unconnected to other emotions: "attitude" involves a whole constellation of feelings and their expressions.) "Attitude" may not imply "ingratitude," but the components of the reaction and the rhyme clearly point in its direction. "Attitude" has proud and independent connotations (the word was first applied to the behaviour of athletes, whose sensibilities it might have been wise to soothe), and these highlight modernity's tendency often to let ingratitude pass, to see its point, even to admire it, rather than excoriate it.

Stein describes receiving from some of his clients rude demands, complaints, and no thanks: "Having [served the meal] I left their table . . . As I was walking away, the oldest girl said, 'Hey . . . Hey, I don't like this color cheese—go to the kitchen and get me something else.'" His own angry reaction to this was what interested him; he wanted to know why he felt it. Here was someone who had shown up at the establishment's door in order, as we easily say, "to get something for nothing." She then, as he eventually realized, disappointed expectations—his own expectations!—by refusing, as he puts it, to "pay" in an affordable and acceptable "currency," namely gratitude. A volunteer, he says, may in such circumstances feel "short-changed." People want to be "paid"—recompensed, recognized—for their benefactions; the money metaphors are telling. Their desire for gratitude is liable, if refused, to elicit from them comments such as "So that's all the thanks I get."

Stein then muses on the difference in status between the patrons of the soup kitchen and the volunteers, coming as they did from "different worlds." He concludes that volunteer activity could be described as "the democratized version of *noblesse oblige.*" It is freely given, by people whose status in society is both high and assured, and who, having performed it, can escape afterwards into their normal comfortable surroundings. The clients, however, experience in their lives constant frustrations, discomfort, powerlessness, and stress; it is much harder for them to behave well. They resent their general lack of choices in life and translate this into anger at not being able to choose what they eat. Many of them have never learned how to mollify others and smooth rough passages in life through the usages we call "manners." Misunderstandings can arise through differences of class and manner; on occasion, Stein notes, people might not have meant to be ungrateful at all. But "the receiver acts on the giver through the manner of acceptance," and it is almost impossible not to react in annoyance at what one perceives as a display of ingratitude. It represents rejection of oneself and one's own self-image—here, as Stein puts it, that of "a good person."

The brothers and nuns and professional staff who worked permanently in the soup kitchens, he found, were apt to say things like, "I'm doing this more for me than for them," or to think that it was their clients' right to receive food. In both cases the result was that they did not feel that the clients owed them anything. (One staff member did say with a sigh that "just one 'thank you' would make my day.") But it turns out that in the author's experience gratitude was actually quite common. He states this extraordinary fact in passing: "In most cases the distribution of food was routine, and clients' responses ranged from benign neutrality to extreme thankfulness."

Marcel Mauss launched sociological research into gifts and gratitude by interesting himself not in infractions but in the norm: he thought that why people on the whole "give back" was more mysterious than why givers were outraged on occasions when they received no response from their beneficiaries. Social scientists have gone on to examine the "production" of gratitude as a form of social repression, a "management of our hearts"[8]—in other words, manipulation and a limit placed on freedom. Most of us, meanwhile, still take it for granted that felt gratitude for favours is both fair and desirable for both parties. We become angry when people fail to provide it.

Gratitude takes time, and gratitude is thoughtful involvement with other people. But we live in speed-driven, unthinking separation from one another, each ignoring the interests of others in order to pursue his or her own. We are often, therefore, ungrateful ourselves, and frequently experience ingratitude from others; we may even become cynically inured to it. People forget that favours have been done for them, or have no time to respond. They wish, often, that others would not try to limit them by means of commitments and ties. It is now easy to get away, disappear from view, and therefore not have to witness any hurt or annoyance that our ingratitude has caused. The next step is for people to desist from doing favours in the first place. Precisely because relationships now count for so little, giving, receiving, and gratitude—which might have encouraged these ties—become harder to perform and to feel. Lack declines into further deficiency as the fabric unravels. We should not forget either that ingratitude as not responding, not feeling, and not doing is essentially inert. Indifference demands less energy and less imagination than is required by either concern or thankfulness.

Meanwhile, the lack of meaningful interrelationship leaves an emptiness that people try to fill with buying things. Objects are simpler than people, shopping easier than conversation or attempts to understand others' needs. Being able to buy becomes the great consolation. One must have enough money for recreational spending, of course. And one must remain persuaded that everything worth having can be bought. The world of commerce thrives on all of this, making preferences and decisions apparently simple and controllable for the customer. It glitters with the power of attraction and temptation, and puts the toils and intricacies of giving and gratitude in the shade, relegating them to our "mysterious" private lives, where we seem to remain unmodern and therefore "mystified" in the sociological sense, meaning labouring under illusions.

Modern society has worked hard to reduce the sphere itself in which favours and counter-favours operate; we have cut back on the number of occasions where gratitude can arise or be considered an appropriate response. The "societies of the Gift" studied and admired by Mauss depended on gift exchange for many of their material necessities. The modern world has money—and that mostly means money *instead*. Our lives are divided into "commercial" and "benevolent" spheres. Money rules completely in the first, although it operates in both: gifts usually have to be bought. It makes the second sphere look hazy, weak, messy, and problematic in comparison with the "hard facts" of wages and prices. We remember how Stein himself uses money metaphors for thanking and recognition in his account of the soup kitchen.

People often feel that money is not an appropriate gift: it is not personal enough and it comes from the wrong sphere, that of exchange and not that of gifts. Paying money for a service removes most of our feelings of gratitude for receiving it. ("She's only doing her job" means she gets paid, so what more could she ask for?) Waiters and other service workers are paid a salary, and therefore modern customers frequently balk at giving a tip. Moreover, money explicitly encourages the discontinuities characteristic of modern life. Paying a price that has been bargained for and agreed on in advance completes a transaction: payment is an ending. It is a "closed deal," over and done with, and nothing personal. Giving, receiving, and gratefully giving back, on the other hand, are expressions of ongoing personal relationship—a continuity. (In old folktales, when money is left for the gift of services they have provided, the fairies disappear.)

In our society, individuals are protected against some of the encroachments of others by means of human rights. People then feel entitled to demand and protect their rights: they hold a "title" to them, as a landowner does to his land with its frontiers marked out and physically strengthened by walls, barriers, and fences. Rights say to other people, "This far and no farther." Each person is expected to recognize the rights of others as well: justice for all is largely a matter, for us, of rights. We are not normally *grateful,* however, for what we have a right to possess. We presume that what we have a right to is ours already, and would be enraged if someone else tried to take it away. For example, if someone receives an inheritance he believes to be his due, he will possibly be glad, but may feel little or no gratitude to the testator. He would, however, be angry *not* to inherit what he thinks he was entitled to. The respect and restraint that protect rights are essentially negative, like the laws that place conditions on our actions. The Silver Rule is the one governing rights—"Do *not* do to others what you would *not* have them do to you."

Other people are obliged to leave us free to enjoy our rights, and we have a duty to respect theirs. Rights and obligations interlock. But where there is duty, entitlement, and obligation, people quickly cease to feel grateful.

The diagrammatical metaphor for rights,[9] of boundaries and the spaces they protect, does not describe persons. It is utterly abstract, a matter purely of principle; therein lies its value. Gratitude, on the other hand, pre-eminently concerns a relationship between persons. Rights as limits and "fences" form a metaphor of enclosing and excluding rather than of opening and sharing, of keeping separate rather than relating. They are there to keep us all safe from unreasonable demands as well as unjust encroachments. But the price of this protection is a temptation once again to see ourselves as isolated from and impermeable to one another.

After the still recent retreat from colonialism, we have come also to reject paternalism. The term reminds us once again of the family (the word refers to fathers) and its inevitably hierarchical arrangements. Children are for many years smaller and weaker than—physically unequal to—their parents, and dependent upon them for their survival, nurturing, and instruction. *Paternalism* is showing "provident fostering care that is apt to pass into unwelcome interference," according to a dictionary definition in 1961. Since then, the word's meaning has become more pejorative. By 2005 being provident and fostering are no longer mentioned. *Paternalism* is said to be "the policy or practice of restricting the freedoms and responsibilities of subordinates or dependants in what is considered or claimed to be their best interest."[10] Paternalism most simply means treating adults as though they were children. Even when well-meaning, it reduces or ignores what in adults is a right to autonomy (their right to direct themselves), their dignity as the paternalist's equals, and their freedom. Paternalism ignores another cardinal modern demand: that for consent when two parties interact. When ingratitude is the response to paternalism, therefore, nobody should feel surprised.

Should the recipient of paternalistic attentions discover and admit later that "it was good for me, although I didn't see it at the time," does she let the paternalist off the hook? The answer, argues a recent social analyst,[11] is no. The paternalist was still wrong to insist on interfering, since the person who was the object of his efforts, unwilling at the time, "cannot consent to something retroactively." And in any case, "whether . . . my paternalism was or was not justified, your later saying 'thank you' will not tell me." If it should be the case that good has been done, its object's happy discovery later should not be considered gratitude, but simply gladness for a fortunate event; for gratitude would have to be granted *to the giver,* the paternalist. This account fails to picture giving-and-gratitude as a movement back and forth between two people, each of whom has a virtue particular to his or her role. Gratitude being the virtue of the receiver, this person should be allowed to feel grateful if he thinks the paternalist meant well—or the reverse. The author is right, however, that the giver—here the paternalist—bears her own responsibility for how and why she gave.

La Rochefoucauld remarked in 1664 that "an ungrateful man may be less to blame for his ingratitude than is the person who did him a favour."[12] What he almost certainly had in mind was an unwanted but deliberately imposed and binding obligation, created by the bestowal of a gift. His maxim has nevertheless a highly modern ring, deriving chiefly from his readiness to find the giver, not the receiver, guilty when ingratitude arises.

Modern people tend to deny any connection between acts of justice and occasions for being thankful. Justice has in the past always been thought of as prior to and more important than gratitude, but also a part of it—and the more so the more "giving back" leaned towards the obligatory. It is still felt to be "only fair" to thank people for favours, and to return good for good received. But having sharply distinguished benevolence from justice, and if presented with a choice, people would rather have the latter, of course. They prefer to be given what they need because they have a right to it, and not to have to depend on the goodwill of others. We recall those who served in the soup kitchen full-time, who believed that their clients had a right to the food they were given and therefore owed them nothing. Yet apparently most of the clients responded by being grateful. Many sociologists would conclude that they had been worn down, their hearts "managed," into gratitude-as-submissiveness.

A totally different way of seeing gratitude is not as the secret and forcibly maintained underpinnings of injustice, but rather as an equally invisible binding power that serves to hold our otherwise atomized world together. During the Middle Ages and the Renaissance, when there was a great deal more hierarchy and obligation than we would put up with today, and much less conviction that ideally each person should be self-sufficient, it was still believed that there was a need for something more—a fundamental bond known as *concordia,* "all being of one heart." This bond operated between and among strangers within one's own society,[13] wherever political bonds of loyalty and obligation, family ties, and friendships were lacking. In many ways ingratitude was horrific because it was not only specifically the opposite of gratitude, but was also thought to undermine the overall harmony that was *concordia.*[14]

The metaphors used to describe gratitude as a modern social phenomenon are telling: they suggest reasons why gratefulness survives as a fundamental value. The most ancient metaphor is that of systems of "ties" and "bonds" of obligation. In an individualistic society these become myriads of actions freely performed by independent persons, all adding up to cohesion if not unity. Georg Simmel[15] spoke of "threads" created by giving, gratitude, and return, which help produce a stable social life. The filaments are slender and the stitches constantly repeated by each of us, for example, in the frequent saying of "thank you" in everyday life. Each time, each stitch "knits" together two parties (giver and receiver, receiver and giver), and then, ideally, each member of this couple turns to others and gives again. No law can force us to perform these actions, which are on the whole voluntary. Giving and gratitude are necessary because they can motivate and enable people to achieve intimate *concordia* with each other. They reach into hearts and into activities where the law cannot penetrate, where it has no authority whatever. The picture of knitting, weaving, sewing, or lacework is that of the "fabric" of society, and gratitude's linking role in it. Ingratitude, on the other hand, prevents the "stitching," creates holes in the "knitting." It uncouples, loosens, and unravels.

Another metaphor is that of soil, from which concrete actions "grow." This image refers to the disposition of a person to be grateful, and his freedom to choose not to be.[16] He is able to "cultivate" in himself a grateful disposition, and an ability to judge what merits his being thankful. He can even learn to notice, to look out for opportunities to feel the pleasurable emotion of gratefulness for real benevolence. An ungrateful disposition, by contrast, is hard and dry, not easily moved by kindness, unwilling to be kind in turn, and generally averse to the production or increase of goodwill. In European languages people often talk of poor soil as "ungrateful."

Gratitude is a social "lubricant" when thought of as correct and polite behaviour. It makes things move smoothly; after all, giving and giving back are movements back and forth. Because we have no obligation to be grateful, people can be unsure how to react and what to do; a receiver cannot even be absolutely certain about the all-important intentions of the giver of a favour. (The giver herself may not be perfectly clear about the springs of her action; her conscious motives may not be all that "pure" either—which does not mean she is entirely calculating.) "Manners" tell us in advance how to behave, both in the moment of receiving and later when giving back, so as to express adequately and not excessively what we feel, not too soon and not too late. Relationship is an extremely complex business; a "lubricating" expression of gratitude prevents a perfectly thankful person from appearing to be ungrateful, disguises for the time being any reservations he may have, and gives him time to think—that indispensable preliminary to feeling true gratitude. Where there is no gratitude, there is no meaningful movement; human affairs become rocky, painful, coldly indifferent, unpleasant, and finally break off altogether. The social "machinery" grinds along and soon seizes up.

Another group of metaphors for gratitude performs an opposite role from that of lubricating: gratitude is "glue." The image points again to the social cohesion that gratitude supplies. Modern society is experienced as fragmented, in danger of flying apart; giving, receiving, and gratitude for both favours and gifts keep people relating. When speakers and writers become especially aware of the interstices left vacant in the social fabric by the present grand schemes of commercial exchange, the metaphor becomes ultra-modern: gratitude is "a kind of plastic filler," "an all-purpose moral cement,"[17] a sort of magic paste that is amazingly malleable, squeezing itself into the cracks and then solidifying and so strengthening the social structure. Gifts and gratitude—sidelined, privatized, relatively unassuming as they are—from this point of view receive the credit for cementing the whole frenzied edifice together. The glue is "all-purpose" because when people look at what gratitude means and how it works, they are quickly dizzied by its complexity and amazed by the number of functions it is called upon to perform.

Gratitude, however, still has to survive surprisingly venomous hostility. Some believe that there is no such thing as a gift, let alone gratitude, since any sort of reward—even any awareness of having given—is thought to disqualify a gift. The idea that giving is good for us is thus made to undermine the possibility of giving. It is often assumed that the only rational action is one taken out of self-interest: by implication, irrationality must be what governs giving, receiving, and gratitude. And the claim of gratitude to require liberty and equality—the ideals of modernity—is denounced as false. Status is presumed to be what we are all inevitably after, in an endless battle with our fellows, and here gratitude is conceded a role—in the reproduction of inequality. We often forget that it is not gratitude and giving, but advantages taken for granted (that is, received without gratitude, as if they were one's due), and then unshared, that are much likelier to produce and encourage both differences of status and injustice.

24

The Poisoned Gift

The city of Troy, like many cities in the ancient world, was fated to survive just as long as it guarded in its citadel a sacred image. In Troy's
case this was a small wooden statue of the goddess Athena, standing erect in
her armour. This figure, called the Palladion, "was" the safety of Troy. Two
heroes of the Greeks, whose army was besieging the city, succeeded in stealing it. After this, Troy was doomed. The theft of the Palladion ensured that
Fate—the fall of Troy—would be fulfilled. But, as so often, Fate was both
overdetermined and a mechanism set going well in advance.

The first event in Troy's fated destruction had occurred ages before, when
Phoenician merchant sailors kidnapped a Greek princess called Io and carried her off to Egypt.[1] Just as reciprocity in giving begins with a first gift,
cycles of vengeance are presumed to start with a first encroachment, a first
outrage that cries out for revenge. Io was a woman of Greece who had been
made to enter "Asia"; she left behind her a gap—a hole in their honour—
that the Greeks would have to fill. Honour fought for customarily belongs to
men; women merely embody it.

The Greeks took revenge for the theft of Io by carrying off Europa,
daughter of the Phoenician king of Tyre.[2] This, says Herodotus, was giving
"tit for tat," "equal for equal." Herodotus is of the opinion that men should
not get too exercised over the rape of women: he says they are not abducted

unless they want to be. "Rape" in the ancient world meant "snatching away," depriving men of their wives. Sexual violation, and indeed the opinion and point of view generally of the women involved, were very minor aspects of "rape." Women, as we saw earlier, were in important respects "gifts" from one household to another, their role being to create between two families ties that would be embodied by children born of both bloodlines. They could, like other precious property, be stolen. They could also turn out to be disastrous figures of destruction in the house into which—"foreigners" as they were, from another family—they had been introduced.

Next, the Greeks stole another woman from the East: Medea, princess of Colchis. They were asked by the king, her father, to give her back, but refused. Asia retaliated when Paris, Prince of Troy in Asia Minor, kidnapped Helen of Sparta and took her home with him. The Greeks then fought a war to recover Helen, and so it came about that Troy fell. Behind the story of honour lost and recovered lies the relentless pattern of Fate; honour and its obligations cause Fate to come to pass.

The theft of Athena's statue, after many years of this war, meant that the safety of Troy had deserted the city. It remained only for the Greeks to enter her walls. This they did by pretending to want to "replace" the Palladion. They offered a "gift," a huge wooden Horse, which they built and wheeled up to within sight of the city's perimeter. They then ostensibly sailed off home to Greece. In fact, they hid their ships behind the island of Tenedos and waited. They had also hidden Greek warriors inside the gigantic, apparently kindly-meant wooden Horse. The Trojans were at first suspicious of the gift. Should they reject it—hurl it into the sea, set fire to it, pierce it through with their spears? These were alternatives to Fate, and of course the narrative could not allow them.

The priest Laocoön[3] begged his people to refuse the gift: "Do you think any gifts from Greeks could be free from trickery?" he cried. "Trust not the Horse, oh Trojans . . . I fear Greeks, even when bringing gifts!"[4] And he hurled his spear at the wooden Horse, which "groaned within." But the gods and Fate, aided by the foolishness of men,[5] were not to be averted. Laocoön was silenced by giant serpents that came up out of the sea to strangle him and sink their poisonous fangs into him and his sons. The snakes were sent by Athena, implacable in her hatred of Troy. They were also figures of Fate, like Furies enraged by attempts to upset the preordained and relentless Pattern of Events.

The Trojans rushed out of their city and drew the Horse into it, breaching their own walls when they saw that the great gift needed more space in order to get in. They longed to replace the lost Palladion, to offer the Horse to Athena in expiation for it. The Horse, accompanied with hymns of joy, entered a city decked with flowers to receive it. The Trojans struggled and toiled to drag the monster up to their citadel. When night fell, the warriors crept out of the Horse and gave the signal to the army waiting out at sea. The Greeks swarmed into Troy, massacred its men, carried the women off to slavery in Greece, and burned the city to the ground.

The Horse was for Troy's citizens a poisoned gift—evil disguised as good, a tempter and destroyer. The Trojans, in receiving it, had gone temporarily insane: their memories deserted them, Virgil wrote, and they were "blind with frenzy."[6] Receivers, as his Roman audience knew, have to *think* before they accept gifts: they have to be aware that people might be "giving" with wicked intentions. The Trojans should not have imagined that their enemies would leave them a true gift, an expression of goodwill. The correct response—if Fate had allowed the Trojans to make one—would have been intelligent reflection and then rejection: in a word, ingratitude for a "gift" that was no gift.[7] Like gratitude, wise rejection or ingratitude should follow recollection: a plunge into the waters of memory. The Trojans could not perceive their danger, however, in their relief at seeing the Greeks depart and in their longing to replace the Palladion. The Horse, suggesting itself as the answer, in fact brought the enemy inside the walls—with the eager help of the Trojans themselves.

The myth of the Trojan Horse is about gifts experienced as deceptive and dangerous invasions. A gift is something that comes to the receiver "from without." Somebody has intruded on my "space" by proposing a relationship with me through doing me a favour. An object as "first gift" often arrives unasked for and unannounced. It expresses the giver's desire for consequences, whether they be fruitful or destructive. From a psychological point of view, which the myth dramatically expresses, people often accept propositions fraught with danger for themselves because they are needy and afraid. The wise person on the receiving end must be cautious and discriminating, which includes knowing how to reject a gift if necessary, when to be ungrateful, and why.

Greek and other mythology often eddies around gifts—foreign bodies entering—which import destruction. (Modern feelings about disease and pollution are presaged by ancient ideas like these.) Human beings could themselves belong to the "invasive gift" category, as people who entered the "space" of others: strangers, guests, suppliants, and even wives. These had to be handled with circumspection, for all of them were potentially dangerous, their loyalties being impossible to ascertain in advance; the rules governing their treatment and behaviour were therefore intricate, and to be flouted at one's peril. In Greek epic Helen, the woman who left her "place" at the side of her husband, was brought to Troy—one figure in a long narrative of recurring outrage and vengeance—to provoke destruction. (Helen is never blamed in the *Iliad* for the damage she caused; she was born portentously beautiful and so was doomed to be an instrument of Fate.[8]) She was, says Aeschylus in *Agamemnon,* like a baby lion cub torn by a hunter from its mother's breasts and brought home to be his family's pet. The children played with it, cradled it like a baby, fed it milk. But in time, when it grew up, the lion's true nature broke out, and it killed its "hosts"; the house ran with their blood. Gratitude for kindness is, naturally, not to be looked for in a lion.[9]

Some doom-bearing gifts are literally poisoned,[10] like the Robe and the Crown that Medea sent as murderous wedding presents to Jason's bride. Or the Shirt of the centaur Nessos, soaked in a poison that the wife of Herakles believed to be a love potion: she gave it to her husband, who put it on and died in agony. (He had caused her anguish first, by bringing into the house a slave woman to be his concubine.) The Necklace that Cadmus gave his wife Harmonia caused death on death, until it was finally dedicated as a votive offering at Delphi, to keep it out of mischief. In 356 BC a mercenary soldier stole the Necklace from the sanctuary and gave it to his wife. Soon afterwards his son burned his house to the ground and his wife, mother to his son, died in the flames.[11] Mythological gifts like these easily take on daimonic personalities with wills and resentments of their own. They resemble in this the gifts of the Maori and others, which were said to moan and complain and make demands to go back home or to leave for other owners. They are cousins too of articles such as the Ring of the Nibelung, or the Handkerchief in Shakespeare's *Othello;*[12] the theatre, in particular, loves visible objects that not only advance the action but concentrate and embody the desires and the history of the characters on stage. No wonder concrete gifts and their passage from hand to hand fascinate us and invite commentary the way they do: they "stand for" favours and feelings, memories, relationships, and gratitude that should issue in response. Gifts, whether given or refused, have power to influence the future.

In the Greek and Roman stories, gifts encouraged reflection on the difference between appearance and reality, on the ease with which a receiver can be deceived by a malevolent pretense of generosity, and on the operation of such deceit in the fulfillment of Fate. Such gifts are often involved in taking revenge, the polar opposite of the friendly relationship that everybody knew the Gift was supposed to promote. All such stories counted on their hearers knowing the rules of obligation that helped run a well-oiled mechanism of "gift"-giving, the taking for granted of which rendered it ripe for abuse. In a different tradition the tale is told of a king of Siam who crushed his courtiers by giving each of them a costly present: a white elephant, the expense of whose care and upkeep would invariably ruin them. This dire gift they could not refuse; neither could they criticize its "generous" giver. And they were forced to show "gratitude" by treating his gift with due respect.

Our own culture tells fewer tales of poisoned gifts, simply because we have less sense of an overwhelming duty that must be "discharged" by giving back something when we have accepted a gift. We do, however, certainly know this pressure, and the way in which unwariness can precipitate disaster. One example in story form occurs near the beginning of Robert Louis Stevenson's novel *Kidnapped*.[13] The young hero, David Balfour, narrowly escapes being murdered by his evil uncle Ebenezer. The manoeuvre begins when this miserly old man astonishes David by suddenly giving him money. "I want nae thanks," says the uncle, "I do my duty; I'm no saying that everybody would have done it, but for my part (though I'm a careful body, too) it's a pleasure to me to do the right by my brother's son; and it's a pleasure to me to think that now we'll agree as such near friends should." The uncle adds "And see here, tit for tat!"—for Ebenezer wants David to do him a favour in return. David accepts the proposition: "I told him I was ready to prove my gratitude in any reasonable degree."

The uncle asks him to go to the top of a tower and fetch him a chest with papers in it that is kept there. David has already found out that his uncle is too stingy to allow lights in his house at night. The boy goes out into a pitch-dark stormy night, opens the tower door, and slowly, step by step and feeling his way, climbs the turning stair. A flash of lightning reveals to him the plot: the stairway is broken off and incomplete. It is clear that his uncle had sent David to fall to his death in the dark. The mean old man had parted with the golden coins in order to ensure that the boy would do what he asked and mount the deadly stairs. If he had had his way, he would have recuperated his "gift."

People have always known that gifts and gratitude can be abused: gifts, being symbols and proposals of goodwill, can pretend to be what they are not. Disguised and deceiving, an invasive gift can be brought to bear on the behaviour of others, making them "take the next step" out of an unthinking compliance with the rules of decency—and do what the "giver" wants. Just as people can mistakenly or for reasons of personal or social insufficiency accept evilly intentioned and dangerous "gifts," so gratitude itself can be felt for the wrong reasons. People can be thankful, for instance, for useful actions with their roots in evil: to an iniquitous regime that nevertheless makes the trains run on time; or to violent repressers of hooliganism, who beat people into submission but never address the reasons for the bad behaviour. Gratitude, in other words, is not a good thing *in itself.* Its virtue is always dependent on what the reason is for a grateful response. A bad reason vitiates gratitude in advance, sincerely felt though it may be.

No matter how useful real thankfulness might be, where expressions of gratitude are forced from people, there is no gratitude. Those who use and enforce gifts and gratitude are very knowing, of course, about how the mechanism works and what it can effect. Large-scale, conscious manipulation of the principle of gratitude was carried out during the twentieth century in the course of one of the great experiments in modernity, the practice of Communism.

After achieving the monopoly of information through censorship, begun by Lenin, the Soviet system set about making positive demands as well: it moved from the mere silencing of inconvenient opinions to forcing people to say what the regime wanted to hear. In the late 1920s, after having liquidated his rivals, Stalin began to legitimize his power by claiming for himself the role of "first giver": he had bestowed peace, order, and security upon Russia, and he expected to receive from the people both their work and the expression of their gratitude as "return gifts." Jeffrey Brooks, who catalogues the process in his book *Thank You, Comrade Stalin!* (2000), shows how lies, fear, and carefully marshalled ritual performances expressing "gratitude" were deployed to keep Stalin in power. Despite the regime's cruelties and failure, as living standards collapsed, millions died, and voices raised in protest were brutally suppressed, the government saw to it that the State—and Stalin, in particular—received only adulation. In 1932, after a declaration of the success of the first Five Year Plan, Stalin began to claim through the media the indebtedness, not only false but also passive and perpetual, of the people to their leader. The State's duty to allocate resources became Stalin's kindly beneficence: "gifts" and obligatory "gratitude" were substituted for rights.

Kept in considerable ignorance of the painful facts and figures, many were genuinely in favour of what they were told and promised.[14] It was an official core value of the Soviet State—formulated, again, by Lenin—that citizens were immeasurably beholden to the Revolution, the Party, the Leader, and the State. Stalin took the lion's share from that list for himself. It was possible to promote fawning on the leader because Russians had been accustomed to adulating the Tsar; it was possible to propose false gratitude because the genuine article was a deeply rooted Christian virtue. Communist regimes often used rhetoric that laid claim to Christian moral values, even as they attempted systematically to wipe out religion. Stalin in particular, the ex-seminarian, knew what notes to play. He tried, as dictators will, to replace God with himself.

The State instituted orchestrated performances of ritual thanksgiving to Stalin in person. On December 30, 1936, for example, the leader was pictured in the newspapers as Grandfather Frost, Russia's Santa Claus. A "New Year's tree," replacing the Christmas tree, was decorated with gifts and surrounded by brightly smiling children. Stalin had become the country's benefactor; the people henceforth owed him immeasurable gratitude. A tribute to him in *Pravda* proclaimed in 1943, "Thank you, dear Marshal, for our freedom, for our children's happiness, for life!" Eulogies like these became an obligatory choral refrain. On his seventieth birthday in December 1949, Stalin received trainloads of "gifts," in return for his "favours" to the people. But even these could never be thought enough, for how could school buses and public buildings, for example, or sausages, smoked fish, oranges, and other increasingly scarce foods that appeared in large cities on holidays ever be recompensed? Stalin had always "given" first, and had always given "more."

In these ways hierarchies with "Comrade" Stalin at their pinnacle were blurred and justified, with the help of manufactured gratitude, which gave to the "giver" obsequious gift-laden flattery while those designated as "receivers" in fact gave everything and got less and less in return. Meanwhile, elaborate systems of rewards, favours, and bribery operated behind the public facade, to "lubricate" the grinding top-down economy. Stalin kept firm control over his own cult, personally picking everyone who received prizes or were declared heroes, and killing off unwilling courtiers. The constant ceremonies of public thanking of the leader pretended to mean "personal ties" with him. He even stole for himself the credit for victories in the war against the Nazis: "We won because we were led by the captain of genius and marshal of the Soviet Union, Stalin," declared a compliantly grateful minion at the parade in Red Square in 1945, and the next day Stalin was made generalissimo. As the Soviet empire grew, Stalin expanded the "gratitude" theme, eventually invoking filial piety as well: he was to become "the Little Father of the Peoples." After the war, it was heavily impressed on satellite countries that they now owed endless gratitude to the Soviet Union, for saving them from the Nazis and bringing them Communism instead.

In the Communist German Democratic Republic too, people were compelled to swallow an artificial rhetoric of the Gift.[15] One of the rules of interaction with the Soviet Union was that East Germans were not to try to lay claim to being "givers." They were perpetual receivers, never allowed to equal in generosity their "big brother." Gratitude was used as well in a highly conscious attempt to "cement" society together. In the 1950s and early 1960s, for example, salaried workers from the cities were sent into the countryside on "interventions" or "insertions" (*Einsätze*) that were specifically meant to link town and country. The incomers donated voluntary labour or provided such services as choirs and bands for the new State festivals. Most importantly, they contributed their support for collectivization, and offered "the gift of socialism." The peasants, since "gifts create obligation," had to respond by handing over compulsory "return gifts" (cost unmentioned) from their crops, and then selling to their benefactors, whenever they wanted to buy, at whole-sale prices. One is reminded of the "gifts" of produce that peasants "owed" landlords in France, England, and Italy as late as the nineteenth century.

Recent research among the careful documents kept in the G.D.R. has revealed many complaints from city workers that they were not paid properly for their "volunteer" work, and reports of a lack of appreciation or plain hostility from the farmers and villagers, who systematically fought off the obligatory "gifts" (with their demands for "returns") from their socially and economically privileged "guests." Within the workers' brigades, on the other hand, at a personal and voluntary level, people genuinely helped one another—and were grateful. The "glue" that gratitude provides in society, even where its desirability is understood, is a personal and individual affair, and it cannot be demanded or controlled. People may overtly obey "gratitude" rules out of fear, but the result will be a boiling resentment, which can only prevent or dissolve solidarity. Gratitude is sincere and freely granted, or it is nothing. Indeed, when enforced it easily becomes its bitter opposite.

The "insertion" into another's life of a different kind of malevolent gift belongs to the strategy we call bribery, a phenomenon that is found worldwide and throughout history.[16] A bribe, designated as it is in English by its own term, is not a gift, even though it is an object bestowed on one person by another. The word comes from Middle English *brybery,* meaning "roguery" and "fraud."[17] A bribe is not in itself deceptive; it is the briber and the bribee who link up to deceive people other than themselves. A bribe depends for its efficacy on the bribe-taker's response—his apparent obligation to "give back." For this reason, modern writers on "the Gift" have not been above seeing bribery as a proof that "there is no free gift."[18] But the opposite is the case: the true nature of the gift is revealed precisely by the mechanism of the bribe, in which an ostensible gift is twisted or "poisoned."

We should note from the start that a bribe has to be accepted in order to do its work, and ethically speaking, no acceptance, no response, and no gratitude are required where a "gift" is seen to have an ulterior motive—in other words, to be no gift.[19] It is no wonder that bribes are often reinforced by blackmail and other threats that seek to enforce acceptance where temptation is not enough. There is some family resemblance between blackmail and bribery, in the false reflection each of them presents of gift-giving and gift-return. Blackmail, now meaning any payment extorted by intimidation or threat, was originally a tribute paid by farmers to plunderers, in return for protection or immunity from molestation.[20] A mafia-like closeness between the exerter of pressure and the "giver," the payment for something extorted with no contractual assurance that the "return" will be received, even the secrecy imposed by a blackmailer who holds information that the victim herself wants kept secret—all these characteristics make blackmail a cousin of bribery. Because bribes and blackmail are manipulative and malevolent, because they have nothing to do with either freedom or equality, because they are about money and not friendship, they are not gifts. Neither bribes nor blackmail inspires feelings of gratitude: they fail the litmus test for whether something handed over is a gift or not.

We see a person who has been bribed as having been "bought" or hired to do the giver's will. In perhaps its clearest form, a bribe induces an office-holder[21] to act against the public interest for which he ostensibly works, and in favour of the private person or group who has paid him to betray the trust placed in him when he took up his post. The word *office-holder* is useful because it reminds us of the role-related obligations that a person accepts along with the principles governing office-holding. For example, gratitude that causes an office-holder to make use of his office in order to return a personal favour becomes a source of immorality. Even if someone has saved the boss's life—or become the boss's wife—she should not be given a salary increase on that account.[22]

A successfully bribed office-holder prefers money or other rewards to performing his office as other people trust him to perform it: bribery undermines trust. Gratitude, on the other hand, like one of the Three Graces, "holds hands" with faithfulness and trust; she, like them, is "naked" because she is open and honest. A bribe is invariably an underhanded thing: the payment is out of sight to everyone not involved in the transaction. The word *suborn* (to bribe or to get someone to commit perjury) is from Latin *ornare*, "equip," and *sub,* "under"—as we might say, "supply the necessary price, under the table." A bribe is secretive because it has to be: should an office-holder be seen taking a bribe, she would forfeit the trust placed in her, and this disgrace could actually make her dishonest services on behalf of those who bought her impossible to perform. Deception and hypocrisy are part of bribe-taking, and these inevitably give rise to lies.

As far as bribe-givers are concerned, the point of the reward, whether handed over in advance or after the event, is coercion of the receiver. There is no love, no benevolence, involved: bribes aim at the interest of the giver, not that of the receiver. All the briber needs to ascertain is the receiver's "price." He will have a specific end in view, and his bribe is offered in order to attain that end: the bribe-taker has no choice about what to "give back." Relationship is not the aim: the "return favour" is. Bribes usually have to be paid back very soon; there is no optional waiting period. That is because bribery is a matter of loveless compulsion: gratitude would be entirely inappropriate. The briber as paymaster has no interest in waiting around.[23]

An excellent exploration of the injustices, insults to freedom, and inequalities involved in bribery is provided in Billy Wilder's movie *The Apartment* (1960). Four insurance company managers, and finally the boss himself, take turns using the hero's convenient Manhattan apartment as a venue for their extramarital rendezvous. C.C. Baxter, the apartment's tenant, is a lowly clerk in the firm, submissive before the managers' power and easily persuaded into compliance by his "returns": complimentary work reports and promises of promotion. He has to stay out all night often, walking the streets or sitting on a lonely bench in the cold. The company director, Sheldrake, borrows the apartment on Christmas Eve and uses it to seduce Baxter's love, Miss Kubelik. Instead of a Christmas present Sheldrake gives her money, whereupon, the truth of the situation is revealed to her, appropriately enough through the contrast between Gifts and Payment. Miss Kubelik tries to commit suicide. When Sheldrake demands the apartment again for New Year's Eve, Baxter stands up to the briber, cleverly confounds him, and quits his job, the outcome of the scene invariably moving the film's audience to laughter and exultation. The young couple are now penniless—but happy. Baxter declares his love for Kubelik as they sit playing gin rummy in the apartment together. The most important effect on the audience's emotions has already been achieved, through the round rejection of bribery and its power to subjugate: Miss Kubelik cuts the sentiment, and lets us know that the couple's love is founded on rock, with the film's famous last line: "Shut up and deal."

It is often claimed, in our modern anxiety not to offend by criticizing the customs of other cultures, that bribery is all right if it can be considered a norm in the culture in question.[24] Bribery is called "grease" in English slang; the expression points to the "lubricating" effect a bribe can have. A "value-free" stance towards cultures whose structures are being studied from without leads some to believe that what are bribes for us are only "group interaction," "lubrication," or the provision of "flexibility" for other societies. What *we* object to, in other words, is acceptable and even useful for *them*.

Where bribery occurs, in all societies without exception, damage is invariably done. And when a great many people have become involved in the breakdown in trust and the bondage it creates, corruption is exceedingly difficult to unravel. People who think that bribery is all right for other cultures—"them"—are not listening to the language of societies today who fight desperate battles against *corruption,* a word now almost synonymous with *bribery,* and which means literally "breaking up completely." (*Corruption* is *con,* an intensive meaning "completely," plus *rupture.*) "Complete rupture" happens to a decaying body. The word *corruption* means "breaking up morally" when the "body" is the structure of society. Gifts and gratitude hold societies together and help them to go on working; they create links. Bribery and corruption make for unwanted ties that constrain; they simultaneously gum up the works and rend the social fabric apart.

Bribery sees to it that people do what is desired by those with the deepest pockets; it ensures that power is based ever more tenaciously upon money. Ideal qualities such as fairness and truth being set aside, equality is soon ruled out as well, and we have seen that equality and freedom are prerequisites for what we mean by "gift." Frequently it is private influence with someone "high up" that is paid for with cash or other rewards. And in the modern globalizing world, the people with the deep pockets are often powerful foreign "invaders" gaining, by means of bribery, unfair access to markets, for example, or paying influence-pedlars.

Bribery shades off in various ways towards gift-giving, and these variations are also illuminating. Tipping, for example, exhibits some of the attributes of bribery, where it seeks to make someone—by means of a "gift"—try harder to please the giver. A tip (diminutiveness is inherent in the word) must be small: a large sum is not a tip, but either a gift or a bribe. It is bribery, and hence immoral, to buy a democratic citizen's vote, yet rich people may be allowed to contribute funds to political campaigns, while poor people are usually unable to stretch their chances in this manner. The conventions of a culture may be disputed: to many, such donations look unfair, and a large contribution is dangerously close to a bribe. Yet these sums are openly given because they are considered legitimate, and because of this openness they are not thought of as bribes. We mentioned access to markets. Where access payments of any sort are small, open (that is, accountable), and equal for all contenders, they are no more unfair than are entrance fees. But a large, secret "access payment," especially if the amount varies according to who is being paid and for what, is a bribe. It ensures inequality, and both direct and overall injustice.

Most injuriously to the ideal of equality, a briber and his catch are not accountable to the public, but *to each other*. Their mutual advantage is gained at the expense of the interests of others, who remain both outside and ignorant of the "deal." Bribery is exclusive: one interest manipulates another by means of the temptations of personal profit, in a move that will be prejudicial to the chances of others; that is an important reason for keeping it secret. Even in societies where corruption is so far-reaching that everybody knows that a bribe is expected or no services will be forthcoming, people keep the action quiet and discreet, or complain about it surreptitiously. In any event they are never proud of it, never praise it—and probably always resent it. Bribees themselves are often compelled to take bribes (as waiters are sometimes made to pressure the clients for tips) because of more foundational injustices, such as payment for their work being impossible to live on without extra bonuses. Because of its exclusivity and its frequent creation of power elites based on money and private influence, bribery will most certainly be detrimental to the common good.

Bribery—and in this it is like gift-giving—creates ties, or rather, involvements, that exclude other people. Here it can throw light on what, as we shall see later, is a limitation inherent in the concept of gratitude. A person is grateful for something, *to somebody else in particular;* thankfulness expresses a relationship between two parties. There has necessarily been, for gratitude to occur, a prior benefit, which qualifies the other person as a benefactor, and it is to this person and no other that gratitude is owed. A person should help anybody who is in trouble, but *especially* someone who once helped her. Adam Smith points out, furthermore, that "if the person to whom we owe many obligations is made happy without our assistance, though it pleases our love, it does not content our gratitude." We ourselves have to be the ones to make him happy if we are to return the benefit.[25]

Other people have "no business" between these two, the favoured and the one who has shown favour, encountering one another face to face. But bribery does everything it can to keep onlookers in the dark. Since gift-givers and receivers concentrate on each other, they are rarely interested in onlookers—which is not the same thing as working hard to deceive them. Onlookers approve of gratitude when they witness it, and disapprove so profoundly of ingratitude that they often intervene—but with reproaches only, because force is off-limits in matters of gratitude. Yet these others have not been *favoured*—a word that also conveys "preferred," with its implication of leaving everyone else in the shade. Both favour and gratitude are partial, and to that extent exclusive, but they are extremely useful to society.

Out of each individual's free will, gratitude participates in justice (it is "only fair" to thank a benefactor and to return a favour), and other people want to be thanked too when they help their fellows. For them it is a kind of duty—and in their self-interest—to encourage the virtue of gratitude and keep it flourishing. Gratitude makes everyone's life easier; bribery's injustice and its manipulations threaten the well-being of all, even those who are not (at the moment) being bribed.

We all know that we should found our ethical choices on moral principles rather than on personal relationships. But we also know that, as persons, we depend on other persons; we need depth of relationship, which cannot exist in the abstract. Having learned to live by impersonal laws in all their objectivity and universality, we are puzzled when we start thinking about unconditional loyalties such as those to one's own family, and about the exclusive nature of intense preferences such as those that govern our friendships.[26] Ancient Greek drama struggles with this problem, setting out its paradoxes as bloody conflicts between the City and the Family, the Individual frequently being torn apart by the difference. The problem has not diminished in complexity for us today, despite the individualism, the mobility, and the anonymity of modern lives, our greatly loosened ties of commitment, and our devotion to money. We have, indeed, produced our own version of the problem by calling the opposition "public versus private," and then relegating gift-giving and gratitude to the latter, the hidden aspect of modernity.

But somehow we have to live with both the rules of impartiality and the need for special treatment. A parent must be partial, but an office-holder must remain deliberately impartial—even when dealing as an office-holder with her own children. We privilege the interests of our own parents—not the parents of other people. We tend to ask to dinner people we already know and like, or people who have previously invited us: reciprocal relationships easily become exclusive. But there are limits to preferential treatment for our family or our community or our country: gratitude to them should not overwhelm other, more fundamental commitments such as those to truth or to justice. Normally, such problems do not arise; normally, we do not have to wonder whether it is right to benefit somebody who has done us a favour. But sometimes we do.

Gratitude in action, being partial, is not always either morally right or appropriate. It cannot stand on its own, but needs to grow from other virtues, principally love and justice, that must come first. Without these preceding virtues and the awareness they supply, gratitude can blight our understanding, prevent us from seeing injustice in ourselves or in others, induce us to do wicked things. It can make us so preferential towards "our own" that we ignore both moral principles and the common good. Gratitude can be false or manipulated; it can be used to put other people down or to keep them submissive and dependent; it can destroy initiative. Showing favour and gratitude exclusively to "our own," especially if we are well off, is an easy and a selfish option. We have to feel gratitude sincerely—even as we step back and think about it sharply, with a circumspection that is very different from the calculation of profit. Gratitude is a deep emotion that derives from the past and has consequences for the future; it is inextricable from thinking.

PART VI

∞

Recognizing

25

Gratitude Instead

C osmology is the art of picturing the universe as a whole. The primary meaning of the Greek word *kosmos* is "order" and consequently "beauty." The assumptions underlying endeavours to envision a cosmology are that the universe is orderly—a "cosmos"—and that human beings can find the order in it, see it whole even if not in all its detail, and contemplate it with admiration. Cosmology, however, as a human point of view, has always tended to project the social organization and even the ethical ideas of its own time onto the structure of the universe.

The earliest written attempt at cosmology in the West was probably that of Anaximander of Miletus, who died not long after 547 BC. Only one sentence from his book *On the Nature of Things* (*Peri Physeos*) has come down to us.[1] Anaximander said that all existing things come into being and pass away,

in accordance with Necessity; for they make reparation to one another for their injustice according to the ordinance of time.[2]

It is interesting for our purposes that Anaximander the Greek saw the continuance of the cosmos as a kind of ongoing vicious circle, a concatenation of acts of the equalizing-through-punishing version of justice that we call vengeance. One entity transgresses (literally, from Latin, "steps across") into the "area" of another, and the encroached-upon element fights back against "injustice" later on, when it has gathered its forces, by transgressing in return. "Injustice" is imagined as a physical invasion, rather like the incursion of the Horse through the walls of the city and into Troy, a poisoned "gift" designed to destroy the receiver, or the first "rape" or snatching-away of a woman from her man, in the long series of similar transgressions that according to Herodotus led up to and caused the invasion of Greece by Persia.

The honour system by which the ancient Greeks lived meant that, in this extremely competitive society, honour could be wounded, "smirched," or subtracted from the injured party; his identity as "honourable" was thereby impugned. The honour "taken" increased that of the winner—his power, his "extent." Honour in such a system *must* ("in accordance with Necessity") be retrieved by the dishonoured man in the very name of his own claim to an honourable identity: it has to be taken back, reintegrated into the robbed "territory," to restore the original "size" of the one suffering the first encroachment. Vengeance is from this point of view a question of balance and fairness, a primitive form of justice. But then vengeance must without fail be taken again, from the other side: reparation has of necessity to be demanded by the one now offended and "reduced" by injustice. The "taking" of revenge is accomplished by "giving" blow for blow. "Take that!" is the typical cry; it parodies the bestowal and reception of a gift. Vengeful reactions, back and forth, can continue for generations. A period of resentment follows each transgression. This protracted sense of indignation eventually boils up into rage; arousal issues in a fight for reparation. Anaximander's vision is an explanation of why the cosmos both changes and continues.[3]

This diagram of cosmic Continuance through Change might have meant something different—even as it kept its structure of boundaries reciprocally crossed and recrossed. It could have been about gifts rather than thefts. Friedrich Nietzsche saw the similarity, also in geometrical terms. For him, gratitude was another name for vengeance; power was the point in both cases. "The reason a man of power is grateful is this," he writes. "His benefactor has through the help he has given him, as it were laid hands on the sphere of the man of power and intruded into it: now, by way of requital, the man of power in turn lays hands on the sphere of his benefactor through the act of gratitude. It is a wilder form of revenge."[4]

Both vengeance and gift-exchange, as we saw earlier, are social strategies-with a strong tendency to last. Peace among human groupings has long been achieved by gift exchange based on obligation: the people to whom a gift has been bestowed *must* give back, on pain of ill feelings that easily erupt into war. Ceremonial gifting-and-returning begins with risk, in the hope that it will solidify eventually into enduring trust. Time is taken after each gifting occasion. During that time the two sides are friends, until the next ceremony during which they will express and prove their friendly intentions again. The Greek maxim "Love your friends and hate your enemies" remains easy to understand.[5] Before vengeance is actually taken, it is frequently nursed ("according to the ordinance of time"): people who have suffered injury spend time hating their enemies and plotting revenge. People love their friends: they take time for appreciating favours, until the moment comes to "give back." "Friendship time," especially between rival social groupings, is also time during which fighting and invasion will not—if the system is working—take place.

Gift exchange *replaces* violence and hostility; it fits perfectly into the "space" left by a vengeance mechanism because—structurally speaking—it is similar: it is a give-and-take between specific parties. People choose it instead of its opposite. This strategy is not the prerogative of small, pre-modern "societies of the Gift." The founding idea of the European Union is that if countries trade with one another, discuss disagreements and try to achieve a consensus, and go on to exchange benefits and knowledge, they will learn to trust one another also. Peace after long war is the result.

Anger aroused by injustice can fuel revenge. Anger, as modern scientific researchers into the emotions tell us, is a "basic" emotion. Thomas Aquinas, who believed, with Aristotle, that humankind is naturally good,[6] explained why anger is found in human beings and animals alike. "There is a special inclination of nature to remove harm," he writes, "for which reason animals have the irascible power distinct from the concupiscible."[7] Anger is natural, as desire is.

Modern scientists of the emotions sometimes say that the opposite of gratitude is anger. That is because anger is what they describe as "negative feelings" towards a specific person: whoever has harmed or is trying to harm oneself. Gratitude is both similar and opposite to anger: it is "positive feelings" towards that person in particular who has done me a favour, or meant to do me a favour. (If people get angry with an object—a computer, for example, that is not working properly—they are ipso facto personalizing that object, thinking of it as an agent that is willfully misbehaving. If people discover that an agent did not intend an injury—or a benefit—their feelings of either anger or gratitude are greatly reduced. They recall that a computer, or some other object, has no will and is therefore not, morally speaking, praiseworthy; nor can it be "to blame.")

People get angry because what should have been done, or what should have been the case, was not. They are grateful often because, owing to the action of another person, the present state of affairs is better than it might have been. But anger is far simpler than gratitude because thinking about oneself is usually easier, more "natural," than thinking about somebody else. Anger towards someone (or some personalized object) rises up almost automatically in response to harm and frustration: anger is nature's way of readying us with the energy necessary, should we need to fight back. Angry people long to strike at and break things to dramatize their experience of being walled in by obstacles: if given the choice, they fling plates and glasses rather than pillows and they pound their fists on the table.[8] Gratitude, as we have seen, is a linking and constructing rather than a sundering and smashing impulse. Thankfulness is about feeling fine—and *still* thinking of another person if he deserves the credit for it. There is no physical necessity to think of someone else, and indeed it is "only natural" simply to take and enjoy what one has been given, to revel in the satisfaction of one's needs, without a further thought.

The thinking aspect of gratitude considers the past and looks to the future; it reflects on what the response shall be to the benefactor. Gratitude is not automatic like anger. But the receiver of a gift "immediately while receiving should turn his thought to repaying."[9] Seneca is speaking here of the man who "intends to be grateful," meaning one who is aware of an "obligation," a principle he has previously adopted, always to repay a gift. The receiver of a slight or a blow will similarly think at once about repaying it in kind, and if he can, he will do so. Anger is immediate and violent, with physical consequences not only for its victim but for the one who feels it, whose face turns red, whose heart pounds; it typically occurs almost simultaneously with the hurt that provokes it. Gratitude is a relatively calm emotion, intense but happy and peaceful, and not a matter of simple arousal, even though it often begins to be felt at once. Laboratory experiments have shown that deep appreciation enormously decreases stress. It is therefore good for one's physical health.

There exists also what we call a "simmering" anger that lasts, or more accurately that is kept available "on the back burner," and many times reheated and refuelled by ruminations about past events and all the possible future exactions of revenge for them. The name for this kind of anger is *resentment*, literally meaning "feeling back at" someone. Resentment involves feeling again—and again.[10] It is this emotion that issues in vengeance. Time is taken with a view to revenge when there are no immediate or appropriate opportunities to hit back—when the offence is not physical violence, for instance. The offended person is likely to utter dark threats, such as "You'll be sorry," partly to recuperate something of his honour, and partly to make his tormentor uncomfortable and maybe afraid for as long as possible, even before he performs his act of vengeance. The grateful person, on the other hand, at once says "thank you" for a good thing received—and later responds with a gift or favour. The first giver, meanwhile, having received an assurance of the other's pleasure, enjoys thinking of the good deeds he has done, quite apart from any return gift she might receive.

There are many signs in our culture that demonstrate the closeness of vengeance and gratitude in people's minds—our awareness of the difference, and at the same time a sort of shuddering at the similarity. Gratitude is about memory; so is revenge. ("Remember me!" cries the ghost of Hamlet's father.[11]) And gratitude (*charis,* "pleasure" in Greek) gives joy—but so does revenge. This is one deep source for the many-levelled horror of the scene in the *Agamemnon* when queen Clytemnestra, covered in blood, exults over the body of her husband and that of the prophetess Cassandra, both of whom she has hacked to death. She begins by calling to mind her long resentment, and goes on to speak of her revenge as a jubilant "thank-offering" of blood outpoured:

> Thus to me
> the conflict born of ancient bitterness is not
> a thing new thought upon, but pondered deep in time.
> I stand now where I struck him down. The thing is done. . . .
> I struck him twice. In two great cries of agony
> he buckled at the knees and fell. When he was down
> I struck him the third blow, in thanks and reverence
> to Zeus the lord of dead men underneath the ground.
> Thus he went down, and the life struggled out of him;
> and as he died he spattered me with the dark red
> and violent driven rain of bitter savored blood
> to make me glad, as gardens stand among the showers
> of God in glory at the birthtime of the buds.[12]

On a more common, everyday level, people sometimes speak of returning a favour as "revenge." *Revanchieren* in German (from French *revanche*) means both "to take revenge" and (colloquially) "to return a kindness." "*J'accepte ton aide à charge de revanche"* in French means "I'll let you help me but on condition that you let me return the favour sometime." And so ingrained is the idea that revenge (like gift-giving) is alternation, that *en revanche* in French means simply "on the other hand."

The receiver of a gift should recognize the giver. It has often been considered a kind of "return" to enhance the giver's reputation by telling everybody else about how generous she has been. Seneca suggests the following as a compliment to be offered to the giver: "I shall never be able to repay to you my gratitude, but, at any rate, I shall not cease from declaring everywhere that I am unable to repay it."[13] A person taking revenge thirsts for his victim's knowledge of just who has caused him pain: vengeance would not be "sweet" otherwise. Therefore Odysseus, who has blinded the one-eyed, man-eating Cyclops, boasts aloud of what he has done, calling out his name to the monster so that there can be no mistake about who has taken revenge: he considers this proclamation worth his while despite the pleas of his men, even though it incites the Cyclops to fling rocks at the departing boat.[14] And Hermione, in Racine's *Andromaque* (1667), wants to kill the man, the *ingrat,* who does not love her in return. She insists that he be told just who has ordered his death: "My vengeance is wasted if he is not aware, as he dies, that I am his killer!"[15] A revenger concentrates on his victim's awareness, but is often not averse to everyone else knowing as well. Vengeance is part of honour culture, after all, the lifeblood of which is what other people think and say; perfect revenge will, in the right cultural circumstances, also produce a generalized fear, respect, and acknowledgement of power.

In our own individualistic culture a gift returned must, as we have noted, be different from what was originally given. This is in part because of the necessary recognition that every person is different, and a giver wants to take into account the receiver's tastes and needs. Choosing a gift or a favour, and the timing of the return, are signs of the giver's freedom, and proofs that the return favour, like the first favour, is a gift. Money payment is equivalency, and a gift must not be anything like a price, a bribe, or a settling of accounts—therefore, a different object (not money) should be given in return. And finally, "paying back" and "settling accounts" refer not only to the discharge of a monetary debt, but also to revenge. The resemblances in structure between gift exchange and vengeance demand a punctilious recognition that they are in fact polar opposites.

An action performed in revenge is most successful when the doer of harm receives back what he meted out: measure for measure, tit for tat. A long rehearsal of wrongs in the mind of the vengeful one should find a perfectly *appropriate* revenge—that is, the most exact equivalence possible. Vengeance, like gift-giving, often encourages imagination and creativity, the punishment should fit the crime. W.S. Gilbert's song of the Mikado, in the opera of the same name,[16] is funny because it reminds the audience of its own common irritations and then provides "harmless merriment" by suggesting an exquisitely suitable revenge for every annoyance:

All prosy dull society sinners
Who chatter and bleat and bore,
Are sent to hear sermons
From mystical Germans
Who preach from ten till four.
The amateur tenor, whose vocal villainies
All desire to shirk,
Shall, during off-hours,
Exhibit his powers
To Madame Tussaud's waxwork,

and the list continues. Victorian parents could consider it righteous as well as vividly fitting to punish their children—for biting people, say, or for using "dirty" language—by washing their mouths out with soap and water.[17] Vengeance should force the offender to feel what it was like to suffer his offence. It is an important part of what René Girard calls "mimetic violence," where each side obsessively mirrors the behaviour of the other. Gratitude, on the other hand, is not violent, and gifts exchanged should be different, that is, not mimetic doubles of each other. Any "return" of a gift or favour that gratitude gives rise to, however, reflects the original movement of giving, and in that sense is also imitative.

One of the reasons for taking revenge can be a kind of virulent didacticism: the avenger wants the original perpetrator to *learn*. "I'll teach him!" she cries, and "Who does he think he is?" (meaning that he has not understood what his position in the pecking order is and now must find out). There is a desire to counteract misconceptions, including any idea the offender might entertain that the one now taking revenge is afraid of a fight. An avenger is typically convinced that hitting back is right and proper; he is invariably sure that the other "started it." A grateful person who returns a favour, on the other hand, is not explicitly trying to teach a lesson. She is more likely to be happy about what she has herself, sometimes unexpectedly, discovered through receiving a favour; she will be impressed by the giver, rather than anxious to protect and strengthen her own status. (The opposite point of view sees her as *needing* to "give back" on pain of remaining in the "lower" position relative to the giver.) She does, however, want to give a sign of her own benevolence towards the giver. And both parties "learn," as they deepen their relationship.

Where ingratitude, as we saw, is often thought to be monstrous because unjust as a response to a benefaction, and "cold," vengeance immediately taken is "hot" because angry, and easily considered to be a proud attempt to recreate equivalence: "getting your own back" (with its implication of a previous theft of honour) and "getting even." Vengeance makes a claim to be just, and societies structured by honour often, secretly if necessary, approve of it. Gratitude, we saw, is also "only fair." But its justice is response—a new gift—rather than requital. Giving in gratitude carefully avoids strict copying so that the return favour will be a true gift—that is, a new and free action.

And where vengeance, springing from pride and hate, is felt to be necessary for the restoration of honour as "largeness," gratitude deliberately accepts the temporarily "lower" place out of regard for the other.

If gratitude emerges *instead* of vengeance, how does this switch come about? We saw ceremonial gift-giving as a choice made, to substitute peaceful exchange for fighting among neighbouring peoples. But once violence is installed, a return to, or the invention of, peace is infinitely more challenging. The parties may come to realize that revenge is in fact an exchange of losses, and that it leads ever downward and finally into anarchy. They may simply get tired of the pain and long to stop. An immense amount of wisdom and generosity will nevertheless be needed to bring the cycle to an end, and a letting-go of resentments for real harm done.

Of course, it is much more difficult to invent anything new than to go on imitating one another by taking revenge. Aeschylus ends his trilogy, the *Oresteia,* with a scene in which Vengeance agrees to give way to Blessings. The Furies, goddesses of Vengeance and Kin Murder, turn into Eumenides (Kindly Ones). They are eventually persuaded that it would be better for them to accept honour for their power to bring fertility to the land than to live in perpetual rage, producing blight. The arguments on either side—the scene also provides a mythical first trial by jury—are unconvincing. What happens is that Persuasion (who had a cult as a goddess in Athens) mysteriously *changes the minds* of the Furies. All at once[18] they decide to transform themselves from one polar opposite into the other: the vengeance fiends become promoters of peace. They are granted (a "first gift" to them from the Athenian citizens) genuine powers of beneficence in the city, and also honour and respect. They promise in return to prevent civil war. At the end of the play they change the colour of their robes from black to red: they become peaceful immigrants (wearing the distinctive clothing of metics, or "resident aliens") in Athens. They retain the possibility, however, of changing back again into bat-winged and iron-footed Furies should the citizens ever be tempted to betray Benevolence towards one another.

The Eumenides promote togetherness within the city—by uniting it against its enemies. We have seen that Greek "gratitude" is pleasure shared between or among givers and receivers:[19] as such, it is for those within the circle of reciprocities, and excludes those without. So the chorus of Eumenides sings:

> Let us not give bloodshed for bloodshed,
> But rather give joy for joy.
> Let love be their common will;
> Let them hate with single heart.[20]

"Gratitude" to one another as "vengeance replaced" overcomes civil strife by projecting the citizens' hostilities outwards; this orientation in itself makes of them a group "with single heart" rather than many individuals with different points of view, who are therefore in danger of fighting one other. But it is precisely this strategy that "works" so triumphantly in the mechanism of scapegoating, where all turn on a common enemy, somebody who is "to blame" for the strife of the group—and find themselves, miraculously, united thereby. Belonging can easily come to seem more important than justice. "Much wrong in the world is thereby healed," sings the chorus of converted Eumenides.[21] They remain partial and limited, Furies at heart.

A remarkable proposal of gratitude as the answer to vengeance is given in the ninth-century Irish poem *The Voyage of Máel Dúin*. Transcendence is achieved through the tumultuous living of the hero's life, until he decides that, after all, he has so much to be thankful for that he simply need not take revenge. The story is about a young man who sets out in a boat with twenty companions to find and wreak vengeance on the robber who had killed his father before he was born. Almost at once the crew reaches the Island of Murderers where Máel Dúin's enemy now lives, but a storm drives the boat back out to sea. It sails on, from peril to peril and undergoing adventure after adventure, to the Island of the Enormous Ants, the Island of the Horselike Monster, the Island of the Revolving Beast (which turns its bones while its skin stays still)—and so on, thirty-three marvellous and terrifying islands in all. Finally the boat comes round to the Island of Murderers once more. The heroes are welcomed by the inhabitants with feasting, and asked to tell their amazing stories. Máel Dúin, confronting his father's murderer, decides finally to take no vengeance but to forgive him, out of gratitude to God for his own deliverance from so many great dangers.[22]

Regret is another opposite of gratitude, even though it may lack the malevolence of resentment and its culmination in revenge. Regret concentrates on what we would have liked, but has not come to pass. Gratitude dwells on the good things we have been given. A decision to concentrate on, by deliberately recalling, what others have done for us can give a new point of view on one's life in general, a far more fruitful one than that of only remembering and regretting failures.

Gratitude, replacing selfishness, greed, and disregard, will in my opinion have to be called upon to help us surmount the ecological crisis that now threatens our very existence. Fears of disaster and the laws we make to protect the environment will certainly be necessary as both pressure to act and restraint from further abuse. But fear and the law will not be enough. What is required is nothing less than a conversion: a turning-around of our ideas, a change of heart, an agreement to see things from a new point of view. Fear can cause rather than avert abuses, and there are infinite numbers of ways to get away with selfish convenience or greed if people care only for their own personal interests.

We saw earlier how gratitude is necessary for the functioning of a healthy society, precisely because it reaches into areas of life that the law can neither control nor inspire. As Charles Taylor reminds us, "High standards need strong sources."[23] One such source is our knowledge of what it is like to be grateful. We have to retrieve now and bring back into the light something that gratitude entails: *respect for what is there,* love for it (for itself and not for what we can gouge out of it). Grateful people make good use of the gifts they have been given, out of respect for the giver. To be ecologically aware we shall need to be thankful for what we so continually and lavishly receive, and feel the need to "give back" and restore the earth's ravaged bounty. It is an attitude to nature that our most "primitive" forebears intensely understood. We should also remember that we inherited a rich and beautiful earth, which it is "only fair" to hand on to our children.

G.K. Chesterton speaks of "the ancient instinct of astonishment": the surprise and wonder that turn quickly into gratitude. A cultivated disposition to be grateful encourages awe in us. Gratitude for the earth arises from a profound belief, an agreement with God, that the world is "very good," as the Book of Genesis puts it in the story of Creation.[24] And every one of us, in person, is responsible for its well-being. The London *Times* once asked a number of writers for essays on "What Is Wrong with the World." Chesterton's reply was shortest and most to the point:

Dear Sirs:
I am.
Sincerely yours,
G.K. Chesterton.

If we truly appreciated the earth, we would be able to find, as Chesterton writes, that "the greatest of poems is an inventory."[25] Gratitude occurs when people receive good things which they do not feel are theirs by right, or that they have deserved. And "there is no way in which a man can earn a star or deserve a sunset."[26] Believing that the gifts of the earth are of inestimable value would convince people never to destroy them or waste them heedlessly.

The "givenness" of the world is apparent even to people who reject belief in God: we human beings are not, after all, the cause of our own existence. We shall need to work together if we want to survive the crisis we have created. And what will connect us in this common endeavour? Grateful wonder at the world's magnificence and vulnerability would certainly help—and justice, which can no longer be dissociated from ecological concerns. Gratitude, the "cement" of societies, is a visible aspect of love, and the enemy of greed and envy.

Envy is malevolence towards another because of his superior advantages. A common method of overcoming it is deliberately to compare one's own relatively fortunate lot with that of somebody manifestly less well off, as Jean-Jacques Rousseau recommends we should do. Pity, for Rousseau, is the opposite of envy. "Pity," he writes, "is sweet because in putting ourselves in the place of one who suffers, we nevertheless feel the pleasure of not suffering as he does. Envy is bitter because the sight of a happy man, far from putting the envious man in his place, makes the envious man regret not being there."[27] Far better, then, to turn to one worse off and pity him, thereby deliberately reversing our envy for someone fortunate. Rousseau's virtuous pity and its pleasures reflect envy's obsession with status and comparison. But his entire concern is with the relative comfort, the "sweetness," of pitying rather than envying. Substituting the vice of envy with satisfaction at his own superiority is Rousseau's solution; there is apparently no concern for the one "pitied" at all.

Kant believed that young people in particular are prone to honour/shame "cravings." They should therefore be directed towards magnanimity as a substitute for envy. Later, with age and experience, people become capable of deliberately replacing envy with benevolence and gratitude.[28] Gratitude is perhaps most malignantly opposed by envy, and is also perhaps the most total reversal of this fundamental vice. In his very conventional sermon, Chaucer's Parson makes envy rather than ingratitude "the worste synne that is."[29] Envy is one of gratitude's shadows.

Thankfulness begins with paying attention to one's benefactor and her gifts and favours, and with appreciating her generous qualities; it then produces a desire to give something to her in return. We saw that on receiving a gift or favour, a grateful person very often looks into the giver's eyes. The word *envy* is from Latin *invidia,* deriving from *videre,* "to see." *Invidia* is "seeing with intensity," paying meticulous and malevolent attention, eyeing in order to measure and compare one's own lot with that of another, while feeling, if the other is deemed to be better off, the injustice of the difference. (The Greek goddess Nemesis envied good fortune. For this and other reasons, she carried as an attribute a measuring rod.) The person in the grip of envy then longs to destroy the lucky one because he has what she wants. She plots to take away from her rival, or to spoil, an offending object, advantage, or position in life.

An ancient and widespread superstition in European and Semitic cultures is fear of the evil eye. Here a person has the power to cause harm to another merely by looking at or praising that person or his property. The victim becomes ill or loses the love of his wife; the walls of his house might crack, or its roof fall in. People protect themselves by wearing amulets, reciting counter-charms, making specific apotropaic gestures, or spitting, to avert the eye's power. Or they may "spoil in advance," but benignly, their child or property: putting a smudge behind a child's ear, or a mark on a white dress, or a scratch on a new bicycle.[30] Ancient Romans believed that an erect phallus had the power to avert the evil eye; they carried in the celebratory processions called "triumphs" a *fascinus* (the word meant both the evil eye itself and a charm against it)[31] in the form of a giant phallus, to protect from the forces of Invidia the victorious chariot-born general who was the focus of all the glory. The envy likely to be inherent in or aroused by staring (or the gaze of the populace) is a large part of what is feared, and therefore to be parried and fought off. Sigmund Freud thought that a fortunate person "projects onto [others] the envy he would have felt in their place."[32]

Both envy and gratitude are *thoughtful* emotions; both of them involve paying attention and making comparisons. They frequently employ what virtue analysts call "counter-factuals," meaning what it is possible to envision yet is not the case: both gratitude and envy encourage plenty of imagination. While the person feeling grateful often finds a place for the realization that "it could have been different," the person envying fastens on the life of the other and wishes for her removal and replacement by himself: "It could have been me." Or he blames the regrettable constitution of the society he lives in: "In a different world the advantage could have been mine." An envier feels that the gap between his own lot and that of his furious obsession is an undeserved trick of either fate or injustice. A grateful person too feels that she does not deserve the favour she has been given. (Indeed, if she thinks she is responsible for and therefore entitled to the good things that come her way, she might feel pleased, but will not be grateful.) Gratitude causes a receiver to look beyond the gift to its giver. A person sufficiently envious is also capable of pushing what is coveted almost out of the picture: she may eventually focus entirely on the hated rival, the person with the (by now mysterious) power to cast her into the shade.

Envy and gratitude are similar—but contrary to each other. Where envy is discontent and a search for redress in the future, gratitude is pleasure with what has already been received. Envy needs to reach for superiority, since it springs from feeling badly done by. (One of the defences against falling into the pain of envy is seeking to make oneself enviable to others; ranking is essential to envy.) A grateful person, on the other hand, accepts the initially "lower" place of the receiver, and the strategy of an eventual overall equilibrium of general equality (not the particularity and exactitude of the equality imposed by revenge). Despising and otherwise devaluing something desirable that is not in one's possession is another common "spoiling" strategy of envy. Gratitude, on the contrary, deliberately adds value to a gift, seeing in it (whatever it is) the benevolence of the giver.

Anger and envy are a terrible mix, envy being a long "simmering" and anger a sudden "boiling over": anger can precipitate action, bringing the seething malevolent dreams of envy to concrete performance.[33] Envy, since it is desire for something one does not have, is related to greed. (It should be distinguished from jealousy, however, which is essentially a fear of loss, especially the loss of somebody's love. Jealousy usually involves three people, not two: lover, beloved, and rival.) Gratitude, on the other hand, is a form of generosity: it wants not only to "give back" but ideally to share with others (not only "us two") the good things received. That is why a pretense of being grateful out of an entirely loveless greed, in the belief that an apparently thankful response will produce further favours, is excoriated when discovered: it is a vice parading as its absolute opposite.

During the Middle Ages ingratitude was, in addition to so much else, a form of avarice: a closed heart, imaged forth as a closed purse.[34] Gratitude, the reinforcement of links among persons that is created by gifts and favours, still means in our own day "openness" to others. "Closed" individuals cut themselves off, increase and protect what they have, and think they owe nothing to other people, to their culture, or to the past. Gratitude is neither self-sufficiency nor self-satisfaction, but recognition that pleasure and satisfaction have come through the benevolence of others. Generosity and humility are aspects of gratitude. Their opposites, Greed and Pride, are two more of the five Deadly Sins that ingratitude covers. They are both implicated, along with Hypocrisy, in Ambrose Bierce's definition from his *Devil's Dictionary:*

> Ingratitude: A form of self-respect that is not inconsistent with
> acceptance of favours.

Superiority, narcissism, a sense of entitlement, and selfishness are all opposites of gratitude. And so are thoughtlessness and forgetfulness. "One squeezes the orange and at once discards it" went the hard-hearted utilitarian maxim of Gracián, with its implicit understanding that this is no way to treat a human being.[35]

When we consider how many evil options gratitude "turns down," we begin to see how desirable a virtue it is. And the monstrousness of ingratitude for Shakespeare and his contemporaries comes much closer home. What is it that enables somebody to replace a mountain of wickedness and misery with a grateful disposition? Before we attempt to answer this question, we must look further at gratitude's preferentialism and at gratitude as "grace." Under what conditions can gratitude remain genuine and still reach for impartiality?

26

Partiality and Transcendence

There are in English apparently only three adjectives describing emotional feeling that can be followed by "to." They are: *sympathetic* (to), *devoted* (to), and *grateful* (to).[1] We never say "delighted to someone," for example, or "angry to someone"; neither do we use "to someone" with *surprised* or *upset* or *disgusted*. "To" implies motion—and here *emotion*—towards. All three of the terms that can be followed by "to" characterize sentiments directed forcefully towards specific persons—or towards objects that are being personified, that is, credited with thought and will.

We use "for" to introduce the reason for gratitude, and when we do so, "for" implies that someone else has been involved in or is responsible for the action: "We were grateful for the fruit" entails somebody else having provided it. ("Sorry for" is similar: "She was sorry for being late" indicates that someone else has been inconvenienced by her lateness. Once again, remembering how the Japanese say "I am so sorry" where we would say "I am grateful," we notice that apologizing and being grateful share a deliberate turning to and consideration for other people.) If I say I am grateful *to* a tree *for* its shade, I am thinking of the tree as wanting to be useful; I then use "for" to explain what the tree is "giving." But if I say simply that I am grateful for the shade of a tree, the implication is that someone (unnamed) has provided the tree and its shade—whether by planting it in the right spot, or by creating trees in the first place. If nobody but myself and the tree is involved, then I may be pleased to have shade, but I am not strictly speaking grateful for it. An inexact use of the word *grateful* here may arise from the fact that gratitude often includes relief, arising from comparison with a less desirable alternative—in this case most probably the heat of the sun. But gratitude can refer only to the agency of somebody other than the speaker.

Adding "to" to the three words of sentiment mentioned addresses them to persons who have not only intentions but *good* intentions. That is why we are not "upset to" or "angry to" but angry (or upset) *with* or *at* a person (or with a tree for dropping its fruit on my head, as though the tree meant to be disobliging). Being *delighted* is definitely a pleasant emotion in the person who feels it, but the word says nothing about the delightful person's intentions to please. I am therefore delighted *at* or *by* or *with* something Alfie has done, rather than "to" him. It is also possible to be grateful *for* Alfie in himself, meaning for his very existence; Alfie is then in the nature of a gift to my life. It is possible to be grateful *to* artists and other people personally unknown to us for what they have contributed to our lives. We can also be grateful *for* somebody like Bach, not only for his great gifts and his generous deployment of them, but also for his very existence—a precious reality we could not ourselves have brought about. My gratitude is always for something that comes to me *from without*. As Thomas Aquinas points out, one cannot be grateful to oneself.[2]

Being thankful means that I do not feel, with Emerson, that "it is not the office of a man to receive gifts. How dare you give them? We wish to be self-sustained. We do not quite forgive the giver. The hand that feeds us is in some danger of being bitten. . . . We sometimes hate the meat which we eat, because there seems something of degrading dependence in living by it."[3] Gratitude includes accepting—not resenting—dependence on something provided by someone who is not ourselves. It means concentrating on that person and on her kind intentions, just as she has concentrated her attention on me. Accepting a true gift can itself be a grateful act; gratitude is virtue in the receiver. And sometimes accepting a gift can be more generous than giving one.

Because human beings are intelligent, they are always prone to compare and contrast themselves with others—to measure their advantages and mishaps against those of their neighbours, to feel either envious or triumphant because of the differences, and to identify themselves and others both by the slots they occupy in the social hierarchy and by the things they possess. Comparison—status, the desire at least to draw equal and if possible to outshine—is "natural," and the motivation of much of human striving; the subject has often come up in this book. But there is another force that is equally common: it is the entirely natural desire of human beings to belong to a group, to identify with it and find profit and protection within its ranks. Groups are created by links forged among their members, one of the most efficient connections being established by the performance of favours and return favours.

And there is plenty that is reasonable about partiality. The excesses of modern individualism can make belonging an especially valuable because a relatively rare thing. After all, we give to people "using our reason," as Seneca puts it. He is aware that motives are seldom pure: "You inquire where and how you should bestow a benefit, which there would be no need of doing if giving a benefit is something that is desirable in itself."⁴ And almost immediately, even simultaneously, the principle of exclusion will kick in, to create and fortify a new couple's or a new group's identity. Gift-giving and mutual favours continue between and among the members, but a wall between those inside and those without comes to seem essential to the entity's existence and continuance.

Gifts are exchanged inside this boundary. Only very formally and infrequently will they cross over to make contact with outsiders, the unpreferred, and this crossing itself is likely to be accompanied by reminders to everyone of the continuing difference between those "in" and those "out." The give and take inside the stronghold may even come gradually to seem more important—and more profitable—than rules of law and morality that are supposed to apply to everybody. Group members will protect and help one another out, not only to the exclusion but also at the expense of outsiders; we looked at this mechanism when considering bribery and corruption. Anthropologists describe this favouring and gratitude reserved to the group as "tribal loyalty" or "amoral familism," because tribes and families are obvious examples of unconditional belonging by birth; race is another.

Such preference is *partiality,* a word that comes from "part." It refers to the way people have divided up into sections the society they live in, the metaphor being that of lines cutting up and enclosing areas within boundaries. Each person, in this model, is thought of as self-enclosed and forming a whole. He or she then becomes, through allegiance or through simple belonging, a "piece" of a larger whole—a group—divided from the rest of society. Gift-giving and favours mutually performed strengthen the links created among "pieces" of a grouped "department" of the whole. Gratitude in all of its aspects—memory, praise and rejoicing, consideration, return of favours, pleasure, freedom, equality, continuance, and the rest—then completes and further strengthens these gift-formed relationships. The combination of gifts and gratitude, strongly expressed in the structures of reciprocity, formal and often amoral as they are, comes to imply exclusivity: an inner circle, a brotherhood, a closed shop.

The "linking" function may be selected out of all the meanings of gratitude and used entirely to promote group cohesion; the "ungrateful"—those who do not play along—will be by definition excluded. In Proust's *Remembrance of Things Past,* Swann is denounced by the Duc de Guermantes because he makes no secret of his belief in the innocence of Dreyfus.[5] No matter what he thought the truth was, Swann ought, in the duke's opinion, to have openly condemned Dreyfus for high treason, and cut himself off not only from supporters of the Dreyfus cause, but also from Jewish society (Swann, like Dreyfus, is himself a Jew). In the duke's mind, as Proust's narrator remarks, this would have been the least Swann could do to express his gratitude to the aristocratic circles of the Faubourg Saint-Germain for having been so good as to invite him to their dinners, their soirées, and their outings. For the duke, "gratitude" merely means submitting one's conscience to the interests of the group.

But society must somehow achieve a binding together of the groups that constitute it; otherwise, it will break apart. We have noted before that one point of view on marriage sees it as a way out of family partiality: incest (sex and reproduction remaining within the family group) being forbidden, a woman is "given away" by her father to a man of a totally different "house" and bloodline. Marriage links, and the engendering of children through them, serve to bind family groups together, to form a society. (And nature itself approves of social prohibitions that ensure variety in the genetic pool.) We have also seen that one of the oldest human strategies for the creation of unity threatened by dissolution is that of scapegoating: the expulsion from the group of someone designated as a common enemy. Societies themselves may practise exclusion to the extent that enemies are actually useful for their self-definition and their solidarity: they "hate with a single heart."

Formally speaking, gifts given and accepted and given again can achieve three things: create or strengthen links, invite an outsider to join the group, and petition a group for admission. The offering and then the acceptance of gifts passing "over the wall" let the outsider in; it is an open-hearted move in either case. For risk is involved on both sides. An outsider, a "guest" allowed in, could be dangerous and disruptive; asking for permission to enter the group could easily result in rejection. We ended the last section with the advisability of replacing vengeance, regret, pride, envy, avarice, anger, and greed with gratitude, the opposite of them all. But there is also a requirement to "rise above" the partiality inherent in gratitude itself.

Gratitude might not be relevant to the situation at all—in which case everything becomes much clearer. The Soviet poet Marina Tsvetaeva protests in her diary[6] that justice and rights come first, and that personal preference, where justice is the point, is totally out of place—and so is gratitude: "When I give bread to a person, I give to a hungry person, that is, to the stomach, not to him. His soul doesn't have anything to do with it. . . . I don't want to believe that anyone, in giving to my stomach, would demand something in return from my soul. . . . It would be strange to prefer one stomach to another, and if a preference is to be made—then the hungrier one. . . . Thus, having established the giver (the hand) and the receiver (the stomach), it is strange to expect one piece of meat to be grateful to another piece of meat. . . . If we give to whom *we* want, we would be the most thorough scoundrels. We give to the one *who wants*. His hunger (will!) elicits our gesture (bread). Given and forgotten. Taken and forgotten. No strings, no kinship. Having given, I refuse to acknowledge. Having taken, I refuse to acknowledge. *Without consequences.*" There is a heart-wrenching revulsion in this passage for gratitude, perceived as a demand made from the powerful to the needy (that is, as the creation of an obligation and a proof of inequality), and as a sign of partiality.

Behind Tsvetaeva's words lies the Gospel precept that we should give so that "the left hand does not know what the right hand is doing."[7] This exhortation is a warning that giving to the poor should never be done for the giver's self-aggrandizement, by drawing attention to the act and so winning other people's admiration. Complicated calculations as to where the giver's self-interest lies are to be ruled out in advance. The fact that there exists what we call "a crying need"—a *person's* need, not a mere empty space in the abstract—is enough. Giving is a direct and simple act, from one person to another; the phrase does not mean that the giver is only a hand, any more than that the receiver is a mere stomach. Need must elicit giving (as Tsvetaeva sees so clearly)—and also love for one's neighbour, a notion she scorns to consider in her desire to exclude "soul." In the parable of the Good Samaritan, the self-righteous characters who ignore the wounded traveller and walk on past him think of their purity and the busy-ness of their lives; the Samaritan (who in the context is a social pariah) sees the suffering man and his need, feels compassion, and helps him without a second thought. He is the one, therefore, who obeys God's command both to *be* a neighbour even to those not "our own," and to love those neighbours.[8]

One problem with the quotation from Tsvetaeva's diary—perhaps it is merely a matter of translation—is that she seems to make no distinction between giving and sharing. Giving is what elicits gratitude. Justice does not require it. And justice must be demanded, as neither gifts nor gratitude can be. Nevertheless it is possible for a person (though not for "a stomach") to feel grateful when justice has been carried out, and also when rights have been observed, for we all know that what should be the case is not always so. Fairness demands not giving but sharing. Sharing should not, however, be made to obliterate the idea of giving. Friendship, after all, is in the realm of the gift. "If men are friends," writes Aristotle, "there is no need of justice between them." He adds that even if everybody were just, there would still be a need for friendship.[9]

A gift is not a share. A group of friends pool their money and send out for a pizza. They cut it up and share it out. While they are eating, another friend arrives, unexpected and late. They allow her, one way or another, to have some pizza. Her helping—unpaid for, un-"accounted" for, and "extra"—is a gift, not a "just slice" or share, since the friend presumably is neither destitute nor starving. There is equality among these people, an equality that is important for what we mean by gratitude. Despite her intimacy with the group, she might even say "thanks" for the pizza and also be grateful *for having these friends.* She would not be *obliged* to say "thanks," but her consciousness of the goodness of her friends (and not because they demand her gratitude) would unquestionably give her pleasure. Gifts and gratitude reach into places where justice—essential though it is—cannot go. Their results are unpredictable and inadequately expressed by the word *consequences.* But would this happy circle of friends agree to allow a stranger—and especially one socially defined as unequal, without power, and not an obvious "asset"—to join the party?

How does a group break the boundaries of "familism"? And why would it want to do so? To begin with method: one way is to create a link where none has previously existed. The Emmaüs Movement in France gives jobs and lodging to those in need; its members collect second-hand goods and repair and freshen up these objects for sale in the popular Emmaüs stores that are found all over France. Its members include its beneficiaries; people have only to have a need for employment, or want to help people in need, in order to belong. It began in a moment of shock, when a woman died of cold in the streets of Paris in 1954. In outrage at the cruel lot of people like her, the Abbé Pierre appealed over the radio to the people of France to unite with him to confront injustice; he began to search for ways to house the homeless. He later describes how a suicidal man, just out of prison, came to see him one day to ask for help. Instead of simply bestowing aid, the Abbé asked the man instead to lend a hand: "First come and help me rehouse these families who have nowhere to live, and we'll look after you later." The man did so, and in the end became one of the Abbé's closest collaborators. What makes people turn to those in need is outrage at injustice, together with an awakening to openness, love, and respect. The secret of the success of Emmaüs at integrating the stranger into the group is that the members turn to those who have nothing—and ask them to give.

In this manner people become associates rather than mere recipients. Members stand side by side, rather than face to face at different levels of social status. Since this is a religious movement, all of them feel equal before God, who alone is "highest."[10] They then find it possible to give as God gives, not to "get something back," but simply out of love, part of which consists in inviting and encouraging receivers to join in giving as well. Emmaüs calls itself a group in which "people decide to unite their will and their actions in mutual aid."[11] Justice and giving do not cancel but complement each other. Nobody feels "beholden." Gratitude depends on the perceptions and feelings of each individual receiver, and in the Emmaüs Movement there is plenty of gratitude. Many who are not in physical need, and who might therefore be thought to be only givers, would not accept that as their exclusive role. Comparatively speaking, they have been fortunate, and that in itself makes them want to "give back". They also know that despite appearances and advantages they are themselves dependent and in need. They receive immense benefits from the complex relationships they have with people they would never otherwise have met. They feel grateful to the movement for its very existence and, since they too have been "let in," for the chance to participate.

The partiality one feels for "one's own" is ideally based on love and on constant interactions with him or them. It involves concentrating on this person and ignoring (for the moment, at least) all others. Gratitude is always a matter of paying attention, deliberately beholding and appreciating the other. One cannot concentrate without excluding the irrelevant; "one thing at a time" is necessary to concentration. Gratitude is also remembering, often for a long time after the giving has occurred. The receiver of a gift freely consents to entering into a relationship with this donor. (That is why accepting a gift can sometimes be a more generous action than giving one.) He might also decide to become a full participant in the way of life that gift-giving itself proposes. The concentrating is on something other than oneself, and the consent is not only to a gift or favour but to a new future that a gift and its grateful reception initiates, but which is mostly unforeseeable.

This giving up of control, this change in one's fortunes that the gift announces, becomes far more dramatic when more than two people are involved, when it is a question of "inviting others in" or wanting to be admitted to a group of friends. As if gratitude were not in these cases a change of direction extraordinary enough in itself, we have in the surmounting of social barriers something that can only be called a transcendent (literally an "up-and-across") ideal. But the first step must be relationship with one other person: if you cannot recognize and love one other person, you cannot begin. As we have noted, gratitude causes the receiver to look beyond the gift to the giver. This movement in itself transcends the object or favour given; it "opens" the receiver to the person of the other. One starts by being partial to another—and remains "partial" in this sense to the end, for loving is concrete and particular before it is generalized. People who eventually learn to love everyone, beyond social structurings, still love their friends in a special way.

And being loved themselves enables them (often in gratitude) to love others to whom they might well not be "partial."

The word *gratitude* stands for the process—freely undertaken and therefore hard to pin down with definitions and generalized explanations—by which a person's attitude changes. It marks, first, the move from the perception of meaning to an emotional response to it—a feeling that seeks expression. A person watching and aware of another's kindly actions and motives in relation to himself takes a further step and, similarly well-wishing, acts upon what he has seen; he moves, most specifically, from receiving to giving something back. Why he should imitate his benefactor's action in this manner will remain inexplicable until gratitude is taken into account. From the smallest event that elicits a felt "thanks" to an appreciation of kindness that totally opens someone's heart to another, gratitude is a transcending movement, one that "rises to the occasion."

The "upward" aspect of the word *transcendence* derives from the metaphor again of an area divided by lines into parts. Not only is this figure flat—two-dimensional—but it is also limited and motionless. A wall or frontier surrounds all of the groups inside; there is only the area enclosed to deal with—to deal out, in fact, into divisions with boundaries of their own. One dimension (the "dot" that is literally the "undivided"—the individual) is given two dimensions in order to create this flat and fenced-in diagram. "Transcendence" is moving from one dimension to two, and then from two dimensions to three. The giving, gratitude, and return of gifts or favours, when they are offered freely, respectfully, and in thankfulness, are ritual and deeply felt markers of these pivotal moments. The circumference may then become a movement, spiralling upwards. It opens out, rises above, and crosses the boundaries of human social structures, even those that may serve to define our society and its culture. A moving spiral of giving replaces the static boundary line enclosing those "in" and excluding those "out."

Neither gratitude nor gifts make profits or merely "have consequences"; the metaphors appropriate to them are of "engendering" and "bearing fruit."

There will surely be increase, but neither one nor the other controls what appears or happens next. Refusing to give or to be grateful is not immoral, as being unjust is immoral; it is rather a limitation, a closure against other people and a desire for nothing new, a failure to grow, a resolution against transcendence. Giving and gratitude, on the other hand, are the beginning and the stuff of transcendence: a free response in love to another person, to the group to which one belongs, to all groups in society including one's own, to humankind as a whole, to the earth, to the universe, and—both finally and first—to God. In 1953, during a moment when he was reflecting on the inevitable coming of death, Dag Hammarskjöld wrote:

> "—Night is drawing nigh—"
> For all that has been—Thanks!
> To all that shall be—Yes![12]

Willing acceptance of everything to come—as for all of his past—is his thankful and trusting response to God for the givenness of his life.

I mentioned earlier that one of the concepts that contributed to the notion we call "gratitude" was what Christians designate as "grace." Grace is for Christians the self-communication of God to human beings, their experience of God. As such, it is a gift, the quintessence and highest mode of giving. Grace is unexpected—often over and above what was previously thought possible—and unmerited. Since its sphere is spiritual, not material, it provides the kind of plenty that goes beyond physical objects, limited goods, economic scarcity, and all our partialities (the circular pizza as a symbol of "all there is"). Grace is overflowing, abundant, always enough. It is experienced as dynamic, energetic, supple, joyful, enabling, generous to the point of extravagance; where a quiet virtue such as patience is needed, grace provides the strength to be patient.

Grace often disturbs human arrangements, and both suggests and invites a creative response in the receiver. It is given *gratis,* and human beings are permitted to accept or to refuse it. This is one sense in which divine grace contains the idea of equality:[13] God and the conscious human being are both free. God did not have to create us, and we are free not even to believe he exists. Peggy Lee's song "Is That All There Is?"[14] presents a jaded, disappointed, and "flat" worldview that precludes any perception of grace, turns down the possibility of transcendence—and so forgoes gratitude. And finally, grace is light as opposed to heavy. Simone Weil makes a philosophy of this view of supernatural grace as the opposite of the Necessity that governs the physical world, in her book entitled *La pesanteur et la grâce,* translated into English as *Gravity and Grace.*[15]

Gratitude, from a Christian point of view, is most importantly a freely rendered and loving response to grace. Those who have received much or who are by nature "gifted" should give most.[16] Cooperation with grace—recognizing the gift and putting it to use—is what enables people to abandon dead structures (to "give them up") and do something new. Pardon is a gift from the person wronged who can find it in himself to forgive; Christians see grace as the mysterious strength that enables someone to perform this difficult letting-go, an act that nobody can demand and only the giver can give, the absolute opposite of vengeance. Grace is essential to conversion, the soul's turning away from pride, envy, anger, and the rest, and replacing them with gratitude—in the first instance, gratitude to God for the grace received.

Grace is generosity that goes beyond "just deserts." In the Gospel story of the labourers hired by the hour to work in the vineyard, each man is engaged as he arrives on the scene.[17] Finally some are hired at the last possible moment—at the "eleventh hour"—so that by nightfall they have worked far less than anybody else has. But they are paid the same amount as those who have worked all day. A listener to this story is called upon to recognize the great generosity of the master of the fields, to realize that it is never too late for grace, and to see in himself the "worker of the eleventh hour," the one who receives a reward that he could not have foreseen and does not deserve. The other labourers are furious that the latecomer got as much as all of them had contracted to be paid, while they themselves had not received more. Envy of this kind is, in the Gospels, one of the least attractive of human traits. It is a sin of self-righteousness, a fixation on comparison and measurement, and above all a failure to be grateful for what the enviers themselves have already received. For human beings know that we have always already received. God is invariably the first giver, of our lives, talents, opportunities, and faith, as well as of his grace. This means that every gift we choose to give is already a counter-gift. "How can we ever be the sold short or the cheated," demands Meister Eckhart, "we who for every service have long ago been overpaid?"[18] We ourselves, like everything else in the universe, are givens. We are neither self-sufficient nor our own doing.

Gratitude is important enough in Christianity for people sometimes to say that it is Christianity's chief or central virtue. But love is the central Christian virtue.[19] Love is prior to giving and the reason for giving in the first place. Gratitude is important because it is born of love. The philosopher Jean-Luc Marion points out that a true lover loves without demanding a return.[20] Someone who is truly grateful loves too, with a love that is a gift in its own right, although it is a "return" gift. The gift of gratitude itself does not ask for anything back. And a disposition to gratitude helps and encourages a person to carry out her responsibility in life, which is to grow in love.

We have seen enough of gratitude to realize that it can actually be not only inappropriate but inimical to virtue: only gratitude that is both clear-eyed and informed by love is virtue. The saints go further and express their love of God in gratitude for God's grace, no matter what their circumstances. The Letters of the New Testament tell the early Christians to "thank God at all times"[21]—that is, even when life is painful—because nothing can alter God's love for them. The theme is repeated down the centuries. Julian of Norwich, for instance, received a revelation of God's "blessed power, wisdom, and love. By these he keeps us just as tenderly, gently, and surely when the going is hard, as he does when we are experiencing comfort and consolation."[22] And we recall the modern Mexican woman who had promised a votive offering if her sick husband lived. He died—but she gave it anyway.

"Grace" is a distinctively Christian concept, but other religions have ideas that are similar: Judaism has *hesed,* God's loving kindness, the original of "divine grace," and Islam has *baraka.* Indeed, grace—roughly speaking, the spiritual or non-material aspects of giving and gratitude—is found in abundance in all societies, including modern secular ones. If it were not, these societies, as we saw earlier, would begin to fall apart. It has been pointed out that giving and gratitude as mutual favour are, like friendship, universal; it is the legal contract that is relatively modern, unique, and in need of explaining.[23]

Whatever good-heartedness is offered and returned beyond what is deserved or due is grace. Like divine grace, it is no one's right; it therefore transcends reciprocal exchange, and it can also transcend both partiality and legalism. Grace includes acts of "ordinary" kindness such as forbearance, disinterested encouragement of others, taking someone else's part and not because it is in one's interest to do so, making decisions out of confidence in another's worth, opening oneself to somebody not "one of us." These and thousands like them are daily acts that call forth gratitude, the reflection of grace received. They go to create the "fabric" of decent social relations, helping to "knit" societies together. Grace (like Greek *charis*) is also charm—not beauty but an *addition* to beauty, something undefinable about a face, a pose, or a gesture that makes the person gifted with it irresistible. It gives delight to the onlooker without a thought of "getting back" pleasure in return; graceful people are the more graceful for being uncalculating of their gift.

People who love God do God's will and love to do so, even when it is painful. "All is grace"[24] is the mystical insight achieved in those who reach full realization that, no matter what happens to them, they are creatures—children—of an all-giving, all-loving God. Such people are grateful even in hardship and sorrow—freely and profoundly grateful, incredible as it can seem to ordinary people who have not travelled the distance. "The love of God is pure when joy and suffering inspire an *equal* gratitude," writes Simone

Weil.[25] Etty Hillesum, a young Jewish woman confined to the transit camp of Westerbork in eastern Holland, where she worked tirelessly to comfort her fellow prisoners before being transported to Auschwitz herself and murdered there, wrote to her friend Henny Tideman in August 1943, enclosing a prayer she had just written in her diary: "You have made me so rich, oh God, please let me share out Your beauty with open hands. My life has become an uninterrupted dialogue with You, oh God, one great dialogue. Sometimes when I stand in some corner of the camp, my feet planted on Your earth, my eyes raised toward Your heaven, tears sometimes run down my face, tears of deep emotion and gratitude. At night, too, when I lie in my bed and rest in You, oh God, tears of gratitude run down my face, and that is my prayer . . ."[26]

Etty said she wanted to be "the thinking heart" of the death camp. Gratefulness is perfectly captured in her phrase "the thinking heart."

27

Recognition

The word *give* implies at least a potential response from the receiver. One does not *give* a pot to the kitchen counter; one merely sets it down there. I might, of course, give it, or pass it, to the chef. We give to people—or to animals and plants, should we hope for a response from them: one gives food to a cat, water to "thirsty" herbs. True, we may "give" a wall a coat of paint, perhaps with the thought that it "needs" painting: at the back of our minds there is probably a hint of personalization of the wall. But generally speaking, a giver expects an active response or at least a reaction from the receiver, who similarly presumes that the giver is capable of such an expectation.[1]

Giving becomes meaningful through active receiving; it is the receiver's acceptance—his response—that converts a mere thing, however generously handed over, into a gift. He has, thereby, already "given back" something to his benefactor. Merely saying "yes" to a gift is already to enter into the action, where giver, gift, and receiver are parts of one performance—which could be the first in a series of such events. A small drama is enacted, complete with roles and action, motivations, intentions, and significance. The meaning, the goal, the reasoning, and the emotion of first the giver and then the receiver all attach themselves to and in that sense "ride" the favour done; where the favour is embodied in an actual present, the object in question symbolizes the rest.

What is symbolized is, of course, what is most important. Each person taking part in gifting receives more than he or she gives: this is an aspect of the "overflow" that is part of the meaning of *grace*. Recognition occurs for the receiver and the giver, a recognition that can widen into gratitude simply for the being of the other.[2] Mutuality—a concurrence of wills—is another level of recognition, which may be expressed in the return of the gift. If a receiver, having given back if he can, goes further and gives to someone outside the "see-saw" that is reciprocity, then the gifting process begins to spiral not only upwards but outwards, avoiding many—ideally all—of partiality's limitations.

It is unkind—though it might be generous—to give to someone while making it plain that this person cannot give anything back, that she has nothing to offer that the giver wants. Such a bestowal is largesse, not a gift: it slights the possibilities of mutuality in recognition. *Largesse* means most literally "largeness"—that is, the magnificent "size" of the giver. It has little to do with the receiver. It is not as bad as obliging the other to make a return whether he wants to or not, but still it declares inequality and refusal of relationship, and therefore deserves no gratitude. Yet the receiver might be grateful all the same: gratitude is the receiver's to give, if she chooses.

Gratitude is a reflection of gift-giving—it is in itself a kind of gift. Feeling often issues in action: further gift-giving often arises from gratitude felt. But gratitude comes second; it is a response to what is accepted as a gift, and to the giver's goodness. "*Jeder Dank ist Antwort*," the Germans say: "Gratitude is always a reply." The most admirable gift, indeed, is given in such a way that the other can (if she wants) give too. The receiver is invited to "join in." Gratitude makes her want to imitate, in her own way, the giver's action. Should she wish to, she "agrees to play" and, herself, gives.

The first giver may feel, and make it clear that he feels, that the receiver's acceptance means a lot to him: just taking his gift then becomes a gift in itself. He may give simply out of love for the receiver, "because it's her";[3] she need make no return (but she may nevertheless in gratitude give back). Giving, like gratitude, is primarily *because* and not *in order that*—out of what is already the case, and not out of a desire to control or steer the receiver, or to demand consequences—even non-specific ones. Some givers feel grateful themselves for a chance to help. They might want, for instance, to reduce situations of injustice. They might feel grateful for having already received so much in life that they want to share their good fortune. People to whom the spiritual is important often feel that anything they give is actually "giving back," a counter-gift in gratitude, for everything they have received. Saint Paul reminds his readers of the giftedness of human existence: "What do you possess that was not given to you?"[4]

The receiver should treat any gift with respect, not because the gift remains in some way part of the giver, but simply out of consideration for her and for her motives, should they be believed to be benevolent. He also recognizes that life has somehow changed for the better *thanks to* the giver and her benevolence. "Thanks to" (Latin *gratia* "by grace of") here means simply "because of." But it is the recognition of that "because of" that gives rise to the actions of gratitude: appreciating the giver's kindness, saying "thanks," using the gift well out of respect for its meaning, and, if possible, giving something in return.

But "thanks to" gifts received, people often give to others who have not given to them. Having accepted a gift, they then (after having "given back" if they can) "turn around" and give to someone else. By becoming themselves first givers they are more exactly imitating the person to whom they are grateful for a gift. "Freely give what you have freely received":[5] where freedom is an essential part of the gift, an imitation of it must itself include freedom. People who feel gifted by God, as we saw and as this saying means, always think of themselves as making gifts out of already being receivers; they often feel no need to get anything back. They may be hurt if their gift is not accepted because refusal implies the rejection of the giver. And they will be delighted to receive any response that demonstrates the other's pleasure. (Respect in a giver first requires him to find out what the other *wants,* what will please her; giving is for the receiver's sake, to enrich the receiver, not the giver. It would be patronizing in him to give entirely because he feels she should have his gift, whether she wants it or not.)

Giving to someone else (not to the first giver) may occur out of an impossibility of return. Someone drops all her papers and parcels in the street. An unknown passerby helps her pick them up, and leaves. The receiver of this favour can do nothing but quickly thank him before he goes on his way. (Giving him money would be entirely wrong, because it would "pay for" and so nullify his gift; he acted freely and did not do what he did for money.) Her response now should be to do the equivalent, when she has the opportunity, for somebody else. Imitating his gift will have the effect of an increase and continuance of goodwill and consideration, that "cementing" of society that characterizes gifts and gratitude.

Transcendence occurs when people seek for ways to spread around the benefits they themselves have received. The last of the Twelve Steps of Alcoholics Anonymous—reached when the alcoholic has stopped drinking and found his serenity—is this: "Having had a spiritual awakening as the result of these Steps, we tried to carry this message to others, and to practise these principles in all our affairs." Bringing the benefits received to others is regarded not only as a pleasurable thing to do, but as essential for further personal growth. No gratitude is expected, no "returns" demanded: the giver gives because he himself has received. Where he sees there is a need, he helps because he can. And he is now, because of what he has learned, uniquely qualified to do so. Partiality shuts nobody out from his concern. If he failed to share his gift, he would be demonstrating that he had not understood his good fortune and his own continuing need.

Delight (Greek *charis*) is one of the component meanings of "gratitude." It is specifically a pleasure shared between giver and receiver; mutuality is essential to it. And *charis* (which is also the Greek word for theological grace) overflows; it is abundant, eschews measure, and wants others to experience its own happiness. Giving, receiving, and giving back are consequently festive in nature; that is why they so often accompany holidays and celebrations. They are not about justice, or arguments, or sternness generally. Instead, they constitute together a performance that loves excess and the refusal of calculation, a ritual affirmation of mutual acceptance. For abstract arguments the giving-and-receiving process substitutes action—a demonstration of trust, despite the risks of error and the possibility of refusal, hypocrisy, or abuse. A sense of expansion and enrichment is the result when things go well, although what will flow from the expansion can be neither calculated nor foreseen. Gratitude does involve an admission of dependence on the goodwill of others and a temporary acceptance, as receiver, of the lower place, including as it does a free concession of "first place" to the giver. But the humility required by gratitude is itself joyful. If no joy is experienced, then the gift is a poisoned one and—or—the gift's reception has nothing to do with gratitude.

Deeply felt gratefulness is a species of awe, and as such requires humility. It implies a sense of one's littleness before the wonder of the universe, of the earth and all of nature, of one's own life—and before the goodness of others. Awe, like gratitude, is the opposite of what we call "taking things for granted," which is receiving and not seeing why one should be grateful; it pays intense attention to something beyond oneself and one's immediate self-interest. It is the proud and the self-centred, after all, who are anxious to be unimpressed, and it is the voracious who have no use for beholding without snatching up and consuming or exploiting. Gratitude, like awe, is a matter of looking, and ultimately of insight.

G.K. Chesterton was convinced that gratitude, springing from an entirely natural pleasure in nature, is a kind of irreducible mystical propensity in human beings. He writes that in his nihilistic days he was saved by the results of wonder. "I invented a rudimentary and makeshift mystical theory of my own," he explains. "It was substantially this: that even mere existence, reduced to its most primary limits, was extraordinary enough to be exciting. . . . I hung on to the remains of religion by one thin thread of thanks. I thanked whatever gods might be, not like Swinburne, because no life lived for ever, but because any life lived at all."[6] Profound thankfulness makes people happy.

And the reverse is also true: gratitude arises so immediately and naturally from happiness that it becomes joy's seal and proof: "The test of all happiness is gratitude."[7] In an early notebook Chesterton expresses the kind of joyful amazement that is a catalyst to gratitude:

Evening
Here dies another day,
During which I have had eyes, ears, hands
And the great world round me;
And tomorrow begins another.
Why am I allowed two?[8]

The cosmic awe that prompts Chesterton's question is a long way from worrying at Mauss's chestnut, the inscrutable because isolated "Why give back?" Lévi-Strauss[9] feels uncomfortable about Mauss's taking seriously the Maori explanation that a *hau* in the gift demanded reciprocity from the receiver; he substitutes for it, as a third force, an abstract relationship between the givers that includes the requirement of a return gift. The idea in essence is that above givers and receivers stands a law, as merciless as it is abstract, which participants in gift exchanges unquestioningly obey, even though they are nearly always unconscious of its social mechanisms or the reasons for them: If you receive a gift, you must later on reciprocate with another one, different but roughly equivalent in value, whether you want to or not. This chastely structuralist picture of autonomous circularity has had many followers among searchers for the answer to the Maussian enigma.

A law of reciprocity undoubtedly exists, where people give and return out of obligation, when a society sets up for itself, for various reasons, areas in which a reciprocal exchange of goods and favours is systemic: exchange is so good for society's coherence that people should be obliged to perpetuate it. Here duty rather than sentiment is the point—something done rather than something felt. (Not giving and not thanking are "simply not done.") And the more obligatory, formal, and mannerly the offering and the return, the less the sentiment of gratitude is felt. People start to speak of the duty, the action of "giving back," as what is meant by "gratitude." But true gratitude is both feeling and action. It does not sit enthroned "over" people, as a law requiring them to give to one another. It takes place *between* them. There is mutual recognition between or among *persons,* who are unique and irreplaceable. The gift is both itself—the present, the hospitality, the favour—and also symbolic, a vehicle of meanings and feelings between the acting partners.

A gift may be given to someone who is called in the Gospels one's "neighbour." This person need not be one of those defined as the giver's "own"; she might not even be someone with whom he was previously acquainted, although this unknown person is *recognized* by the very fact of the favour given or done. Where there is no recognition, there can be no love and no gift. There is, invariably, at least an element of *agape*—of a love indifferent to "getting something back"—in any true gift. (Pure *agape* is rare; normally givers, like receivers, have mixed feelings, mixed motivations. This does not mean that anything less than pure *agape* disqualifies a gift from having been given.) *Agape* is without comparison and without calculation; it is personal recognition without extra ends in view. *Agape* is a love that declares itself rather than explains itself; it is expressed in deeds more than in words. Therefore free giving is a natural expression of it. As far as the giver in *agape* is concerned, there need be no return.

The anthropologist Raymond Firth, investigator of the New Zealand Maori and the Melanesian people of Tikopia, once described his journey to Tikopia as a young scientist in the early 1930s.[10] He depended, as so many anthropologists do, upon the missionaries already present in the area for practical help: "On my way through the Solomon islands to Tikopia I had to rely for transport and hospitality on the Melanesian Mission, and for some weeks was the guest of the head of the Mission, Bishop Steward, on the Mission yacht *Southern Cross*. As we travelled together among the islands we discussed many problems of human relationship in the island communities.

Malinowski had only recently published his book *Crime and Custom in Savage Society* in which he stressed the importance of reciprocity as a force of binding obligation in Melanesian social organization. . . . The Bishop borrowed the book from me, read it, and strongly disagreed. He argued vehemently that Melanesians, like other people he said, performed many acts for others freely and without thought for return. Giving, not reciprocity, was the prime motive of service, he held. . . . We argued amicably about this and other themes, and I think came to respect each other—partly perhaps because being more detached I could question his views more stoutly than could his clergy." Firth was convinced that he had much to teach this man who had lived among the Melanesians for many years.

"At last the time came," Firth continued, "for him to land me on the beach of Tikopia and leave me to my fate. He had shown me many kindnesses, which I could not repay. This was his last trip on the *Southern Cross;* he was retiring from the Mission after many years and we both knew it was unlikely we should ever meet again—and we never did. As he said goodbye, leaving me alone in this remote community he shook me firmly by the hand, said gruffly 'No reciprocity!,' turned his back and walked off down the beach to the boat. This was his way of hiding his emotions with a joke—but his words were also a reaffirmation of a moral viewpoint." At least Firth was generous enough to recount this story. In doing so, he might even have been making the bishop some return for his kindness. But the bishop clearly thought—and we might reflect upon his opinion—that the Melanesians would probably have done as much for Firth, even though there might be no return, and even should they realize that Firth, as an enlightened Westerner, was committed to "seeing through" their motives, and prone inevitably to the suspicion that they must be calculating their own advantage.

In French, gratitude is *reconnaissance,* which also means "recognition": French is one of the rare languages that honour in the very etymology of their word for "gratitude" the deep relationship between the two.[11] Knowledge (*con-*

naissance in French), and not only feeling, is part of being grateful. Germans speak of *Dank* (which became English *thank*), derived as it is from *denken,* "to think." At a transcendental level, gratitude and insight were linked in the experience of the English mystic Julian of Norwich: "Thankyng is a new, inward knowing," she writes.[12] "New" here is close in sense to "lively" and "vivid,"[13] and hence has a feeling component, which at once turns to "gret reverens and lovely drede" ("great reverence and loving fear"): gratitude is a species of awakening in the self.[14]

"Thankyng," Julian goes on, "turns us with all our powers to do whatever our good Lord indicates." She here explains why, in a context of religious faith, a feeling of gratitude rouses people to respond in kind: being aware of goodness received makes the "knowing" mind want to find out where more good is needed and to do it, in response. Love's insight turns, through the pivotal feeling of gratitude, into love's action. Later, Julian will tell us something else she knows: that God himself "takes as great pleasure and delight as if he were indebted to us for all the good we do. And yet it is he who actually does it!"[15] And God's pleasure in our response will be part of his own "everlasting gratitude."[16] This is the language of gratitude as grace: *acceptance* of the gift of grace is what a human being has in her gift; God himself cannot force her to receive grace or to respond by giving to others. Both gratitude and grace are freely given, and a joy that is shared. God being eternal, this joy is shared forever.

This "new, inward knowing" is a profound and intense version of *reconnaissance,* the knowing being recognition of the goodness of the other, who was the first to recognize: giving is itself a voluntary sign of recognition. And returning out of gratitude (*reconnaissance*) is a gift that echoes the first giver's recognition (*reconnaissance*). Paul Ricoeur[17] speaks of recognition as having evolved in the human psyche, from the basic identification of objects—knowing what they are and are not—to a reflexive consciousness, a recognition of the self by the self. The third stage is mutuality: the recognition, in intimacy, of one person by another, and recognition in return. For there is in human beings a powerful longing to *be recognized*—an important move from the active to the passive voice. Recognition is not something one inherently has; it must *be given*.

Self-recognition involves memory of the past and, as Ricoeur points out, the capacity to make promises: it implies consistency in the future. We have noted the essential role that memory plays in gratitude. Readiness to achieve completion through returning a favour later on corresponds to Ricoeur's "promises." Whereas memory in the individual is self-bound, promises are made *to others*. As with promises made, where gifts and favours are concerned social pressure may be exerted too. Influence can be brought to bear, via their approval or disapproval, by others outside the performing partnership, who feel it is "only fair" for the receiver of a favour to do something for the giver, and at the very least to thank him, just as it is "only right" that promises should be kept. The health of society depends on the continuance of reliability and voluntary gratitude for favours. The keeping of ordinary promises, like gifting, cannot be controlled by law; social pressure takes up some of the slack. But mostly, decisions to "follow through" are taken in freedom by the givers of return gifts, or the makers of promises. With promising, the first, antecedent promise has already been made: always to keep one's word. Gratitude, similarly, springs from a cultivated disposition to be grateful; one is in some sense grateful *in advance* of any gift or favour, because one is prepared to recognize goodness and be grateful for it.

The fundamental human struggle for identity, relationship, and belonging is practised and expressed in the reiterated drama of giving, receiving, gratitude, and returning the favour, where one recognizes and is recognized at each stage of the action.[18] We all learn that another person is from many points of view essentially unknowable. Yet we also realize that she is a person, a subject like myself, a centre of her own world, a being that calls forth my own recognition of her, in fraternity with her, and in love. We are given to perceive that she is like me, through her expressive looks, postures, gestures, and what she says. But the process of linking through giving, receiving, being grateful, and giving back preserves the fact that she is Another—one who also deserves the distancing effect of respect for her difference. Recognition is a positive act, not merely a negative one like tolerance. There is infinitely more respect in recognition than in tolerance.

Mutual, impartial recognition is the real root of human rights, such as those to life, liberty, and property, *for all*. It might one day bring us to the point where we begin to combine political rights and freedoms with a fair distribution of basic goods, for all. Recognition in our day already requires of us respect for and an attempt to understand cultures different from our own, and the humility and patience to ask other peoples to take our cultural norms into account as well: dependence on the goodwill of the other is the ancient risk inherent in both giving and receiving. It is above all the non-material favours that are commonly asked for: we ask another person to be good enough to listen to us, to help us, to forgive us; it is permissible to ask to be given consideration or another's patience. That is because such asking acknowledges need and (inter)dependence. It is important to realize that weakness and dependence are not the same as unworthiness, whether in ourselves or in anybody else; that the type of pride that is "vainglorious" is not only a source of pain, but an enemy to truthfulness. Gratitude's humility and acknowledgement of dependence are part of its strength, its "thinking heart" the secret of its ability to replace many of the causes of misery so readily grouped at the time of Shakespeare under the heading "Ingratitude." Disrespect and violence can and must yield to giving and gratitude. We have to learn to give and let give.

Gift-giving is the opposite of commodification. It has what we might call an "anti-economy," because its condition is one of surplus, not scarcity.[19] But even commerce needs goodwill, and sellers often want their customers to maintain human as well as monetary relations with them. In the food markets of Barcelona, for example, parsley is never sold. It is set aside from the other produce and designated as a gift—to symbolize, when given and received, the contentment and fidelity of the customer, and everything that is not venal in the seller. After the customer's purchases of meat, fish, or vegetables have been asked for, priced, and collected in a pile, comes the question: "Parsley?" The buyer nods, and a bunch of parsley lands on top of the heap, gratis. The adding *on top* of everything else is characteristic of *charis* and of the gift; non-payment for it is the medium of attachment and recognition between partners in the sale, and of hope that the relationship will continue.

In the "anti-economy" that is the realm of the gift, people do not hang on to what they have, nor do they seek profit above all else. Instead, having recognized the extent to which they have been gifted themselves, they pay attention to the needs of others and recognize—look squarely—not only at the problems, but at those who are suffering injustice or are just plain suffering. Because there is a need, and because they have, they give. They gain thereby, although profit for themselves is not what they sought. They do not feel that what they have given away is something they have lost. Life is not for them only unrelenting physical Necessity in the form of economic scarcity, like a pizza with an unforgiving circumference, portions cut out of it and gaps left on the plate for every slice. Instead, in the gifting scenario the whole is greater than the parts.

This is, for example, the original meaning of giving presents at Christmas. The significance of the festival is that the baby Jesus is the first Christmas gift, inspiring everybody else to give to one other out of joyful gratitude. The Christmas story and its celebration demonstrate God's love and express his desire that we should now "turn around" and give to others, wherever an opportunity for giving arises, and especially where people are most in need. If we all do this, there will be enough to go round. We ourselves shall satisfy our need to give, the source of which is not merely the result of social pressure, but arises out of recognition and the desire to be recognized, out of the gratitude that unites these two, and the wish to imitate goodness we have known. We shall also be rewarded, in ways we cannot foresee. "At the end of the day," writes Saint John of the Cross, "you will be examined in love."[20] And the fruits of our loving, our giving, and our gratitude will provide the evidence: "Only what you have given, be it only in the gratitude of acceptance, is salvaged from the nothing which some day will have been your life."[21]

Notes

1: "What Do You Say?"

1. Mrs. Humphry, *Manners for Men*. Exeter: Webb and Bower, 1897, p. 136.
2. Esther Blank Greif and Jean Berko Gleason, 1980, p. 162.
3. A great deal depends, of course, on the amount of effort previously put in by the parents. In the experiment performed by J.A. Becker and R.C. Smenner in 1986, 37 percent of the children studied gave spontaneous thanks at the age of four.
4. Esther Blank Greif and Jean Berko Gleason, 1980, p. 163.
5. See Margaret Visser, 1991.
6. One study of preschool middle-class American families found that during a meal children said "thank you" on average once every 3.75 minutes. They said it more often than did the parents, who prompted them relentlessly to produce the expression. Gleason, Perlmann, and Greif, 1984, pp. 495–96.
7. Emile Benveniste (1973, Chapter 6) argues that the root *do-* in Indo-European could mean "give" or "take" depending on the grammatical construction.
8. Nickie Charles and Marion Kerr, 1988, p. 189.
9. Esther Blank Greif and Jean Berko Gleason, 1980, p. 166.

2: No Thanks

1. See, for example, David Crantz, *The History of Greenland*. Vol. I, London 1820, p. 175; H. Ling Roth, *The Aborigines of Tasmania*. Halifax, England: F. King, 1899, p. 49; William Edward Parry, *Journal of a Second Voyage for the Discovery of a North-West Passage from the Atlantic to the Pacific*. New York: Greenwood, 1824, pp. 521–26.

2. Samuel Hearne, *A Journey from Prince of Wales's Fort in Hudson's Bay to the Northern Ocean in the Years 1770, 1771, and 1772*. New York: Da Capo Press, 1968, p. 306.

3. Richard F. Burton, *Personal Narrative of a Pilgrimage to Al-Madinah and Meccah*. 2 vols. New York: Dover Publications, 1964. First published 1893. Vol. 1, p. 51.

4. H. Ling Roth, note 1 (p. 394), pp. 47–48.

5. Ibid., p. 51.

6. Washington Matthews, "The Study of Ethics among the Lower Races," *The Journal of American Folk-Lore* 12(1899) 1–9. See also E. Casalis, *The Basutos, or twenty-three years in South Africa*. Facsimile reprint. Capetown: C. Struik, 1965, p. 307.

7. Alexander Mackenzie, *Voyages from Montreal on the River St. Lawrence through the Continent of North America . . . in 1789 and 1793*. Vol. 3. Edmonton: M.G. Hurtig, 1971, pp. 137–8. See also Walter Burchell, *Travels in the Interior of Southern Africa*. London: The Batchworth Press, 1953. First published 1822–24. Vol. 2, p. 29: "I saw a tear of joy and thankfulness moistening her anxious eye," he said of a mother whose child he had attended.

8. Walter Burchell, note 7 (p. 394), p. 28.

9. Audrey I. Richards, *Land, Labour and Diet in Northern Rhodesia*. Oxford University Press: International African Institute, 1969. First published 1939. pp. 196–97.

10. For various examples, see Margaret Visser, 1991, pp. 228–32.

11. William Edward Parry, note 1 (above), p. 525.

12. See for example, D. Damas, "Central Eskimo Systems of Food Sharing," *Ethnology* 11(1972) 220–40.

13. Audrey I. Richards, note 9 (above), p. 197.

14. H.B. Guppy, *The Solomon Islands and Their Natives*. London: Swan Sonnenschein, Lowrey, 1887, pp. 127–28.

15. Jean-François de Galaup, Comte de La Pérouse, *Voyage autour du monde, pendant les années 1785, 1786, 1787, et 1788*. Paris: Cercle du Bibliophile, 1970, p. 129.

16. William Edward Parry, note 1 (p. 394), p. 521.

17. H.B. Guppy, note 14 (above), p. 127.

18. Ibid.

19. For more on the complex laws of hospitality, see Margaret Visser, 1991, p. 91, chapter 3 and passim.

20. William Edward Parry, note 1 (p. 394), p. 526.

21. Edwin W. Smith and Andrew Murray Dale, *The Ila-Speaking Peoples of Northern Rhodesia*. London: Macmillan, 2 vols., 1920. Vol. 1, pp. 364–65, vol. 2, pp. 315–16.

22. Peter Freuchen, *Peter Freuchen's Book of the Eskimos*. Cleveland: World Publishing, 1961, p. 154.

3: IT'S ONLY NATURAL

1. Robert L. Trivers, 1971, pp. 35–57.

2. Lexa Grutter, interviewed on ABC TV *Science* in May 2002. ABC's homepage, s.v. "cleaner wrasse." www.abc.net.au.

3. Lexa Grutter, ibid., p. 2.

4. J.E. Randall, "Fish Service Stations," *Sea Frontiers* 8(1962) 44.

5. Irenäus Eibl-Eibesfeldt, "Über Symbiosen, Parasitismus und andere besondere zwischen-artliche Beziehungen tropischer Meeresfische," *Zeitschrift für Tierpsychologie* 12(1955) 208.

6. Robert L. Trivers, note 1 (above), p. 45.

7. Ibid., p. 38.

8. Ibid., p. 50.

9. J. Wallace and E. Sadalla, "Behavioral Consequences of Transgression: The Effects of Social Recognition," *Journal of Experimental Research in Personality* 1(1966) 187–94.

10. J.L. Freedman, S.A. Wallington, and E. Bless, "Compliance without Pressure: The Effect of Guilt," *Journal of Personality and Social Psychology* 7(1967) 117–24.

11. For example, A. Tesser, R. Gatewood, and M. Driver, "Some Determinants of Gratitude," *Journal of Personality and Social Psychology* 9(1968) 232–36.

12. D.G. Pruitt, "Reciprocity and Credit Building in a Laboratory Dyad," *Journal of Personality and Social Psychology* 8(1968) 143–47.

13. Robert L. Trivers, note 1 (above), p. 50.

14. Ibid., p. 49. Glenn E. Weisfeld, a modern ethologist, writes that gratitude "seems to be a recent innovation in vertebrates." It was "perhaps the main transitional event" in the evolution of human social systems from animal dominance hierarchies. He means by "gratitude" a reciprocating action. He also finds a place for gratitude as an emotion, but when he does, he calls it "an unpleasant feeling that is expiated only by fulfilling one's obligations." This discomfort had been created in us by our genes in order to pressure us into relieving it through gratitude defined as returning gifts. This aspect of gratitude in turn existed to ensure a future "payoff" for so-called altruists, so that they would keep giving and reciprocating. The reward was either material goods, or "an insurance policy" of goodwill and prestige, expressed as praise and thanks and promises. (1980, pp. 280–86)

15. Robert L. Trivers, note 1 (above), p. 54.

16. Merlin Donald, *Origins of the Modern Mind: Three Stages in the Evolution of Culture and Cognition.* Cambridge, MA: Harvard University Press, 1991. Précis of the book, with Open Peer Commentary, *Behavioral and Brain Sciences* 16(1993) 737–91. See also *A Mind So Rare: The Evolution of Human Consciousness,* 2001.

17. H. Hediger, "Putzerfische im Aquarium," *Natur und Museum* 98(1968) 89–96.

18. Merlin Donald, 1993, p. 776: " . . . heaven forfend that I should imply that humans are even slightly superior to beavers, budgie birds, or tree frogs; we are just, well, different. There is no need for value judgments here; but I insist that ethologists and comparative psychologists must realistically confront the richness of human cultures, and not underestimate the gulf between human cultures and those of other species. Teleology does not come into it, however."

19. See the Open Peer Commentary, 1993, note 16 (p. 396), p. 764.

4: "I'm So Sorry"

1. See, for example, Claude Hagège, *Halte à la mort des langues.* Paris: Odile Jacob, 2000.

2. The example is from Tetsuo Kumatoridani, 1999, p. 625.

3. Florian Coulmas, 1981, pp. 69–91. His article is called "Poison to Your Soul: Thanks and Apologies Contrastively Viewed." An important earlier discussion was Takie Sugiyama Lebra, 1976, chapter 6.

4. Three outstanding examples in English are Atsushi Takagi, 1995, Risako Ide, 1998, and Tetsuo Kumatoridani, 1999. Naomi Sugimoto, ed., *Japanese Apology Across Disciplines.* Commack, NY: Nova Science Publishers, 1999, is a book-length index, with commentary, of books and articles up to that date, including many on apologies-as-thanks in Japan.

5. Takeo Doi, 1973, pp. 11–12.

6. Atsushi Takagi, 1995, pp. 29, 165–66.

7. Ruth Benedict, 1946. My remarks relate mostly to chapters 5, 6, and 7.

8. This is one of the keys to Amélie Nothomb's novel, *Stupeur et tremblements.* Paris: Albin Michel, 1999.

9. One is reminded of Socrates' attitude towards Athens and its laws in Plato's *Crito.*

10. For more on this subject, see Jane Bachnik, "The Two 'Faces' of Self and Society in Japan," *Ethos* 20(1992) 3–23.

11. Risako Ide, 1998, p. 512, and p. 524, note 15. This is a rule in transition: see Risako Ide, p. 511, note 2.

12. Erving Goffman, 1971, chapters 3 and 4.

13. I have taken examples, adapted for brevity, from Risako Ide's article (1998), which is an analysis of conversational exchanges recorded at the counter of an ophthalmological clinic in downtown Tokyo.

14. Risako Ide, 1998. The professor, incidentally, denies that the Japanese psyche is rooted in the obligations called *giri* and *on,* as Benedict said it was fifty-two years earlier; he

believes that she and people who agree with her are "rather biased." Risako Ide, 1998, p. 525, note 15.

15. Florian Coulmas, 1981, p. 83.

16. This and the following examples are from Tetsuo Kumatoridani's article (1999), which is a study of how, why, and where *sumimasen* is placed in conversational exchanges.

17. Tetsuo Kumatoridani, 1999, p. 637.

18. Atsushi Takagi, 1995, pp. 34, 38.

5: "Thank You Very Much Indeed"

1. Eirlys E. Davies, 1987, p. 87.

2. Ibid., p. 83.

3. Ibid., pp. 74–88.

4. Florian Coulmas, 1979, p. 253.

5. J.L. Austin, 1962, pp. 159–60. These William James Lectures, delivered at Harvard University in 1955, were seminal for the elaboration of the discipline of pragmatics.

6. Karin Aijmer, 1996, pp. 34–35; John Searle, 1969, p. 63.

7. Karin Aijmer, 1996, p. 75.

8. Charles A. Ferguson, "The Structure and Use of Politeness Formulas," in Florian Coulmas, 1981, p. 24.

9. E.B. Hale and M.W. Schein, "The Behaviour of Turkeys," in E.S.E. Hafez, ed., *The Behaviour of Domestic Animals.* London: Baillière, Tindall and Cox, 1962.

10. Erving Goffman 1976, p. 69.

11. Miriam Eisenstein and Jean Bodman, 1993, pp. 71–72.

12. Raja Ram Mehrotra, "How to Be Polite in Indian English," *International Journal of the Sociology of Language*, 116 (1995), esp. pp. 105–06. He points out that "the practice of saying a phrase equivalent to 'thank you' was almost nonexistent in ancient India."

13. See Joan Manes and Nessa Wolfson, in Florian Coulmas, 1981, pp. 115–32.

14. Catherine Kerbrat-Orecchioni, 1994, p. 243.

15. Ibid., p. 241.

16. John Gumperz, 1974, p. 19.

17. Karin Aijmer, 1996, p. 40.

18. Sarah Buss, "Appearing Respectful: The Moral Significance of Manners," *Ethics* 109 (1999) 795–82, esp. p. 802.

19. Karin Aijmer, 1996, pp. 61–62. This is a recording of a real conversation. The notes are my own.

20. Ibid., p. 64.

21. Florian Coulmas, 1981, p. 91.

6: WHY GIVE BACK?

1. Friedrich Nietzsche, 1883–1892 (1961 edition in English), p. 208.

2. See, for example, Bartolomé Clavero, 1990, trans. into English, 1996, and Alain Caillé, 2000.

3. A newspaper report in the *New York Times* was entitled, "Why We're So Nice: We're Wired to Cooperate." 23 July 2002.

4. Marcel Mauss, *The Gift. The Form and Reason for Exchange in Archaic Societies.* Trans. W.D. Hall, with a foreword by Mary Douglas. London and New York: Routledge 1990, republished Routledge Classics, 2002.

5. See Mary Douglas, foreword to the above edition, p. xxi.

6. See C.A. Gregory, 1982, p. 180.

7. "What motivates reciprocity," writes Annette B. Weiner, 1992, "is its reverse—the desire to keep something back from the pressures of give and take," (p. 43). See further pp. 64–65.

8. See chapter 2, "No Thanks," citing H. Ling Roth, *The Aborigines of Tasmania,* 1899, pp. 47–48.

9. Julian Pitt-Rivers has suggested that in a similar fashion the Stone of Scone for a long time made felt its imperious desire to be returned to Scotland. 1992, p. 237.

10. Marshall Sahlins (1972), pp. 79–83, points out that the context of Ranapiri's words was the *hau* of the forests and the birds in it, and so concluded that the *hau* must have had to be returned so that the fowl could replenish themselves in the forest. Indeed, Mauss seems to have thought of this himself. He speaks of the Chukchee after their thanksgiving ceremonies casting into the sea or scattering to the winds the remains of the banqueting sacrifice; these "return to their land of origin, taking with them the wild animals killed during the year, who will return the next year."

11. Lewis Hyde, 1979, pp. 26–27.

12. The best known early account is that of Bronislaw Malinowski, 1922, pp. 81–104.

13. Shirley F. Campbell, 2002, plate 17.

14. "The mass re-production of capitalism, with its need to generate obsolescence, continually challenges the privileged position of inalienable possessions, but the intense longing for possessions to mark who we are has not abated." Annette Weiner, note 7 (above), p. 154.

15. Karl Marx, *Capital,* chapter 1 (1867). See Marshall Sahlins, 1972, pp. 93–95.

16. By Raymond Firth, 1972, and Marshall Sahlins, 1972, pp. 70–83.

17. The Roman philosopher Seneca, as early as AD 64, produced a detailed account of giving, receiving, and returning in seven books, called *De Beneficiis*. It is astonishing how little this work is used by modern social scientists. Mauss himself never mentions it, despite his evincing an interest in the ancient Romans.

7: ALL WRAPPED UP

1. Raymond Firth, 1972, pp. 410–11.

2. The *w* replaces the Greek sound called a rough breathing, which is expressed as an *h* in a word like *rhapsode*, "a sewer of odes" (meaning a creator and singer of songs), and its derivative, *rhapsody*, a stringing-together of poems or tunes.

3. Millie Creighton, 1991, pp. 679–80.

4. Joy Hendry, 1993, pp. 58–59.

5. This is the subject of Joy Hendry's book, *Wrapping Culture*, 1993.

6. Harumi Befu, 1974, p. 216.

7. Aafke Komter, in Robert A. Emmons and Michael McCullough (2004), speculates that this rule is really designed to keep the recipient's possible disappointment hidden from the giver. p. 195.

8. For more on the gift-bearing tree and the present-bestowing Santa Claus, see Margaret Visser, 1994, pp. 32–36, 202–206.

9. Theodore Caplow, 1984, p. 1311.

10. Ibid.

11. Arlie Russell Hochschild, 1983, pp. 76–86, calls polite dissimulation "psychological bowing," and an "offering" or return gift to people who expect "sincere display" from us. She believes that "we keep a mental ledger with 'owed' and 'received' columns for gratitude, love, anger, guilt, and other feelings." p. 79.

12. Sometimes people carefully fold up and keep wrappings thought to be especially pretty—and even use them again for their own gift-giving. They are showing thereby their appreciation of the beauty of the packaging (they set aside the wrapping often in the presence of the giver) and their determination not to waste it—even to hand it on.

8: THE THREE GRACES

1. *De Beneficiis*, ca. AD 64, 1.3.2–1.4.2.

2. Seneca is here describing a second scheme, where the Graces represent persons rather than obligations or actions. *De Beneficiis* 1.3.3.

3. *Incorrupta sunt et sincera et omnibus sancta.* Virginity, as the etymology of each of these adjectives intimates, is symbolic of being "unmixed," uninvaded, or single of heart. See further, Margaret Visser, *The Geometry of Love,* 2000, pp. 237–57.

4. "*Hai Charites gymnai,*" Greeks would say.

5. Erasmus, *Adages* 2.7.50.

6. *De Beneficiis* 1.3.5.

7. Georg Simmel (1858–1918), English edition of 1950, p. 392. Simmel undoubtedly knew his Seneca.

8. See chapter 7, "All Wrapped Up," p. 83, and note 6.

9. Joy Hendry, 1993, p. 65.

10. Frédéric De Garis, 1934, p. 43.

11. Mary Douglas, foreword to Marcel Mauss, *The Gift.* 1990, p. ix.

12. Ralph Waldo Emerson, "Gifts," 1844 (1968 edition), p. 359.

13. Aristotle, *Nicomachean Ethics* (fourth century BC) 5.5.7.

14. Plato (fifth–fourth century BC), *Crito.*

15. Strictly speaking, it is misleading to use the English word *gratitude* here, as we shall see later. What Socrates does instead is speak of himself as the child of Athens and its laws: his decision becomes a matter of filial piety, another subject we shall consider later. Plato is much criticized by modern philosophers for seeing an analogy between a correct attitude towards the State and loyalty to one's parents. For further discussion on this, see A.D.M. Walker, 1988 and 1989.

16. Richard Korn and Lloyd W. McCorkle, "Resocialization within Walls," *Annals of the American Academy of Political and Social Science,* 293(1954), p. 90. Quoted by Barry Schwartz, 1967, p. 4.

17. This is another maxim, like *nudae gratiae,* that could mean something very different. The emperors Septimius Severus and Caracalla used the adage to warn the governors of Roman provinces not to overindulge in corruption and so inflame the citizens: not to take everything, always and everywhere, from everyone. *Digesta* 1.16.6.3.

18. Frédéric De Garis, 1934, p. 43.

19. Claude Lévi-Strauss, 1949, chapter 5.

20. Charles Lamb, *Essays of Elia and the Last Essays of Elia.* Popular Fallacies: XI. "That We Must Not Look a Gift-Horse in the Mouth." First published 1820–1833. pp. 376–79.

21. See, for example, Jonathan Parry, 1986, with the references he gives.

22. Charles Lamb's essay (note 21 above) describes his joyful and unashamed enjoyment of victuals given him according to this custom.

23. Edward, Lord Herbert of Cherbury (1583–1648), *Autobiography.* Whitefish, MT: Kessinger Publishing Company, 2007. First published 1764.

24. John Gillis, 1996, p. 185.
25. Lewis Hyde, 1979, p. 16.

9: GIVE IT AWAY

1. See chapter 7.
2. Marcel Mauss, 2002, first published 1925, p. 29.
3. For example, it is a duty in Islam publicly to proclaim benefactions received, as well as publicly to acknowledge the obligations incurred. See A. Kevin Reinhart, "Thanking the Benefactor," in John B. Carman and Frederick J. Streng, 1989, pp. 115–33.
4. Marcel Mauss, 2002, pp. 47–48.
5. In seventeenth-century France, Antoine de Courtin advised that one should not praise something too much or look at certain things too curiously, in case one was thought to be "aiming one's gun at them like a hunter." p. 163.
6. Raymond Firth, 1972, pp. 410, 430, 432.
7. An exception is at special gift-giving events such as Christmas, or schoolchildren's in-class gift-exchanges on Valentine's Day, where the giving is simultaneous.
8. Raymond Firth, 1972, pp. 411–12.
9. Compare Edward Lear's limerick:
   There was an Old Person of Buda
   Whose conduct grew ruder and ruder;
   Till at last, with a hammer,
   They silenced his clamour
   By smashing that Person of Buda.
10. Aristotle, *Nicomachean Ethics* (fourth century BC) 5.5.
11. René Girard, 1999, pp. 23–36.

10: THE GIVE-AND-TAKE OF EVERYDAY LIFE

1. Rena Lederman, 1986, 236–37.
2. Claude Lévi-Strauss, 1969, p. 56.
3. J. Isaacs, *Bush Food: Aboriginal Food and Herbal Medicine.* Sydney: Weldons, 1987. Other examples, apart from the sharing of the seal among the Copper Eskimo described earlier, are in M. Gast, "Partage de la viande à Idélès," *Libyca,* 11(1963), 235–44, and R.L.

Zumwalt, "The Return of the Whale," in A. Falassi, ed., *Time Out of Time: Essays on the Festival*. Albuquerque, NM: University of New Mexico Press, 1987.

4. Seneca, *De Beneficiis* 2.17.3–4. Seneca is speaking here of the skill required in keeping up the game. He is not asking *why* the ball (the gift) is returned; he merely assumes that it is because that is how the game is played.

5. See Jacques Derrida, 1992. Derrida says elsewhere that gift-giving is unjust if it is not irrational: gifts should be "without exchange, without circulation, without recognition or gratitude, without economic circulation, without calculation and without rule, without reason and without rationality." ("Force of Law: The Mystical Foundation of Authority," *Cardozo Law Review* 11:5–6(1990), p. 965.)

6. Katharine Whitehorn, *Whitehorn's Social Survival*. London: Methuen, 1968, p. 16.

7. Shakespeare, *Hamlet*, 1.3.75, 3.4.216.

8. See Antoon Vandevelde, 2000 (a), p. 4.

9. *Hamlet* 1.3.76–77.

10. "To borrow" in Spanish is *tomar prestado,* "to take something loaned." The French have a word, *prestation,* which is closer to "loan" than is the word "gift" in English, or *don* ("gift") in French. *Prestation,* used instead of *don,* helped Mauss to import an idea of stern obligation into our concept of the gift. English-speaking anthropologists used to employ the rare English word *prestations* in translations, in order to accommodate Mauss; it was also used in other descriptions of societies who practise group "giving" of a compulsory nature. This word—which at least served to signal the addition of something foreign to the normal meaning of "gift"—seems now to be less common in anthropological texts. W.D. Halls never uses it in the translation of Mauss's book (Marcel Mauss, 2002).

11. David Cheal, 1987, p. 103.

12. David Cheal, 1988, p. 19. The Winnipeg Cycle produced the following definition of the modern gift economy: it is "a system of redundant transactions within a moral economy, which makes possible the extended reproduction of social relations."

13. David Cheal, 1987, p. 100.

14. Ibid., p. 105.

15. See Barry Schwartz, 1967.

16. For more on dinner gifts, see Margaret Visser, 1991, 111–12.

17. First cited by Margaret Mead, *Sex and Temperament in Three Primitive Societies*. London: Routledge, 1935, p. 83.

18. Claude Lévi-Strauss, 1969, p. 62.

19. For a full discussion of the British Pakistani wedding, see Pnina Werbner, 1990.

20. Luke 6:38. Rewards for giving and for virtue generally are frequently promised in the Gospels. Often the reward will be spiritual, not material: again and again we hear that someone "has his reward already" if it is merely material or a matter of status. See Matthew 5:46; 6:1; 6:2; 6:4; 6:5; 6:16; 6:17–18; 19:29, etc. In Hinduism, Mauss notes (typically speaking of the gift as itself performing an action), "The thing that is given produces its rewards in this life and the next." Marcel Mauss, 2002, p. 72.

21. For tensions between Opposites as constitutive of culture, see Margaret Visser, *Beyond Fate,* 2002, pp. 123–27.

22. James Carrier, 1995, p. 180.

23. Ibid., p. 160.

24. Ibid., p. 158.

25. For an extensive exposition of this theory of the foundations of modernity, see Jacques T. Godbout, 2007, pp. 21–101. The theory tends to leave out Marxist analyses of capitalist power and class struggle, which are based on a vision of humanity's need to correct crying inequalities.

26. Pierre Bourdieu 1977, 1990, 1997.

27. This is not necessarily the case in Japan: see Millie Creighton, 1993, p. 5, where a homemade chocolate heart was offered on Valentine's Day: "He said he didn't want it and gave it back on the spot." It is not clear from the article how far this constitutes an infraction of rules of politeness; it certainly cuts off the possibility of relationship. Similar behaviour, of course, is not unknown in the West.

28. David Cheal, 1987, p. 105.

29. C.J. Healey, 1985, p. 138.

30. R. Dyson-Hudson and R. Van Dusen, 1972.

31. See Marcel Hénaff, 2002, pp. 175–98. The point is also made by Marcel Mauss, p. 17.

32. Alvin Gouldner (1960), p. 175, describing the *vartan bhanji,* a form of reciprocity practised in Pakistan and India. His source is Z.E. Eglar, *Vartan Bhanji: Institutionalized Reciprocity in a Changing Punjab Village.* PhD thesis, Columbia University, 1958.

33. Deuteronomy 19:21.

34. Tobit 4:15.

35. Matthew 7:12, Luke 6.31.

36. Matthew 5:43–48.

37. Luke 6:28. It is notable that the Golden Rule, "Do to others as you would have them do to you," is placed just *after* "Love your enemies" in Luke. Paul Ricoeur sees this as precluding a tit-for-tat reciprocity that some have suggested is latent in the Golden Rule. 1991, pp. 196–97.

38. Jeffrey Fadiman, 1995, pp. 403–4.

39. Rena Lederman, 1986, pp. 82, 95–96.

40. Alvin Gouldner, 1960, p. 174.

41. Aristotle, *Nicomachean Ethics* 4.3.24. Compare the giving of extra sweets in order to obligate the departing wedding guest, p. 134 and note 32 (p. 404).

42. Marcel Mauss, 2002 (1923), pp. 46–47: "Now, the gift necessarily entails the notion of credit."

43. François de La Rochefoucauld, *Maximes,* 1664, no. 226: "*Le trop grand empressement qu'on a de s'acquitter d'une obligation est une espèce d'ingratitude.*"

44. Pierre Bourdieu, 1990, p. 142.

45. Pierre Bourdieu, 1977, p. 176.

46. David Cheal, 1987, p. 103.

11 : Votive Offerings

1. *The Charioteer,* now in the Delphi Museum, once stood in a bronze horse-drawn chariot. The figure, fragments of the rest of the monument, and part of an identifying inscription were unearthed in 1896. Another famous example of a Greek votive offering is the stone Victory of Samothrace in the Louvre. Visigothic votive crowns can be seen in the Archaeological Museum in Madrid.

2. Johannes Maringer. *The Gods of Prehistoric Man.* New York: Alfred A. Knopf, 1960, pp. 38–49.

3. Where people lived on root crops (such as potatoes) that were left underground and collected as needed, in South America for example, there were no traditions of harvest festivals and first-fruits. Thanksgiving festivals celebrate a particular, and climactic, moment of the year, in cultures where food is harvested all at once and stored for the winter months.

4. Latin *mirari:* to wonder at; *mirus:* astonishing; *miraculum:* a prodigy. *Mir-*, with an *s*-prefix (*smei-*) gives Sanskrit *smayate,* "he smiles," Old English *smearcian,* Middle English *smilen,* "to smile." *Smearcian* also becomes *smirk*—which now means "smile, but with an irritating complacency."

5. John Ferguson, 1989, pp. 76–77. He points out that the fact that the oracle, in its responses to questions, sided with Persia in the war with Greece did not prevent Greeks from expressing gratitude at Delphi for their victory over the Persians.

6. Greeks built temples as votive offerings, such as that of Apollo at Bassae for deliverance

from the plague. In Europe, large numbers of chapels in churches are dedicated to the plague saints, Rocco and Sebastian.

7. The present statue is an eighteenth-century work by Pietro van Verschaffelt, substituting for the original sixteenth-century stone one by Raffaello da Montelupo, which now stands in a courtyard of the Castel S. Angelo. Gregory the Great's vision occurred in the sixth century.

8. Van Dyck: *Madonna del Rosario,* 1627, made in gratitude for the end of a plague in Palermo. Mantegna: *La Madonna della Vittoria,* 1506, in the Louvre.

9. Venice, Accademia. 1576.

10. Apocalypse 12:1.

11. Pinacoteca Vaticana. 1512.

12. Votives were condemned, for example, at the sixth-century Synod of Orleans. A thousand years later Saint Charles Borromeo, in the context of the Council of Trent, protested in his *Instructiones fabricae ecclesiasticae* that votive offerings were "often false, indecorous, base, and superstitious."

13. Eileen Oktavec, 1998, pp. 27–28, 155. Another priest said simply, "This is what the people want to do." p. 183. See also p. 185. I depend on Oktavec's excellent study for much of the following.

14. Ibid., p. 162. "The bell had such a sweet sound," said a silversmith, "because it was made of so many kinds of metal in the milagros."

15. Ibid., p. 165.

16. Anne Betteridge, 1985, especially pp. 197–99.

17. The central scene of the frieze on the Athenian Parthenon, at the east side of the temple, shows young girls handing over to the priests a new robe which they have spent nine months weaving as an offering to Athene, for her statue to wear.

18. Oktavec supplies photographs, on pp. 23 and 190. There are well-documented examples—though Oktavec says it does not happen at the shrines she describes—of people who become angry with saints slow to hear them, or who threaten their powerful interlocutors to make them comply.

19. Eileen Oktavec, 1998, p. 39.

20. Saint Charles Borromeo, note 11 (above).

21. Eileen Oktavec, 1998, p. 19. It should be added that many devotees at the Mission confuse Saint Francis Xavier with Saint Francis of Assisi. They are apparently quite unconcerned about the vagueness; both, after all, are great saints and worth praying to. Oktavec explains how the confusion arose; the historical account is instructive in itself, and a fascinating example of the impossibility of reducing hagiography to a matter of facts, names, and dates.

22. Ibid., pp. 37–8.

23. Ibid., p. 38.

12: Unpacking "Gratitude"

1. Deuteronomy 26:5–10.

2. Deuteronomy 5:8; Exodus 20:4–5.

3. The final shape of the Book of Deuteronomy can be dated to ca. 560 BC, but the work was gradually created from older sources.

4. In the great city states of the Middle East during the second millennium BC, the founding myths spoke of a primeval cosmic struggle among the gods, in which light and order were pitted against darkness and chaos, good against evil, life against death. A hero god conquered the darkness, and his mighty deeds were the subject of cultic celebrations on earth. It was the divine realm—reflected in the earth's dying and coming to life every year, in the phases of the moon every month, and every day in the setting and the rising of the sun—that overwhelmingly counted.

5. For a brief account of how this slowly came about, see Harvey H. Guthrie, 1981, pp. 31–69.

6. See Anna Wierzbicka, 1992.

7. See Claus Westermann, 1981, p. 25.

8. "Thanking [as opposed to praising] presupposes that the community is no longer primary and no longer self-evident," Westermann writes. "It presupposes that the community is no longer prior to the individual." 1981, p. 28.

9. Other quite different offerings were the daily holocaust, the daily cereal offerings, sin offerings, reparation offerings, and peace offerings. For details see Leviticus, chapters 6 and 7.

10. *Psalm* is from a Greek word meaning "to pluck the strings of a musical instrument."

11. Psalm 29/30:11–12.

12. Psalm 114–15/116:12–19.

13. Psalm 50/51:16–17.

14. Deuteronomy 8:11–19.

15. Paul Joüon, 1923, p. 382.

16. Anna Wierzbicka, 1991, p. 122.

17. See Claude Moussy, 1966, p. 37.

18. The word *gratitudo* was formed much later, in the thirteenth century AD. We shall look further at this development.

19. See Claude Moussy, 1966, p. 52.

20. "*O decus Italiae virgo, quas dicere gratis/ quasve referre parem?*" Book 11, lines 508–9. As we

might put it, "What can I say to express my gratitude, and what can I do in return?" The word *gratis* is the accusative of the somewhat archaic plural noun *grates.* It is not the same as *gratis,* "for free."

21. *De beneficiis dicendum est et ordinanda res, quae maxime humanam societatem alligat.* "It is essential to have a discussion of benefits, and a systematization of the rules for a practice that constitutes the chief bond of human society." 1.4.2. Cicero, in *De inventione,* says that gratitude is the foundation of natural law (2.65, 66, 161).

22. *Charis* is not etymologically connected to the word *charity,* which comes from Latin *caritas:* "high regard, affection."

23. On saying "thank you" in ancient Greek conversation, see J.H. Quincey, 1966.

24. Bonnie MacLachlan, 1993, pp. 27, 147.

25. *Mercy* in English comes from an older meaning for French *merci,* which signified *miséricorde,* the heart's sympathy with and pity for another's pain, before it began to be used for the kind of appreciation that is thanking.

26. In Homer, *charis* was "poured over the head and shoulders" of Odysseus by Athene, so that he became beautiful to behold. *Odyssey* 8:19.

27. *Glad* is from Old English *glaed,* "shining" and therefore joyous. A "glade" is an open space in a dark wood where the sunshine can pour in.

28. Bonnie MacLachlan, 1993, p. 149.

29. The French word *prestige* comes from illusions produced by conjuring tricks (prestidigitation). It now means a kind of aura, similar in some respects to that of *charis.*

30. *Glamour* is said to derive from *grammar: grammarye* was magic power, formerly attributed to learned people, Greek *grammatike* being the art of reading and writing.

31. Claude Moussy, 1966, pp. 409–11. He denies any etymological link between the two words; *gratia* made a "sense borrowing," no more.

32. The sacrament Christians call "Communion" and "the Eucharist" is *eucharistia* ("gratitude") in Greek. (Modern Greeks say "*efcharisto*" for "thank you.") The institution of the sacrament of the Eucharist at the Passover meal called the Last Supper began with Jesus blessing the bread and wine and giving thanks to God. In the Catholic Mass, which is a sacred meal remembering the Last Supper, a solemn "grace" or thanksgiving is said—or sung—twice, at the beginning of the central part of the ritual, and again at its end.

33. Early German had its own independently evolved version of "gratitude" as praise-for-favours. The Gothic expression for thankfulness was *awiliup. Awi* means "favour." *Liup* (a word that evolved into German *Lied*) means "song." Thankfulness was expressed, as in Sanskrit *gir* and Old Testament *todah,* by a "chant of favour." It later translated the Greek term *charis.* See Emile Benveniste, 1973, p. 160.

34. See note 25 (above).

13: The Fourth Law of Nature

1. Feudal law was never uniform, nor was it universally applicable: each grouping made its own rules. An excellent account of the feudal era of Poland, which gives a remarkably clear sense of what such a period was like, is Norman Davies, *God's Playground: A History of Poland*. New York: Columbia University Press, 2005. Volume 1, chapter 3. First published 1980.

2. Tacitus, *Germania*. AD 98, chapter 14. Trans. Harold Mattingly and S.A. Handford, Penguin Books, 1971.

3. *Beowulf and the Fight at Finnesburg*. Fr. Klaeber, ed. New York: D.C. Heath, 1936, lines 20–24a. Trans. Andrew Galloway, 1994, p. 366.

4. *The Historia regum Britanniae of Geoffrey of Monmouth*. Neil Wright, ed. Cambridge University Press, 1985, vol. 1, p. 101. Trans. Andrew Galloway, 1994, p. 367.

5. John 18:36; Matthew 6:24.

6. I take this phrase from the French article by Anne Lombard-Jourdan, 1997, p. 525.

7. See Emile Mâle, *L'art religieux du XIIIe siècle en France*. 1923, reprinted Paris: Armand Colin, 2007, p. 56.

8. Aquinas calls "gratitude" both *gratia* and *gratitudo,* and sometimes also *recompensatio.* Thomas Aquinas, *Summa,* Question 106. *Summa Theologiae Secunda Secundae, De Gratia sive Gratitudine,* CVI. Ottawa: Commissio Piana, 1953, Tome 3, 1973b–1979a.

9. Dante, *Inferno,* canto 34. See the notes of Charles S. Singleton, *Dante Alighieri, The Divine Comedy. Inferno.* Princeton, NJ: Princeton University Press, Bollingen Series LXXX, 1970, pp. 630–33.

10. William Langland (ca. 1330–1386). A.V.C. Schmidt, ed., *William Langland: The Vision of Piers Plowman.* London: J.M. Dent: Everyman, 1995, 9.25 and following.

11. Geoffrey Chaucer, Langland's contemporary, already uses *kynde* only in the modern sense, restricting it to benevolent personal behaviour that has nothing to do with kin.

12. Quoted from the original manuscript by Ellen Dunn, 1946, p. 89.

13. Shakespeare, *Julius Caesar* 3.2.

14. Shakespeare, *King Lear* 2.2.75.

15. Ibid., 4.3.43–4, 2.4.135–6, 1.4.296–8.

16. Ibid., 2.4.179–183

17. Ibid., 2.4.46–51.

18. Ibid., 1.2.1–4.

19. Ibid., 1.2.191.

20. Ibid., 3.4.110.

21. Marshall Sahlins (1972, pp. 83–95) has found much similarity between Hobbes and Marcel Mauss.

22. Thomas Hobbes, 1950, first published 1651, p. 66. Notice the resemblance to Lear's "poor, bare, forked animal," and also his "Allow not nature more than nature needs,/ Man's life is cheap as beast's" (*King Lear* 2.4.266–9). Shakespeare's remedies for the human condition are, of course, completely different from those of Hobbes.

23. Thomas Hobbes, 1950, p. 69. Hobbes knew, or at least had closely read, Scripture.

24. Ibid., 1950, p. 78. (The italics are Hobbes's.)

25. Ibid., p. 169.

14: AFTER ALL

1. Gregorio Morán, "¿Qué hacemos con la abuela?" ("What shall we do with Grannie?"). Barcelona, *La Vanguardia,* 24 January 2004, p. 20.

2. Closer to modern times, Honoré de Balzac's novel *Le Père Goriot* (1835) contains the story of a father who gives his two daughters everything he has, and they are utterly ungrateful. Balzac is thought to have based his story on *King Lear;* he provides no Cordelia.

3. Shakespeare, *King Lear* 2.4.252.

4. *King Lear* 1.5.40, 3.4.14–16.

5. Despite the validity of this general rule, we realize, of course, that it is not always kept. See, for example, Yasujiro Ozu's classic film *Tokyo Story* (1953). The unkind treatment of the old couple in the film is for Ozu's Japanese audience deeply shocking, and shows up the saintly qualities of the heroine. We are able to understand.

6. On April 9, 2007, the Chinese government decided that job promotions should be denied to people who failed to look after their parents adequately; it felt that modern social attitudes were undermining this traditional practice, and that the State was in danger of having to pick up the slack.

7. Xenophon, *Memorabilia* 2.2.13. Filial misconduct entailed religious impurity: the city could not allow a man guilty of failing to treat his parents well to offer sacrifices on behalf of the State. Failure to look after his parents' graves was also a black mark in the official preliminary investigation of a candidate's fitness for office.

8. Exodus 21:16–17.

9. Plato, *The Laws* 11.930e–932d.

10. Polybius, *The Histories* 6.6.2–8.

11. *pietas* sometimes meant specifically religious practice, but Cicero distinguishes religion from it in *De Inventione rhetorica* 2.66.

12. Virgil, *Aeneid* 2.705–746.

13. Aelian, 10.16.

14. See Plutarch, "The Comparison of Theseus with Romulus" 6.4, in his *Lives of the Noble Greeks and Romans.*

15. Aristotle (fourth century BC), *Nicomachean Ethics* 8.14.4. Aristotle says that a son, therefore, should never disown his father although a father may disown his son. He adds two cynical afterthoughts. First, a father would never actually do this, because "natural affection apart, it is not in human nature to reject the assistance that a son will one day be able to render." Second, bad sons, on the other hand, are likely to try to avoid looking after their fathers, "for most people wish to receive benefits, but avoid bestowing them, thinking them unprofitable."

16. Seneca, *De Beneficiis* 3.29.2–3.38.3. For the flies and worms, see 3.30.4 and 3.31.4.

17. Compare *Gulliver's Travels,* note 21 (below). Swift may well have remembered this idea from Seneca.

18. See Michael Slote, "Obedience and Illusions," in O. O'Neill and W. Ruddick, eds., *Having Children: Philosophical and Legal Reflections on Parenthood.* Oxford University Press, 1979, 319–26.

19. For example, Norman Daniels, "Family Responsibility Initiatives and Justice Between Age Groups," *Law, Medicine and Health Care* 13(1985), 155.

20. Michael Slote, note 18, p. 321. See further Martin R. Levy and Sara W. Gross, "Constitutional Implications of Parental Support Laws," *University of Richmond Law Review* 13(1979) 523–28.

21. Nancy S. Jecker, 1989, p. 74. Jonathan Swift in *Gulliver's Travels* (1726) has the Lilliputians object to filial piety on the grounds that "Men and Women are joined together like other Animals, by the Motives of Concupiscence; and that their Tenderness towards their Young, proceedeth from the like natural Principle. For which Reason they will never allow, that a Child is under any Obligation to his Father for begetting him, or to his Mother for bringing him into the World; which, considering the Miseries of human Life, was neither a Benefit in itself, nor intended so by his Parents, whose Thoughts in their Love-encounters were otherwise employed." Part I. *A Voyage to Lilliput,* chapter 6. The Lilliputians would have made appreciative readers of many a sociological text.

22. David Archard, "Filial Morality," *Pacific Philosophical Quarterly* 77(1996) 179–192. (Archard lists these arguments as a foil for the ideas of Confucius.) We might also imagine the dismay with which children might receive a bill from their parents for expenses incurred in their upbringing. The great French painter Jean Siméon Chardin (1699–1779) did precisely this: he presented his son, aged twenty-six, with accounts

for the cost of his guardianship. Chardin *père* was not a poor man. (Charles-Nicholas Cochin, "Essai sur la vie de M. Chardin," 1780.)

23. Jane English, "What Do Grown Children Owe Their Parents?" in O. O'Neill and W. Ruddick, eds., *Having Children: Philosophical and Legal Reflections on Parenthood*. Oxford University Press, 1979, 351–56.

24. Nancy S. Jecker, 1993, p. 279, summarizes these arguments, but does not think them sufficiently "encompassing." See further Martin R. Levy and Sara W. Gross (note 20, p. 411).

25. Nancy S. Jecker, 1993, p. 279.

26. Seneca mentions this possibility in *De Beneficiis* 3.31.3, without mentioning the issue of gratitude from a child whose life has been permitted by his father. A father has claimed responsibility for his son's success. The son says he would prefer to have been exposed to being told that his father should have the credit for his achievements.

27. Thomas Hobbes, 1950, first published 1651, p. 182.

28. Nancy S. Jecker, 1989, p. 74.

29. Samuel Beckett, *Endgame,* 1957.

30. In early Roman law, the father of a family was the only fully legal person in it. A father could put a grown son to death as well as expose at birth children he did not want; he could also sell his children, because they were his property.

31. Seneca, *De Beneficiis* 6.4.2–6.5.1.

32. I rely for supporting research in this section on Myra Lewinter, 1999, pp. 58–63, 272–87.

33. Vladimir Jankélévitch, 1968, vol. 2, p. 926. First published 1949.

34. Matthew 25:31–46.

35. See Daniel Callahan, 1985, and the references there given.

36. Both Myra Lewinter, 1999 (note 32, above), and Daniel Callahan, 1985, advocate this idea. Lewinter describes the unconditional provisions made for the elderly by the citizens of Denmark, and shows the practical benefits of the plan.

15: TIPPING

1. The Latin term *gratuitus,* from which we get *gratuitous* in English, was influenced by Christian translations into Latin of the Old Testament. Hebrew *hinnam,* "without paying," also means "with no reason, profitless, in vain," and Latin added the latter meanings to *gratuitus,* "for free." The English word now means "done for nothing," "without reason," and so "uncalled for" (although not "in vain"). French *pour rien,* like Latin *gratuitus,* means not only "for free" but also "in vain" (as can English *for nothing*).

Pierre Bourdieu denied that a gift could be freely given: a gift *pour rien* included its being given "in vain," which seems to imply calculation in the giver (see, for example, Bourdieu, 1994). For the etymology, see further Claude Moussy, 1966, pp. 332–43.

2. Seneca, discussing whether or not a slave could give anything at all, decides that indeed a slave can give. "When he supplies more than a slave need do, it is a benefit or favour . . . it ceases to be called a service when it passes over into the domain of friendly affection. . . . What a slave supplies, not from obedience to authority, but from his own desire, will be a benefit." And a benefit deserves gratitude, which should give rise to a return favour. *De Beneficiis* 3.8.21.1, 2.

3. Boas Shamir, 1984, p. 65. For the economists' view, see, for example, Batifoulier, Cordonnier, and Zénou, 1982, p. 930.

4. George M. Foster thinks that "a tip, clearly, is money given to a waiter to buy off his possible envy, to equalize the relationship between server and served." 1972, p. 181. He also believes that "to tip" comes from *tipple,* a drink.

5. John Reed, *Ten Days That Shook the World.* New York: Vintage, 1960, p. 14.

6. Michael Lynn, George M. Zinkhan, and Judy Harris, 1993, p. 482.

7. See further William Joseph Reader, *Professional Men: The Rise of the Professional Classes in Nineteenth-Century England.* London: Weidenfeld and Nicolson, 1966. See also Margaret Visser, 1994, pp. 122–6.

8. Seneca describes the tipping of professionals, from boat pilots to teachers and physicians, in *De Beneficiis* 6.16.4. He says that "a man is ungrateful if he thinks that he owes such people no more than he bargained for." "The price of his mind" is owed to the service provider, over and above the set fee, when the provider has given "something of himself," *ipsis aliquid.* 6.17.1.

9. Examples, chosen because the titles of these articles are expressive: Kimberly Garrity and Douglas Degelman, "Effect of Server Introduction on Restaurant Tipping," *Journal of Applied Social Psychology* 20(1990) 168–72; Kathi L. Tidd and Joan S. Lockard, "Monetary Significance of the Affiliative Smile: A Case for Reciprocal Altruism," *Bulletin of the Psychonomic Society* 11(1978) 344–46; April H. Crusco and Christopher G. Wetzel, "The Midas Touch: The Effects of Interpersonal Touch on Restaurant Tipping," *Personality and Social Psychology Bulletin* 10(1984) 512–17; Jacob Hornik, "Tactile Stimulation and Consumer Response," *Journal of Consumer Research* 19(1992) 449–58; Renée Stephen and Richard L. Zweigenhaft, "The Effect on Tipping of a Waitress Touching Male and Female Customers," *Journal of Social Psychology* 126(1986) 141–42; Michael Lynn and Kirby Mynier, "Effect of Server Posture on Restaurant Tipping," *Journal of Applied Social Psychology* 23(1993) 678–85; J.D. Fisher, M. Rytting, R. Heslin, "Hands Touching

Hands: Affective and Evaluative Effects of an Interpersonal Touch," *Sociometry* 39(1976) 416–21; J.W. Stillman and W.E. Hensley, "She Wore a Flower in Her Hair: The Effect of Ornamentation on Non-verbal Communication," *Journal of Applied Communication Research* 1(1980) 31–39; Bruce Rind and Prushant Bordia, "Effect of Server's 'Thank You' and Personalization on Restaurant Tipping," *Journal of Applied Social Psychology* 25(1995) 745–51.

10. Bruce Rind and Prushant Bordia, note 9 (above), 1995, p. 746.

11. See further G. Mars and M. Nicod, *The World of Waiters.* London: Allen and Unwin, 1984.

12. Boas Shamir, 1984, pp. 69–71.

16: Freedom and Equality

1. Immanuel Kant, *The Metaphysic of Morals.* 1964. First published 1797. p. 117. See further Thomas E. Hill, 1971.

2. Arjun Appadurai, 1985, is my source for what follows. See further Arjun Appadurai, 1990. On *"nanri,"* see Appadurai, 1985, pp. 236–37, and note 2 on p. 245. He says it has been suggested that *"nanri"* for "thanks" might be "a product of early missionary efforts to find a reasonable Tamil lexeme for the relevant Christian conception."

3. Katherine Rupp, 2003, pp. 40–50.

4. Ibid., p. 109, note 6.

5. We recall how Takeo Doi felt he could not say "thank you" to his American university supervisor because he was not his equal. (See chapter 4, "I'm So Sorry," 38)

6. Aristotle, *Nicomachean Ethics* 4.3. 1–38, esp. 24–25.

7. Aristotle describes also the man "of great munificence, conspicuousness, and splendour," the *megaloprepes* or "magnificent man" (4.2.1–19). He says that "a poor man cannot be magnificent." The size of the amount given is essential to the concept.

8. Seneca held the opposite view, and was quoted by Thomas Aquinas because of his agreement with the Christian view of giving and gratitude: "The rule for doing favours is that one person quickly forget what he has given, and the other long remember what he has received." *De Beneficiis* 1.4.5; 7.16.1; 2.10.4: *alter statim oblivisci debet dati, alter accepti numquam; Summa Theologica* Question 107, 3. See also Demosthenes, *On the Crown* 269. It is difficult not to wonder whether Aristotle might be poking gentle fun at his *megalopsychos.* But no sign is given that he is.

9. Aristotle, *Topica* 4.4, 125 a 18. In *Posterior Analytics and Topica.* Trans. E.S. Forster. Loeb Classical Library. London: Heinemann, 1960.

10. *Vulgar* is from Latin *vulgus,* "crowd." The vulgar are the opposite of the "elite," which

means "those chosen or picked out"—that is, out of the crowd—and set apart. Such people are necessarily few, and "honourable" because they are honoured.

11. Thomas Aquinas (thirteenth century), *Summa Theologiae,* Question 106.

12. Acts 20:35.

13. Thomas Hobbes, 1950, first published 1651, p. 50.

17: GESTURES

1. Dante, *Inferno.* 34.11–15. The interpretation of these postures was that of early commentators such as Bernardino Daniello da Lucca. See Ellen Catherine Dunn, 1946, p. 66, note 73.

2. See chapter 3, "It's Only Natural," p. 28 and note 2.

3. See M.H. Siddiqi, 1989. A special form of prostration to express thanks to God for personal good fortune and for military success, *sujud al-shukr,* is recorded in Muslim traditions as a favourite of the Prophet Muhammad. It was inherited from pre-Islamic practice, and included two acts of bending. See further Roberto Tottoli, 1998.

4. Genesis 48:12. Joseph's brothers repeatedly prostrate themselves not in gratitude but in homage to Joseph in Egypt, not knowing that he is their brother. Genesis 43:26, 28; 44:14.

5. Ruth 2:10.

6. II Kings 4:37. She presumably thinks that Gehazi has performed the miracle.

7. Luke 17:16.

8. I Samuel 20:41. David may have meant his prostrations to be to God rather than to Jonathan.

9. See Esther Goody, 1972.

10. We recall that in European languages, and most especially in English, saying "thank you" is a means of ending a conversation.

11. For an analysis of the ritual of suppliancy, see John Gould, 1973.

12. See Richard Broxton Onians, 1951, pp. 175–8, 180, 185, 491.

13. Homer, *Iliad* 1.500–501. At *Iliad* 8.370–72, Thetis *kisses* his knees and takes his chin in her hand. See Richard Broxton Onians, 1951, pp. 132–3, 232–3, for the meaning of male chins, which was similar to that of knees.

14. Homer, *Iliad,* 24. 468–506, esp. lines 478–79.

15. *Funk and Wagnalls Standard Dictionary of Folklore, Mythology, and Legend.* 1972, p. 589.

16. Boye Lafayette De Mente, "*Ojigi:* From Kowtowing to Bowing," *NTC's Dictionary of Japan's Cultural Code Words.* Lincolnwood, IL: National Textbook Company, 1995, pp. 288–89.

17. From Naomi Sugimoto, ed., *Japanese Apology Across Disciplines*. Commack, NY: Nova Science Publishers, 1999, p. 216; A. Matsunaga, "Kodomo (yoji) no sekai no shazai," in *Nihongo Gaku* (Special Issue: Apology expressions), 12(1993) 84–92.

18. Erasmus, *De civilitate morum puerilium libellus*. Froben, Bale, 1530. Vol. 25 of *Collected Works of Erasmus,* 1985, p. 278.

19. Raymond Firth, 1970, p. 203. See Margaret Visser, 1991, pp. 71–74, et cetera, on the uses of deliberately making polite movements difficult.

20. Nodding has long signified agreement, as when Zeus nodded to Thetis. Disagreement— saying "no"—in Greece today is the opposite of a nod: throwing the head briefly backwards while clicking the tongue.

21. For a description and explanation of table manners, including bowing, at a Japanese meal, see Harumi Befu, 1974.

22. Henry Norman, 1908, pp. 28–29.

23. *Li Chi*. Trans. J. Legge, 2 vols., New York University Press, 1967. Vol. 2, 435–39, 456.

24. Jean-Baptiste de la Salle, *Les règles de la bienséance et de la civilité chrétienne*. Rouen, 1713, 1729, quoted by Jean-Claude Bonnet, "La Table dans les civilités," *Marseille* 109(1977), 100.

25. The reason for this is that the left hand is taken to be inadequate and impure; it may also be disqualified as profane. This is true in many cultures, though often to a lesser extent: in English, for example, "sinister" and "gauche" mean literally "left," a word which comes from Anglo-Saxon *lyft,* "weak" or "worthless." *Right,* meanwhile, is synonymous with *correct.* See further Robert Hertz, *Death and the Right Hand.* Trans. Rodney and Claudia Needham, Glencoe, IL: Free Press, 1960 (originally published 1925); Margaret Visser, 1991, pp. 170–72, and 1994, pp. 127–31.

26. Robert A. Barakat, 1972–73.

27. Samuel Richardson, *Clarissa*. London: Viking, 1985. First published 1747–48. Vol. 1, p. 138.

28. S. Chimombo, "Riddles and the Representation of Reality," *Africa* 57(1987) 314–315.

29. *Funk and Wagnalls Standard Dictionary of Folklore, Mythology, and Legend,* 1972, p. 603.

30. Herodotus 1.134.

31. The word is probably onomatopoeic and related to Greek "*euoi!,*" a ritual cry at Bacchic festivals. The theatre was from the beginning sacred to Dionysus, also known as Bacchus.

32. See Dennis Kurzon, 1996.

33. "La pesadilla de Guantanamo llega a los escenarios de Londres," *El Pais,* 30 May 2004, p. 53.

18: MEMORY AND NARRATIVE

1. *Was heisst Denken?* 1954, pp. 91–5; trans. *What Is Called Thinking?* 1968. Part II, Lecture 3.

2. *Im Dank gedenkt das Gemüt dessen, was es hat und ist.* p. 93.

3. Or at least important aspects of the concept: see chapter 12, "Unpacking 'Gratitude.'"

4. Joseph William Hewitt, 1927, p. 149.

5. Masatoshi Nagatomi, 1989, pp. 77–78.

6. Terrance McConnell, 1993, pp. 70, 73.

7. From Latin *cognoscere,* "to know," and English *cognition.* See the last part of this book, "Recognizing."

8. See Seneca, *De Beneficiis* 6.43.2: *Egi illi gratias, id est, rettuli.* "I said 'thank you' to him, which means to say that I made a return."

9. *De Beneficiis* 4.10.2–4; 4.9.2.

10. Mark 4:3–20; Luke 6.35–36; Matthew 5:45.

11. Georg Simmel (1858–1918), "Faithfulness and Gratitude," in Kurt H. Wolff, trans. and ed., *The Sociology of Georg Simmel,* 1950, 379–395. Simmel, as a sociologist, is interested almost exclusively in the external aspects of gratitude and faithfulness, and their strength as social stabilizers today.

12. See, for instance, the Spanish proverb:

    La memoria del mal, es por vida.

    La del bien, presto se olvida.

13. *De Beneficiis* 7.28.1–3.

14. *De Beneficiis* 1.12.1–2. Later Seneca advises us to choose something rare to bestow as a gift, "because anyone can endure being indebted for that!" 1.14.2.

15. Rena Lederman, 1986, pp. 85, 232.

16. Alasdair MacIntyre, 1999, p. 216.

17. James Alison, *Raising Abel: The Recovery of the Eschatological Imagination.* New York: Crossroad, 1996, p. 111.

18. See, for example, Xenophon, *Constitution of the Spartans* 13.2–8; Plutarch, *Lycurgus* 21.4.

19. The word *prize* comes from German *Preis,* which means not only "prize" but also "price," "praise," and "glory."

20. Homer, *Odyssey* 24.80–94. For more on this subject see Sitta Von Reden, 1995, pp. 28–30.

21. I am indebted for much of what follows to Alex King, 1998.

22. Statues on war memorials in Western Europe after the First World War tend to show soldiers pensive, silent, on watch, rather than in the glow of active aggression (see Alex King, 1998, pp. 176–79, with photographs). The Soviet Union, however, kept alive the tradition of triumphant statuary—of men bounding forward howling with righteous

rage, brandishing their flags and their weapons. A collection of such figures, fascinat-
ingly outdated as they are, have been relegated together to Szoborpark, the Park of
Statues, in Budapest.

23. Seneca, De Beneficiis 4.11.4–6. "If we give only when we may expect some return," he
writes at the end of this passage, "we ought to die intestate!" Seneca ignores the sensa-
tions of power that can bring glee to the maker of a will.

24. See Dan P. McAdams and Jack J. Bauer, "Gratitude in Modern Life," in Robert A.
Emmons and Michael E. McCullough, eds., 2004, pp. 81–99.

25. Luke 10:29–37. See also, in part, Seneca, De Beneficiis 4.12.2.

26. Warren E. Roberts, 1958, gives a detailed examination of the variants and the differences among them. See further his "Special Forms of Aarne-Thompson Type 480 and
Their Distribution," Fabula 1(1957) 85–102.

27. A kairos was what we might call a "loophole" or a "window of opportunity." It was a
concrete metaphor, possibly derived from weaving, where the creator of a length of
textile had to throw her shuttle at the very moment when the threads on the loom
opened, not before and not after, for fear of ruining the cloth. See Richard Broxton
Onians, 1951, pp. 343–48.

28. Mark Twain, The Tragedy of Pudd'nhead Wilson. Cutchoque, NY: Buccaneer Books, 1976,
p. 122. First published 1894.

29. Aelian, 8.3.

30. Aulus Gellius, Attic Nights (AD 180), 5.14, quoting from a lost work by the first-century
Greco-Egyptian scholar, Apion; Aelian 7.48.

31. The location of the event in the Circus Maximus is from Gellius. For further developments of the story during the Middle Ages, see Arthur G. Brodeur, 1924. Bernard Shaw
wrote a play based on it.

32. At least two of these have survived: Pliny the Elder, Natural History 8.56, has the hero
Mentor the Syracusan; at 8.57–58 the hero is Elpis of Samos. Stories about other
Grateful Animals survive from antiquity. For example, a man saves an eagle from being
strangled by a snake. Later, at dinner, the eagle swoops down and dashes his cup from his
hand. The man is outraged at this apparent ingratitude and hostility. But he lives, thanks
to the quick thinking of the grateful eagle, whereas his companions perish, because in
their cups is snake poison, deposited there before the snake died. (Aelian 17.37–38.)

33. The story is told by John Moschus (ca. 545–619 or 634) in his Spiritual Meadow.

34. Mark 9:37; Luke 9:48.

35. The Hindu God Krishna also showed his generous love for human beings through his
gratitude to them. See Vasudha Narayanan, 1989, pp. 24–28.

36. Isaiah 11:6–9.

37. Homer, *Iliad,* 20.163–75.

38. Alison Goddard Elliott, 1987, p. 196.

39. Chrétien de Troyes, *Chevalier au Lion,* line 3392.

40. *La Queste del saint Graal,* ed. Pauphilet, 1980, pp. 94–101. For more on animals in stories of the saints, see Alison Goddard Elliott, 1987, and Helen Waddell, 1934.

41. Fyodor Dostoyevsky, *The Brothers Karamazov.* Trans. David McDuff. London: Penguin, 2003. First published 1880. pp. 650, 861–62.

42. Luke 17:11–19.

19: EMOTIONS

1. Anna Wierzbicka, 1985, pp. 168–69.

2. See Dean Barnlund, "Communicative Styles in Two Cultures: Japan and the United States," in Adam Kendon, Richard Harris, and Mary Ritchie Key, eds., *Organization of Behavior in Face-to-Face Interaction.* The Hague, Paris: Mouton, 1975, pp. 427–56. See further Edward T. Hall, *The Hidden Dimension.* New York: Anchor Books, 1969, pp. 149–154. 1973.

3. Anna Wierzbicka, 1999, p. 18.

4. William James, *The Principles of Psychology.* Cambridge, MA: Harvard University Press 1981, p. 485. First published 1890.

5. Paul Heelas, 1986, p. 238.

6. Anna Wierzbicka, 1992, pp. 119–24; 1999, p. 32. The point about grasping emotion concepts even if we have not experienced them ourselves is made by Peter Goldie, 2000, p. 32.

7. Anna Wierzbicka, 1992, pp. 136–79.

8. Takeo Doi, 1981. The entire book is on the concept of *amae.*

9. Michelle Rosaldo, *Knowledge and Passion: Ilongot Notions of Self and Social Life.* Cambridge: Cambridge University Press, 1980.

10. Catherine Lutz, *Unnatural Emotions.* Chicago: University of Chicago Press, 1988, pp. 121–37.

11. Paul Heelas, 1986, p. 235.

12. For much of what follows, see Zoltán Kövecses, 1990.

13. The earliest and literal meaning of *emotion* was "a moving out, migration, transference from one place to another." For more on the transition from "passions" to "emotions," see J.M. Barbalet, 1998, introduction, and Thomas Dixon, 2003.

14. *Passion* is from the past participle of Latin *patior,* the root of the word *patient.*

15. See Anna Wierzbicka, 1999, pp. 2–5.

16. J.M. Barbalet, 1998, p. 13.

17. See Marshall Sahlins, 1972, p. 89. Consider the tale, for example, of a history of peace, embodied in a New Zealand Maori greenstone weapon called a *mere,* which received a personal name, "Hine-nui-o-te-paua." The adventures of this *mere* begin with its being given by the Kawerau people, eight generations previously, to Ngati-Paoa as a token of peace. The greenstone object subsequently travelled from group to group as a gift, "trying to secure peace"; every occasion, every person involved, every movement of the *mere* together with the feasts and other circumstances of the transfer, and the reasons of those who gave it, was remembered in story. The old people knew all the details and handed them down to the young. The stone object became ever more redolent of peace, and expressive of joy for the presence of peace. Finally the Kohimarama people, then holders of it, presented it to Governor Grey as a token of their desire to keep peace with the white people. "It was shown to us by Governor Grey at Te Kawau, and we wept over it," a Maori informant recorded in the 1920s—such is the affection of the Maori for ancient heirlooms. (Raymond Firth, 1972, p. 415, quoting from John White's recounting of the story of Ponga and Puhihuia.) This story is irresistible to both Maori and foreigners. The tale now includes these tears shed over the stone and its history: a new episode has been added to the chronicle of Hine-nui-o-te-paua. It also leads to those who listen to it being, as we say in English, "touched."

18. David Cheal, 1987, p. 169.

19. Charles Darwin, 1873.

20. For the following see Paul Ekman, 1994, and the references there given.

21. Other scientists have different lists: Theodore D. Kemper, 1987, for example, has four physiological or "autonomic" emotions: fear, anger, depression, and satisfaction. But he admits "social components" that add to these four surprise, disgust, guilt, shame, and pride in achievement. He publishes a table (p. 266) of other scientists' lists of emotions; only fear and anger are in all of them.

22. Ekman presumably means the "Duchenne Smile" (named after the nineteenth-century French doctor Guillaume Duchenne), which is a sincere smile, not a matter of artificial politeness, in which the corners of the mouth turn up and crinkles appear at the corners of the eyes.

23. Catherine Lutz and Geoffrey M. White, 1986, p. 405. Much of what follows is indebted to this review article.

24. See Sarah Tarlow, "Emotion in Archaeology," *Current Anthropology* 41(2000) 713–46.

25. Jon Elster, 1999, p. 403.

26. Robert C. Solomon, 2003, and "Emotions and Choice," *The Review of Metaphysics* 27(1973) 20–41.

27. Peter Goldie, 2000, p. 140.

28. Catherine Lutz and Geoffrey M. White, 1986, pp. 419–20, 414.

29. Anna Wierzbicka, 1992, pp. 119, 126.

30. Catherine Lutz and Geoffrey M. White, 1986, p. 422.

31. Ibid., pp. 415–16.

32. See, for example, Michael E. McCullough, Jo-Ann Tsang, and Robert A. Emmons, 2004.

33. E.L. Rosenberg, "Levels of Analysis and the Organization of Affect," *Review of General Psychology* 2(1998) 247–70. Rosenberg defines emotions as "acute, intense, and typically brief psychophysiological changes that result from a response to a meaningful situation in one's environment." p. 250.

34. The example is taken from Peter Goldie, who gives it in detail (2000, pp. 149–50).

35. Michael E. McCullough, Jo-Ann Tsang, and Robert A. Emmons, 2004, p. 296.

36. One best-selling book on this subject is Martin E.P. Seligman, PhD.: *Authentic Happiness: Using the New Positive Psychology to Realize Your Potential for Lasting Fulfillment,* 2002. The movement was presented to the scientific community in Martin E.P. Seligman and Mihaly Csikszentmihalyi, "Positive Psychology: An Introduction," *American Psychologist* 55(2000) 5–14.

37. Rollin McCraty and Doc Childre, "The Grateful Heart. The Psychophysiology of Appreciation," in Robert A. Emmons and Michael E. McCullough, eds., 2004, pp. 230–58.

38. Ibid., p. 232.

39. This is known to psychophysiologists as Pribram's Theory, expounded in K.H. Pribram and F.T. Meges, "Psychophysiological Basis of Emotion," in P.J. Vinken and G.W. Bruyn, eds., *Handbook of Clinical Neurology,* vol. 3. Amsterdam: North-Holland Publishing, 1969, pp. 316–41. Peter Goldie, 2000, refers to Proust: The habitual expressions on our faces "are hardly more than gestures which force of habit has made permanent. Nature, like the destruction of Pompeii, like the metamorphosis of a nymph, has arrested us in an accustomed movement." *A la recherche du temps perdu. A l'ombre des jeunes filles en fleurs.* First published 1918. Pleiade edition, 1954, vol. 1, p. 909.

20: FEELING GRATEFUL

1. Social scientists still feel they cannot answer Mauss's question, "Why give back?" See, for example, Barbara L. Frederickson in Robert A. Emmons and Michael E. McCullough, eds., 2004, p. 150.

2. Marcus Tullius Cicero (106–43 BC), *De Officiis* 1.15.47; 2.18.63.

3. Seneca, *De Beneficiis* 2.22.1.

4. Matthew 7:16.

5. Thomas Aquinas (1225–1274), *Summa Theologica.* Question 106, Article 3, Reply to Objection 5. (Aquinas here calls gratitude *recompensatio.*) Article 5: "because gratitude regards the favour inasmuch as it is bestowed gratis, and this regards the disposition of the giver, it follows again that repayment of a favour depends more on the disposition of the giver than on the effect: *gratiae recompensatio attendit magis affectum dantis quam effectum.*" The Latin prefixes in *affectum* and *effectum* vividly point to the difference between motivation and deed.

6. Mark 12:41–44; Luke 21:1–4.

7. Thomas Hobbes, 1950, first published 1651, p. 78.

8. Jean-Jacques Rousseau, *Second Discourse on Inequality.* Trans. G.D. Cole in *The Social Contract and Discourses.* London: J.M. Dent, 1913, first published 1755, p. 230.

9. Adam Smith, author of *The Wealth of Nations* (1776) with its emphasis on self-interest and on the unimportance of people's intentions to such economic matters as prices, profits, interest rates, or divisions of labour, wrote *The Theory of the Moral Sentiments* in 1759. It was published in 1790.

10. "*Tous ceux qui s'acquittent des devoirs de la reconnaissance ne peuvent pas pour cela se flatter d'être reconnaissants.*" La Rochefoucauld, *Maximes* 224. First published 1664.

11. For examples of hedging and the importance of small verbal politenesses in modern informal conversational English, see Penelope Brown and Stephen C. Levinson, 1987, and Margaret Visser, 1994, 57–61, 217–21.

12. I Corinthians 13:1–3. There are many demands for sincere feelings in the Bible. See, for example, the Book of Joel, where people are exhorted to feel sorrow rather than merely demonstrate it: "Let your hearts be broken, not your garments torn!" Joel 2:13.

13. Emily Dickinson, Poem No. 1192 (ca. 1871).

14. Erving Goffman, *Asylums.* Chicago: Aldine, 1962, p. 115.

15. For the importance of the casual and informal in modern manners, see Margaret Visser, 1991, pp. 378–96, and s.v. "informality."

16. See Laura M. Slatkin, 1991, chapter 2. So few and so oblique are Homer's references to the story of Peleus and Thetis that not everybody believes, as I do, that the "gratitude" of Zeus underlies the plot of the *Iliad* and adds profound resonance and pathos to the figures of Achilles and his mother. Jennifer R. March, for example, believes that Pindar, much later, invented this story: see "Peleus and Achilles" in *The Creative Poet: Bulletin of the Institute of Classical Studies* Supplement 49(1987) 1–26. We should recall that Homer lacked a word for "gratitude."

17. Marcel Proust, in *A la recherche du temps perdu,* gives an example of this, when Gilberte Swann looks with a greater degree of intimacy at the novel's Narrator and smiles as

she begins to call him by his first name. She expresses intimacy, consciousness, pleasure, and gratitude. "*Son regard, se mettant au même degré nouveau d'intimité que prenait sa parole, m'atteignait aussi plus directement, non sans témoigner la conscience, le plaisir et jusque la gratitude qu'il en avait, en se faisant accompagner d'un sourire.*" *A l'ombre des jeunes filles en fleurs.* (1918) Paris: Pleiade (1954), vol. 1, pp. 403–4.

18. Shinichiro Okamoto and W. Peter Robinson, 1997, pp. 411–33.

19. The oldest version we have already appears to be a specialized variant. It forms part of the deuterocanonical Book of Tobit (fifth to fourth centuries BC, although the story is set about two hundred years earlier), where the angel Raphael takes the place of the figure of "the Grateful Dead." The folktale "Jack the Giant-Killer" belongs to the group as well, and the English playwright George Peele reshaped the story in *The Old Wives' Tale* (1595). For a complete account of this folktale and its variants, see Gordon Hall Gerould, 1908.

20. A similar literalness appears in Shakespeare's *The Merchant of Venice,* where "a pound of flesh" has been promised in recompense for a debt unpaid. The same kind of relentlessly material reasoning is used *against* the demander of his pound of flesh: let him take the flesh, but *without any blood.* The impossibility of carrying out the precise terms of the contract saves the debtor.

21: LEARNING AND LASTING

1. Andrew Ortony, Gerald L. Clore, and Allan Collins, 1988, pp. 147–48.

2. George Simmel, 1950, ed. and trans. Kurt H. Wolff, first published ca. 1918, p. 393.

3. David Steindl-Rast, 1984, has excellent pages on this subject.

4. See, for example, Karl Halvor Teigen, 1997.

5. Melanie Klein, 1957, pp. 176–235.

6. Saint Augustine (354–430) writes in his *Confessions* that he saw a jealous infant (*zelantem parvulum*), not old enough to talk, glare at his foster-brother at his mother's breast with a "pale, bitter expression" (1.7). And we recall Proust's misery as a child when he thought he would not receive his mother's kiss; both he and his Narrator were to be tormented by jealousy for the rest of their lives.

7. Robert C. Solomon, "On Emotion as Judgments," in *Not Passion's Slave,* 2003, insists that we are responsible for our emotions, and ought to be, because of the central roles they play in our moral and social lives. He agrees that emotions must be sincere. But "we do need to learn them, and to learn how to 'do' them." p. ix.

8. The metaphor is to be found in Plato's *Phaedrus* (fourth century BC) 246a–d, 253c–254e.

9. Rollin McCraty and Doc Childre, in Robert A. Emmons and Michael E. McCullough, eds., 2004, pp. 235–44. The article is called "The Grateful Heart: The Psychophysiology of Appreciation."

10. Martin E.P. Seligman, 2002, pp. 72–74.

11. Aaron Ben-Ze'ev, 2000, p. 76.

12. Chapter 39 and following.

22: THE MARBLE-HEARTED FIEND

1. Morris Palmer Tilley (*A Dictionary of the Proverbs in England in the Sixteenth and Seventeenth Centuries,* Ann Arbor: University of Michigan Press, 1950) lists the still-surviving adage as Number 166. Bernard of Clairvaux (1090–1153) wrote a discourse on ingratitude, "the worst of vices." See also his *Sermones in Cantica Cantorum,* in Jacques Paul Migne, *Collection des Auteurs Sacrés* (1846–48), Col. 827.

2. John Lydgate, *Fall of Princes* 3.718, lines 1651–52.

3. Thomas Aquinas, *Summa Theologica* (1266–1273), Question 107, and Seneca, *De Beneficiis,* 3.1.2–5.

4. See, for instance, Psalm 38:19–21; Mark 3:22–30; Matthew 12:31–37. Close to our own time, an author who knew of and presented for our inspection examples of this extreme form of ingratitude was Charles Dickens. Read, for instance, *Our Mutual Friend* (1864–65) part 3, chapter 14.

5. "The debt of gratitude flows from charity, which the more it is paid the more it is due." And he quotes Paul's Letter to the Romans 13:8: "Owe no man anything, but to love one another." Question 106, article 6. See the rest of the Romans passage, 13:9–10.

6. For Kant's contemporary, the poet Christopher Smart (1722–1771), "the sin against the Holy Ghost is ingratitude" (*Jubilate Agno* B2 306). He is referring to Matthew 12:31–37 and Mark 3:28–30.

7. Immanuel Kant, *The Doctrine of Virtue.* Part 2 of *The Metaphysic of Morals,* 1797. See also *Lectures on Ethics,* 1780, p. 218. David Hume has written that "of all crimes . . . the most horrid and unnatural is ingratitude." *A Treatise of Human Nature* (1739–1740) 3.

8. We have seen that there were in the ancient world instances of laws forbidding filial impiety—but this has always been a special instance of ingratitude, complete with its particular name.

9. A slave, any slave, but especially one taken in war, was called in Latin a *servus:* he had been pre*served* from death. Such a slave could therefore be thought to owe gratitude to his Roman conqueror for his survival, and his owner remained in this sense always

a "first giver." A slave could collect money and buy his freedom if his master let him do so, even though he had strictly no right to own money: the master might therefore consider himself again a "giver." See Wolfgang Waldstein, 1992. Cicero wanted to re-enslave two freedmen who had let him down (*Letters to Atticus* 7.2), but it is clear from the context that he had no legal right to do so.

10. See François-Régis Chaumartin, 1985, pp. 313–35, and the references there given. Helmuth Berking (1999) says that modern German law "turns donations into a con-tractual relationship by making a gift *revocable* if the recipient commits a gross transgres-sion." pp. 26–27.

11. Ammianus Marcellinus writes that the Parthians "stand in special fear of the laws, among which those dealing with ingrates and deserters (*ingratos et desertores*) are particu-larly severe." Traitors are what he presumably means by *ingratos*. He adds that the guilt of one "ungrateful" Parthian meant that all his relatives were put to death and his slaves as well (*Julianus* 23.6.81). Seneca says the Macedonians were an exception among states because they punished ingratitude by law (*De Beneficiis* 3.6.2).

12. Part I. *A Voyage to Lilliput,* chapter 6. (1726).

13. Xenophon, *Cyropaedeia* 1.2.16; 8.8.11. See also Herodotus 1.138, Ammianus Marcellinus, *Julianus* 23.6.75, and Athenaeus, *The Deipnosophists* 8.345c.

14. Xenophon, *Cyropaedeia* 1.2.3–6.

15. Seneca, *De Beneficiis* 1.10.4.

16. "*Omne dixeris maledictum, cum ingratum hominem dixeris.*" *Publilii Syri Mimi Sententiae* (first century BC–first century AD). Leipzig: Teubner, 1880, p. 26. The English version is from the sermons of Edwin Sandys. See Ellen Catherine Dunn, 1946, p. 9.

17. Shakespeare, *King Lear* 4.2.40.

18. Virgil, *Aeneid* 4. 365–367. Dido, as we should expect, calls Aeneas treacherous, base, and a perjurer rather than ungrateful—although she certainly deserves his gratitude. See also Shakespeare, *Coriolanus* 5.3.178–80.

19. In Swahili, *Fadhili ya punda ni mashuzi.*

20. *King Lear* 1.4.257.

21. *Coriolanus* 1.1.162; 1.9.82, 89–91; 3.3.124, 134–35.

22. *King Lear* 3.2.16–19 (see 1–24).

23. *Coriolanus* 3.1.287–91.

24. Seneca makes a passing reference to people who consider the givers of benefits their worst enemies out of "natural depravity" or perhaps "natural perverseness," *pravitate naturae,* whereas most people just tend to be forgetful. 3.1.2.

23: WE ARE NOT GRATEFUL

1. Ambrose Bierce, *The Enlarged Devil's Dictionary.* Penguin, 1967. First published 1906. Compare de La Rochefoucauld: "The gratitude of most men is only a secret desire to receive greater favours." *La reconnaissance de la plupart des hommes n'est qu'une secrète envie de recevoir de plus grands bienfaits.* Maxim 298.

2. "*On respecte tout, de nos jours, pour n'avoir plus rien à admirer.*" Alain Finkielkraut, *Ingratitude.* 1999, p. 208.

3. *To admire* also means literally "to look at."

4. Edmund Burke (1729–1797), "Letter to a Noble Lord," *The Writings and Speeches of Edmund Burke,* 12 vols. Toronto: George Morang, 1901. Vol. 5, pp. 210–12.

5. This is an ancient Roman phrase for a custom involving a whole repertoire of measures intended to delete the memory of a famous person; a man's first name might be forbidden to be carried in his family, for example. Often *damnatio memoriae* was, and indeed still is, carried out by political and other rivals and enemies.

6. *The Letters of Samuel Johnson.* Ed. R. W. Chapman. Vol. 1. Oxford: Clarendon Press, 1952, Letter no. 61, pp. 64–65. Written in 1755.

7. Michael Stein, "Gratitude and Attitude: A Note on Emotional Welfare," 1989.

8. The phrase comes from the title of Arlie Hochschild's book, *The Managed Heart,* 1983.

9. On this spatial metaphor for rights, see Margaret Visser, 2002, pp. 102–108, 128, 133.

10. *Chambers's Twentieth Century Dictionary,* 1961; *Oxford English Dictionary,* 2005.

11. Tziporah Kasachkoff, 1994.

12. *Tel homme est ingrat, qui est moins coupable de son ingratitude que celui qui lui a fait du bien.* François de La Rochefoucauld, Maxim 96.

13. In practice, *concordia* was goodwill arising from a common humanity, and encouraged by such circumstances as residence in the same town or country, or similarity in leisure activities and interests.

14. See Ellen Catherine Dunn, 1946, pp. 24–29. *Concordia's* link with gratitude was confirmed by Seneca, who in a famous passage condemns ingratitude as destructive of *concordia* in all society: "Ingratitude is something to be avoided in itself because there is nothing that so effectually disrupts and destroys the harmony (*concordiam*) of the human race as this vice." *De Beneficiis* 4.18.1.

15. Georg Simmel, 1950, first published ca. 1918, p. 395.

16. The metaphor is related to a biblical parable of different human souls: gifts are showered on all of them, but not all respond or continue to be faithful. Mark 4:3–20; Luke 8:4–15.

17. Alvin W. Gouldner, 1960, p. 175.

24: THE POISONED GIFT

1. Herodotus, *Histories* 1.1–2. This theft of a woman was "the first of the injustices" that were to lead eventually to the invasion of Greece by Persia, which started the war that was the subject of the *Histories.* It was the Persians, says Herodotus, who, with this claim, put the blame on the Phoenicians for the whole appalling chain of events. *Histories* 1.3–5.1.

2. This is an alternative to the story of Zeus falling in love with Europa, turning himself into a bull, and swimming away to Crete with the girl on his back.

3. Laocoön was the uncle of Aeneas, the future founder of Rome. It was fated that Rome should arise and therefore that Troy's tragedy should force Aeneas to leave—in order to found Rome.

4. This last sentence, *Timeo Danaos et dona ferentis,* became proverbial. It reminded Romans (and later other Europeans who learned the Latin saying) to be careful of normally hostile gift-givers, their intentions, and their tactics. See Virgil, *Aeneid* 2.49 (lines 13–267) for the whole story.

5. Virgil, *Aeneid* 2.54. Virgil adds yet another reason for the Trojans' fateful decision: a deceitful Greek who lied to them and persuaded them to take in the gift. He let the hidden warriors out of the Horse when the time was ripe.

6. *Immemores caecique furore. Aeneid* 2.244.

7. The adage *Hostium munera non munera* ("Gifts of enemies are no gifts") is recorded by Erasmus in the sixteenth century. *Adages* 1.3.35.

8. Helen herself wishes she had died before she could leave her bridal-chamber for Troy, and calls herself a "savage dog" for the damage she has done. *Iliad* 3.173–76; 24.764; 6.344, 350.

9. Aeschylus, *Agamemnon,* lines 717–736. This view of lions as inherently ungrateful remained a foil for the later tradition of stories of "The Grateful Lion"—tales meant, as we saw, to be reproaches to ungrateful human beings.

10. Marcel Mauss (1924) was struck by the German word *Gift,* meaning "poison." (German for "gift" is *Gabe,* from *geben,* "to give.") *Gift* is a medical term, a loan translation from Greek *dosis* (English "dose")—an amount of medicine (or poison) administered, from the Greek for "an act of giving." German *Mitgift,* "dowry," keeps the original idea of "giving" and "gift." See Emile Benveniste, 1973, p. 55. German *Geschenk* means "gift," but literally signifies a liquid poured out—so commonly did Germans offer each other steins of beer.

11. Plutarch, *On the Delays of Divine Vengeance* 553E; Diodorus 16.64.2. The speciality of the Necklace was precipitating the deaths of mothers at the hands of their sons.

12. Richard Wagner, *The Ring;* Shakespeare, *Othello* 3.4.55–75.

13. Robert Louis Stevenson, *Kidnapped*. Penguin, 1993, pp. 23–27. First published 1886. The author's real surname was Balfour.

14. Influential political and intellectual leaders in the West, such as Winston Churchill and George Bernard Shaw, also raised their voices in admiration of Stalin.

15. See Sandrine Kott, 2001.

16. On this subject, see the excellent book by John T. Noonan, 1984.

17. The word may derive from French *bribe*, "little thing, trifle," the diminishment being intended to express contempt. In French a bribe is often called a *pot de vin,* "a jug of wine"—a small thing, as though it were a tip. Bribes, of course, often involve large amounts of money.

18. See, for example, James G. Carrier, 1995, p. 147.

19. See Paul F. Camenisch, 1981, p. 11.

20. The *-mail* component of this term was an Old English and Scottish word meaning "tribute" of the kind described.

21. John T. Noonan, 1984, insists on the term *office-holder* because it usefully implies both clarity of duty and the trust of those who give someone an office to perform. The term *office-holder,* however, stands for anyone in whom trust is invested, or whose faithfulness is innocently relied on.

22. See further Terrance C. McConnell, 1993, chapter 4.

23. Yunxiang Yan, 1996, p. 226, remarks that "instrumental" giving demands a response in the short term; it is "expressive" giving that involves waiting and taking time before the receiver gives back.

24. For an example, see *The Oxford Classical Dictionary,* 1996, s.v. "corruption."

25. Adam Smith, 1790, p. 95.

26. In philosophical circles in Scotland during the eighteenth century, "there arose like a spectre the suggestion that Gratitude itself, and not its universally disclaimed opposite, was vicious." This was because of gratitude's personal character, its partiality. For the debate, which eventually came down on the side of gratitude, see Charles Stewart-Robertson, 1990, 189–205, esp. 201.

25: GRATITUDE INSTEAD

1. This is probably the oldest surviving sentence in European prose, poetry being an older form of literary composition than is prose.

2. Simplicius quoted these words—part of a sentence, really—in his Commentary (ca. AD 540) on Aristotle's *Physics,* 24, 18 (DK 12 B1). By "all existing things" Anaximander

meant the Opposites—hot and cold, wet and dry, light and dark, and so on—which had separated themselves out from the *apeiron,* meaning "the infinite" or "endlessness."

3. We know more about Anaximander's cosmology from other indirect sources.

4. *Human, All Too Human.* (1870). Trans. Marion Faber and Stephen Lehmann. London: Penguin, 1994, p. 44.

5. See Matthew 5:43–48, where the adage is quoted in order to be revoked and replaced.

6. Aristotle, *Nichomachean Ethics* 2.1.

7. Thomas Aquinas, *Summa Theologica,* Question 108, p. 68.

8. Fritz Herder, 1958, p. 271.

9. Seneca, *De Beneficiis* 2.25.3.

10. Max Scheler (1874–1928) used the French word *ressentiment* to denote the powerless rage, envy, and vengefulness that produced the modern fascist personality, in a series of essays collected as *Das Ressentiment im Aufbau der Moralen.* Trans. William W. Holdheim as *Ressentiment.* New York: Schocken Books, 1972. First published 1915.

11. Shakespeare, *Hamlet* 1.5.91.

12. Aeschylus, *Agamemnon* lines 1376–1392. Trans. Richmond Lattimore.

13. Seneca, *De Beneficiis* 2.24.4. See also 2.22.1 and 2.23.1. We noted earlier that Jesus often told those he healed *not* to publicize what happened.

14. Homer, *Odyssey* 9, 475–542. Part of Odysseus's subterfuge involved calling himself "Nobody," so he has an even sharper need to proclaim that he is "somebody."

15. *Ma vengeance est perdue*

    S'il ignore en mourant que c'est moi qui le tue.

    (Jean Racine, *Andromaque* 4.4)

16. W.S. Gilbert and Arthur Sullivan, *The Mikado.* 1885.

17. See, for example, Gwen Raverat, *Period Piece. The Cambridge Childhood of Darwin's Granddaughter.* London: Faber and Faber, 1952 (2002 edition), p. 58. She gives further examples.

18. This event takes place after 87 lines of dialogue: *Eumenides,* lines 885–972, culminating in the joyful cry of Athene: "I admire the eyes of Persuasion, who guided the speech of my mouth toward these, when they were reluctant and wild!" (Notice that Athene does not *thank* Persuasion but praises her.)

19. Strictly speaking, the play is not about what we mean by "gratitude"; we noted earlier that this was not a major preoccupation of the Greeks, who did not have a word that precisely corresponds to the concept. The term used by the Eumenides for the opposite of vengefulness is *charmata,* "joys" or "delights."

20. Aeschylus, *Eumenides,* lines 980–87.

21. Ibid., line 988.

22. For the poem, its translation into English, and a commentary on it, see Hans Pieter Oskamp, 1970.

23. Charles Taylor, *Sources of the Self: The Making of the Modern Identity.* Cambridge, UK, and New York: Cambridge University Press, 1989, p. 516.

24. Genesis 1:31.

25. Cited by David W. Fagerberg, 1999, p. 452.

26. G.K. Chesterton, *St. Francis of Assisi. Collected Works.* San Francisco: Ignatius Press, 1986, p. 73. First published 1923.

27. Jean-Jacques Rousseau, *Emile.* Trans. Allan Bloom. New York: Basic Books, 1979, p. 221. First published 1762.

28. Immanuel Kant, *The Metaphysic of Morals,* 1797, and *Education.* Trans. Annette Churton. Boston: D.C. Heath, 1900, sections 98–100. First published 1803. Kant speaks both of beneficence (doing good) and of benevolence-and-gratitude (having goodwill and giving back).

29. Geoffrey Chaucer, "The Parson's Tale," *Canterbury Tales,* ca. 1390. X(I), lines 484–511.

30. Alan Dundes suggests that the modern rich may dress in torn old jeans to avert the evil eye of others, and that people, when asked how things are going, make deprecatory and therefore safe remarks such as "Not too bad" or "I'm not complaining." See "Wet and Dry, the Evil Eye," in his *Interpreting Folklore.* Bloomington: Indiana University Press, 1980, p. 94.

31. The English verb *to fascinate* originally meant "to cast a spell over."

32. Sigmund Freud, "The 'Uncanny.'" *Collected Papers* Vol. 4, New York: Basic Books, 1959, p. 393.

33. Feelings of envy shift and change with circumstance. An excellent description of the ugliness and torture that is envy is provided in Ovid, *Metamorphoses* 2. 760–832. Envy causes so many changing attitudes and emotions that its appropriate punishment is immobility: the envious one is metamorphosed into black stone.

34. Andrew Galloway, 1994, p. 371.

35. *"A peine a-t-on pressé l'orange qu'on la jette."* Baltasar Gracián y Morales (1601–1658), *Maximes* #5, Paris: Rollin fils, 1730.

26: PARTIALITY AND TRANSCENDENCE

1. Meredith Osmond, 1997.

2. Thomas Aquinas, *Summa Theologiae,* Question 106, 3.

3. Ralph Waldo Emerson, 1844, p. 324.

4. Seneca, *De Beneficiis* 4.9.2.

5. Marcel Proust, *Sodome et Gomorrhe. A la recherche du temps perdu.* 1913–1927. Paris: Pleiade, Vol. 2, p. 677. Alfred Dreyfus, imprisoned for high treason in 1894, was eventually proven not guilty.

6. Marina Tsvetaeva, 2002, pp. 118–19. The italics are hers.

7. Matthew 6:3.

8. Luke 10:25–37. There is a *command* to love one's neighbour and see to his needs; love of God is meaningless without it, and transcendence cannot begin without it either. See Leviticus 19:18, quoted in the Lucan passage together with Deuteronomy 6:5.

9. Aristotle, *Nicomachean Ethics* 8.1.4. In the same passage he says that "friendship appears to be the bond of the state; and lawgivers seem to set more store by it than they do by justice," because they wish to promote social concord, which is akin to friendship.

10. The ancient Christian prayer the *Gloria* grants to Christ, as God, the highest place: *tu solus altissimus*—"you alone are highest." This condemns in advance the claims of anyone else to the summit of power.

11. "Pour s'entraider." Manife*ste universel du Mouvement Emmaüs.* Paris: Emmaüs France.

12. Dag Hammarskjöld, 1965, p. 89.

13. Christians also believe that God came to live among us, made himself our brother in Jesus, and so gave human beings a new, previously unheard-of intimacy with himself.

14. The lyrics for the song, written by Jerry Leiber and Mike Stoller in 1969, are indebted to Thomas Mann's short story *"Enttäuschung,"* "Disillusionment" (1896). The disillusioned man in the story, however, remembers seeing the sea for the first time, and he "did feel a sudden tremendous craving for freedom, for a sea without a horizon."

15. Paris: Plon, 1988. First published 1947. *"Aucun événement n'est une faveur de Dieu,"* she writes, *la grâce seule.* "Grace is the only event that is a favour from God." The rest is "gravity" or "weight." p. 129.

16. Luke 12:48.

17. Matthew 20:1–16.

18. Cited by Dag Hammarskjöld, 1965, p. 61.

19. Thomas Aquinas, *Summa Theologiae.* Tome 1, Questions 37, 38. See most succinctly 1 John 4:8: "God is love."

20. See Jean-Luc Marion, 2003.

21. 1 Thessalonians 5:18; Ephesians 5:20; Colossians 3:15–17.

22. Julian of Norwich, ca. 1393, chapter 62. "God is kynde in his being," says Julian. "He is the same thing that is kindhede, and he is very fader and very moder [very father and mother] of kynde." For "kynde" see chapter 13, "The Fourth Law of Nature," pp. 183–84.

23. Julian Pitt-Rivers, 1992, pp. 235–36. He adds that that is what Marcel Mauss is really

doing in *The Gift:* explaining the evolution of the notion of contract. He regrets that Mauss lacks a notion of grace, and believes that the Maoris' famous *hau* in fact embodied the abstract principle of the gratuity of grace. Pitt-Rivers is one of a very few social scientists who have begun to study grace in conjunction with "the Gift." Another is Camille Tarot, 2000.

24. "*Tout est grâce*" was a favourite saying of Saint Thérèse of Lisieux.

25. Simone Weil, 1988, first published 1947, p. 75.

26. Etty Hillesum, 1943, p. 332. The final words in the last book of her diary to survive are "We should be willing to act as a balm for all wounds." p. 231. The final volume perished with her in Auschwitz.

27: RECOGNITION

1. See Risto Saarinen, 2005, p. 10.

2. Marina Tsvetaeva wants to do away with gifts, favours, and other expressions of love altogether: "Thank you—for being. Everything else, whether from me to another person or vice versa, is an insult." 2002, p. 119.

3. Montaigne, mourning his dead friend Etienne de La Boétie, describes how their love had made them one soul, although they remained two distinct people who each felt the other's uniqueness: "In the friendship I speak of, our souls mingle and blend with each other so completely that they efface the seam that joined them and cannot find it again. If you press me to tell why I loved him, I feel that it cannot be expressed, except by answering 'Because it was he, because it was I.'" *The Complete Essays of Montaigne.* Trans. Donald M. Frame. Stanford: Stanford University Press, 1957, p. 1239. First published 1595.

4. 1 Corinthians 4:7.

5. Matthew 10:8.

6. G.K. Chesterton, *The Autobiography.* Thirsk: House of Stratus, 2001, p. 58. First published 1936.

7. G.K. Chesterton, *Orthodoxy.* New York: Doubleday, 1990, p. 52. First published 1908.

8. Cited by David W. Fagerberg, 1999, p. 453, and by Philip Yancey in his introduction to Chesterton's *Orthodoxy* (note 7, above), p. xiv.

9. Claude Lévi-Strauss, 1950.

10. Raymond Firth, 1973, pp. 400–401.

11. Paul Ricoeur, 2004, p. 8.

12. Julian of Norwich, fourteenth century, chapter 41. Julian does not use the relatively

new scholastic word *gratitude*. The early English and Germanic *thankyng*, with its strong thoughtful and insightful component, is her term for the concept. See chapter 13, "The Fourth Law of Nature," pp. 181–82.

13. Clifton Wolters, in the Penguin modern English version of Julian's book, translates *new* in this passage as *real* (p. 125). But see the *Oxford English Dictionary*, s.v. "new," paragraph 9.

14. See Hans-Georg Gadamer, 1992, p. 35.

15. Julian of Norwich, chapter 43.

16. Ibid., chapter 41.

17. The main body of Paul Ricoeur's book, 2004, recounts this process: pp. 23–246.

18. Recognizing was for Thomas Aquinas the highest level of gratitude. The lowest depth of ingratitude was not recognizing. See chapter 22, "The Marble-Hearted Fiend," pp. 303–304. *Summa Theologica*, Question 106.

19. Stephen H. Webb, 1996, p. 157.

20. "*A la tarde se examinarán en el amor.*" Saint John of the Cross (1542–1591), *The Collected Works*. Washington, DC: The Institute of Carmelite Studies, 1979, p. 672, #57.

21. Dag Hammarskjöld, 1965, p. 38.

Bibliography

Aelian (Claudius Aelianus), (AD 165/170–230/235), *On the Characteristics of Animals*. 7.19, 23, 48; 8.3; 4.44; 10.16; 17.37–38.

Aeschylus (fifth century BC), in David Grene and Richmond Lattmore, eds. and trans., *Greek Tragedies*, Volume 1. Chicago: University of Chicago Press, 1991.

Aijmer, Karin, *Conversational Routines in English: Convention and Creativity*. London and New York: Longman, 1996.

Anspach, Mark R., *A charge de revanche: figures élémentaires de la réciprocité*. Paris: Seuil, 2002.

Anthony of Taizé, "Shakespeare's Monsters of Ingratitude," *The Shakespeare Review* (1990) 1–10.

Appadurai, Arjun, "Gratitude as a Social Mode in South India," *Ethos* 13(1985) 236–45.

———, "Topographies of the Self: Praise and Emotion in Hindu India," in Catherine Lutz and Lila Abu-Lugod, eds., *Language and the Politics of Emotion*. Cambridge, UK: Cambridge University Press, 1990. 92–112.

Apte, Mahadev L., "'Thank you' and South Asian languages: A Comparative Sociolinguistic Study," *International Journal of the Sociology of Language* 3(1974) 67–89.

Aquinas, Thomas (1225–1274), *Summa Theologiae*. Tome 1, Questions 37, 38; Tome 3, Questions 106, 107, 108. Ottawa: Commissio Piana. Trans. The Fathers of the English Dominican Province, *The Summa Theologica*. 1953.

Aristotle, 384–322 BC, *Nicomachean Ethics*. Trans. H. Rackham. Loeb Classical Library. Cambridge, MA: Harvard University Press, 1999.

Audet, Jean-Paul, "Esquisse historique du genre littéraire de la 'Bénédiction' juive et de l'Eucharistie' chrétienne," *Revue biblique* 65(1958) 371–99.

Augustine of Hippo (AD 354–430), *De correptione et gratia*. George Folliet, ed., *Sancti Augustini Opera*, Volume 42. Vienna: Österreichische Akademie der Wissenschaften, 2000.

Austin, J.L., *How to Do Things with Words*. Oxford: Clarendon Press, 1962.

Averill, James R., "The Acquisition of Emotions during Adulthood," in Rom Harré, ed., *The Social Construction of Emotions,* 1986. 98–118.

Barakat, Robert A., "Arabic gestures," *Journal of Popular Culture* 6(1972–73) 749–87.

Barbalet, J.M., *Emotion, Social Theory, and Social Structure: A Macrosociological Approach.* Cambridge, UK: Cambridge University Press, 1998.

Barnett, Homer G., "The Nature of the Potlatch," *American Anthropologist* 40(1938) 349–58.

Batifoulier, Philippe, Laurent Cordonnier, and Yves Zénou, "L'emprunt de la théorie économique à la tradition sociologique: Le cas du don contre-don," *Revue économique* 43(1992) 917–46.

Baumeister, Roy F., and Stacey A. Ilko, "Shallow Gratitude: Public and Private Acknowledgement of External Help in Accounts of Success," *Basic and Applied Social Psychology* 16(1995) 191–209.

Bäuml, Betty J., and Franz H. Bäuml, *A Dictionary of Gestures.* Metuchen, NJ: The Scarecrow Press, 1975.

Becker, J.A., and R.C. Smenner, "The Spontaneous Use of *Thank You* by Preschoolers as a Function of Sex, Socioeconomic Status, and Listener Status," *Language in Society* 15(1986) 537–46.

Becker, Lawrence C., *Reciprocity.* London: Routledge and Kegan Paul, 1986.

Befu, Harumi, "An Ethnography of Dinner Entertainment in Japan," *Arctic Anthropology* 11 (Supplement, 1974) 196–203.

———, "Gift-giving in a Modernizing Japan," in Takie Sugiyama Lebra and William P. Lebra, eds., *Japanese Culture and Behavior.* Honolulu: University of Hawaii Press, 1974. 208–21.

Benedict, Ruth, *The Chrysanthemum and the Sword: Patterns of Japanese Culture.* Cambridge, MA: Houghton Mifflin, 1946.

———, *Patterns of Culture.* New York: Mentor, 1960.

Benveniste, Emile, *Indo-European Language and Society.* Trans. Jean Lallot. London: Faber and Faber, 1973. 53–70, 159–62.

Ben-Ze'ev, Aaron, *The Subtlety of Emotions.* Cambridge, MA: MIT Press, 2000.

Berger, Fred R., "Gratitude," *Ethics* 85(1975) 298–309.

Berking, Helmuth, *Sociology of Giving.* Trans. Patrick Camiller. London: Sage, 1999.

Berkwitz, Stephen C., "History and Gratitude in Theravada Buddhism," *Journal of the American Academy of Religion* (2003) 579–604.

Bernasconi, Robert, "What Goes Around Comes Around: Derrida and Levinas on the Economy of the Gift and the Gift of Genealogy," in Alan D. Schrift, ed., *The Logic of the Gift,* 1997. 256–73.

Berns, Laurence, "Gratitude, Nature, and Piety in *King Lear,*" *Interpretation* (The Hague) 3(1972) 27–51.

Betteridge, Anne H., "Gift Exchange in Iran: The Locus of Self-identity in Social
Interaction," *Anthropological Quarterly* 58(1985) 190–202.

The Jerusalem Bible, Old and New Testaments. New York: Doubleday, 1968.

Bickerman, E.J., "Bénédiction et prière," *Revue biblique* 69(1962) 524–32.

Blau, Peter M., *Exchange and Power in Social Life.* New York: John Wiley, 1964.

Bonnie, Kristin E., and Frans B.M. de Waal, "Primate Social Reciprocity and the Origin of
Gratitude," in Robert A. Emmons and Michael E. McCullough, eds., *The Psychology of
Gratitude,* 2004. 213–29.

Bourdieu, Pierre, *Outline of a Theory of Practice.* Trans. Richard Nice. Cambridge, MA:
Cambridge University Press, 1977.

———, "The Work of Time," in *The Logic of Practice.* Trans. Richard Nice. Cambridge, MA:
Polity, 1990. First published 1980. 98–111.

———, "Un acte désintéressé est-il possible?" in his *Raisons pratiques: Sur la théorie de l'action.*
Paris: Seuil, 1994. Chapter 5.

———, "Marginalia—Some Additional Notes on the Gift," in Alan D. Schrift, ed., *The Logic
of the Gift,* 1997. 231–41.

Bremer, Jan-Maarten, "The Reciprocity of Giving and Thanksgiving in Greek Worship," in
Christopher Gill et al., eds., *Reciprocity in Ancient Greece,* 1998. 127–37.

Brodeur, Arthur G., "The Grateful Lion. A Study in the Development of Mediaeval
Narrative," *PMLA* 39(1924) 485–524.

Brooks, Jeffrey, *Thank you, Comrade Stalin!: Soviet Public Culture from Revolution to Cold War.*
Princeton, NJ: Princeton University Press, 2000.

Brown, Penelope, and Stephen C. Levinson, *Politeness. Some Universals in Language Usage.*
Cambridge, UK: Cambridge University Press, 1987.

Burkert, Walter, *Greek Religion.* Oxford: Blackwell, 1985. 66–75.

Caillé, Alain, *Anthropologie du don: le tiers paradigme.* Paris: Desclée de Brouwer, 2000.

Callahan, Daniel, "What Do Children Owe Elderly Parents?" *Hastings Center Report* 15(1985,
April) 32–7.

Camenisch, Paul F., "Gift and Gratitude in Ethics," *Journal of Religious Ethics* 9(1981) 1–34.

Camerer, Colin, "Gifts as Economic Signals and Social Symbols," *American Journal of Sociology*
94 (Supplement, 1988) 180–212.

Campbell, Shirley F., *The Art of Kula.* Oxford and New York: Berg, 2002.

Caplow, Theodore, "Rule Enforcement Without Visible Means: Christmas Gift Giving in
Middletown," *American Journal of Sociology* 89(1984) 1306–23.

Card, Claudia, "Gratitude and Obligation," *American Philosophical Quarterly* 25(1988) 115–27.

Carman, John B., and Frederick J. Streng, *Spoken and Unspoken Thanks: Some Comparative
Soundings.* Dallas: Center for World Thanksgiving, 1989.

Carrier, James G., *Gifts and Commodities: Exchange and Western Capitalism since 1700*. London and New York: Routledge, 1995.

Chaumartin, François-Régis, *Le 'De Beneficiis' de Sénèque, sa signification philosophique, politique, et sociale*. Paris: Les Belles Lettres, 1985.

Cheal, David, "'Showing Them You Love Them': Gift Giving and the Dialectic of Intimacy," *Sociological Review* 35(1987) 150–69.

———, *The Gift Economy*. London: Routledge, 1988.

Clark, Herbert H., and J. Wade French, "Telephone Goodbyes," *Language in Society* 10(1981) 1–19.

Clavero, Bartolomé, *La Grâce du don: anthropologie catholique de l'économie moderne*. Foreword by Jacques Le Goff; trans. Jean-Frédéric Schaub. Paris: Albin Michel, 1996. First published in Spanish as *Antidora, 1990*.

Cobbi, Jane, "Don et contre-don. Une tradition à l'épreuve de la modernité," in Augustin Berque, ed., *Le Japon et son double*. Paris: Masson, 1987. 159–68.

———, "L'obligation du cadeau au Japon," in Charles Malamoud, ed., *Lien de vie, noeud mortel. Les représentations de la dette en Chine, au Japon et dans le monde entier*. Paris: EHESS, 1988. 113–65.

Coulmas, Florian, "On the Sociolinguistic Relevance of Routine Formulae," *Journal of Pragmatics* 3(1979) 239–66.

———, ed., *Conversational Routine: Explorations in Standardized Communication Situations and Prepatterned Speech*. The Hague, Paris: Mouton, 1981.

———, "Poison to Your Soul: Thanks and Apologies Contrastively Viewed," in his *Conversational Routine, 1981*. 69–92.

Cousin, Bernard, *Le miracle et le quotidien: Les ex-voto provençaux, images d'une société*. Aix-en-Provence: Edition Sociétés, Mentalités, Cultures, 1983.

Creighton, Millie R., "Maintaining Cultural Boundaries in Retailing: How Japanese Department Stores Domesticate 'Things Foreign,'" *Modern Asian Studies* 25(1991) 675–709.

———, "'Sweet Love' and Women's Place: Valentine's Day, Japan Style," *Journal of Popular Culture* 27(1993) 1–19.

Cropp, Glynnis, *Le vocabulaire courtois des troubadours à l'époque classique*. Geneva: Droz, 1975. 174–80.

Darwin, Charles, *The Expression of the Emotions in Man and Animals*. London: John Murray, 1873.

Davidson, William L., "Gratitude," in James Hastings, ed., *Encyclopaedia of Religion and Ethics*. New York: Charles Scribner, 1921. Vol. 6, 390–92.

Davies, Eirlys E., "A Contrastive Approach to the Analysis of Politeness Formulas," *Applied Linguistics* 8(1987) 75–88.

Davis, Natalie Zemon, *The Gift in Sixteenth-Century France.* Madison, WI: University of Wisconsin Press, 2000.

De Courtin, Antoine, *Nouveau traité de la civilité.* Ed. Marie-Claire Grassi. Clermont-Ferrand: L'Université de Saint-Etienne, 1998. First published 1672.

De Garis, Frédéric, *We Japanese.* Miyanoshita, Hakone, Japan: Fujiya Hotel Ltd., 1934.

Derrida, Jacques, *Given Time: I. Counterfeit Money.* Trans. Peggy Kamuf. Chicago: University of Chicago Press, 1992.

DeSilva, David A., *Perseverance in Gratitude: A Socio-rhetorical Commentary on the Epistle "to the Hebrews."* Grand Rapids, MI: Wm. B. Eerdmans, 2000.

Dillon, Wilton S., *Gifts and Nations: The Obligation to Give, Receive and Repay.* La Hague-Maris: Mouton, 1968.

Dixon, Thomas, *From Passions to Emotions: The Creation of a Secular Psychological Category.* Cambridge, UK, and New York: Cambridge University Press, 2003.

Donald, Merlin, "Origins of the Modern Mind: Three Stages in the Evolution of Culture and Cognition," *Behavioral and Brain Sciences* 16(1993) 737–91.

Douglas, Mary, "No Free Gifts." Foreword to Marcel Mauss, *Essay on the Gift.* 1990.

Dunn, Ellen Catherine, *The Concept of Ingratitude in Renaissance English Moral Philosophy.* Washington, DC: The Catholic University of America Press, 1946.

Dyson-Hudson, R., and R. Van Dusen, "Food Sharing Among Young Children," *Ecology of Food and Nutrition* 1(1972) 319–24.

Eibl-Eibesfeldt, Irenäus, "Social Interactions in an Ethological, Cross-Cultural Perspective," in Fernando Poyatos, ed., *Cross-Cultural Perspectives in Nonverbal Communication.* Toronto: C.J. Hogrefe, 1988.

Eisenstein, Miriam, and Jean Bodman, "'I Very Appreciate': Expressions of Gratitude by Native and Non-native Speakers of American English," *Applied Linguistics* 7(1986) 167–85.

———, "Expressing Gratitude in American English," in Gabriele Kasper and Shoshana Blum-Kulka, eds., *Interlanguage Pragmatics.* New York: Oxford University Press, 1993. Chapter 3.

Ekman, Paul, "All Emotions Are Basic," in Paul Ekman and Richard J. Davidson, eds., *The Nature of Emotion: Fundamental Questions.* New York and Oxford: Oxford University Press, 1994.

Elliott, Alison Goddard, *Roads to Paradise: Reading the Lives of the Early Saints.* Hanover and London: Brown University Press, 1987.

El-Sayed, Ali M., "Politeness Formulas in English and Arabic: A Contrastive Study," *Indian Journal of Applied Linguistics* 15(1989) 96–113.

Elster, Jon, *Alchemies of the Mind: Rationality and the Emotions.* Cambridge, UK, and New York: Cambridge University Press, 1999.

Emerson, Ralph Waldo, "Gifts," in *Ralph Waldo Emerson: Essays and Journals*. New York: Doubleday, 1968. 322–25. First published in *Essays, First and Second Series*, 1844.

Emmons, Robert A., and C.A. Crumpler, "Gratitude as Human Strength: Appraising the Evidence," *Journal of Social and Clinical Psychology* 19(2000) 56–69.

———, and Michael E. McCullough, eds., *The Psychology of Gratitude*. New York: Oxford University Press, 2004.

English, Jane, "What Do Grown Children Owe Their Parents?" in Onora O'Neill and William Ruddick, eds., *Having Children*. New York: Oxford University Press, 1979.

Erasmus, Desiderius, *De conscribendis epistolis* and *De civilitate morum puerilium libellus*. Froben, Bale, 1530. Trans. B. McGregor, in *Literary and Educational Writings*, Vol. 25 of *Collected Works of Erasmus*, ed. J.K. Sowards. Toronto: University of Toronto Press, 1985.

———, *Adages*. Vols. 34–36 of *Collected Works of Erasmus*.

Fadiman, Jeffrey A., "A Business Traveler's Guide to Gifts and Bribes," in William H. Shaw and Vincent Barry, eds., *Moral Issues in Business*. Wadsworth Publishing, California, 1995. 400–08.

Fagerberg, David W., "Gratitude as the Basis for Asceticism in Chesterton," *The Chesterton Review* 25(1999) 451–77.

Ferguson, John, *Among the Gods. An Archaeological Exploration of Ancient Greek Religion*. London and New York: Routledge, 1989.

Ferguson, Kennan, "The Gift of Freedom," *Social Text* 25 (2007) 39–52.

Finkielkraut, Alain, *L'Ingratitude*. Paris: Gallimard, 1999.

Firth, Raymond, "Postures and Gestures of Respect," in Jean Pouillon and Pierre Maranda, *Échanges et communications: Mélanges offerts à Claude Lévi-Strauss*. Tome I. The Hague, Paris: Mouton, 1970. 188–209.

———, *Economics of the New Zealand Maori*. Wellington: A.R. Shearer, 1972.

———, "Symbolism in Giving and Getting," in his *Symbols, Public and Private*. London: Allen and Unwin, 1973. 368–402.

Fitzgerald, Patrick, "Gratitude and justice," *Ethics* (1998) 119–53.

Foster, George M., "The Anatomy of Envy: A Study in Symbolic Behavior," *Current Anthropology* 13(1972) 165–202.

Freud, Sigmund, "Further Recommendations in the Technique of Psycho-Analysis," 1913, in *Collected Papers* Vol. 2. New York: Basic Books, 1959. 342–65.

Funk and Wagnalls Standard Dictionary of Folklore, Mythology, and Legend. Sacramento, CA: HarperSanFrancisco, 1972.

Gadamer, Hans-Georg, "Danken und Gedenken," in Josef Seifert, ed., *Danken und Dankbarkeit*, 1992. 27–36.

Galloway, Andrew, "The Making of a Social Ethic in Late-Medieval England: From *Gratitudo* to 'Kyndenesse,'" *Journal of the History of Ideas* 55(1994) 365–83.

Garrity, Kimberly, and Douglas Degelman, "Effect of Server Introduction on Restaurant Tipping," *Journal of Applied Social Psychology* 20(1990) 168–72.

Gerould, Gordon Hall, *The Grateful Dead. The History of a Folk Story.* London: David Nutt, 1908.

Gill, Christopher, Norman Postlethwaite, and Richard Seaford, eds., *Reciprocity in Ancient Greece.* Oxford: Oxford University Press, 1998.

Gillis, John R., *A World of Their Own Making: Myth, Ritual, and the Quest for Family Values.* New York: Basic Books, 1996.

Girard, René, *Je vois Satan tomber comme l'éclair.* Paris: Bernard Grasset, 1999.

Gleason, Jean Berko, and S. Weintraub, "The Acquisition of Routines in Child Language," *Language in Society* 5(1976) 129–36.

Gleason, Jean Berko, Rivka Y. Perlmann, and Esther Blank Greif, "What's the Magic Word: Learning Language through Politeness Routines," *Discourse Processes* 7(1984) 493–502.

Godbout, Jacques T., and Alain Caillé, *L'Esprit du don.* Montréal: Boréal, 1992.

———, *Ce qui circule entre nous: Donner, recevoir, rendre.* Paris: Seuil, 2007.

Godelier, Maurice, *L'Enigme du don.* Paris: Flammarion, 1996.

Goffman, Erving, "The Nature of Deference and Demeanor," *American Anthropologist* 58(1956) 473–502.

———, *The Presentation of Self in Everyday Life.* New York: Doubleday Anchor Books, 1959.

———, *Behavior in Public Places: Notes on the Social Organization of Gatherings.* New York: Macmillan, The Free Press, 1963.

———, *Interaction Ritual.* New York: Doubleday (Anchor), 1967.

———, *Relations in Public: Microstudies of the Public Order.* New York: Harper and Row, 1971.

Goldie, Peter, *The Emotions: A Philosophical Exploration.* Oxford: Oxford University Press, 2000.

Goodin, Robert E., "Do Motives Matter?" *Canadian Journal of Philosophy* 19(1989) 405–19.

Goody, Esther, "'Greeting,' 'Begging,' and the Presentation of Respect," in J.S. La Fontaine, ed., *The Interpretation of Ritual: Essays in Honour of A.I. Richards.* London: Tavistock, 1972. 39–71.

Gould, John, "*Hiketeia*," *Journal of Hellenic Studies* 93(1973) 74–103.

———, *Give-and-take in Herodotus.* The Fifteenth J.L. Myres Memorial Lecture. Oxford: Leopard's Head, 1991.

Gouldner, Alvin W., "The Norm of Reciprocity: A Preliminary Statement," *American Sociological Review* 25(1960) 161–78.

Greenberg, Martin S., "A Theory of Indebtedness," in Kenneth J. Gergen, Martin S. Greenberg, and Richard H. Willis, eds., *Social Exchange: Advances in Theory and Research.* New York: Plenum, 1980. 3–26.

Greenberg, Martin S., and Solomon P. Shapiro, "Indebtedness: An Adverse Aspect of Asking for and Receiving Help," *Sociometry* 34(1971) 290–301.

Greenberg, Martin S., and David R. Westcott, "Indebtedness as a Mediator of Reactions to Aid," in J.D. Fisher, A. Nadler, and B.M. DePaulo, eds., *New Directions in Helping: Recipient Reactions to Aid.* New York: Academic Press, 1983. 85–112.

Gregory, C.A., *Gifts and Commodities.* London: Academic Press, 1982.

Greif, Esther Blank, and Jean Berko Gleason, "Hi, Thanks, and Goodbye: More Routine Information," *Language in Society* 9(1980) 159–66.

Gumperz, John, *Discourse Strategies.* Cambridge, UK, and New York: Cambridge University Press, 1974.

Guthrie, Harvey, *Theology as Thanksgiving: From Israel's Psalms to the Church's Eucharist.* New York: Seabury Press, 1981.

Haight, Roger, *The Experience and Language of Grace.* New York: Paulist Press, 1979.

Halkin, Léon, *La supplication d'action de grâces chez les Romains.* Paris: Les Belles Lettres, 1953.

Hammarskjöld, Dag, *Markings.* Trans. Leif Sjöberg and W.H. Auden. New York: Alfred A. Knopf, 1965.

Harkins, Jean, and Anna Wierzbicka, eds., *Emotions in Crosslinguistic Perspective.* Amsterdam: Mouton de Gruyter, 2001.

Harré, Rom, "Emotion Talk Across Times," in Rom Harré, ed., *The Social Construction of Emotions,* 1986. 220–33.

———, ed., *The Social Construction of Emotions.* New York: Blackwell, 1986.

Healey, C.J., "New Guinea Inland Trade: Transformation and Resilience in the Context of Capitalist Penetration," *Mankind* 15(1985) 127–44.

Heelas, Paul, "Emotion Talk Across Cultures," in Rom Harré, ed., *The Social Construction of Emotions,* 1986. 234–66.

Heidegger, Martin, *What Is Called Thinking?* Trans. J. Glenn Gray and Fred D. Wieck. New York: Harper and Row, 1968, Part II, Lecture 3. First published as *Was Heisst Denken?* Tübingen: Max Niemayer, 1954.

Hénaff, Marcel, *Le Prix de la vérité: le don, l'argent, la philosophie.* Paris: Seuil, 2002.

Hendry, Joy, *Wrapping Culture: Politeness, Presentation and Power in Japan and Other Societies.* Oxford: Clarendon Press, 1993.

Henrich, Dieter, "Gedanken zur Dankbarkeit," in Reinhard Löw, ed., *Oikeiosis. Festschrift für Robert Spaemann.* Weinheim: VCH Verlag, 1987. 69–86.

Henry, O., "The Gift of the Magi" (1905), in *The Four Million.* New York: Doubleday (Doran), 1919. 16–25.

Herbert, George (1593–1633), *The English Poems of George Herbert.* Ed. C.A. Patrides. Everyman's Library. London: J.M. Dent & Sons Ltd., 1974. "Gratefulness," "The Thanksgiving," "Ungratefulness."

Herder, Fritz, *The Psychology of Interpersonal Relations.* New York: John Wiley, 1958. 265–76.

Hewitt, Joseph William, "On the Development of the Thank-Offering Among the Greeks," *Transactions of the American Philological Association* 43(1912) 95–111.

———, "The Thank-Offering and Greek Religious Thought," *Transactions of the American Philological Association* 45(1914) 77–90.

———, "Some Aspects of the Treatment of Ingratitude in Greek and English Literature," *Transactions of the American Philological Association* 48(1917) 37–48.

———, "Gratitude and Ingratitude in the Plays of Euripides," *The American Journal of Philology* 43(1922) 331–43.

———, "The Development of Political Gratitude," *Transactions of the American Philological Association* 55(1924) 35–51.

———, "The Terminology of 'Gratitude' in Greek," *Classical Philology* 22(1927) 142–61.

———, "Gratitude to Parents in Greek and Roman Literature," *American Journal of Philology* 52(1931) 30–48.

Hill, Jr., Thomas E., "Kant on Imperfect Duty and Supererogation," *Kant-Studien* 62(1971) 55–76.

Hillesum, Etty (1914–1943), *An Interrupted Life. The Diaries, 1941–1943, and Letters from Westerbork.* Trans. Arnold J. Pomerans. New York: Henry Holt, 1996. First published in Dutch, 1981.

Hobbes, Thomas, *Leviathan, or the Matter, Form, and Power of a Commonwealth, Ecclesiastical and Civil.* New York: Dutton, 1950. First published 1651.

Hochschild, Arlie Russell, *The Managed Heart: The Commercialization of Human Feelings.* Berkeley: University of California Press, 1983.

———, "The Economy of Gratitude," in David D. Franks and E. Doyle McCarthy, eds., *The Sociology of Emotions: Original Essays and Research Papers.* Greenwich, CT: JAI Press, 1989. 95–113.

Hohendahl-Zoetelief, J.M., *Manners in the Homeric Epic: The Uses of Literacy.* Leiden: Brill, 1980. Chapter 4.

Hyde, Lewis, *The Gift: Imagination and the Erotic Life of Property.* New York: Vintage Books, 1983. First published 1979.

Hyde, Michael J., *The Life-Giving Gift of Acknowledgement: A Philosophical and Rhetorical Inquiry.* West Lafayette, IN: Purdue University Press, 2006.

Ide, Risako, "'Sorry for Your Kindness': Japanese Interactional Ritual in Public Discourse," *Journal of Pragmatics* 29(1998) 509–29.

Jankélévitch, Vladimir, *Traité des vertus.* 3 vols. Paris, Montréal: Bordas, 1968. First published 1949.

Jecker, Nancy S., "Are Filial Duties Unfounded?" *American Philosophical Quarterly* 26(1989) 73–80.

————, "Justice and Mother Love: Toward a Critical Theory of Justice between Old and Young," in T.R. Cole, W.A. Achenbaum, P. Jakobi, R. Katenbaum, eds., *Voices and Visions of Aging: Toward a Critical Gerontology.* New York: Springer, 1993.

Johnson, Samuel, Letter to Chesterfield, February 7, 1755, in R.T. Davies, ed., *Selected Writings of Samuel Johnson.* Evanston, Illinois: Northwestern University Press, 1965.

Joüon, Paul, "Reconnaissance et remerciement en hébreu biblique," *Biblica* 4(1923) 381–85.

————, "*Reconnaissance et action de grâces dans le Nouveau Testament,*" *Recherches de Science Religieuse* 29(1939) 112–14.

Julian of Norwich (1342–post-1413), *A Revelation of Love.* Ed. Marion Glasscoe. University of Exeter: Exeter Medieval English Texts and Studies, 1986. Ms. completed post 1393. Modern English edition, *Revelations of Divine Love.* Trans. Clifton Wolters. London: Penguin, 1982.

Kant, Immanuel, *Lectures on Ethics.* Trans. Lewis Infield. London: Methuen, 1930. First published 1780.

————, *The Doctrine of Virtue.* Part 2 of *The Metaphysic of Morals.* Trans. Mary J. Gregor. Philadelphia: University of Pennsylvania Press, 1964. First published 1797.

Kasachkoff, Tziporah, "Paternalism: Does Gratitude Make it Okay?" *Social Theory and Practice* 20(1994) 1–23.

Kemper, Theodore D., "How Many Emotions are There? Wedding the Social and the Autonomic Components," *American Journal of Sociology* 93(1987) 263–89.

Kerbrat-Orecchioni, Catherine, *Les interactions verbales.* Vol. 3. Paris: Armand Colin, 1994.

King, Alex, *Memorials of the Great War in Britain: The Symbolism and Politics of Remembrance.* Oxford and New York: Berg, 1998.

Klein, Melanie, "Envy and Gratitude," in *Envy and Gratitude and Other Works 1946–1963.* First published 1957. London: Virago, 1988. 176–235.

Komter, Aafke E., "Reciprocity as a Principle of Exclusion," *Sociology* 30(1996) 299–316.

————, ed., *The Gift: An Interdisciplinary Perspective.* Amsterdam: Amsterdam University Press, 1996.

————, "The Social and Psychological Significance of Gift Giving in the Netherlands" and "Women, Gifts and Power," in her *The Gift: An Interdisciplinary Perspective.* 1996. 107–31.

Kott, Sandrine, "Le don comme rituel en R.D.A. 1949–1989: Instrument de domination et pratiques quotidiennes," *Le Mouvement Social* 194(2001) 67–83.

Kövecses, Zoltán, *Emotion concepts.* Berlin, Heidelberg and New York: Springer, 1990.

Kumatoridani, Tetsuo, "Alternation and Co-occurrence in Japanese Thanks," *Journal of Pragmatics* 31(1999) 623–42.

Kurzon, Dennis, "The White House Speeches: Semantic and Paralinguistic Strategies for Eliciting Applause," *Text* 16(1996) 199–224.

Lacroix, Michel, "L'art de remercier," in *De la Politesse: Essai sur la littérature du savoir-vivre.* Paris: Commentaire/Julliard, 1990. 375–81.

Laidlaw, James, "A Free Gift Makes No Friends," *Journal of the Royal Anthropological Institute* 6 (2000) 617–34.

Lamb, Charles, *The Essays of Elia and The Last Essays of Elia.* "Grace Before Meat," 132–40; Popular Fallacies XI: "That We Must Not Look a Gift-Horse in the Mouth," 376–79. London: Oxford University Press, 1964. First published 1820–33.

Laporte, Jean, *Eucharistia in Philo.* New York and Toronto: Edwin Mellen, 1983.

La Rochefoucauld, François de, *Maximes et réflexions diverses.* Paris: Gallimard, 1976. First published 1664.

Laughlin, Charles D., "On the Spirit of the Gift," *Journal of the Indian Anthropological Society* 2(1986) 156–76.

Lazarus, Richard S., and Bernie N. Lazarus, *Passion and Reason: Making Sense of Our Emotions.* NY: Oxford University Press, 1994.

Lebra, Takie Sugiyama, *Japanese Patterns of Behavior.* Honolulu: University Press of Hawaii, 1976. 90–109.

Leddy, Mary Jo, *Radical Gratitude.* Maryknoll, NY: Orbis, 2002.

Lederman, Rena, *What Gifts Engender: Social Relations and Politics in Mendi, Highland Papua New Guinea.* Cambridge, UK, and New York: Cambridge University Press, 1986.

Leech, Geoffrey N., *Principles of Pragmatics.* London: Longman, 1983.

Leithart, Peter J., "City of In-gratia: Roman Ingratitude in Shakespeare's *Coriolanus,*" *Literature and Theology* 20(2006) 341–60.

Lévi-Strauss, Claude, *The Elementary Structures of Kinship.* Trans. James Harle Bell, John Richard von Sturmer, and Rodney Needham. Boston: Beacon Press, 1969. First published as *Les structures élémentaires de la parenté.* Paris: P.U.F., 1949. Chapter 5.

———, "Introduction à l'oeuvre de Marcel Mauss," in Marcel Mauss, *Sociologie et anthropologie.* Paris: P.U.F., 1985, ix–xii. First published 1950.

Lewinter, Myra, *Spreading the Burden of Gratitude: The Elderly between Family and State.* Copenhagen: University of Copenhagen Press, 1999.

Liljeblad, Sven S., *Die Tobiasgeschichte und andere Märchen mit toten Helfern.* Lund: P. Lindstedt, 1927.

LiPuma, Edward, *The Gift of Kinship. Structure and Practice in Maring Social Organization.* Cambridge, UK, and New York: Cambridge University Press, 1988.

Locke, John, *The Second Treatise of Government* in *Two Treatises of Government.* New York: Cambridge University Press, 1960. First published 1690. Section 66.

Lombard-Jourdan, Anne, "L'invention du 'roi fondateur' à Paris au XIIe siècle: De l'obligation morale au thème sculptural," *Bibliothèque de l'Ecole des chartes* 155(1997) 485–542.

Lutz, Catherine, and Geoffrey M. White, "The Anthropology of Emotions," *Annual Review of Anthropology* 15(1986) 405–36.

Lynch, Owen M., "The Social Construction of Emotions in India," in Owen M. Lynch, ed., *Divine Passions: The Social Construction of Emotions in India.* Berkeley: University of California Press, 1990.

Lynn, Michael, George M. Zinkhan, and Judy Harris, "Consumer Tipping: A Cross-country Study," *Journal of Consumer Research* 20(1993) 478–88.

Lyons, Daniel, "The Odd Debt of Gratitude," *Analysis* 29(1969) 92–97.

MacIntyre, Alasdair, *After Virtue.* London: Duckworth, 1999. First published 1981.

MacLachlan, Bonnie, *The Age of Grace: Charis in Early Greek Poetry.* Princeton, NJ: Princeton University Press, 1993.

Malamoud, Charles, *Lien de vie, Noeud mortel. Les représentations de la dette en Chine, au Japon, et dans le monde indien.* Paris: Editions de l'Ecole des Hautes Etudes en Sciences Sociales, 1988.

Malinowski, Bronislaw, *Argonauts of the Western Pacific: An Account of Native Enterprise and Adventure in the Archipelagoes of Melanesian New Guinea.* London: Routledge and Kegan Paul, 1922.

Manes, Joan, and Nessa Wolfson, "The Compliment Formula," in Florian Coulmas, ed., *Conversational Routine,* 1981. 115–32.

Maraniello, Gianfranco, Sergio Risaliti, Antonio Somaini, eds., *Il Dono. Offerta, ospitalità, insidia.* Milan: Charta, 2001.

Marion, Jean-Luc, *Etant donné: Essai d'une phénoménologie de la donation.* Paris: P.U.F., 1997. Trans. *Being Given: Toward a Phenomenology of Givenness.* Stanford, CA: Stanford University Press, 2002.

Marshall, Lorna, "Sharing, Talking, and Giving: Relief of Social Tensions among !Kung Bushmen," *Africa,* 31(1961) 231–49.

Martin, Judith, *Miss Manners Rescues Civilization from Sexual Harassment, Frivolous Lawsuits, Dissing, and Other Lapses in Civility.* New York: Crown, 1996.

Martin, Mike W., *Love's Virtues.* Lawrence: University Press of Kansas, 1996. 164–77.

———, "Good Fortune Obligates: Gratitude, Philanthropy, and Colonialism," *The Southern Journal of Philosophy* 37(1999) 57–75.

Mauss, Marcel, *The Gift: The Form and Reason for Exchange in Archaic Societies.* Foreword by Mary Douglas. London and New York: Routledge, 2002. First published 1923.

———, "Gift, Gift," trans. Koen Decoster, in Alan D. Schrift, ed., *The Logic of the Gift,* 1997, 28–32. First published in *Mélanges offerts à M. Charles Andler par ses amis et ses élèves,* 1924.

McConnell, Terrance C., *Gratitude.* Philadelphia: Temple University Press, 1993.

McCraty, Rollin, and Doc Childre, "The Grateful Heart: The Psychophysiology of

Appreciation," in Robert A. Emmons and Michael E. McCullough, eds., *The Psychology of Gratitude,* 2004. 230–58.

McCullough, Michael E., Robert A. Emmons, Jo-Ann Tsang, "The Grateful Disposition: A Conceptual and Empirical Topography," *Journal of Personality and Social Psychology* 82(2002) 112–27.

———, Jo-Ann Tsang, Robert A. Emmons, "Gratitude in Intermediate Affective Terrain: Links of Grateful Moods to Individual Differences and Daily Emotional Experience," *Journal of Personality and Social Psychology* 86(2004) 295–309.

Meilaender, Gilbert C., *The Theory and Practice of Virtue.* Notre Dame, IN: University of Notre Dame Press, 1984. Chapter 7.

Milbank, John, "Can a Gift Be Given?" in Gregory Jones, ed., *Rethinking Metaphysics.* Cambridge, MA: Blackwell, 1995. 119–61.

Montandon, Alain, ed., *Etiquette et politesse.* Clermont-Ferrand: Association des Publications de la Faculté des Lettres et Sciences Humaines de Clermont-Ferrand, 1992.

Morris, Ian, "Gift and Commodity in Archaic Greece," *Man* 21(1986) 1–17.

Moussy, Claude, *Gratia et sa famille.* Paris: P.U.F., 1966.

Nagatomi, Masatoshi, "Gratitude as Thanksgiving and Thanksgiving as Gratitude," in John B. Carman and Frederick J. Streng, eds., *Spoken and Unspoken Thanks: Some Comparative Soundings,* 1989. 76–80.

Narayanan, Vasudha, "Reciprocal Gratitude: Divine and Human Acts of Thanksgiving," in John B. Carman and Frederick J. Streng, eds., *Spoken and Unspoken Thanks: Some Comparative Soundings,* 1989. 23–31.

Nietzsche, Friedrich, *Thus Spoke Zarathustra.* Trans. R.J. Hollingdale. New York: Penguin, 1961. First published 1883–92.

Noonan, John T., *Bribes.* London: Macmillan, 1984.

Norman, Henry, *The Real Japan.* London: T.F. Unwin, 1908.

Norrick, Neal R., "Expressive Illocutionary Acts," *Journal of Pragmatics* 2(1978) 277–91.

———, "The Speech Act of Complimenting," in E. Hoodhaugen, ed., *The Nordic Languages and Modern Linguistics.* Oslo: Universitetsforlager, 1980. 296–304.

Okamoto Shinichiro, and W. Peter Robinson, "Determinants of Gratitude Expressions in England," *Journal of Language and Social Psychology* 16(1997) 411–33.

Oktavec, Eileen, *Answered Prayers. Miracles and Milagros Along the Border.* Tucson: University of Arizona Press, 1995.

Onians, Richard Broxton, *The Origins of European Thought about the Body, the Mind, the Soul, the World, Time, and Fate.* Cambridge, UK: Cambridge University Press, 1988. First published 1951.

Ortony, Andrew, Gerald L. Clore, Allan Collins, *The Cognitive Structure of Emotions.* Cambridge, UK, and New York: Cambridge University Press, 1988.

Oskamp, Hans Pieter, *The Voyage of Máel Dúin: A Study in Early Irish Voyage Literature.* Gröningen: Wolters-Noordhoff, 1970.

Osmond, Meredith, "The Prepositions We Use in the Construal of Emotion: Why Do We Say *fed up with* but *sick and tired of?*" in Susanne Niermeier and René Dirven, *The Language of Emotions.* Amsterdam and Philadelphia: John Benjamins, 1997. 111–33.

Parry, Jonathan, "The Gift, the Indian Gift, and the 'Indian Gift,'" *Man* 21 (1986) 453–73.

Paul, Ellen Frankel, Fred D. Miller, Jeffrey Paul, eds., *Altruism.* Cambridge, UK, and New York: Cambridge University Press, 1993. Chapter 13.

Pitt-Rivers, Julian, "Postscript: The Place of Grace in Anthropology," in J.G. Peristiany and Julian Pitt-Rivers, eds., *Honor and Grace in Anthropology.* New York: Cambridge University Press, 1992. 215–46.

Quincey, J.H., "Greek Expressions of Thanks," *The Journal of Hellenic Studies* 86 (1966) 133–58.

Raheja, Gloria Goodwin, *The Poison in the Gift: Ritual Presentations and the Dominant Caste in a North Indian Village.* Chicago, IL: University of Chicago Press, 1988.

Richards, David A.J., *A Theory of Reasons for Action.* Oxford: Clarendon, 1971.

Riches, David, "The Obligation to Give—An Interactional Sketch," in Ladislav Holy and Milan Stuchlik, eds., *The Structure of Folk Models.* London: Academic, 1981. 209–31.

Ricoeur, Paul, "Love and Justice," in Werner G. Jeanrond and Jennifer L. Rike, *Radical Pluralism and Truth.* New York: Crossroad, 1991. 187–202.

———, *Parcours de la reconnaissance: Trois Etudes.* Paris: Stock, 2004. Trans. David Pellauer, *The Course of Recognition.* Cambridge, MA: Harvard University Press, 2005.

Roberts, Robert C., "Therapies and the Grammar of a Virtue," in Richard H. Bell, ed., *The Grammar of the Heart: New Essays in Moral Philosophy and Theology.* San Francisco: Harper and Row, 1988. 149–70.

———, "Virtues and Rules," *Philosophy and Phenomenological Research* 5 (1991) 325–60.

———, *Emotions. An Essay in Aid of Moral Psychology.* Cambridge, UK, and New York: Cambridge University Press, 2003.

———, "The Blessings of Gratitude: A Conceptual Analysis," in Robert A. Emmons and Michael E. McCullough, eds., *The Psychology of Gratitude.* 2004.

Roberts, Warren E., *The Tale of the Kind and the Unkind Girls.* Berlin: de Gruyter, 1958.

Rouse, W.H.D., *Greek Votive Offerings.* Cambridge, UK: Cambridge University Press, 1902.

Rupp, Katherine, *Gift-Giving in Japan: Cash, Connections, Cosmologies.* Stanford, CA: Stanford University Press, 2003.

Ruth, Julie A., "It's the Feeling That Counts: Toward an Understanding of Emotion and Its

Influence on Gift-Exchange Processes," in Cele Otnes and Richard F. Beltramini, eds., *Gift Giving: A Research Anthology.* Bowling Green, OH: Bowling Green State University, 1996. 195–211.

Saarinen, Risto, *God and the Gift: An Ecumenical Theology of Giving.* Collegeville, MN: Liturgical Press, 2005.

Sahlins, Marshall, "The Spirit of the Gift," in his *Stone Age Economics.* Chicago: Aldine, 1972. 70–99.

Sankowski, Edward, "Responsibility of Persons for Their Emotions," *Canadian Journal of Philosophy* 7(1977) 829–40.

Sarbin, Theodore R., "Emotion and Act: Roles and Rhetoric," in Rom Harré, ed., *The Social Construction of Emotions,* 1986. 83–97.

Schieffelin, Edward L., "Reciprocity and the Construction of Reality," *Man* 15(1980) 502–17.

Schmidt, Leigh Eric, "Practices of Exchange: From Market Culture to Gift Economy in the Interpretation of American Religion," in David D. Hall, ed., *Lived Religion in America: Toward a History of Practice.* Princeton, NJ: Princeton University Press, 1997.

Schrag, Calvin O., *God as Otherwise than Being: Toward a Semantics of the Gift.* Evanston, IL: Northwestern University Press, 2002.

Schrift, Alan D., ed., *The Logic of the Gift: Toward an Ethic of Generosity.* New York and London: Routledge, 1997.

Schwartz, Barry, "The Social Psychology of the Gift," *American Journal of Sociology* 73(1967) 1–11.

Schwarz, Balduin V., "Some Reflections on Gratitude," in *The Human Person and the World of Values.* Westport, CN: Greenwood Press, 1960. 168–91.

———, "Der Dank als Gesinnung und Tat," in Josef Seifert, ed., *Danken und Dankbarkeit,* 1992.

Searle, John R., *Speech Acts: An Essay in the Philosophy of Language.* London: Cambridge University Press, 1969.

Seifert, Josef, ed., *Danken und Dankbarkeit: Eine Universale Dimension des Menschseins.* Heidelberg: Carl Winter Universitätsverlag, 1992.

Seligman, Martin E.P., *Authentic Happiness. Using the New Positive Psychology to Realize Your Potential for Lasting Fulfillment.* New York: Free Press, 2002.

Seneca, Lucius Annaeus, *Ad Lucilium epistulae morales* LXXXI. (ca. AD 60) Trans. Richard M. Gummere. Loeb Classical Library. Cambridge, MA: Harvard University Press, 1962.

———, *De Beneficiis.* (ca. AD 60) *Moral Essays,* Vol. 3. Trans. John W. Basore. Loeb Classical Library. Cambridge, MA: Harvard University Press, 2001.

Shamir, Boas, "Between Gratitude and Gratuity: An Analysis of Tipping," *Annals of Tourism Research* 11(1984) 59–78.

Sharp, Ronald A., "Gift Exchange and the Economics of Spirit in *The Merchant of Venice*," *Modern Philology* 83(1986) 250–65.

Sherry, John F., "Gift Giving in Anthropological Perspective," *Journal of Consumer Research* 10(1983) 157–68.

Siddiqi, M.H., "Thanksgiving in Islamic Thought," in J.B. Carman and F.J. Streng, eds., *Spoken and Unspoken Thanks: Some Comparative Soundings,* 1989. 145–54.

Sidgwick, Henry, *The Methods of Ethics.* Indianapolis, IN: Hackett, 1981. First published 1907.

Silber, Ilana, "Beyond Purity and Danger: Gift-Giving in the Monotheistic Religions," in Antoon Vandevelde, ed., *Gifts and Interests,* 2000.

Simmel, Georg (1858–1918), "Faithfulness and Gratitude," in Kurt H. Wolff, trans. and ed., *The Sociology of Georg Simmel.* New York: Free Press, 1950. 379–95.

Simmons, A. John, *Moral Principles and Political Obligations.* Princeton, NJ: Princeton University Press, 1979.

Sittl, Karl, *Die Gebärden der Griechen und Römer.* Leipzig: G. Olms, 1970. First published 1890.

Slatkin, Laura M., *The Power of Thetis: Allusion and Interpretation in the Iliad.* Berkeley: University of California Press, 1991.

Smith, Adam, *The Theory of the Moral Sentiments.* Ed. Knud Haakonssen, Karl Ameriks, and Desmond M. Clarke. Cambridge, UK: Cambridge University Press, 2006. First published 1790.

Soellner, Rolf, *Timon of Athens: Shakespeare's Pessimistic Tragedy.* Columbus: Ohio State University Press, 1979.

Solomon, Robert C., *Not Passion's Slave: Emotions and Choice.* Oxford and New York: Oxford University Press, 2003.

———, *In Defense of Sentimentality.* Oxford and New York: Oxford University Press, 2004. 101–7.

Sommers, Christina Hoff, "Filial Morality," *The Journal of Philosophy* 83(1986) 439–56.

Spinoza, Benedictus de, "Ethics," in Michael L. Morgan, ed., Samuel Shirley, trans., *The Essential Spinoza: Ethics and Related Writings.* Indianapolis, IN: Hackett, 2006. First published 1677.

Starobinski, Jean, *Largesse.* Paris: Gallimard, 2007. (Enlarged edition of the catalogue of the Louvre exhibition of 1994.)

Stein, Michael, "Gratitude and Attitude: A Note on Emotional Welfare," *Social Psychology Quarterly* 52(1989) 242–48.

Steindl-Rast, David, *Gratefulness, The Heart of Prayer: An Approach to Life in Fullness.* New York/Ramsey: Paulist Press, 1984.

Stewart-Robertson, Charles, "The Rhythms of Gratitude: Historical Developments and Philosophical Concerns," *Australasian Journal of Philosophy* 68(1990) 189–205.

Strathern, Marilyn, *The Gender of the Gift*. Berkeley: University of California Press, 1988.

Strawson, Peter F., "Freedom and Resentment," in his *"Freedom and Resentment" and Other Essays*. London: Methuen, 1974.

Sugimoto, Naomi, ed., *Japanese Apology Across Disciplines*. Commack, NY: Nova Science Publishers, 1999.

Takagi, Atsushi, *A Cross-Cultural Analysis of Thanks and Apologies by Native and Non-Native Speakers of Japanese*. Thesis. La Trobe University, Melbourne, Australia, 1995.

Tanaka, N., "Politeness: Some Problems for Japanese Speakers of English," *The Japan Association of Language Teachers Journal* 9(1988) 81–102.

Tarot, Camille, "Gift and Grace: A Family to Be Recomposed?" in Antoon Vandevelde, ed., *Gifts and Interests*, 2000. 133–55.

Teigen, Karol Halvor, "Luck, Envy, and Gratitude: It Could Have Been Different," *Scandinavian Journal of Psychology* 38(1997) 313–23.

Titmuss, Richard M., *The Gift Relationship: From Human Blood to Social Policy*. London: George Allen & Unwin, 1971.

Toffin, Gérard, "Hiérarchie et idéologie du don dans le monde indien," *L'Homme* 30(1990) 130–42.

Tottoli, Roberto, "The Thanksgiving Prostration (*sujud al-shukr*) in Muslim Traditions," *University of London School of Oriental and African Studies Bulletin* 61(1998) 309–13.

Trivers, Robert L., "The Evolution of Reciprocal Altruism," *Quarterly Review of Biology* 46(1971) 35–57.

Tsvetaeva, Marina, *Earthly Signs: Moscow Diaries, 1917–1922*. Trans. Jamey Gambrell. New Haven, CT: Yale University Press, 2002. 115–21.

Vacek, Edward C., "Gifts, God, Generosity and Gratitude," in James Keating, ed., *Spirituality and Moral Theology*. New York: Paulist Press, 2000. 81–125.

Vandevelde, Antoon, ed., *Gifts and Interests*. Leuven: Peeters, 2000.

———, "Towards a Conceptual Map of Gift Practices," in Antoon Vandevelde, ed., *Gifts and Interests*, 2000. 1–20.

Visser, Margaret, *The Rituals of Dinner*. Toronto: HarperCollins, 1991.

———, *The Way We Are*. Toronto: HarperCollins, 1994.

———, *The Geometry of Love*. Toronto: HarperCollins, 2000.

———, *Beyond Fate*. Toronto: Anansi, 2002.

von Hildebrand, Dietrich, *Über die Dankbarkeit*. St. Ottilien: Eos Verlag, 1980.

von Reden, Sitta, *Exchange in Ancient Greece*. London: Duckworth, 1995.

Waddell, Helen, *Beasts and Saints.* London: Constable, 1934.

Waits, William Burnell, *The Modern Christmas in America: A Cultural History of Gift Giving.* New York: New York University Press, 1993.

Waldstein, Wolfgang, "*Ingrati accusatio* im Römischen Recht," in Josef Seifert, ed., *Danken und Dankbarkeit,* 1992. 135–47.

Walker, A.D.M., "Gratefulness and Gratitude," *Proceedings of the Aristotelian Society* 81(1980–81) 39–55.

———, "Political Obligation and the Argument from Gratitude," *Philosophy & Public Affairs* 17(1988) 191–211.

———, "Obligations of Gratitude and Political Obligation," *Philosophy & Public Affairs* 18(1989) 359–64.

Wall, John, "The Economy of the Gift: Paul Ricoeur's Significance for Theological Ethics," *Journal of Religious Ethics* 29(2001) 235–60.

Wallace, John M., "*Timon of Athens* and the Three Graces: Shakespeare's Senecan Study," *Modern Philology* (1986) 349–63.

Webb, Stephen H., *The Gifting God: A Trinitarian Ethics of Excess.* New York: Oxford, 1996.

Weil, Simone (1909–1943), *La pesanteur et la grâce.* Paris: Plon, 1988. First published 1947. Trans. as *Gravity and Grace.* New York: Routledge Classics, 2002.

Weiner, Annette B., *Inalienable Possessions: The Paradox of Keeping-While-Giving.* Berkeley: University of California Press, 1992.

Weisfeld, Glenn E., "Social Dominance and Human Motivation," in Donald R. Omark, F.F. Strayer, and Daniel G. Freedman, eds., *Dominance Relations: An Ethological View of Human Conflict and Social Interaction.* New York: Garland, 1980. Chapter 15.

Weiss, Roslyn, "The Moral and Social Dimensions of Gratitude," *Southern Journal of Philosophy* 23(1985) 491–501.

Wellman, Christopher Heath, "Gratitude as a Virtue," *Pacific Philosophical Quarterly* 80(1999) 284–300.

Werbner, Pnina, "Economic Rationality and Hierarchical Gift Economies: Value and Ranking among British Pakistanis," *Man* 25(1990) 266–85.

Westermann, Claus, *Praise and Lament in the Psalms.* Trans. Keith R. Crim and Richard N. Soulen. Atlanta: John Knox Press, 1981.

Westermarck, Edward, *The Origin and Development of the Moral Ideas.* London: Macmillan, 1917. Vol 2. 156–66.

Wicclair, Mark R., "Caring for Frail Elderly Parents: Past Parental Sacrifices and the Obligations of Adult Children," *Social Theory and Practice* 16(1986) 163–89.

Wierzbicka, Anna, "Different Cultures, Different Speech Acts," *Journal of Pragmatics* 9(1985) 145–78.

————, Cross-Cultural Pragmatics: The Semantics of Human Interaction. Berlin: Mouton de Gruyter, 1991.

————, Semantics, Culture, and Cognition: Universal Human Concepts in Culture-Specific Configurations. New York: Oxford University Press, 1992.

————, Emotions across Languages and Cultures: Diversity and Universals. Cambridge, UK, and New York: Cambridge University Press, 1999.

Wilhite, Margaret, "Children's Acquisition of Language Routines: The End-of-Meal Routine in Cakchiquel," Language in Society 12(1983) 47–64.

Yan, Yunxiang, The Flow of Gifts: Reciprocity and Social Networks in a Chinese Village. Stanford, CA: Stanford University Press, 1996.

Index